Arab Culture
Exploring the Arabic-speaking World through Cartoons, Satire, and Humor

By:

Tarek Mahfouz

Copyright © 2011 by Tarek Mahfouz

Copyright, Legal Notice and Disclaimer:

This publication is protected under the United States Copyright Act of 1976 and under all other applicable international, federal, state and local laws. All rights are reserved. No part of this book may be reproduced or transmitted in any form, by any means (electronic, photocopying, recording, or otherwise) without the prior written permission of the publisher.

Limit of Liability and Disclaimer of Warranty:

Tarek Mahfouz and the Publisher have used their best efforts in preparing this book, and the information herein is provided as is. They make no representation or warranties with respect to the accuracy or completeness of the contents of this book, and specifically disclaim any implied warranties of merchantability or fitness for any particular purpose. They shall in no event be liable for any loss of profit or any other commercial damage, including but not limited to special, incidental, consequential, or other damages.

Trademarks:

All brand names and product names used in this book are trade names, service marks, trademarks, or registered trademarks of their respective owners. Tarek Mahfouz is not associated with any product or vendor mentioned in this book.

Written by: Tarek Mahfouz

Edited by: Thane Floreth

Cover Design: Tarek Mahfouz

ISBN: 978-0-557-85489-9

First edition: January 2011

Printed in the United States of America

About the Author

Tarek Mahfouz is an innovator in the field of Arabic language and cultural studies. He has many years of experience as an educator about Arab culture, and he has long sought ways to enhance the learning of Arabic to make it more engaging. He has authored a number of popular and pioneering books that give students a new perspective on the language and how to internalize and absorb it. He also firmly holds the view that culture is even more important than language, which is the reason behind this book.

Why I wrote this book

In talking with people over many years, both as a teacher and just as an Arab, I have been aware of two particular groups that I have felt for and wanted to help. The first includes those who have a sincere and abiding interest in the Arab world and its civilization but do not have means or time to go there and discover more. For them, the book opens up this world and will give a real sense of it. The second group are students of Arabic, both those at home and those who have the chance to spend time in Arab countries. I have found that learners want to complement their study of classic, standard Arabic—the Arabic used in the media—with the Arabic of the streets; but there are few places to see everyday, colloquial Arabic written down, and there is none that covers the whole range of the Arab world, while even advanced students need some help in dealing with such a diversity of dialect and region. This book is the missing resource: idiomatic Arabic from the whole variety of dialects and regions written down and explained in English. The speech used also consists of concise and useful phrases that are readily used in real-life situations, so worth attention and learning, and the picture often shows the context and manner of address better than any explanation. I also meet students who have spent anything from a few weeks to a year, even more, studying in an Arab country, but have never really had an opportunity to get up close to the culture of the place where they are. Their contact is often confined to the Westernized and cosmopolitan people who are attracted to them, and even if they have the chance to meet ordinary people, their very presence is likely to change the situation—and they may find that they are viewed as an object of curiosity or an opportunity for English practice—so that at the end, they return much as they went and have never penetrated very far into Arab culture. The two volumes of this book, therefore, aim to offer a deep and thorough insight into the Arab world, one that a foreigner might spend years living in an Arab country without being able to attain. For all, I believe that culture still hasn't been given its rightful place in language learning, and that lack of awareness of culture has potentially far more serious consequences than simple ignorance of language. Technological advance may one day remove the obstacles of not speaking a foreign language, but knowledge of the culture, from which these words spring, must be acquired at an individual and human level.

Tarek Mahfouz

I am happy to be reached at: tm5522@yahoo.com

Acknowledgements

My sincere appreciation is due to the many editors, cartoonists and students who have contributed suggestions to make the book more interesting, understandable and practical for those who want to learn about Arab culture. As a result of their very helpful recommendations, the book will better satisfy the learning needs of students.

Table of Content

Introduction iv
How to Use This Book vi
A Note on the Text viii
Prologue 1
1 — Sagging and Swagging 11
2 — Social Life 21
3 — Kissing 56
4 — Dating and Getting Married 61
5 — Family Life 113
6 — The Big Problem of Obesity 158
7 — Domestic Violence 165
8 — Underage Marriage 182
9 — Women 188
10 — Arab Leaders 219
11 — Terrorists 249
12 — How Arabs View America 284
13 — Sand Clock 328
14 — Mazayen al-Ebel, the Camel Beauty Show 329
15 — Soccer 336
16 — Education 348
17 — High School Exam 386
18 — Work Place and Bureaucracy 396
19 — Immigrants 414
20 — Religion 423
21 — Begging 443
22 — The Internet 451
23 — Heat 454
24 — Reminiscing 458
Topics in Volume Two 468
Index 469

introduction

Arab Culture aims to introduce the reader to the wealth and variety of life and attitudes in the Arab world, providing a guide through its complexity, that has come from an intimate knowledge and a life-long involvement in explaining and interpreting its language and culture. The book does not seek to present a thematic argument, but to use each cartoon as the starting point for a new conversation with the reader, presenting the ideas and material in an accessible and enjoyable manner. You would have to spend many years living in Arab countries, talking to people and noting their customs, to gain the wealth of insight that is offered in the book's two volumes.

The book is directed toward two kinds of reader in particular: firstly, those who are learning Arabic and want to find out more about the cultural framework within which the language works, and secondly, those who may not need or want to learn the language but who have a deep interest in the Arab world and want to gain a depth of knowledge about the Arab world that can only come from understanding how people's minds, words and attitudes combine within a culture.

Arranged around a core of some thousand cartoons from the Arabic language press, selected to show customs, ways of life and attitudes to a wide variety of topics from across the modern Arab world, this study is both light-hearted and deeply serious. The cartoon is a particularly rich form: it has a message but also shows a context. To its audience, the cartoon conveys its viewpoint with a simplicity that is vivid and direct, often with humor, but also sometimes with the satirist's "savage indignation." That immediacy is sometimes equally clear to the outsider, but often refracted or obscured by cultural elements that are more or less opaque and need explanation. The cartoon, as a simplified caricature, often also reveals much about the context of ordinary life and the body language that accompanies speech, showing aspects that probably pass almost unnoticed by the native readers and just seem "right," while outsiders will usually not know what to look for and often miss the telling details. The analysis here shows how to read the cartoon, pointing out elements of interest, from dress and gesture to customs and characteristics, and maybe also inviting readers to recognize their own assumptions and how their background influences their approach.

Cartoons are particularly important for students of Arabic, because they are one of the only places where they will see the colloquial Arabic written down, expressing the dialect of a particular region. This book collects examples from across the whole Arab world to give the student a full sense of the diversity of spoken Arabic. What's more, the language is presented in short "chunks" and phrases appropriate to common situations that can be learned and used directly.

The cartoons are organized into topical groups and areas, but their richness cannot be contained in simple categories, so that each one is taken as the starting point for an easy and discursive consideration of the issues it raises rather than straitjacketed into a thematic argument. The cartoon itself is often like an anecdote and can provoke a variety of different lines of thought, even other anecdotes in turn. For this reason, the treatments that fall under a topic heading may often be rather unexpected and provide something of a sideways look, but will also mean that the reader gains a far broader and more nuanced appreciation of the subject.

Every cartoon is given a translation that is literal enough to help students of Arabic to see how the colloquial language works, but also clear enough that the reader without Arabic will have no problem understanding the ideas and what is being expressed. Where relevant, particular points of language and usage are considered in more detail and in a way that will be of interest to both Arabic speakers and those without Arabic, who will gain a greater understanding of the cast of mind through an idiom or turn of phrase. The broader consideration of the cultural material is not only focused through the topics of the cartoons, but also deliberately digressive, like a conversation between friends — so consideration of how America is like an onion will take in Arab ideas about America, but also the role of the onion in Arab life, its proverbial use, how married couples talk to each other, and whatever else seems pertinent. Where the humor may be hard to see for an English-language reader, the joke is explained.

To some extent it is now easier than ever to find out about other societies as the internet makes a range of resources available anywhere and travel is generally easier. Arab culture in particular is becoming more homogeneous than at any time in history, as satellite television, modern communication devices and telephony, and interactive media use classical or standard Arabic to make sure that they can reach all Arab countries. Emigration and travel within the Arab world have also led to cross-fertilization of strands within the Arabic-speaking world. The cartoons here cover the whole region and are selected as representative of universal elements, but are drawn particularly from Egypt, the Gulf and Jordan.

This book does not therefore seek to give information that can be found readily on the internet or in standard reference works, aiming rather to draw out what would be impossible to find without help and that even an expert Arabic-speaker might have problems researching. However, if a topic is raised and you wish to find out more, there is an abundance of good material on the worldwide web — as well as plenty of dross — including press, film, song, and comment.

A glance at the contents of the two volumes will show that there a wide variety of topics are covered in each, and that each contains a mixture of broader themes. To some extent the first volume leans more toward the perennial elements within Arab culture, while the second looks at topics that are particularly current or problematic, but to avoid making either volume too monotonous the elements are deliberately intermingled.

For students of Arabic, the book shows real colloquial language as it is used in everyday speech, often lively and blunt, from the whole range of Arab countries. Even the beginner will find a rich source for study as the text is usually short and pithy, which means that a cartoon is often portraying few or even just one speech act, in context with other elements. Anyone who has studied a language for any time will be aware of how inseparable the culture is from the language and vice versa. It is commonly said that more than half of communication is non-verbal — the percentages mentioned vary from 55% to 95% — but it is certainly true that much of what we express relies upon shared assumptions and references, body language and elements that are often unspoken. Though there are many introductions and guides to Arabic and its dialects, no book has sought to give such a thorough grounding in the culture that goes with this language. Though this book cannot provide the sounds and smells of an Arab city, in other aspects it is as if the reader had had the benefit of living in the Arab world for many years, and a knowledge of Arabic doubles its usefulness.

The book aims to be as balanced and comprehensive as possible, but there is also a distinct voice and character to the presentation, which makes it engaging and readily accessible.

How to use this book

Throughout the book, cartoons are first displayed by themselves, inviting students to bring their knowledge and insight to them as raw cultural artifacts. Explanation and interpretation then follow in four categories: "Translation," "Humor," "Language," and "Culture." First comes the graphic…

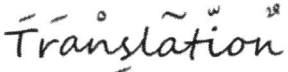

The text is given in full in English, arranged as a kind of play script, with descriptions and labels in italics, and brackets where appropriate, and with the speech balloons as spoken dialogue in inverted commas (where needed to distinguish it from labels and comments).

> *Title*: It happens these days
> *From outside the panel:* Would you like to eat something, my beloved?
> *Man:* Give me an orange.
> *Voice off (as orange hits his face):* Take it!

In general the material is taken from right to left, as it is read in Arabic. The translation is as close to a literal translation as possible, to give students of Arabic a sense of how the language functions, but aims to be readable and comprehensible English. (Where the scene may need a little further interpretation, there is also more extended description after the translation.) The literal translations may not always make immediate sense to those who are not intimately familiar with Arabic, and in such cases, the reader proceeds to the next section, marked by the graphic…

Language

This heading appears only when relevant, to explain idioms, obscure phrases and points of general interest. Idioms are notoriously tricky — from opening a can of worms to throwing in the towel — and though some are surprisingly similar across barriers of language and culture, others need quite a leap of imagination.

Language also deals with the contexts in which certain idioms are used or the different import of the same phrase depending on context (such as "*Ya salaam,*" literally "Oh peace," which varies from "How wonderful!" to "Wow, really!?" to "Really??" to "How terrible!" and more).

The principles of transliteration followed here are *broadly phonetic*, seeking to indicate the sounds of the Arabic words as far as the simple Roman alphabet allows, given that Arabic contains a number of sounds that do not exist in English. Two conventions are worth noting, the use of a c-shaped inverted comma ʻ for *ayin*, and a capital H for the emphatic *ha*.

When you understand every word and every expression yet are still baffled as to why anyone would find a cartoon funny, you should look for the humor graphic:

Most of the cartoons are meant to be funny, and in most of those the themes are universal enough that the humor is immediately recognizable. In some, however, what the original audience would find funny is far from evident to the reader who doesn't share that background or world. Where this happens, there is a symbol of a smiley face in a *guthra* or headdress, and at least something of the joke is explained according to what an Arab would find funny — though Arab readers are as different in what they find funny as anyone else. (And of course, a joke that has to be explained is seldom hilarious and you may still find the humor hard to see, but at least you'll have an idea of what's going on.)

For more in-depth analyses that flesh out the reader's understanding and explore matters touched on in the cartoon, you then proceed to…

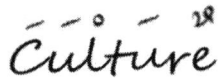

The section on "Culture" is the core of the book, interpreting the cartoons and drawing out the themes that are presented, to illustrate aspects of Arab life and shed light on the people and their attitudes. These sections range from a few lines of comment to a few pages, but always try to keep the treatment to a manageable length, while doing justice to topics that are often complex.

Since it is impossible to isolate any area from others, no attempt has been made here to deal with any topic once and for all in a single entry. Rather, in the case of the most important themes, elements will be found throughout the two volumes, as a strand that reappears and related to the many other areas where they impinge. Thus, although the books are arranged in small units, and there is no fixed sequence in their ordering, it is best to read the material from beginning to end as arranged, in order for the method of presentation to be most effective. The index at the end of each volume enables the reader to trace an idea through its various appearances, and cross-references are provided where there is a clear connection between two topics.

The approach is to present the way that Arabs think as directly as possible, while at the same time offering some touchstones for reference and contrast, but without constantly pointing up qualifications or caveats. Therefore comments may sometimes appear politically incorrect in their viewpoint, sexist, traditionalist and anti-Western, particularly in more controversial areas, as they try to convey people's thinking accurately — it is left to the reader to add "but this may not be/is not accurate/fair/valid." Nothing is included simply to be offensive: if readers find themselves feeling hostile to what is being expressed, the important thing is to recognize that it is the expression of an attitude that exists, to try to understand it, see where it is coming from and why it provokes hostility.

Where there are useful comparisons with American culture that are not too limited in application, they are introduced briefly and in such a way that the argument does not depend upon familiarity with a particular point of comparison. Currency conversions are not usually made, since the values vary and can readily be checked online in whatever currency the reader feels most comfortable with.

Within a group of cartoons on a broad theme, if the point that a cartoon makes is fairly obvious and follows treatment of other cartoons with similar content, there may be little or no comment, though usually there will be a brief note to confirm that what seems obvious genuinely is so. Otherwise the comment may focus on a secondary element within the cartoon. Many cartoons raise a number of important issues, and different topics are separated with a crescent symbol…

 To indicate a change of tack.

One may have learned what the words say in "Translation," and one may have learned what they mean in "Language," but only someone who has the knowledge and recognizes the attitudes that inform a native Arab's reading of it can be said to understand it. That understanding is the mission of the "Culture" section and the purpose of this book.

A Note on the Text

Given the nature of the book, it is worth mentioning that, in the Arabic world, excessive mirth is thought generally unseemly. Numerous proverbs and hadith discourage such displays ("immoderate laughter," reads one, "kills the heart"), and many Arabs will close a fit of laughter with the utterance, "may God make it goodness" — the mentality being that, having encountered undue joy, undue tragedy surely lurks nearby. An Arab person would probably describe some of the cartoons that follow as inciting "laughter like weeping" — because, as another proverb holds, the very worst calamities make you laugh, not cry. (Of all Arab countries, Egypt is thought to have the most generous sense of humor. And the most frequent advice an Egyptian will receive upon finding work in Saudi Arabia is, simply, to be serious.) First and foremost, the Arab people derive their understanding of humor, mirth and laughter from the Muslim faith. The Qur'an is a serious, eminently sobering text, containing both the standards of behavior that a person should strive to achieve, and the dire consequences of failing to do so. And while it does enjoin practitioners to appreciate their share of earthly life, the emphasis is placed on things eternal. Secondly, one cannot discount the impact of the geography (the smoldering heat, the vast deserts) and the current geopolitical situation on the Arab mentality.

In a way, this is a book about advice. The elaborate economy of advice-giving is one of the central features of Arab culture: in Arab countries, people will regularly tell others how to live, where to live, and who to live with — and that's just the tip of it. In such places, this sort of advice is not the province of busybodies (as a Westerner might object), but is rather an ethical duty shared by all. This sense of responsibility is nurtured by the Qur'an, which holds that we are all responsible to return those who have gone astray to the right path. It is similar to the Western dictum that we are our brothers' keepers — only elaborated, and elevated to a cultural hallmark. But is not only about giving advice — that is, it is not only about keeping track of our brothers — but rather about eagerly accepting advice too, about letting our brothers take care of us.

Prologue

Translation

Both Arab men are thinking: Son-of-a-gun! His English drives me wild, but it's his hair [style] that's really crazy! I have to do my hair like that, starting tomorrow!

[*The salesman is identified as a foreigner.*]

Caption: Instead of admiring extraordinary industrial technology and trying to imitate this mighty scientific progress, our countrymen admire the most trivial dimensions of situations.

[*N.B. The English text in the cartoon is part of the original.*]

Language

The phrase here rendered as "Son-of-a-gun" more literally translates as, "O son of those who," though the sense of wondering admiration is the same. Whereas in English the use of the vocative particle "O" to introduce a direct address is largely either anachronistic or used to place emphasis on the act of getting attention, the corresponding Arabic particle *Ya* is generally used whenever introducing conversations or calling someone by name.

The two men are not interested in the product demonstration but instead in the man's hair and his good English. The machine's ability to make coffee and heat food is not meant to depict it as outlandish but to demonstrate the men's lack of interest even when the machine's functions are worth paying attention to.

Culture

The enthusiasm that these men display at hearing the salesman's good English reflects the high regard in which skill in foreign languages is generally held in the Arab world. Before the discovery of oil, many Arab nations had become isolated from the larger international community, and the memory of this has engendered a passionate enthusiasm amongst Arabs for joining the wider milieu and participating in global culture and commerce.

Proficiency in foreign languages is a potent signifier of sophistication and education, and it is a vital qualification for many professions. Ambitious Arabs are keen to hone their language skills in modestly priced classes at the many cultural centers that foreign governments maintain in urban areas, such as the German Goethe Institute, the Spanish Cervantes Center, the Alliance Française, and the British Council. These prestigious institutions employ native speakers of their respective languages so that students become accustomed to hearing the language spoken properly and naturally, and a native accent is highly prized. English holds a particularly important place as the language of so much international business and so much global media, so a meeting with native English speakers provides students of English with a rare and valuable opportunity to pick up the particularities of accent, phrasing, and idiom, while others will associate the language with the glamour of the movies and internationalism. Until recently, foreigners were rare phenomena in many Arab countries. Though they have begun to integrate themselves into the broader societies, most foreign workers have tended to live in rigidly separated communities, leaving only for professional reasons, and in many countries, tourists are strongly regulated and shepherded. Governments of many countries are suspicious of foreign influences on their populations and scrutinize all interactions between natives and foreigners, even to the point of questioning Arabs seen walking in the company of foreigners.

Arabs use English in advertisements, on signs, and even in their speech as a sign of cosmopolitan sophistication and education. Most of the time, however, their English is not grammatically correct, as is the case with the English depicted in the cartoon above. English is welcomed and widely understood in Arab countries, though, and it is very easy to get around without knowing Arabic in the areas commonly frequented by tourists. In the worst-case scenario, a foreigner in need of directions will have to talk to find a second local to ask if the first person's English is not up to the task or too heavily accented. Many people will volunteer their help, and if a foreigner takes the time to speak slowly and carefully, he or she will encounter little trouble

The widespread comprehension of English in the Arab world is due to a number of factors, tracing back to the days in which the United Kingdom exercised enormous imperial power in the region. Many Arabs speak English because they have studied it, in public schools since the seventh grade and in private schools since the first grade. In addition, American culture and media exert a strong influence. American movies and television series are very popular and are shown and broadcast in English with Arabic subtitles. This has an additional benefit for the American visitor, as America's cultural influence makes the American dialect the most familiar, rather than, for example, British or Australian dialects. Ironically, American English is commonly thought of as a corruption of "proper" British English. Many Arab speakers of English are passionate about maintaining what they have been taught to be correct English and attribute deviations from that standard to the deleterious American influence on British English.

The countries of Morocco, Algeria, and Tunisia, formerly dominated by the imperial power of France, constitute an exception to the general rule of familiarity with English and, in those countries, French is the primary foreign language. Morocco is especially Francophone, with everything from government publications and web sites to many commercial advertisements being written in French. The French influence can also be felt outside that particular bloc in Lebanon, where French, though less dominant than in the other countries, is still likely to take precedence over English as students' first choice for foreign-language study.

If there is an emergency and an English-speaking foreigner needs to go to the hospital, he or she will have no trouble communicating with doctors. Arab doctors all speak English, as the curricula of almost all medical schools are taught and all textbooks are written in English, the only exception being Syria, which is the only country in the world that teaches medicine in Arabic. Furthermore, many of the most distinguished college professors obtained their advanced degrees from America or Britain, and a educational background from those nations carries great cachet. Even outside of academia, English is valued in other fields, such as engineering. Despite efforts to re-write school curricula in Arabic—known as Arabization—, both professionals' need to keep up-to-date with developments and discoveries by their international colleagues and tendency of students to go to English-speaking countries to complete their educations have tended to maintain English as the dominant, professional language.

☪ Throughout the Arab world, there has recently been a proliferation of universities that teach entirely in English. Some are branches of prestigious western institutions, some are Arab universities that have twined themselves with Western partners, and even some are entirely Arab-run schools.

☪ Most travel-related businesses, such as hotels and airports, as well as up-scale shops and restaurants, have English-speaking employees as well as English signs. Foreigners will be aided by the familiar logos of international brands and corporations. Even street and road signs are in both Arabic and English, and the road infrastructure is designed after the American model. In most tourist areas, shopkeepers and those who come into contact with tourists have taught themselves to converse in all the major languages. Foreigners are often amazed at what they have picked up for themselves and humbled by their abilities, especially those who have taken courses or lessons and still cannot carry on a conversation in anything other than their mother tongue.

One difficulty an English-speaking foreigner may encounter is the nuances of how English sounds when spoken with an Arabic accent. The English sound "th," for example, may be spoken as "s" and the letter "p" is pronounced as the letter "b." Arabs may also insert certain Arabic expressions, such as *Wallahi*, which literally means "By God!" and is used to express surprised incredulity, and *Ya* which is used when addressing someone by name. Arabic's grammar and syntax tend to be applied inappropriately to English when it is spoken by native Arabic speakers, leading to potentially confusing constructions, such as when they follow Arabic word order and place adjectives after the noun described rather than before it—speaking, for instance, of the "car blue" rather than the "blue car." Confusion also frequently arises when Arabs attempt to translate literally terms and expressions unique to Arabic into their English speech. For example, in Arabic, "I'll kill you," spoken in the right context, is a friendly expression of bonhomie, but it would be hard for a native English speaker to hear it as other than a threat. Similarly, "You are my liver," would surely baffle any Westerner on a date, but it is, in Arabic, a term of endearment equivalent to the English, "You are my heart," while "my eye" is a more general expression of affection, meaning, "You are as dear to me as my eye."

☪ Westerns may be disconcerted by Arabs' apparent ready hostility and short-temper. Even upon a first meeting, an Arab may pounce upon a new acquaintance for faults like a trivial lateness. These criticisms are not truly meant as attacks, however; rather, they are a playful way of establishing a close social bond. If the Arab were truly offended, he or she would likely respond with stony silence; the sudden, vocal criticism is a public demonstration either of a friendly familiarity or the desire for one.

☪ The Arab men's distraction over the salesman's hair is an instance of what, to Western eyes, can be the puzzlingly homoerotic aspect of Arab male interactions. Many behaviors, which, in the West would be interpreted as signs of homosexuality, e.g., men walking hand-in-hand or arm-in-arm (for which Arabs use a French term, engagé), and kissing on the cheek as a form of greeting are common cultural phenomena in the Arab world and not signifiers of sexual orientation. Indeed, such public displays are emphatically not to be read as indicators of a sexual bond, as heterosexual Arab men refrain from publicly exhibiting the same behaviors with all women, even wives. The casual physical intimacy amongst heterosexual Arab men may, in part, have been a development in response to the strict and carefully maintained distance that Arab culture traditionally imposes between men and women. Most of a man's social life is carried on solely amongst men. The intricate interactions between men and women will also be a recurring theme in this book.

Translation

Title: The Arab Dream
All sing: "This is our dream, our life-long dream, a place to embrace us all."

Culture

In this cartoon, the people waiting in line are wearing the traditional clothing of (from left to right) Jordan, Egypt, Syria, Palestine, Lebanon, Sudan, Morocco, and the Gulf.

☪ After 9/11, the prevailing question among Americans was, "Why do they hate us?" with "they" meaning Arabs and particularly Arab Muslims. American media arrived at a popular and facile answer: Arabs hate Americans' freedom and the American way of life. To judge, however, from the popularity of American movies and TV, Arabs' imitation of American fashion and culture, and the long lines of visa-seekers snaking through American embassies throughout the Arab world, this must be inaccurate. In this cartoon, a line of Arabs from a range of countries sing of it as "a place to embrace us all," meaning that all Arabs will be able to live together in peace and prosper, which is not the case in most of the Arab world. Throughout this book, you will find proof that Arabs like the American way of life and appreciate the opportunities that are available to American citizens regardless of race or creed. This is illustrated by the first cartoon, depicting two Arab men who admire the appearance of the Western, English-speaking salesman. The caption, however, expresses a counter-current of anxiety over this influence, contending that Arabs should admire the science and technology that the Western world has achieved and rather than strive merely for the superficial Western "look."

In the following cartoon, one side shows the American perception of Barack Obama and the other shows the Arab perception of his equivalent, specifically dealing with how a person of Obama's background could become the president of the most powerful nation on Earth.

Translation

American Obama	→ Arab Obama
His father is an African immigrant who abandoned him when he was young.	He does not have lineage (rootless).
A dark-skinned lawyer and civil-rights activist in the Democratic party.	He is a black slave infiltrator who has a foreign agenda.
Was elected a president of the United States of America.	Would not even dream of getting an Arab citizenship.

Culture

Firmly established paternity is very important in Arab countries. Children who have been abandoned by their fathers, as President Obama was, carry with them the blot of being "rootless," unconnected to the familial line and heritage that normally establishes a person's place in society. In order to be a solid member of the society, one is expected to be part of a deeply-rooted family tree.

☪ Amongst themselves, many Arabs habitually refer to ethnically black persons as "slaves." However, the deep-seated cultural aversion to the color black means that, when referring specifically to their skin color, Arabs prefer to call black persons *asmr*, which literally means a lighter, olive-colored skin tone.

☪ The cartoon labels Obama an "infiltrator" because his history of grass-roots political action would, in the context of Arab politics, make him a dangerous subversive rather than an admirable campaigner for social change. In Arab countries with a strictly controlled political arena, it is assumed that anyone agitating for increased democracy is a puppet of interfering, Western powers and, therefore, is to be condemned.

☪ In many Arab countries, people with a foreign parent are not considered full citizens. They may not be able to work, and they pay more for public services than regular citizens do. The case of President Obama, then, is very surprising to Arabs, since the child of a foreign parent would never have the ability to become president in their countries. Indeed, most Arab countries require that one be descended from parents and even grandparents who are all full citizens in order to be eligible for important political or military posts. Even beyond questions of citizenship, Obama is surprising to Arabs because it would be unthinkable for a member of a minority to be elected president—or even given an important government appointment.

Does racism exist in the Arab world?

The short answer is yes: racism does exist in the Arab world. Especially after September 11, 2001, Arabs complain a lot about racism that is directed towards them, but while they do suffer discrimination and complain justly, this can obscure the fact that they are also guilty of racist behavior themselves.

The racism found in Arab culture may most readily be seen in the perception of black Africans and the valorization of fair skin among the Arab population. Even the Arab countries on the African continent see themselves as distinct from rest of Africa, black Africa. In Arab culture, a girl's marriage prospects are directly correlated with the color of her skin: the lighter, the better her prospects are. The dowry that a fair-skinned girl commands is also much higher. Arab men usually prefer to marry a pale girl, a preference commonly made explicit in personal ads. The same holds true for men: a black-skinned Arab will likely find his marriage prospects to be poor, and most Arab women will think twice about marrying a black man. Since marrying off their daughters is so important, and the chances of marrying off a black daughter is so low, an Arab prefers not to have a black child, which is yet another reason to avoid matches with dark-skinned people. The reputation of dark women in Arab countries is so low that they are often seen only as disposable sex objects, with many black female tourists falling victim to harassment in the streets. If an Arab living in Europe or America gets engaged to a black girl, his family will be shocked and will most often try to dissuade him from going through with the marriage.

When Arabs speak among themselves, they usually refer to dark-skinned people as "slaves," as in the cartoon. Usually, African blacks were brought to Arab countries as slaves. Some were put to work with the *hareem*, or the female members of the family. To ensure that no inappropriate relations occurred between these slaves and the women, the black slaves would customarily be castrated. Furthermore, if a free man were to marry a slave woman, then his child would be a slave also. Therefore, despite the importation of black slaves into Arab countries continuing until the early twentieth century, a local population of African ancestry never grew.

Until it was joined in the Arab League in recent decades by Comoros, Djibouti, Mauritania, and S[omalia], the only blacks were from Sudan, and Sudan had joined in the face of fierce opposition because of [its] color led by Lebanon—the fairest-skinned nation in the Arab world. The name "Sudan" means the "[Land] of the Blacks." While the black population has spread into more Arab countries, there is still a noticea[ble] lack of black people in the Arab world. The color and body type of people is generally homogenous, bu[t] there are certain countries, like Egypt, Iraq, and some parts of Saudi Arabia, where black populations do exist. Unfortunately, these people are often treated differently from the rest. For example, in Iraq, some tribal sheiks still keep blacks as slaves, and in Egypt, black-skinned people who hail from Nubia—a region with an ancient culture and language distinct from those of the rest of Egypt—tend only to be considered for certain low-status jobs. Reflecting and thereby further enforcing the stereotype and discrimination, black Nubians are always depicted in movies as servants and doormen. In both movies and real life, one seldom sees a black person working in a prominent career. Because of the long history of mistreatment of Nubians by the rest of the Egyptian population and their historically distinctive culture, the region has a simmering independence movement. They remain, however, a distinctly disadvantaged minority. Similarly, in Saudi Arabia, people with African roots will be treated differently from light-skinned Saudis.

To Arabs, the color black most often has negative connotations. An Arab woman will get angry if someone calls her dark-skinned, and it is nearly impossible for a black person to be considered beautiful by a non-black Arab. Many black Arab girls will resort to chemical processes to make their skin whiter. The most famous and popular product of this sort is "Fair and Lovely," a cream that professes to substantially whiten the skin. Beyond personal considerations, the color of someone's skin can even be used against him or her professionally or politically. For example, when the late Egyptian President Anwar al-Sadat assumed his presidency immediately after the death of Gamal Abdel Nasser, his political opponents used his skin color, inherited from his Sudanese mother, as one of their arguments why he would not be a good leader of Egypt.

Even though the antipathy towards black-skinned people is widespread in the Arab world, a truly devout Arab Muslim does not hold any prejudices about skin color. At the introduction of Islam, the negativity towards blacks was entrenched in everyday thinking due to the institution of slavery, but it is counter to the religion's teachings. The Qur'an states that no person is superior to another person by virtue of his skin color, but only by his devoutness. To a true Muslim, skin color is viewed as a miracle from God and different shades, a testament to the infinite variety of His creation. An Arab Muslim will undoubtedly also cite the example of one of the earliest Muslims, the first *mo'zen* in Islam (caller to prayer), a black man named Bilal. According to the Qur'an, the Prophet Moses was also black—this is evident from the story that one of God's signs that he was a prophet was that he would put his hand into his clothing and when he took it out, it would be white, by implication in contrast to the rest of him.[1] And although an Arab Muslim might never marry a black person, he would certainly befriend one. In fact, friendship with a black person is interesting to an Arab, as it is an opportunity to learn about different cultures and countries, and to gain a reputation as worldly and knowledgeable.

An individual friendship between blacks and Arabs notwithstanding, there is also a great deal of national prejudice. Some springs from economic origins, as Arabs associate certain nationalities with low status, service positions. Saudis and those from other rich Arab nations grow up seeing foreigners as servants

---

[1] "Now put thy hand into thy bosom, and it will come forth white without stain (or harm): (these are) among the nine Signs (thou wilt take) to Pharaoh and his people: for they are a people rebellious in transgression." Al-Qur'an, 027.012 (*An-Naml* [The Ants]).

ceive them that way. If—on an airplane, for example—they should be
foreigner from a country with which they have such associations, such as
a rich Arab is likely to feel uncomfortable, no matter what the
of that foreigner might, in fact, be. These national prejudices can be
widely held to be gullible fools that "Do you think I'm an Indian?" is used to
to fall for that?"² and Bangladeshis have a particularly bad reputation for
...nality.³

...ough, people in the Gulf States tend to look down on all foreigners. For example, though
...even million foreigners working in Saudi Arabia, most Saudis avoid close social relationships
...nem. A Saudi family will almost never invite a non-Saudi family over for lunch or dinner, despite
...e importance of sharing meals in their culture. These feelings extend even into the practice of religion:
Arab Muslims will seldom worship at a mosque that is frequented by non-Arab Muslims. If a foreigner
has been hired "blind" and turns out on arrival to be from a less-favored group, he may well find that his
post is paid less than he expected or that he is not confirmed after his probation period. This can include
an American who is found to be Arab-American rather than white—or even, paradoxically, black (since
this is seen as more authentically American).

☪ Just as Jewish tradition refers to non-Jews as *goyim* or "gentiles," and the ancient Greeks labeled all
foreigners "barbarians" because of their babbling speech, so people in the Arab world refer to non-Arabs
as *ajem*, which literally means, "to speak incorrectly." Of course, even if the foreigner is expertly fluent in
his mother tongue, he is still an *ajem*—because to speak correctly, in this sense, is to speak Arabic.

Translation

President Obama: I studied, and I became a professor in one of the most established universities in the world. I authored two best-selling books, and I became a member of Congress, and I was elected the first black President of America, and I received the Nobel Peace Prize.

What do I have to do next?

Language

Arabs follow British usage and call the document that lists their professional achievements—commonly known in America as a résumé—a C.V., which is the abbreviation for the Latin, *curriculum vitæ*.

---

² See "2 — Social Life," p.46.
³ See "19 — Immigrants," p.415.

Culture

Many Arabs think highly of President Obama and are very impressed with his list of achievements, judging as unfair the attacks that accuse him of not having accomplished anything. One notable comment that accompanied this cartoon upon publication, though, revealed an important facet of the Arab world's appreciation for America's busy president: the commentor offered that Obama's next action should be to visit the commentor's Arab home and thereby spur the government to clean it up a bit. Without the impetus of international attention, too many governments in the Arab world are willing to let apathy and inattention wear away at the infrastructure of citizens' daily life.

Translation

Boy: I want to be like Obama when I grow up.

Father: Lower your voice, kid.

Culture

The father is scolding his son for talking too loudly about his aspirations because it might lead people to think that they are subversives, with inappropriate ambitions that threaten those in power and their plans for the future—including who will be president.

☪ Obama's popularity within the Arab world derives partly from his age: it is rare for an Arab man to achieve so much by his mid-40s. The major exceptions to this rule are members of the royal families and the sons of government leaders. Notable examples from this latter group include Gamal Mubarak, the son of Egyptian president Hosni Mubarak, who holds the title of "Guardian of the National Party's Platform"—a position, in fact, that was invented expressly for him. Meanwhile, the current Syrian president is the son of a former Syrian president, while the son of Libyan president Muamar al-Qazafi has been groomed and is poised to succeed his father in office.

Obama is particularly popular with the young, for obvious reasons: his middle name; his eloquence; his cultural sensitivity; the color of his skin, which is like that of an authentic Arab; and his coming after George W. Bush, who was widely perceived as a nightmarish figure by Arabs. He is generally seen as the polar opposite of Bush. When Obama was elected to office, celebrations occurred in the streets of Arab cities, with people carrying American flags through Cairo and Amman and sending text messages with words of congratulation.

Although Obama has enjoyed a surge of popularity among the Arab population, some remain skeptical of his—and America's—new attitude towards Arab and Muslim society, as depicted in the cartoon of Obama painting a smile on the hooded detainee from Abu Ghraib included later in the book. Many people are still waiting for concrete examples of change from America, but the mood in the Arab street is generally optimistic about the new American attitude.

Obama' victory inspired many candidates running for office in different Arab countries, despite their slim chances of winning, and they looked to capitalize on his popularity by using the campaign slogan "Yes we can," gaining wide publicity, and indeed many won.

The majority of Arabs are predisposed to like America. U.S.AID has a large presence in the Arab world, and their image of two hands, one white and one brown, shaking each other figures prominently on everything sent from America, from school lunchboxes to buses for public transportation. Despite U.S.AID's heightened presence in the Middle East throughout the 1960s, many Arab countries leaned politically towards the Soviet Union.

When Egypt signed the peace treaty with Israel, American consumer goods were the first to arrive and visible evidence of the vaunted "peace dividend": Seven Up trucks in the streets Cairo's slums were an unaccustomed sight for Egyptians, used to drinking local soda, which often contained unwanted ingredients — at the worst, even roaches. Before these goods had only been available when brought back from abroad by a relative or friend and they were now being sold on the street corner. Because of the public transportation crises, America also provided Egypt with buses, but this created some problems: they were automatics, noisy and characterized by jerky movements, and the consensus was that they should not be used by pregnant women for fear that they would lose their babies. Automatic transmission was not suitable for the stop-and-go traffic of Cairo's streets.

1 – Sagging and Swagging

Translation

"Are you drawing the map to your house on your face so that you won't get lost?"

[N. B. Having the collar up, like the man on the left, indicates that he is Saudi, along with his oversize guthra.]

Culture

Traditional-minded Arabs view deviations from conventional choices in appearance negatively and think less of the youth whose style choice is very different from the norm.

Translation

Man in traditional clothes: Watch the pants!

Man in non-traditional clothes: No, Son of lawful – this is fashion.

Language

The basic meaning of "Son of lawful" is a good man.[4] It literally means that the child is legitimate, and both literally and metaphorically therefore the opposite of a bastard. It could be used in a variey of situations, either talking about a third person or addressing someone.

---

[4] See also the explanation in "19 – Immigrants," p.419.

Culture

Revealing Clothing

In some Arab countries, wearing revealing clothes or having extreme hairstyles is viewed as a serious offense. In the Arab world, revealing clothes constitutes something different than it does in America; for instance, "sagging and swagging," the style of wearing one's pants belted low, so that one's boxers are showing above the belt, would be considered too revealing and thus offensive. This type of fashion does not have a single proper name in Arabic, but is referred to in the Gulf countries as "Forgive me, father." Wearing one's hair in a mohawk, afro, or spiked would also be considered offensive to some Arabs, as might wearing excessive amounts of jewelry. Usually security forces and religious police (or self-appointed guardians of morality) will crack down on those who wear these revealing clothes or style their hair in such manners. For a first offense, people will be stopped and advised that their style and behavior is un-Islamic and should be changed immediately. For a second offense, people will be arrested and prosecuted. The punishment for these offenses can range according by country, from scolding or a reprimand to flogging to prison or a combination of both.

In the opinion of certain fundamentalists, Westerners are viewed as infidels—generally in Islam Christians and Jews are considered "unbelievers" but not "infidels," since they are "people of the book" with a single God, but some fundamentalists describe Christians as cross-worshipers, and consequently "infidels."[5] Imitating infidel behavior is prohibited in Islam, and therefore a person who is convicted for dressing in this extreme Westernized fashion will never be allowed to give any legal testimony for the rest of his life on the grounds of having "defective character."

In general, following Western styles is regarded as wrong and imitation of the enemy, because of the West's perceived hostility toward Islam, particularly since the invasion of Iraq and the consequent conflicts.

In America or Europe there are some styles of clothes that are only worn by specific groups of people, such as gays. In Arab countries, sometimes young people will adopt these styles, oblivious of the cultural background and intended meanings of the clothes. An example of this would be another type of offensive jeans that not only have zippers in the front, but also in the back. These specific types of pants are referred to as *Ignore me* pants. The style of sagging originated in the '80s and imitates the appearance of young people apprehended by New York Police Department, who were made to take off their shoelaces and belts, because they might be used in a suicide attempt—not yet in jail, they were in their street clothes and in police custody. Many Arabs note the criminal associations and believe that these clothing styles are degenerate even in the West, and another conspiracy to corrupt their youth.

---

[5] In the Qur'an, God describes Christians and Jews as unbelievers and also as "people of the book." Infidels do not believe in the one God of Abrahamic tradition, but some of the people of the book are described as also infidels, which leaves some Muslims unclear as to whether, in God's eyes, Christians and Jews may also be infidels. The people of the book who are infidels may simply refer to those who have lapsed from their faith, or who have strayed into heresy, but in any case God will not accept anyone who takes a religion other than Islam.

Translation

Boy with cell phone: No grandpa, this is globalization!

[*The grandfather holds a piece of elastic, such as is used to belt underwear or pajamas.*]

Culture

The old man appears not to realize that the boy actually has a belt and is choosing not to use it, offering him elastic. However, the cartoon's target is the boy, whose understanding of "globalization" is reduced to fashion trends and accessories.

☪ These elastic bands are widely available in Arab shops, as the thrifty traditions lead people to repair rather than discard underwear and pajamas that have lost theirs original bands. By using a hairpin as a make-shift needle, the waist on pajamas can readily be fitted with a new band.

Translation

Goat: "He [God] creates 40 nearly identical *hairstyles*"

Language

The goat's comment is a play on the phrase "He [God] creates 40 nearly identical looks," which is used as an excuse when one mistakes a person for someone else. In other words, the close resemblance is something of an uncanny, minor miracle.

Likening someone's appearance to an animal is insulting, and especially a food-animal such as a goat. The cartoon is mocking the man's quiff, and he is identified as someone following Western fashions by his "heart" t-shirt and cell phone. T-shirts, especially those with messages, are not considered appropriate wear in Arab countries.

Culture

Traditional Arab men will often look down on an Arab man who has a metro-sexual Western look, because as said before, Arabs prefer men to be an embodiment of masculinity and not to project any look that could be perceived as feminine. It is important for Arab men to keep up with their appearance, but not to the point of caring too much about the look of their hair or clothes. For Arab women, however, this type of look will not lower their opinion of a man; on the contrary, they may like it, especially younger Arab women. When an Arab man looks down upon another Arab man who has this look it could be interpreted as a sign of jealousy.

Translation

Man on right: "You know brother, those foreigners ruin the morals of the country."

Man on left: "No, Father of Muhammad, this is not a foreigner, this is my son."

☪ Customarily, Muslims use rosaries in mosques in performing supererogatory acts of praising God beyond the prescribed prayers. Outside the mosque, he can extend these devotions by constantly using it as a physical reminder of God and the need to live a holy life. Such a visible symbol may also, of course, be used hypocritically by those who find it convenient to be percieved and respected as devout.

Culture

Young Arabs are most likely to get their role models for imitation from movies or TV shows, which in most cases do not show what the people of their own age in Western countries are really like or what they are wearing.

☪ The presence of Western tourists and expatriates in a country can provoke contempt and disgust in the older generation when their appearance and behavior goes against local custom — with men wearing tank tops, long hair and tattoos, women wearing revealing clothes, and public kissing — while young people very much try to imitate their clothes, body language and behavior. This is combined with a general change in body shape and body language among younger people, so that national types, styles of dress and behavior are being eroded, and foreigners are no longer identifiable by sight, as they used to be.

☪ The government is not passive in response to these Westernized approaches to dressing and appearance, imposing fines and sanctions on offenders.

Translation

Title: The new hairstyle laws and fines

Subtitle (on left): This is a graph of different hairstyle fines according to height.

Longest hair (right to left): Twenty dinars, multiplied by amount of wax.

Shorter: 10 dinar fine, increased by quantity of gel.

Short: 5 dinar fine.

Bald: Exempt from fine, because it is widespread.

Title: Sagging

Right: 5 dinar fine for appearance of top of boxers.

Second from right: 10 dinar fine for top of boxers and buttock crack.

Second from left: 20 dinar fine if buttocks and boxers are shown together at half mast.

Left: Arrest and detention if everything is revealed.

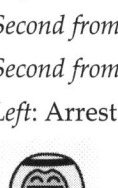 The words for "hairstyle," *tasriHah*, and "fine," *tasHilah*, are similar and juxtaposing them is funny.

Translation

Title: Old Fashion

Man on the right: There is no power or strength except from God. People have stopped covering their shame.

Man of the left: Is this what they call fashion? How disgraceful; these people have no shame.

 When it comes to low-hanging jeans, workmen like these have lead the fashion, though they don't realize it.

Culture

Making vocal criticisms of those who deviate from cultural or religious norms is widely seen as a virtuous act that identifies the critic as a concerned and upright member of society, and many use such denunciations to establish their moral character with new acquaintances. Ironically, a truly devout Muslim, unlike the men in the cartoon, would avert his eyes from the immodest display and refrain from drawing attention to it.

Translation

Title: [My] father allows me

Man on right: Does she have a father to look after her,? Where is her brother? Where is her [male] cousins? I just want to know!

Man on left: Here I am, brother, I am her father—what exactly do you need to know?

Man on right: I just want to know the boutique address so I can get my daughter one like it

Language

The title, "[My] father allows me," is pun on the popular name of this type of jeans, "Forgive me, father," since *samméhli* , "allows me," sounds very close to *samméhni*, "forgive me." It satirizes fathers who allow their daughters to wear this type of clothes.

Culture

Traditonal Arabs will not talk directly to a woman about wearing clothes or behaving in a manner that are deemed inappropriate, but instead to her male relatives, reminding them to uphold tradition and ensure that she is modest. Most men will try avoid talking to a man about the conduct of a female member of his family, and if they do comment they must, of course, be tactful, since any remark supposes that the man will act on it, either defending the woman's honor or correcting her (in the most extreme cases, possibly, by honor killing).

☪ The type of dress exemplified by the girl in the cartoon is not common, but is found most often amongst college students.

Translation

Title: He-mash-cool

Right: With his sister…

"Do you have no shame, going out wearing those clothes? You want to disgrace the family with this getup? You think you are going to the beach [*live by the sea*]? Go and change, the hell with you!"

Left: With his girlfriend…

"I swear on my honor, you are the bomb! I love and respect women with a sense of fashion! Yes, yes, this is the real deal!"

Language

"Disgracing the family" refers to the way that women's conduct or dress reflects on the family, so that their good behavior redounds to the family's credit but their bad behavior disgraces it.

Culture

Brothers are very protective of a sister. They will usually ask her where she is going and where she has been, and will look at her clothes before she leaves the house to make sure that is dressed appropriately. Sometimes, they will go as far as spying on her to assure themselves of her chaste behavior. The brother even looks out for the welfare of his sister after her marriage. For example, he may fight with his sister's husband over the husband's behavior towards his sister. Usually, sisters have a deep admiration and love for their brothers, and when they choose a husband, they gravitate towards a man who resembles a brother. The relationship between brothers and sisters in this culture is much stronger than the same relationship in America. For some girls, their first—and sometimes only—contact with the opposite sex is with their brothers and many girls choose their husband from among their brothers' friends.

☪ The actual reason Arabs are protective and overbearing toward their sisters is for fear of "karmic" retribution of their own misdeeds towards women. Arabs are strong believers in the idea that what goes around comes around: the men know that they have done things that would cause a woman's disgrace and fear that their sisters or mothers will therefore be disgraced in a similar manner.

☪ Girls are generally closer to their mother, while boys are closer to their father. Girls will form the strongest bonds with their mother, then their sisters, then their brothers, and finally their father. Of course, this situation does vary by family, but this trend is fairly common.

Swearing (not cursing)

Arabs swear a great deal—probably more than anyone else— and swear by different things according to the gravity of their oath. At the top, of course, comes Allah. The man in the cartoon swears on his honor, but he could also swear on his mother's honor. Men may also swear by their beard or their moustache (if they have one), whereas women can swear by the side-lock, generally holding it when they utter the oath, *"Wa-hayat maksoosee!"* Both sexes can swear "by bread and salt," reflecting the bond of breaking bread with the other person.

Translation

Title: The shy are dead.

Boy: Do you see, father? This retarded girl is wearing her little sister's dress.

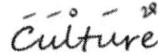 The child does not recognize the clothes as tight and revealing, but thinks that the woman must be stupid to have put on her little sister's clothes by mistake.

Language

When someone uses the phrase "The shy are dead," it expresses shock at those who are not modest and do not shy from wearing revealing clothes or behave in an outrageous way. It is used in the same way that English-speaking people say, "Those people have no shame."

☪ The word *'abit*, here translated as "retarded," literally means soft, unripe, or immature and does not carry the same weight as it does in polite English usage. It is frequently used to describe the behavior of people who act in a foolish or thoughtless manner, more or less "dumb."

Culture

The Arabic proverb that roughly translates to "the shy are dead" comes from an old story. The story tells of a fire in a women's public bath. Because of the fire, the naked women were forced to run out into the streets. However, the women who were too ashamed of their nakedness did not escape and died inside. As a result, all of those who felt shy were dead.

☪ The culture of public baths that is commemorated in the above proverb still exists in many parts of the Arab world, but the spread of sophisticated plumbing has generally rendered public baths superfluous. Now, most customers of public baths are working class, and even they only go for special occasions like marriages or for intensive spa treatments.

Translation

Title: At the marina

Man in hat: What's going on? Toutou, this is the daughter of your doorman.

Man on left: That's right Mido. When she's in Cairo, she's one thing: when she's at the marina, she's something else!

Language

In the second bubble, you will see the phrases *hala hala* and *Yalem Allah*. Like saying "golly" for "God," "Hala" is a polite alteration of "Allah" used to avoid blasphemously uttering His name in vain. *Yalem Allah*, dispenses with these niceties and means, "Allah knows." When a clause beginning with *hala hala* is followed by a clause beginning with *Yalem Allah*, it indicates that what the two statements or things described contradict each other. In the context of the cartoon, Toutou's doorman's daughter is a modest, good girl at home in Cairo but is happy to cut loose and show skin when she is on vacation.

The un-bowdlerized version of *hala hala*—*Allah Allah*—has entirely different meanings. Spoken slowly and reverently, it expresses wonder and praise at a remarkable sight or experience. Pronounced quickly, with measured sarcasm, it is a saying of extreme disappointment and regretful disgust at having come across evidence of some disgraceful moral failing.

Nicknames like "Toutou" and "Mido" automatically register as "preppy" and westernized—at least in their own eyes.

☪ Girls from lowly backgrounds are often overlooked, but can also be exert some fascination over young men, who may fantasize about what is hidden by their dress in a way that they would never view wealthier girls, regarding them as more accessible and likely to put up less resistance as well. It is in many ways comparable to attitudes in Europe and America.in the nineteenth and earlier twentieth centuries.

Summer at the beach is more relaxed and women will show more skin than they would ever dream of at home—so the Arab's worst nightmare—both the woman's and even more her male relative's— is meeting someone whom she knows from home. The cartoon is taken more from the male perspective, though, the men's fascination with how different the girl is and Toutou's pride that it's his doorman whose daughter is hot (which is not very realistic); it also shows the girl's happiness at freedom from the restrictions of her daily life and at being admired.

Translation

Right to left, top then bottom:

Frame 1: New Directions for Contemporary Youth Poetry!!

2: Bursting at reality!

3: Scatterbrained and lost in life!!

4: My life is a mess!!

5: Surrender to reality and go with the flow!!

6: Emptiness and intellectual drought!!

Language

The word for "hair" *sh'ar* and "poetry" *sh'er* are spelled the same with different vowels in Arabic (the only difference is the *Harkat*, the dash the position of which indicates the intended vowel). Also, the word "trend" is literally "direction," so the title plays on new [trends/directions] for [hair/poetry].

Aided by the similarity of the Arabic words for "hair" and "poetry," the portentous title guises the discussion of the frivolous topic of hair styles in the sublime language of poetry.

2 – Social Life

Translation

Title: They know each other!!

[*N.B. The men are sweating with embarrassment, and trying to avoid each other's eyes, because they are accompanied by their wife.*]

Culture

In Arab culture men avoid being seen with female members of their family, and most men will avoid acknowledging acquaintances in their presence. A man is most embarrassed to be seen with his wife, less so with his sister, and least with his mother.

Arab men consider their wives valuable treasures,[6] best kept hidden. There is a very big fear among men that these treasures might be judged, degraded, or stolen if displayed in public. The fear of criticism or lust is particularly strong, as women can be objectified through such "revealing" attire as an incompletely covered face or clothing that is tight enough to reveal the outline of the body.

---

[6] See "10 – Women," p.195.

When an Arab man goes out in public with his wife it is a stressful event, especially within their own neighborhood where recognition is unavoidable. If the couple meets a friend of the husband, it is bad manners for him to do more than nod a salutation, and any show of interest in the wife is rude. If they cannot avoid him, there are two ways to handle the encounter. The traditional approach is for the wife to continue walking as her husband stops to talk to his friend. By continuing her walk, she is indicating to him that he needs to keep the conversation as short as possible, or he may tell her to keep walking for the same reason. In a more modern approach, the wife will stand a short distance away from the men, out of earshot of their conversation. Even in the most Westernized Arab countries (Egypt, Lebanon, Tunisia, and Morocco) these rules are observed to a certain degree. There a wife or sister may stop during an encounter and stand relatively close to the men, but she will rarely take part in the conversation. Usually the friend will end the conversation quickly as a courtesy, so that the couple may continue their outing.

☪Furthermore, an Arab man might not want to be seen with a female relative because he knows she will be seen as an object of sexual desire by any men who are looking on. It would be embarrassing for him to be seen as a man whose wife or sister is coveted.

Translation

Title: The Difference between the Married Man & the Bachelor

Bachelor
1: In girls' eyes: The eye on him

Married Man
1: In girls' eyes: Used

2: Freedom: limitless	2: Freedom: Limited or non-existent
3: In his mother's eye: Satisfied with him	3: In his mother's eye: Very angry with him, because of his wife.
4: In the eyes of society: A Rogue	4: In the eyes of society: Established Man
5: At work: Dismiss him; he can take care of himself.	5: At work: Sin/wrongdoing! A family behind him
6: His mobile: Rich with girls and friends	6: His mobile: Devoid of girls' numbers. Only his wife, mother-in-law, & mother
7: The salary: For himself	7: The salary: For his wife
8: His friends: With them day & night.	8: His friends: He barely sees them, and spending an evening with them? Almost doesn't exist.
9: Social occasion: If he doesn't visit anyone, nobody blames him because he's single.	9: Social occasion: If he doesn't visit anybody, people will be upset with him and stop asking after him.
10: He's always at: malls, coffee shops, or *out on the town*.[7]	10: He's always at: a vegetable market or thrift markets

Language

1: The eye on him means he's desirable

5: "Sin/wrongdoing" is a warning uttered to stop someone from doing something *haram* (wicked or unlawful). The antonym of *haram* is *halal*. "A family behind him" means that he has to support a family. When, in Arabic, something is spoken of as being "behind" someone, it means that the thing is that person's responsibility. For example, "Work behind him," means, "He must do some specific work." The expression can be used to enquire about whether someone is busy at the moment, with the question, "Is there something behind you?"

6: Cellular phones have two names in Arab countries. They are either called, "travellers/rovers," or they're given the British term, "mobile," as in "mobile phone."

Culture

A gulf separates the married from the unmarried man. The married man embodies wisdom, stability, life experience, responsibility, and good moral fiber. The single man, on the other hand, is associated less with these qualities. Being married is a social expectation, and a man of marriageable age who is not married is thought of as being strange. A middle-aged man who has never been married is very rare and sad, as it is assumed that there must be something truly wrong with him. The desire to be married is referred to as the desire to complete the second half of his religion, for being settled in marriage is hoped to keep a man in a righteous and moral lifestyle.

Many Arab people carry their newspaper with them, as in this picture, wedged under their arm. The newspaper has more of a purpose than just to be read; it also acts as a prayer rug, and as a clean surface to sit on anywhere you go. This is especially important to Muslim Arabs, because if they sit on a dirty surface, their clothes will be soiled with impurity and they won't be able to pray. It is also used as an

---

[7] *Dowar Abdoun* is a particular place, here translated as *out on the town*.

umbrella to protect from the sun, or as a fan to cool off. A newspaper in Arab countries will never go to waste, because it is worth money new or old, and on average will be read by seven people, not just the one person who bought it. People then sell their old newspapers by the kilo to grocery stores, restaurants, or sandwich vendors, who use the newspaper to wrap up food or blot oil from falafel or french fries. In the occurrence of a fatal accident in the street, Arab passersby will cover the body with newspapers. Newspapers are the main source of news for people in Arab countries. You can get your newspaper from the vendors, usually located near bus or metro stops, who sell newspapers straight from piles on the sidewalk. You can also get your paper delivered, and the delivery man will encircle the rolled-up newspaper with a strip of cut-up cigarette box, like a napkin ring. An Arab delivery man must have very good aim, because he has to throw the newspaper accurately and far, all the way to balconies on the 5th or 6th floor of buildings.

☪ Many Arabs have a good aim, because throwing stones is the method of choice in defending oneself against stray dogs or human attackers. The stone throwing during demonstrations by Palestinian youths against the Israel Defense Forces (IDF) and civilians defined that violence for many.

☪ Arab young men, like the one in this cartoon, wear backwards caps with the New York Yankees logo, and other clothing styles adopted from the U.S., without really knowing what is behind these cultural symbols.

☪ As the third line tells us, this happy bachelor enjoys the knowledge that he has satisfied his mother. Satisfying the expectations of both one's parents is extremely important to Arabs, but the mother's satisfaction in particular is held to be akin to God's satisfaction. A major step in dying process for Arab parents is to put their children's minds at ease and explicitly state that they are satisfied with them; for one's parents to die without expressing satisfaction in this way is a crushing blow to any Arab.

Translation

A single man being thrown out of town by the people of Riyadh, the capital of Saudi Arabia. He is labeled "single man" on his shirt and the sign reads *al-Roub' al-Khaly*, "The Empty Quarter," the famous desert wilderness of the Arabian Peninsula.

Culture

Single men are often discriminated against and isolated from certain aspects of the society. Family-oriented stores, restaurants, and parks discourage or ban them, mainly because of their behavior. Older single men in particular often seek out the opposite sex to engage in conversation or pay unwanted attention to women who are out with their families, causing annoyance and giving offence. Owners of establishments therefore deter single men from coming to their stores in order to maintain their good name and keep trouble away. Furthermore, the stores want to encourage women and families over groups of single men, since they are more likely to spend money in these establishments.

In many Arab countries, young men have been prohibited from congregating in local malls. Many stores within these malls, particularly the restaurants, cater exclusively to whole families, and both storeowners and mall security fear that these single young men come not to shop, but rather to harass these families' younger female members. An inadvertent result is, in fact, the closure of many shops that market to precisely these young men—which, due to lack of sales, have had to relocate to the street, where their clientele may still browse and buy.

Translation

Title: Who else but you my mother!!

(From top to bottom, right to left)

Man: "My love, may Allah makes you happy, the 'Open Day' is for families only."

Security guard: "Father of youth, not allowed. Today the mall is for families only."

Maitre d': "Sorry mister, the café is for families only."

Bouncer: "Prohibited, father of youth, the party is for 'Couples Only.'"

His mother: "Atwa, why have you come so late dear, I couldn't get to sleep. So I waited to open the door for you."

Language

"My love," "my beloved," *Habiby*, can be said to men to establish camaraderie, even for people who don't know each other, and is mostly used in Levantine Arabic.

"May Allah make you happy" or "may Allah please you" is a form of request for somebody to do something that you want them to do, a kind of "please."

Abu al-shabab, "father of youth," meaning the best of young men, is a phrase used to address young people, mosty used casually and by street-smart types who wish to convey a certain "cred," such as those who use it in the cartoon, a bouncer and a security guard.

Also notice how the English phrases "Open Day" and "Couples Only" are used in speech, although in both phrases the "p" would become a "b."

Culture

This cartoon demonstrates the enormous importance of family in the Arab world. Time and again in this cartoon, the man is rejected because he is attempting to function in society as a lone man, without a family or even a wife accompanying him and following him. Without having the basic interpersonal connections of the family, he cannot branch out and integrate into the wider social connections of society at large.

If he is experiencing some delay starting his own family, the last panel shows that at least he always has a place with the family of his birth. His mother waits devotedly for him, and he will always have a place in her home. This essential family connection is indissoluble, and it gives him both a physical as well as a societal home.

Translation

Title: The Solitary Viewer

Clockwise from upper right:

Man on cell phone: Allo, allo, allo.

Man calling: "Aboud, come over here, there's a seat!"

Man in front row: (sleeping) خ خ خ =zzz

Teenage boys (one with Yankees cap): (snickering) كخ كخ كخ كخ = krr krr krr krr

Woman with baby: "I'm telling you, shut up! Shut up!"

Man handing beverage to friend: "Here you go!"

Man on cell phone: "I can't hear! Hello?"

Woman to child standing on seat: "Tell him what your name is."

Culture

The reasons for going to the cinema may include more than just seeing a movie. Most theaters are air conditioned and provides a sanctuary from the afternoon heat when it is at its worst. One of the most popular reasons to go to the movies is for a nap, and it is common to find several patrons asleep in the theater seats. Like in the Western world, the cinema is widely regarded as a perfect place to meet up with friends. Due to the inherent extroverted and effervescent nature of Arab people, the cinema is a forum for socializing rather than just simply watching the movie. The darkened ambiance provides a perfect opportunity for flirtation with the opposite sex. This situation is especially beneficial for women in a *hijab* since the dim lighting acts as a shield against the shame and criticism she would receive in much more overt settings and makes discretion far simpler. The Arab rating system is far less rigid or stratified than that found in the West. Films generally fall into one of two categories, either general admission or adults only. Most Arab audiences take an immerseive approach to the film and it is common for them to verbally express themselves or talk to the characters on the screen. Moviegoers who prefer a quieter experience can go to what are known as first-class cinemas. Here the environment caters more to viewing the film rather than providing an atmosphere for socializing. Concession stands can be found in the lobbies of the first-class cinemas while in the more sociable cinemas it is common to find vendors passing through the theater selling snacks and drinks. During the summer months, open-air (ceilingless) theaters are most popular.

☪ Note the woman wearing the *hijab* on the fourth row back is kissing a boy—simply wearing this type of attire does not mean that women will not "behave badly," but they need to be hidden from view since otherwise they can be publicly admonished.

☪ Declaring a film "adults only" guarantees its success since the moviegoer will assume that it contains racy, steamy content. In most Arab countries sex is heavily censored so young Arab men will go to a movie with an "adults only" rating in hopes of catching a glimpse of nudity.

Translation

Bar sign: Good Time Bar!

Sign on door: Closed for praying.

In this cartoon, the phrase "Good Time" refers to not just any bit of wholesome, innocent fun, but rather serves as a euphemism for the enjoyably illicit and debauched. In the Arab world, certain familiar phrases can be euphemized in the names of shops and businesses. The situation is similar to that in the West, where publicly presentable, innocuous-sounding names and phrases are regularly used to indicate the illicit nature of the services offered.

The humor in the cartoon above is that it would be unthinkable for an observant Muslim who keeps his prayer schedule to work in a bar.

Culture

In many Arab countries, work stops during prayer time in both the private sector and government circles. If a person is working in a store, he will hang a sign, similar to the one in this cartoon, to indicate that he has gone to pray in a mosque or is praying inside the store. If the store is close to a mosque, a person should go there to pray, instead of remaining inside the store. This advice derives from a saying of the Prophet Muhammad that there is no place for the neighbor of a mosque to pray at but the mosque.

A visitor to an Arab country will rarely see an intoxicated person. Bars are not as plentiful in Arab countries as in other parts of the world. Most of these countries practice Islam, which prohibits any contact with alcohol, including, of course, consumption. There are almost no street bars -, and the bars that do exist are located inside hotels or casinos. Even these few remaining bars are often only allowed because of fears that tourists will not be willing to visit a completely dry country. These fears have not, however been borne out in many cases, such as when Egypt Air stopped serving alcohol. Indeed, one would hope that the lure of 5,000 years of civilization, some of the world's grandest sites, and a place at the crossroads of history might perhaps be sufficient to make up for a few days' temperance.

Unfortunately, Muslims often turn to other substances, such as *qat* in Yemen or *hasheesh* in Egypt, to get the same effects as alcohol.

Hasheesh

Hasheesh use began in the Arab world in the religious practices of Sufis. Their tradition pursues transcendental experience and communion with God—the epiphanic religious experience described by Freud as "oceanic"—and they employ a variety of means to bring them to such a state, including ritual rhythmic chants and movement. Taking hasheesh was found to facilitate and heighten the experience, and it became an important part of many Sufis' religious practice.

Of course, not all drug users are pursuing such exalted aims, and hasheesh came to be abused as a purely recreational drug. Its potent sedative and dissociative effects were great balms to the vast segment of Arab society that sought to escape the conditions of injustice, oppression, and poverty in which they lived through the mellow bliss of the drug. By 1900, the drug's abuse and the social problems it caused had made it one of the most despised substances of abuse in respectable Arab society. The hasheesh user, known in Arabic as a *hashash*, was equated with criminality and social ills, specifically pick-pocketing and theft. The social connotations of its use were soon to undergo yet another transformation, though, as the outbreak of the First World War cut off the supply of fine European wines for the elites in the Arab world. Hasheesh, thereupon, was taken up by inarguably respectable citizens as a replacement, and the stigma vanished. Whereas once a well-appointed home would have included an amply stocked bar, these were quickly replaced by domestic hasheesh dens, called "stitches" in colloquial Arabic. During this period, many a *hashash* was able to maintain his habit by finding employment as a stitch-attendant and taking part of his earnings in drags of hasheesh. Throughout the course of the war, it remained perfectly legal and served an important function in the absence of palatable liquor and the government had plenty to occupy it in defeating the Central Powers. However, when the Great War had ended, the British authorities banned hasheesh in the hopes of restoring alcoholic drinks—imported by the British—to their former popularity. Legal bans on hasheesh, though often initially imposed by Western powers, survive to this day throughout the Arab world.

Nevertheless, the practice of surreptitiously taking hasheesh continues to be widespread. It may strike observers as incongruous that even faithful Muslims who carefully abstain from enjoying the intoxicating effects of alcohol might be so willing to partake of other strong, psychoactive chemicals, but the phenomenon is justified according to a strict and literal interpretation of the Qur'an. Hasheesh was unknown in the Arab world at the time of the founding of Islam and was therefore not explicitly banned—and therefore, so the argument goes, it is not forbidden in Islam.

Because hasheesh lowers one's critical faculties and leads the brain to make apparently random associations, its users, frequently say and do bizarre, ridiculous, or frankly hilarious things, and the conversations of *hashashin* are staples of Arab humor. Hasheesh use, in Arab humor, serves much the same function as "walking into the bar" does in many Western jokes: it is the condition under which normal rules of sense can be bent. Interestingly, by figuring largely in Arab jokes, hasheesh can continue to serve, even for those who do not personally use it, the purpose that it has for centuries. It helps people escape the difficult circumstances of their lives. Across the Arab world, one of the first responses to difficult political, economic, or social circumstances is to meet them with a joke, and often, that joke will involve the little absurdities of a *hashash*.

Translation

Title: Invitations Market

Clockwise from right:

First man in elevator: "By Allah, you are first. Please, go ahead."

Second man in elevator: "You are the one on the right. Please, you go ahead."

Man with chicken leg: "Man, I swore that you will eat it. By Allah's glory, please eat it, good man. According to the poet, Galaxy, I am telling you the last part is the best! "

Man across table from him: "Man, I swear on the honor of my sisters, I am full! I'm telling you I can't!"

Woman on cell phone: "My love, you hang up first! No, you…you!"

Man at cash register with wallet: "This could get serious. *You* stay out of my face! I swear on my honor, you will not pay!"

Man at cash register with cash in both hands: "I swear that I will pay. I told you already, stay out of my face! You will not pay, I'm telling you!"

Man in corner offering cigarette: "Man, I swear to Allah, you will not smoke anything other than the cigarettes I'm giving you!"

Man in hat: "I told you I don't change brands. I don't!"

Who will go first?

Arabs pride themselves as being courteous to others and consider it a very important part of their culture. It is common for them to fight over who will be the more generous. Certain rules apply, such as whoever is standing on the right is always given the privilege of going first. As the right side is considered superior, even if the man standing to the right is behind a man to the left, the man on the left should give way, as with the two men in the elevator here. The look on the face of the woman behind might show simple frustration at being held up or anger that the men are forgetting the tradition of "ladies first."

Who will eat the last piece?

In dining situations, a host will insist on guests eating the last choice piece of the meal — this is usually meat, since it is the most expensive part of the meal and indeed essential to hospitality. This cartoon shows the host getting angry that his guest is declining, and trying to convince him that the last piece is the most delicious, by quoting the authority of poetry and swearing on it. This transaction is considered serious business, and if the guest still declined, the host would be insulted. So the guest must take at least a bite. The host cannot be the one to eat this piece, since it would go against the understanding of hospitality and generosity.

Who will hang up first?

As in the West, lovers will often playfully and flirtatiously argue about who will hang up the phone first. However, for Arab people it is also a matter of courtesy. Finishing any telephone conversation involves a back and forth of good wishes and prayers, with each wish being countered by another until one party finally summons the courage to cut the exchanges off.

Who will pay?

The most contentious fight over generosity usually happens in restaurants when the bill arrives. It is common for people to fight over who will pay it in order to maintain their reputation for generosity and appear courteous—there is nothing worse than a miser or tightwad. It is not unusual to see people, cash in hand, fighting almost hand to hand over who will pay. Sometimes it can escalate into one person throwing money in the cashier's face while the other will try to convince the cashier that the other is younger, from a different city, etc. and should get the money back. This is a vagary cashiers must deal with on a daily basis.

I don't change brands!

People will usually insist on giving cigarettes to their friends. When offering a cigarette, an Arab will usually offer the pack with one cigarette protruding as in the cartoon. The only accepted, respectful way for a person to decline is to claim that they do not want to change brands.

Many people consider this habit as vapid and insincere. From the expression on the cashier's face and his thought bubble containing a hand "flipping the bird," it is obvious that he is one of these critics.

The poet named "Galaxy" is fictitious, and the name is obviously non-Arab, which adds to the humor. Arabs love to pepper their speech with quotations: the first source is the Prophet Muhammad, though the Hadith are often dubious; the second is the Qur'an itself. The same is true in writing, with the addition of poets as a third source, though the rise in religious observance has diminished the importance of this last. Arabs learn this way of writing in school, where their Arabic language teacher will tell them that the more they quote Hadith, the Qur'an or poetry in their composition the higher their mark will be. Quotation is used to reinforce whatever point the speaker or writer wishes to convey. Newspaper articles are similarly reinforced with devout quotation, from the mouths of the stories' persons in the case of factual reports, or from the writer's own pen in the case of columns and opinion.

Translation

Title: The international day of the prisoner

(From right to left)

1. Child. ("Housekeeper" written on woman)

2. Young man

3. Mother

4. Father ("Work" written on briefcase)

5. Grandfather. (Young man in mirror is "The past")

Translation

Title: How everyone perceives you.

(From top to bottom, right to left)

"New Manager"

"Your wife"

"Your girlfriend" [*N.B. man's arm reads "brad pitt" in English*]

"The government: "You still alive?'" [*N.B. spraycan reads: Insecticide*]

"A trader"

"Your son: 'Father is strong'"

☪ The Western reader may be shocked at the depiction of an African woman as a slave in the upper right-hand panel. The grass skirt, primitive nudity and large lips are all hallmarks of racially prejudiced stereotypes. In the Arab world, such stereotypes still thrive, and the shorthand for slave involves this kind of image.

This stereotype does not necessarily result from hate, but also possibly from ignorance (although, it can be argued that the latter, left untreated, leads inevitably to the former). To Arabs, the African is still the preeminent "Other," subjected to an exoticized misunderstanding that arose from a general unfamiliarity with Africans. On the other hand, though, the cartoon *is*, after all, about the vagaries of subjective perception: thus, there is a chance that the gross stereotype is "embedded" within the cartoon expressly in order to criticize those who still buy into its validity. In that case, the depiction is comprehensive in its foolishness because such stereotypes are comprehensively foolish.

☪ Natural gas pipelines are not common. Thus, most homes get their gas from refillable gas cylinders, of the sort depicted in the bottom left-hand panel, often LPG (Liquid Petroleum Gas, mainly propane) or butane. Weighing upward of one hundred pounds, it is no surprise that the young child thinks his dad a superman for lifting one of them.

Gas cylinder storehouses are typically situated in the center of residential areas — presumably, in order to facilitate the retrieval and distribution of these heavy tanks for use within the home. However, the placement of these storehouses has been heavily criticized by the media, who view the presence of an unguarded mass of gas canisters a disaster waiting to happen: a problem with a single cylinder could quickly lead to a chain reaction that, in power, is identical to the detonation of a bomb within this unsuspecting residential district.

Arab Culture

Translation

Title: How the khaligies [people of the Arabian Gulf] look.

Culture

In the Gulf, one can distinguish between people of different countries by their appearance—for example, by the size and shape of the person's *guthra* (headdress), by the style of his dress, or by the nature and breadth of his *iqal*.

Moving clockwise from the top right corner, the first panel portrays an Omani, whose uniquely distinct garments set him far apart from the others depicted; in particular, his headdress and top reveal him to be Bedouin. In the next panel, the man's collar and oversized, checkered-red *guthra* clearly declare him a Saudi: the Saudi collar stands upright with two or three buttons at the neck, while the Saudi *guthra* is larger than those of other Gulf countries and more frequently checkered red (the checkered-red *guthra* is reserved for colder weather, and Saudi Arabia is the coldest country in the Gulf). In the third panel, the man's dress altogether lacks buttons or a raised or standing collar, showing him to be from the United Arab Emirates. The fourth man hails from Kuwait, where men wear just one, centrally placed button on their dress. In the fifth panel, the man's creased, folded collar (similar to that of the American polo shirt) identifies him as Qatari. Finally, one can see from the standing collar and two buttons that the sixth panel also portrays a Saudi; however, the numerous threadbare patches show that, unlike the man in panel two, the man in panel six is impoverished.

From left to right: Abdul Aziz al-Ghurair of The al-Ghurair Family, U.A.E.; His Royal Highness Prince Alwaleed Bin Talal, Saudi Arabia; Mishal Kanoo, of the Kanoo Family, Bahrain; Suleiman al-Rajhi, Saudi Arabia; Rashid al-Galadari, of the Galadari family, U.A.E.

Culture

The photograph above displays five of the fifty wealthiest Arabs in the world. There exists, in the West, a stereotype of the rich Arab man: typically, he is thought to have made his money in the oil industry, and to enjoy a peculiar combination of religious sobriety and luxuriant wealth. But while there is a fair degree of oil wealth circulating throughout the Arab world, the very richest Arabs—including four of the five in the picture above—do not always derive their fortunes from such pursuits. Rather, their money comes from a diversity of assets and holdings in a variety of key industries, such as real estate, construction and, above all, banking.

A biographical study of the men in the photograph—as well as a quick perusal of any of a number of "wealthiest" lists—will reveal that the perhaps crucial prerequisite to fortune-making in the Arab world is a connection to either a royal family or to political leaders. Once one achieves a certain income bracket, it is said, a person's capacity to accumulate wealth begins to increase exponentially. Likewise, if a person with a modest personal fortune forges a relationship with such politicians or royals, he is all but guaranteed enormous returns on his investments, as well as lucrative investment and business opportunities theretofore unavailable.

Such political connections are crucial to a number of Arab industries, particularly those of real estate and construction. Only through the friendly aid of well-placed acquaintances can an entrepreneur in these industries acquire the national (and international) development grants that fuel corporate growth. And once the entrepreneur has begun growing his fortune through the right connections, he will possess the capital sufficient for the purchase of stock and assets in global corporations.

As the reader will surely note, a surprising percentage of the listed "wealthiest Arabs" are not individual people, but rather families. This is a phenomenon uncommon to the Western world. The reason for this is the preponderance of properly family-run businesses within the Arab world. Unlike in the West, where a small business' growth typically results in the company's going public—and, in turn, in the influx of outside businessmen into its newly corporate infrastructure—a traditional, tribal-based mentality makes it such that Arab businesses often keep things decidedly *within* the family, as owners will trust relatives more than other, non-relative workers. Thus, Arab families will often function as individual entrepreneurs, purchasing assets and making investments in the name of a single, family-operated entity.

Men who have become rich are a source of regional pride and interest. In the comments attached to online articles about the very rich one often finds heartfelt pleas for money and assistance, made in the hope that the subject of the article will read the comments and help. Very often, happily, these deserving requests are answered.

Arab Culture

Translation

In circle: "Advertisement"

Counterclockwise from top right square.

"Excellent opportunity for those who like to acquire rare and unusual things."

"For sale, tomato-paste can-opener that can also open tuna cans and cheese cans. / Dead parrot: when he was alive he was worth 5,000."

"Polaroid. When you take your brother's picture, it will print out your cousin. / A black lamp -100. For bedroom. When you turn it on, it makes your room dark so you can sleep well."

"Dozen pallets of tea, buttonhole on the left. / Wall clock, with the wall. / Aquarium fish that can swim in steam. / Outside intercom that, when someone uses it, displays his [government] ID number."

These joke ads give a good sense of Arabs' absurdist humor and their delight in surreal associations, it really is worth taking some time to think about each of them as a key to what Arabs find funny. (Note that the dead parrot would not evoke shades of Monty Python to an Arab reader and that it's not entirely clear if the seller of the can-opener is stupid or just trying to impress a stupid reader with the opener's versatility — to an Arab, cheese is by default feta cheese, which is generally sold in tin-cans.)

Translation

Counterclockwise from top right.

"A golden opportunity. Mercedes Benz 500, Model 1981, upgraded to 2006. To discuss: 1941122"

"Our son, Adheam, please come home, all your requests are answered. That Devil's cell phone #2 [Nokia 6680] — you will find it under your pillow. — Your Family"

"Hurry before it's too late. Bulldozer, yellow, personal, used carefully."

"Elian el-Zohin advertises that his sponsor Iqbal Khan, who works as an engineer, has given him a final exit visa and hasn't yet returned."

Each classified ad shown in the cartoon is funny for its own reasons. The first one is funny because in Arab countries, cars will sometimes be modified to resemble the newer model, e.g. a 1981 car will be given a slight change so that it will resemble the 1982 model. However, the person in the ad is stating that he has modified his car from a 1981 model to a 2006 model, which is excessively ambitious. The second ad states that a young man has run away because his parents will not buy him a better cell phone; the ad is a plea for the son to return because the family has relented and the phone is waiting under his pillow. This is a very paltry reason for a son to run away, which is the source of the ad's humor for Arabs. The third ad is funny because the "slightly used" bulldozer for sale is being advertised as previously being used for personal purposes; few people, especially in Arab countries, would maintain a bulldozer for personal use. In the fourth ad, an employee has given an exit visa to his employer (usually, employers give them to employees) and the employer has yet to return. The names are recognizably Saudi and Pakistani respectively, and if a sponsored person absconded before the end of his contract that would be a reason for publishing his picture and name, to stop others from hiring him.

Culture

The sponsorship system of employment (*kafalah*) in Arab countries requires that foreign workers seeking employment need to put themselves under the sponsorship of their employers. Sponsorship gives employers a huge amount of power over their workers. They can prohibit their sponsored employees from working for other people, hold their passports, control their movements, and have the ability to withhold the permission that the employees need to travel. The sponsors' power, unfortunately, is open to abuse: sponsors might hold their employees' wages, and the employees cannot file complaints against them without their permission. Some even see it as a modern form of slavery. Recognizing the abject and dangerous dependence which this system placed upon foreign workers, opposition to it has grown in recent years and Bahrain has abolished the sponsorship system altogether.

Arab young people are very aware of designer labels, and some prominent Middle Eastern brands enjoy high popularity. Nokia, however, rates number one.

The Sleeping Sponsor

In many Arab countries, especially in the Gulf, foreigners cannot start a business without local partnership. This is mandated by governments for two reasons: to help alleviate rising unemployment and to help the local population gain the knowledge and experience required to run a business. The governments hope that by requiring foreign business owners to work with local partners, the locals will learn the skills needed to start their own businesses in the future. There is no prerequisite to be hired other than nationality. Often times, sponsors are either not interested in learning the profession of their partners, or they are too old to engage actively in the operation of their partner-business. This leads to negligent sponsors who receive payment without actually working. The foreign partners will pay an individual to be a worker in name-only. The governments tacitly allow this loophole to lessen the economic strain on poor families, who need the income that this sponsorship brings.

The sponsor system can be abused by both parties. Citizens can sponsor multiple companies, receiving either monthly stipends from several companies or a percentage of the companies' profits without actively engaging in the operations of the businesses. Usually the contract between the native sponsor and foreign partner includes clauses that absolve the sponsor of responsibility for any illegal action by the foreign company, but the sponsor can be held accountable if their partner does not pay back a loan. It is the local's responsibility to obtain authorization for the company to work in their area; this includes paying taxes and unemployment insurance. Sometimes sponsors neglect to pay the necessary fees, forcing the company to cover expenses. On the other hand, sometimes the sponsor will take all the responsibility for a crooked investor. The partner may leave the country without paying workers' salaries, leaving the sponsor responsible (this is not uncommon in the Arab world and some workers in the Gulf will not be paid for months at a time).

Translation

Title: Sign Language Translation

In American:
Excellent
Victory sign
You're a dead man
Free ride

In Arabic:
I'll give you what's coming your way
Give me a cigarette.
You're invited to eat a mansaf [Jordanian meal].
The boss wants to talk to you.

[N.B. In this cartoon, "Sign language" refers not to the language for the deaf but rather to the hand signals people use in every day interactions.]

Culture

Some hand gestures used in the Arab world look very similar to those used by Americans—but often with very different meanings and with slight differences in how they move or are used. It's worth noting that the first Arabic gesture rocks backwards and forwards at the wrist, and that in the sign requesting a cigarette the fingers are close together, imitating holding a cigarette, with the palm facing the person signing. The sign with two fingers, which looks like the American "gun" sign, indicates "you plural" and is moved from side to side to indicate who is being invited. The thumb sign points over the shoulder, to indicate the boss or whoever might want to talk.

Hand gestures are important in a good number of cartoons and it is worth paying special attention to their meaning and context.

Translation

Angry man: May God run you through the sieve, God willing, I told you don't talk to me while you're sitting in a coffee shop smoking *maasil* [hookah tobacco].

Language

This speaking of running through a sieve refers to a hadith (saying of the Prophet Muhammad) that refers to a time in which rampant loose morals will bring God to test everyone as if through a sieve to distinguish the good from the bad. The wish that the man on the other end of the phone might be tested does not necessarily equate with a wish that the man might be found wanting and be damned; it is a potent enough wish that the man might be put through the agonies and suffering of a thorough testing. It is a very grim curse indeed to wish the trials of Job on someone (Job is known as Ayoub in Arabic).

☪ Arabs often use "God willing", *In sha' Allah,* to wish good things on their friends and family: e.g. "God willing, he'll get a job." It is far more unusual for it to be paired with a curse, as here, and this is surely a sign both of the man's volatile nature and the great provocation of having smoke pour out of his phone.

☪ The first flavored tobacco was molasses or sweet tobacco (molasses is called black honey and eaten with bread the same as bee or white honey, which is more expensive). Four centuries ago, a shipping accident mixed tobacco with molasses. The tobacco would not ignite because it was soaked with this black honey. The merchant attempted to salvage his shipment by placing the tobacco in an earthenware vessel and placing burning charcoal on it to burn. This produced a lovely fragrant smoke and began the custom of smoking sheesha with flavored tobacco.

Translation

My brother, our gathering is over, everyone is gone except you, what are waiting for? You are like the big toe, first in the sandal and the last out.

Culture

Gatherings of friends are frequent and long and usually there will be one friend who is the last to leave. Generally friends leave together, but leaving a gathering takes a long

time since people tend to find subjects to talk about. It is not unusual for people who have started to leave to find themselves still talking hours later, to the extent that the host will tell them to spend the night instead of going home—some will accept the invitation and some will consider it as "Go home, already," and they will leave. A subtle way to suggest that a guest should leave is to suggest a change in the situation, usually by offering something, such as food, drink or accommodation, but with the intention of prompting the guest to think and realize that it really is too late for all these things—and remember that invitations should be declined, at least for the first few times.[8]

Holding the tea pot upside-down means that there is no tea to serve—a less subtle way of indicating that it's time to go, used by good friends. Notice the playing cards on the floor which probably indicate that they have been playing *baloot*. In Saudi and khaligi societies, very few men will not know how to play this type of game.

Translation

"It's the age of hormones!"

Culture

The overpopulation of the Arab world has resulted in a widespread shortage of food, which has necessitated the use of artificial fertilizers and other chemicals in order to produce more crops. In the old days, these methods were not necessary, because the number of people who required food was far smaller. Now, however, the situation is different. In

---

[8] See heat, page 453

many Arab countries, these new agricultural methods have resulted in diminished flavor and an increase in the cancer rate. Because of lack of knowledge and oversight, Arab farmers sometimes use illegal fertilizers that can have harmful effects on human health, as well as on the soil. These types of fertilizers were introduced to the market by corrupt government officials and countries with an interest in harming Arab nations' economies. Steps have been taken to verify the suitability of different fertilizers and methods of genetically altering plants in order to ensure that these substances and methods do not have any long-term effects on the health of either the people or the land.

Translation

On dumpster: "Garbage dumpster."

Man on the right: "Why don't you throw your garbage in its right place?"

Man on the left: "This is my garbage and I am free to dump it wherever I like."

Culture

Since many Arab countries have refuse in the streets, people have no qualms about adding their own garbage, and the government tries to instill within its citizens clean and civilized trash-disposal practices through different mediums, including cartoons like these.

Translation

Executioner: "What is your last wish before we carry out your sentence?"

Prisoner: "I want to check my email."

Culture

Most executions in the Arab world are carried out by hanging. The executioner is called *Ashmawee* after a famous early executioner.

Education in Prison

The condition of prisons in Arab countries varies according to country. They can be very squalid and of poor quality (Egypt, Sudan, Yemen) or they can have very good standards (Dubai, Saudi Arabia)—all depending on the wealth of the country. What is most common is that prisoners can finish their education—or begin it—once they are in prison. Prison education covers the whole range of schooling, from primary school all the way up to completion of college, and is encouraged by prison officials. When the inmate wants to take a final examination at the end of a semester, he is generally escorted to an actual college to take it with other students; the prisoner wearing shackles and shadowed by an armed guard, however, can prove to be a distraction for other students. In America, ex-convicts will have a record. In Arab countries, certain crimes are removed from record to facilitate re-entry into society, because the government wants to aid these rehabilitated criminals in finding work—and references are rarely checked. In Arab countries employers are given tax credits in addition to other benefits as incentive for hiring former inmates. Rehabilitation in Arab prisons includes a moral component. Religious scholars are often brought in to discuss the religious immorality of the crimes a prisoner has committed. Even terrorists undergo this treatment. As is the case in America, Arab prisoners are able to work for small amounts of money. These jobs are often crafts, including purse-making and painting, and these products are then sold by prison officials to an eager public.

In most countries the prison system uses a variation on the slogan "Discipline, Edification and Rehabilitation" (Arabs like to give slogans to any ministry or institution) and Arabs have a genuine belief in the reform of prisoners, but see it as being effected through force. With the rise of radical Islam, combined with 9/11 and the interest of the West in how Arab countries treated their terrorist prisoners, it has become clear that the forceful treatment of prisoners has radicalized them further and been counterproductive. As a consequence, they have introduced a program to build new prisons that are oriented more toward rehabilitation and reform, with greater possibilities for openness and less rigid discipline, as well as building to increase the variety to the prison stock, so that not all prisoners automatically go into the only type of jail available.

Translation

Barber: "Why do you need a second razor?"

Customer: "To defend myself with."

Culture

Arab barber are exactly the same as American barbers: in both places, they are famous for talking a lot. Arab barbers also have a reputation for being staid and unexciting.

While most hair salons in America are small operations, in Arab countries, the salons are much larger and will often be

very high-class establishments, as Arabs pay a lot of attention to their hair. Not all Arab hairdressers, however, will be found in a salon. They can also be found walking on the streets, carrying their equipment and cutting hair while their client sits on the sidewalk. Hairdressers will also sometimes make house calls to their customers. In the Arab world, hairdressers always have Mondays off and are busiest on Thursday nights. The hairdressers in Arab countries sometimes used to perform circumcisions and occasionally still will in rural areas where hospital services are not readily available. Barbers are natural centers of neighborhood gossip and information; they can help set up real estate deals, tell suitors about the reputation and prospects of eligible bachelors and maidens, and even facilitate small-scale trade in illegal drugs.

Female Hairdressers

Even though they cover their hair and faces, women in Arab countries employ the services of female hairdressers. There are far fewer female hairdressers (for women) than male barbers, but female hairdressing businesses are big, and salons have become one of the few places for women to socialize outside the home.

Underneath the covering, many women wear the latest fashions and keep their hair very nicely groomed. Around the time of festivities, in particular the Eids celebrations after Ramadan and after the Hijj, female hairdressers are the busiest. Reservations have to be made months in advance. Most female hairdressers are women, as it is not allowed for a woman to reveal her hair—and in some instances her face—to men who are not members of her immediate family. The most popular request of women visiting the hairdresser is for highlighting. In more conservative Arab countries female hairdressers can be the target of attacks by Islamic extremists, while some are so busy they work around the clock and their income can exceed $5000 per night.

Culture

Although these women are totally covered, their perfume means that they are inviting attention, and some religious people would consider that they are encouraging adulterous thoughts, as this cartoon implies in its title "Perfume's Force of Attraction."

☪ Whereas many women refrain from using perfume because they feel it immodest, most Arab men use cologne liberally, an effect augmented by the hot climate. These scents, of which musk is generally a valued ingredient, can also play a role in religious observances; a respectful Muslim is sure to apply some prior to going to the mosque for Friday noon prayers, and he will use the scented liquid to annoit important shrines or graves of holy men as a sign of respect.

Translation

This cartoon is a rebus — words or parts of words are replaced with pictures, numbers or letters.

Title: This cartoon is for a smart reader who understands it while it's flying.

Woman on right: "Thank you very much, sister Fa-ten, for the dress that you lent me to attend the wedding. Honestly, your dress made me look so beautiful and sassy and every one of those attending fell in love with it. I wish you had come to the wedding to see them.

Woman on left: "You are welcome, sister As-maa, for this sweet talk that you said about my dress. By God, I wanted to come with you to the wedding but my husband stated to me that I don't attend weddings except if I am invited."

Language

"Understand it while it is flying" means that the person doesn't need a full explanation to understand.

Neighborhood weddings are a chance for everyone in the neighborhood to eat and celebrate, by listening to music or watching the singing and dancing, even if they are not invited, since they consider themselves part of the larger family and feel "we don't need an invitation." The host family tolerates uninvited guests and takes them into considration when preparing to distribute dessert by putting it in small boxes and giving it to everyone there, like giving out candy at Hallowe'en. As in the cartoon above, some husbands don't like this habit of gate-crashing a wedding and believe it reflects badly on the family.

2 – Social Life   45

هلا عـَودة كيفك يا MAN... يلعن face abook Apple ليش ما بتسأل؟ ماكونتش هيك لا حس ولا خبر يا زلمة Disney من عندك خلّي الـ BOSS يشغلني عندو... بلكي LACALLE وظيفة خليه يرش علينا شوي من KENZO ماهو انت شايف وضعي ZAY الزفت...مش ضايل غير أطلع في الشارع وأصيح يا ناس YAHOO! شغلوني. و ahli أهلي جننوني بضلهم يحكولي روح دورلو إنك شاطر كان زمان لقيت شغل...نفسي أخذ VISA وأهج من هالبلد...يا زلمة من الزهق قاعد في LIVING ROOM مترمي على Kanabaye ولابس بيجامة Red وعم بشرب عصير MANGO وكنت جايب فليم جت لي THE ONE وإلا بدخلة أبوي... SAAB الغرفة الثانية وقعد عندي يقشر حبة orange وبقلي قوم FEZ روح DELL تاع الـ DIESEL على البيت ....كنت بدي أقلو إحكي PEPSI بس قلت عيب بضل أبوي...بعدين رحت ألعب play ستيشن مع أخوي طلع الـ CD ما بزبط لأنو Virgin ثاني بعديها رحت لعبت Domino's مع أختي ...وشوي وإلا جينا ناس..يا زلمة هو الناس ما إلا في الليل رحت دخلت غرفتي وحطيت الـ iPod على ذاني وقعدت أسمع موسيقى Nai وإلا NOKIA برن طلعت صاحبتي Zain على الخط وكانت الـ Signal ضعيفة شوي ...آه حياتي شو عم تعملي...عم بتفرج على فيديو كليب الـ 4 CAT الجديد على Mazzika ...المهم قعدت تبرم ساعة وتحكيلي عن أصنّية حياتها في المستقبل أنها تزور بلد TCHE EHDT غيڤارا...وفي نهاية التلفون حكتلي نايتي حبيبي حكتلها وين... bossini حكتلي لا خلينا FR·I·E·N·D·S قلت مش ناقص غير توخذيلك chicco Nappi إنو Books & Cafeen ...إسمع إحكي لصاحبك لسة ما إنصرف ليكون مفكرني Hindi بلاش أجرو على الـ POLICE و أ Shell عرضو TGI FRIDAY'S ...ما علينا يا صديقي تصبح على خير ... وخلينا نشوفك يوم الـ

Translation

Man on telephone: Hello, Ouda, how are you man? Curse the face of your father,[9] why don't you ask about me? You weren't like this before. I haven't heard a peep from you. Can you push your boss to let me work at his business? Maybe I can find a job, let him spread the wealth, you see that my situation is like tar, and there's nothing left to do but go in the street and yell, "People, give me a job!" And my family is driving me crazy and keeps telling me that if you were smart, you'd have found a job a long time ago. I wish I could get a visa and just leave this country. Man, because of boredom, I'm in the living room laid out on the couch, wearing red pajamas and drinking mango juice. I got a Jet Li movie, *The One*, and all of a sudden my father left the other room and came to me, and started peeling an orange and telling me "Get up and go and show the diesel seller where we are." I was about to curse him [Pepsi] but I said, no, that's not right, he's still my father. After that I went to play Playstation with my brother, but the CD turned out not to work properly, because it was virgin. Then I went to play dominoes with my sister, and after a while some people came to visit us and, man, why do people only come to visit at night. I then went into my room and put my iPod into my ears and kept listening to some flute music. All of a sudden my Nokia rang and my girl friend Zain was on the line. The signal was a little weak, [I told her], "My life, what are you doing?" and [she said,] "I'm watching the new video clip from "Four Cats" on Mazzika [Channel]." Anyway, she kept blabbing for an hour, telling me that, in the near future, her life's wish is

---

[9] See next cartoon on Arab curses.

for her to visit the country of Che, Che Guevara, and at the end of our conversation, she said goodnight, and I said, "When are you going to kiss me?" and she said, "No, let's still be friends." And I said, "There is nothing left for me but to give you a fist and two slaps."

Listen, tell your friend Naggi that I haven't been able to cash his check—does he think I'm Indian? Otherwise I'll go to the police and disgrace him. Anyway, my friend, goodnight, let us see you Friday.

Language

This cartoon incorporates the logos of many well-known brands, using them in a variety of ways. Some are used straightforwardly, signifying their usual company (e.g. the speaker watches a music video on music television channel, Mazzika). Many Western words have entered demotic Arabic, and so some Western logos in the cartoon signify the thing after which the company is named (e.g. Arabic uses the standard English term for diesel fuel, so the cartoon uses the clothing company Diesel to mean the common variety of petroleum). Other company names have homophones in Arabic (e.g. whereas in English, "yahoo," is either an expression of delight or a Swiftian term for a savage, in Arabic, "yahoo," is a general summons and call for attention). Finally, the familiar Facebook logo has been humorously altered to "Face abook," literally "the face of your father," and "curse the face of your father" is a common term of endearment amongst close friends.

A young Arab man may consider that when a girl is not a "virgin" all forms of "play" are possible, whereas with a "virgin" the options will be limited—and the idea is here transferred to a Playstation CD.

"Let us see you Friday"—Arabs sometimes talk of themselves in the plural.

☪ In Arabic, a comparison to tar indicates that something is deeply unpleasant, rather than, as it might connote in English, primarily that it's sticky. Tar's black messiness is repellent to Arabs.

Culture

This is another game of rebus, where you can recognize brand logos, some of which are famous in the West, while other are only known in the Arab world. It is a word game of considerable complexity, requiring a sophisticated audience, with an ability to read the Roman alphabet, recognize Western brands, and to translate the sounds back into Arabic homophones, often with quite a stretch. It is great fun and flattering for readers who can cope with its international frame of reference.

☪ Arabic logos avoid forms that resemble symbols of any religion other than Islam, nor will they include anything Islamic, which would be cheapening or sacrilegious. Skulls or skull-and-bones are shunned and banned by governments as satanic symbols. People are always on the look-out for potentially offensive forms where commercial logos could resemble words that have a religious significance. Nike inadvertently used a symbol that was thought to have the form of the name of Allah, and it was forced to apologize and explain.

Translation

[The naked woman in the man's speech-balloon refers to the sexual connotations and misogyny of much profanity and the woman's speech-balloon shows a stream of curse-words.]

Culture

Arab cursing

Religion, sex and women: all Arabic curse words revolve around these three areas of what is deeply cherished and what is taboo as ways to insult another person.

There is proverb to the effect that if you really want to humiliate or infuriate someone, which is the purpose of swearing or cursing, you have to mention a female member of his family and that is the usual way — insults will focus on a woman of the family, especially the mother, who is then often combined with reference to sexual body parts to heighten the offensiveness.

Some families will teach their young children curse words, in order for them to show their toughness and make sure that no-one messes with them. The family will be delighted when the child repeats these words and phrases in front of their friends, though this practice is not common outside the lower classes. Women also curse and the lower their social class, the more vicious their choice of terms will be. When women are in a fight or very angry with someone, instead of physical violence they will engage in lengthy streams of vituperation. This is called *radH*, which literally means "long period of time," and is a malicious tirade that describes the other person's deeds and his/her family or background and family members, usually it ends when others intervene, as they always do in this sort of confrontation or more physical fights.

Translation

Man: I played hide-and-seek with my wife once; I hid for seven years.

Language

Note that the man speaking uses an Arabic transliteration of the word *hide-and-seek* rather than the Arabic word, *massaka*. Arabs often use English names for indoor games and card games, and with the introduction of computer games, the phenomenon is growing.

Culture

These two men are sitting in a coffee shop, which is an Arab's first

destination for socializing. People not only drink coffee there, but also smoke hookah and play board games and cards. Until recently, women did not visit coffee shops, but they have begun to do so and the trend is growing. The average amount of time that an Arab person will spend in a coffee shop is much greater than the amount of time an American will spend. Unlike coffee shops in America, the Arab coffeehouse is no place for productive work because of their noise level. When a waiter takes a customer's order, he will shout it to the man working behind the counter, who will then generally shout the order back to him in acknowledgment.[10] This man performs his job with a great deal of showmanship (which is prevalent in all places that prepare food in the Arab world), clanking utensils and pouring tea loudly from a great height.

A certain stigma is attached to frequently passing time in coffeehouses; people who do this are considered to be wasting valuable time and energy. They also naturally take on the character of their neighborhood and clientele, so while some may be fashionable and others artistic, many are feared as rough hangouts for drug dealers, pickpockets, and thugs. Coffeehouses are occasionally the scene of big fights among patrons, in which they attack each other and break chairs to use them as weapons. Breaking chairs (or other things) is also associated with expressing grief, and when Gamal Abdel Nasser died, people marked their anger and grief by breaking their chairs, and for some this sound was the first sign that a national tragedy had occurred.

In the past, coffee shops were primarily patronized by retired men; now, it is mostly young people who visit coffee shops. And because of widespread unemployment, many Arab people spend as much time in coffee shops as possible.

---

[10] See demonstration of this method of calling out orders. "5 — Family life," p.136.

Translation

Man: "You know the guy whose name I saw in 'I want a wife'? Today I saw him in 'He's gone and never came back.'"

Language

In Arabic, the column "I want a wife" is equivalent to the American classified ad "Men seeking Women," while "He's gone and never came back" is equivalent to "Missing People."

Culture

In Arab countries, advertisements seeking mates are very specific in their list of requirements. Ads posted by males will often list age, height, skin color, religion, education, and the wearing of *hijab* as requirements for

their potential mate. Ads posted by women will include these specifications (except *hijab*), but also state whether or not they are willing to be a second wife or willing to marry a man who has had children with another wife. This requirement is one that is of importance, as stepmothers have a bad reputation. It is understood that when a stepmother finally has her own children with her husband, the children from the husband's previous relationship do not enjoy the same privileges and treatment that the wife's biological children do.

☪ In Arab countries, urban areas are crowded, and children often get lost. Parents of missing children take to the streets, either shouting their child's name or broadcasting his name with a microphone attached to a car. If anyone finds a lost child, they will take him to the closest mosque. As mosques invariably possess microphones, they are able to broadcast the name of the child who has been found.

Translation

Titel: The emotions of the Jordanian citizen:

Right to left:

When he is sad.

When he is angry.

When he is happy.

When he is elated.

Culture

Arab Sense of Humor

Sense of humor varies according to country in the Arab world, though most of it is verbal—observational or linguistic—and seldom physical. What makes a Yemeni laugh, for example, will not have the same effect on an Egyptian.

The two previous cartoons are Egyptian and both depict two men laughing at each other's comments, and whenever two Egyptians meet, even if it is only for few minutes on the street, they feel the need to try to make each other laugh, most likely by telling something against themselves, though the humor can also become something of a competition in outdoing the other person. After Egyptians, the Lebanese are regarded as the most humorous Arabs.

Saudis have the least sense of humor, for two main reasons. First of all, there is the sense of responsibility that comes from their country's holding the birthplace of Islam and the feeling that they must conduct themselves in a respectful and serious manner. Secondly, they have historically lived in a harsh and hostile environment that did not lend itself to leisure and joy, unlike the Lebanese and Egyptians whose countries always enjoyed a level of material and cultural comfort.

From the cartoon above, it is not difficult to see that Jordanians also maintain a serious demeanor most of the time.

Political humor is an important element of daily life, voicing the people's frustrations and providing some safety valve. It is taken very seriously by governments, and most countries have a Ministry of National Guidance to inform the rulers of what is being said and how people are responding to the current situation. These jokes can really spur the government into action: in 1967, in Egypt during a rice shortage, the Ministry of Guidance reported a joke about a man from Cairo who heard that there was rice in Alexandria and decided to go there. On the train, the ticket collector asked him where he was going and the man told him he was going to Alexandria to buy rice. Halfway to Alexandria, in Tanta, the ticket collector told him to get off. The man objected that he was going to Alexandria, and the collector said, "Yes, you said that you were going to Alexandria to buy rice. The line starts here." After learning of this joke, the president demanded immediate action to make rice available, and soon after it became far easier to obtain.

Even the jokes originating in a nation's enemies can become well-known in Arab countries; for example, also in 1967 much of the Arab world buzzed with an Israeli joke in which Moshe Dayan, then the Israeli Defense Minister, complained to one of his generals of having nothing to do that day. The general suggested that they occupy an Arab land. Dayan agreed, but then wondered how they would spend the afternoon. The bitter barb was ruefully repeated throughout the Arab lands, and served as a painful reminder of their recent military defeat. Given the Arab love of jokes, a witticism can be a weapon in Arab countries, yet another instrument by which countries compete with and attack one another.

Translation

Types of Backstabbing

Right to left, upper row then lower.

1) *A child backstabber: weak, so the effects go away within a day.*

"Mother, Hamoudah broke the glass and hid it under the bed!"

2) *A scholarly backstabber: medium strength and the effect is gone after the headmaster punishes the other student.*

"Sir, I know the student who was throwing papers at Professor Khalil!"

3) *Backstabbing between friends: the most widespread and effective type.*

"Honestly, Sana, Atta doesn't love you and he knows as many girls as he has hairs on your head. I'm telling you this because, by God, you are dear to me.

4) *Backstabbing between married people: very harmful, can sometimes lead to divorce.*

"I saw your husband at the Gardens with a blonde girl in tight clothes, and your husband was smiling from ear to ear!"

5) *Employment backstabbing: considered the most widespread, it can ruin anyone affected by it.*

"I lost my job, and my house is ruined, because of the guy who wrote the letter"

6) *International backstabbing: the most potent and dangerous and it is prohibited internationally.*

This frame depicts what Arabs feel about their position in international relations. The Arab's desk shows a map of the Arab world, while the Israeli is indicated by his flag and yarmulke, and the American by his flag. The Israeli is whispering to the serious-looking American representative about the Arab, who looks nervous.

Culture

As seen in this cartoon, the practice of backstabbing is alive and well in most Arab countries. In Arabic, this practice is called "hammering a wedge," similar to the English phrase "driving a wedge between people."

Translation

Hell is . . .
An Egyptian wife ([*She says:*] Yes, O soul of your mother!)

An Emirates meal

Lebanese citizenship

Palestinian policeman ([*He says:*] Where is the salary?)

Qatari tourism

Saudi neighbor

Jordanian taxes

Syrian salary

Heaven is . . .
A Syrian wife ([*She says:*]You may put me in the grave)

Lebanese meal

Emirates citizenship

Jordanian policeman ([*He says:*] Move!)

Egyptian tourism ([*He says:*] You light up Egypt!)

A Palestinian neighbor ([*He says:*] Taste this upside-down cake)

Saudi taxes

Qatari salary

Language

The word here translated as "heaven" is *nai'eem,* and does not carry the strictly religious overtones of the English word, though it is often contrasted with "hell." It is an ideal state of bliss, ease, and felicity.

The Egyptian wife's "Yes, O soul of your mother," is the equivalent of the English insult, "mama's boy," meaning "sissy." The Syrian wife, on the other hand, wishes that her husband should live to put her in her grave. This is both a version of the common Arab prayer, "May God grants you long life," and a touching tribute that she would not want to live longer than her cherished husband.

The Egyptian tour guide's, "You light up Egypt," simply means, "You brought good qualities and vivacity to Egypt." The polite response would be that it was lit by its inhabitants.

Culture

This cartoon contrasts a number of features of everyday life in Arab countries, with one column indicating which country is favored with the best and the other column listing the worst in each category. Interestingly, no country is allowed to dominate either list; on the one hand, this simply shows a fair balance, but it is also reveals the deep truth that each country in the Arab world has its beauties and each its flaws.[11]

☪ To start where the cartoon does, Syrian women are reknowned throughout the Arab world for their superlative beauty and their tender personalities. A Syrian woman, so goes the stereotype, will be a generous source of love for her husband. Egyptian women, on the other hand, are thought prone to neglect their looks. Furthermore, they are believed to have strong, forceful personalities that resist the dominating insticts of the typical Arab male, coming from a country with a history of women's emancipation. These harridans are also thought to descend too readily into vulgarity during domestic conflict.

☪ Lebanese food is what most Westerners think of as typical Middle Eastern food, and its vibrant flavors and abundant variety has ensured that Lebanese cooking dominates the other cuisines of the Arab world. Emirates cooking, on the other hand, is notoriously monotonous. Being a desert country it lacked the natural resources to give rise to much range in its cuisine, in stark contrast with lush Lebanon, which also benefited from millennia as a great trading nation.

☪ The United Arab Emirates is internationally recognized as a wildly prosperous country. Accordingly, foreign governments are confident that few who hold an Emirates passport will be eager to leave their homeland; rather, such a visitor is likely to be a cash-laden tourist and is eagerly to be admitted. Lebanon, on the other hand, has long been ravaged by conflict and is the source of many refugees. Furthermore, it is the font of a thriving and pernicious drug trade, so Lebanese travelers are looked at with grave suspicion.

☪ Jordan's security services are much on the model of those in the United States. Fears of the swirling unrest in the region have prompted the Jordanian king to invest very heavily in his small kingdom's

---

[11] There is a similar European list that plays with national stereotypes, so that in heaven the British are the police , the French are the cooks the Germans are the engineers , the Swiss are the administrators, and the Italians the lovers. In hell, the police are German, the cooks are British, the engineers Italian, the administrators French and the lovers Swiss.

security, and his efforts have forged a remarkably efficient force. The problems of Palestinian security are obvious and chronic. They are notoriously underpaid and accordingly often willing to accept bribes, a state of affairs that has produced a security service that has been deeply penetrated by Israeli forces and by organized crime. To crown the sorry state of affairs, treaties with Israel prevent the Palestinian forces from being well armed. (Aside from the general plight of the Palestinian security force, the policeman's cry—"where is the salary?"—alludes to the insolvency of banks within the Gaza Strip, see below.)

☪ In spite, or perhaps because, of the people's troubles, Palestinians are famous for their neighborliness and community spirit. Hospitality is a highly prized virtue throughout the Arab world, so it is high praise that Palestinians should have earned such fame. In contrast, wealthy Saudi Arabians are thought of as terrible neighbors. Saudi society is very restrictive of recreational activities but, rather than do without, those who are prosperous enough have their entertainment installed in their own home. This directs their attention inwards rather than towards the community. Furthermore, neighbors of Saudis have to contend with noisy goings-on and a stream of gas-guzzling cars arriving and departing at all times of day.

Beware: if you do happen to be on the receiving end of this famous generosity (and this applies to all Arabs, not just Palestinians)—don't return an empty plate. Instead, fill the neighbor's dish (which contained that delicious upside-down cake) with some treat of your own making. Otherwise, you'll be considered rude and inhospitable.

☪ The Gulf States famously sit atop enormous oil-wealth, so the governments do not need to bother with taxing their citizenry. Countries less blessed with natural resources, however, naturally need to collect taxes. Many in the West might not be inclined to feel much sympathy over the modest percentages charged, but comparing themselves to their wholly unburdened neighbors, even moderately taxed Arabs feel an understandable envy.

☪ Qatar is the richest country in the Arab world, so it naturally wins for the best place for salary. Syria, while not absolutely the poorest, is the poorest country that is nevertheless considered part of the respectable core of the Arab world, ignoring abysmally poor nations.

Gaza Banks

There is a crisis currently facing banks within Gaza. Gaza's current ruler, the democratically elected Hamas, is considered a terrorist organization by much of the international community. Thus, in order to curtail its authority, numerous countries have placed embargoes and restrictions upon trade and commerce with Gaza's banks. By this point, Palestine's largest trading partner—counter-intuitively, Israel—refuses to deal with Gaza's banks (being one of the many countries to impose an embargo, and unique in considering the routing of funds to any party within Gaza an act of "money-laundering"), and even the West Bank Palestinian Authority shies away from such banks as well. The Palestinian Authority is, in fact, partially responsible for the larger problem (as is Hamas, of course). Although jurisdiction over Palestine is split between the Palestinian Authority and Hamas, Palestine's banking is monitored by a single, overarching entity, the Palestinian Monetary Authority (PMA). Both the Palestinian Authority and Hamas jockey for control over the PMA, and strive to undermine one another's political security through the PMA's activities. For example, the Palestinian Authority convinced the PMA to freeze $800,000 (U.S.D) for Friends of the Infirm, a charity organization with ties to Hamas. When a Palestinian court overturned the freeze, the bank still refused to release the funds. Consequently, Hamas organized a raid on the bank and seized the funds itself. The fear of such raids, logically, does substantial harm to the public trust in Gaza's banking system. In New York, for example, there are currently lawsuits against Gaza banks, which employ the threat of raids to curry favor and support.

The plethora of embargoes, combined with the widespread lack of confidence, has had damaging effects upon the Gaza community in general. Due to a severe lack of opportunities, Gaza's banks invest only 19% of their funds; normal banks, on the other hand, are expected to invest up to 60% of their funds — in order to remain both competitive and to be investors to the community.

In response to these pressures, Hamas itself founded its own bank, the National Islamic Bank. (The presence of the word "Islamic" within the name of a bank signifies that the institution follows Islamic banking laws.) Thus far, however, it has not been recognized by either the PMA or the international community and confines itself exclusively to business within Gaza.

For Gaza's banks, confined to local business, the most lucrative potential clientele are tunnel-businessmen — that is, those who control the (literally) underground trade of goods between Israel and Palestine. However, as such activity is considered illegal, Gaza's closely monitored banks lack the opportunity to engage with these well-known men.

Given the preceding discussion, it is not surprising that the majority of business between Palestine and Israel is conducted in cold, hard cash — millions of shekels in sacks or suitcases, exchanged hand-to-hand in private encounters.

☪ This cartoon's topic is the enormous variety in culture across the Arab world, yet far from challenging the notion of a distinct and coherent Arab culture, the inarguable if indefinable "Arab-ness" of the world-view it expresses speaks to the shared core of Arab culture. Of course, every region, every country, every community, and every person in the Arab world has its individual way to be "Arab," but as in a mosaic, each contributes to the whole.

3 – Kissing

Translation

Title: In an Inferno of Kisses.

Man floating in air: "By God, I have to kiss your hand, my uncle."

Man under him: "No, no, no. I beg forgiveness of God."

Man with checkered headdress: "How are you Father of Muhammad? (mwah). Can you believe it's been *an hour* since I last saw you?"

Two women on right: "(Mwah).

Man kissing other man's head: "Forgive me, Father of Ishmael. By God, I have to kiss your head."

Boy to girl: "Why did you turn on the television to watch that movie full of kisses? I'll tell your father, unless you kiss the contrition."

Young lady: "Welcome, Mahjob. How are you? Long time no see! I haven't seen you in five years. How are you doing?"

Frame on wall: "Tell he who blames [others] for falling in love…" (Incomplete verse)

Language

"In an Inferno of Kisses" is a phrase from a famous poem by Bishara al-Khoury, known as *al-Akhtal al-Saghir*, "His eyelid teaches flirtation" (as is conventional, male pronouns are substituted to protect the woman's honour). As a song by Muhammad Abdelwahab from a movie called *The White Flower* (1933), it became a popular hit. The poet also is know for the line quoted in the framed verse on the wall, which proclaims that people should not be blamed for falling in love. As in the motto of the Order of the Garter, "Shame on him who thinks this shameful."

Muslims believe that saying "*Astaghfir Allah*," or "I beg forgiveness of God" will cancel any venial transgressions. This belief derives from the Qur'an, (Chap. 39, v. 53): "Say, O my servants, who have transgressed against your own souls, despair not of the mercy of God, seeing that God forgiveth all sins [unto those who repent], for He is the Very Forgiving, the Merciful." A very pious Muslim will also say this when he is praised, as the true source of all benefaction is God, and it is He to whom all praise belongs.

The young man is greeting the woman by placing his left hand below his heart, as he is shaking her hand with his right (it would also be possible to use just his right hand in the center of his chest below his heart as a greeting), in both cases tapping it twice.

Terms of kinship can be used quite fluidly. In English they are fairly fluid so that "Gramps" or "Pop" does not need to refer to a person's real grandfather or father, while "brother" or "sister" can refer to almost anyone of the user's age who is close. Arabic takes this kind of usage a few stages further so that what is associated with a term can be transferred fairly readily. The most widely used term is "uncle," specifically paternal uncle, *'amm*, used when addressing older men that one meets regularly, usually of lower status, but showing respect, so that it can be used with store owners, vendors, but also humorously with friends. The word for maternal uncle, *khel*, is used in most of the same cases, but because it is associated with a woman, is less common and implies that the relationship involves an element of compassion. "Brother" and "sister" are used widely for people of one's own age, both friends and strangers. "Mother" and "father" are used for those in an older generation, but tend to be used with strangers and are slightly patronizing; they can also be used between friends, and a woman can even call her own son "mother" when she is emphasizing compassion and similarly a father can call his daughter "father" — look out for this kind of usage in other cartoons, it is not a misprint! "Son" or "daughter" are really only used in a patronizing but friendly way, such as when giving advice. "Cousin" is used like brother and sister, but less often, and there are, of course, different words for male and female cousin, from the maternal and paternal side, and even variations depending on whether the cousin is the child of a brother or a sister, but the pattern is always to favor the male line, so the words that refer to the father's brothers are used a lot more frequently. These words vary according to the dialect of the country and region, so there is no single transliteration to be given here, whereas *'amm* and *khel* are universal.

☪ "Kissing the contrition" refers to a sign of repentance, where a person kisses their index finger and then touches the nose with that finger, as the girl can be seen doing in the cartoon. It might be translated more loosely as "make a kiss of contrition."

It is an irony that the boy is disgusted that the girl watched a romantic movie with kissing on TV and yet is oblivious to all of the kissing going on around him — or, perhaps better, above him.

Culture

In Arab culture, a kiss can take an abundance of forms, and each has a specific contexts and meaning. This cartoon illustrates with some irony the range of kisses and what they can express.

On the extreme right of the cartoon, we see two men engaged in a display of gratitude, deference, and polite humility. The "flying" man has literally launched himself at the grand gentleman in order to kiss his hand and thank him for some favor or kindness. His benefactor demurs politely, asking for God's forgiveness for being the recipient of the thanks which, by right, ought to belong only to Him. However, the flying man insists and piously declares that, "By God," he must kiss his hand. The kiss on the head, demonstrated by the two men towards the left side of the cartoon, is a similar gesture, but he who is giving the kiss on the head does so out of contrition, rather than gratitude.

Amongst this "inferno of kisses," the only couple who are clearly romantically interested in each other are also, strangely, the only ones not involved in kissing. The young lady extends her hand in a gesture known as the fish — palm down and fingers together, so called because of its remeblance to the animal — towards the bashful man whom she is clearly very pleased to see. The gesture simultaneously offers ladies a chance to display their wealth of rings and also maintains their modesty, as it would be improper for a lady to have her hand grasped. The kiss may be a prominent and public gesture in most of Arab life, but decorum demands that the use with which it is most readily associated and observed in the west — i.e. an expression and token of romantic affection — be strictly private. The strict separation of genders can make well-brought-up Arabs like the young man in the cartoon somewhat girl-shy, resulting in the blushing and sweating he exhibits.

One place that Arabs will avoid in their social kissing is the eyelid. A kiss there is considered bad luck, a harbinger of unplanned separation.

One further Arab restriction on social kissing that is more strict than in the west is the kiss of greeting between persons of different genders. Anyone from an Arab culture would be shocked for one man to stand by while another greets his wife with a kiss on the cheek.

When an Arab husband goes to the airport to collect his beloved wife, returned from travels abroad, he greets her with — a firm handshake. This sort of behavior bewilders those Western women married to Arab men, who are accustomed to that rather more lavishly declarative and emotional sort airport reunion so popular in Western media. The Arab husband, on the other hand, will instruct: don't hug, don't kiss me. This is because, in many Arab countries, public displays of affection are not permitted, relegated instead to the private, at-home hours, behind closed doors.

When Arabs don't kiss

Everybody will kiss everybody else in an Arab family except for the husband and wife, and father and daughter. A brother and sister will also probably not kiss, but there is no taboo against this.

It is not unusual for children never to have seen their parents kiss, and even in private, kissing is not an important aspect of a couple's love-life. There are a number of reasons for this situation: Kissing is not a sign of greeting, it implies a very high level of intimacy. Married couples do not kiss openly because modesty is an aspect of their faith. Religiously, many Islamic scholars have forbidden a man from kissing his wife in a public place, so that she is not aroused. In Arab society interaction between the sexes is so restricted that a demonstration of love between a man and woman might also be provocative to the unmarried men in any public space. Arabs are not very romantic people. Women do not have an expectation of romantic seduction or foreplay from their husbands, and are likely to scold a husband who makes amorous advances, even in private.

☪ In some Arab countries, public displays of affection are not only socially unacceptalble, but also illegal. Case in point: in March, 2010, Charlotte Lewis, a 25-year-old British national, was sentenced to one month in prison for allegedly kissing her boyfriend on the lips in a Dubai resort. (Lewis maintained that her boyfriend merely pecked her on the cheek, which is legal under Dubai law.)

☪ In some romantic Arab songs, the masculine gender is applied to the beloved object, who is, nevertheless, a female. This tendency arises, in part, from common etiquette: in many Arab cultures, knowledge of a pre-marital romantic attachment can be hugely detrimental to a girl's reputation. Thus, the polite suitor will keep her identity secret. In doing so, he will even abstain from referring to the girl *as a girl*, achieving this total concealment of identity via the use of the masculine gender.

Arabs are not fastidious about dental hygiene, so one of the reasons for not kissing is awareness that one may have bad breath.[12]

Translation

[Both the cartoon and the photo show the act of "noses' love."]

Culture

Throughout Arab culture, the nose is held to be the symbol of a person's pride, dignity, and virtue. The various civilizations of the Middle East have long held the nose in esteem; consider the practice whereby defeated enemies or disgraced figures would have their statues defaced by having the nose taken. To this day, a great number of Arab proverbs deal with the nose: ranging from the familiar "Don't stick your nose in [a given subject]"; to "I will rub his nose in the sand," meaning "I will humiliate him"; to "Despite his nose!" meaning "to force someone to do something"; and "your nose is your friend," which simply testifies to the symbolic power of the nose.

"Noses' love" is a form of greeting prevalent in many Gulf States. It is considered the most profound form of greeting, evidence of extraordinary respect and love, and it can also be a heartfelt plea for forgiveness. The two participants quickly but tenderly rub their noses one to three times in silence; initiator has the option of placing his right hand on the other's left side of the chest, in which event the other may reciprocate with his right hand. Only once the procedure is complete may the conversation begin. The equality implicit in this exchange means that it would be something of a presumption to do "noses' love" with someone of significantly superior status; a revered elder should be kissed once on the nose followed by a handshake. A father, on the other hand, has his nose kissed once, and then the good son kisses his father's head.

---

[12] See "5 — Family Life," p.155.

The ancient greeting has recently come under some criticism from health authorities as an unhygienic anachronism in the age of flu epidemics, but the custom persists. Many are simply unwilling to relinquish such an important and deep-rooted practice. Still others feel that things such as the transmission of disease are a matter of destiny and that, if they are fated to catch a virulent disease, then they will do so despite precautions.

Culture

Though this is actually a Western cartoon, it reflects an Arab philosophy reflected in the proverb: "If you need something from a dog, call him 'my master.'" Arab culture has a range of gestures whereby one might demonstrate one's respect for another person's authority and prominence, and Arabs are very conscious of self-respect and the deference others show to them.

As common as these outward signs of respect are, they do not necessarily reflect that the person making them genuinely reveres the other. All true power, the Muslim believes, stems from God, and it is He to whom all honor belongs and who controls the behavior of other people. The deepest bows and most prostrate groveling are reserved for God, and obeisance to the petty powers of the Earth is generally instrumental rather than heartfelt. Of course, truly loved and honored figures can also receive elaborate and deeply felt honors, but the primacy of God remains. Furthermore, there is a tendency among Arabs to take the side of the underdog, rather than the person who has the most power or influence: the underdog's success is a demonstration of God's mysterious power over human affairs.

☪ The gesture of kissing an important man's hand is a prominent sign of respect in the Arab world. In modern times, it is generally restricted to rural or very old-fashioned communities, but kissing hands maintains an important symbolic place. The one who is honoring the other takes the right hand of the other and bends to kiss it, but at the last moment that hand is withdrawn, signifying that the soon-to-be kissed man thanks the kisser for the compliment but does not claim to be worthy of such respect. Traditionally, the head of a household would expect to be greeted in this fashion each morning by all the members of the family. Prominent clerics, local politicians, and relatives of a royal house, too, would expect such treatment. The practice is an ancient one that is current throughout the Arab world and not only in Muslim populations; are Arab Christians, for example, notably assiduous in offering this respect to their clergy.

☪ Often, whenever a child greets his father for the first time that day, he will kiss his father upon the pate of his head (as illustrated in the photograph on the right). In some countries, the child will kiss the mother thus too. More often than not, however, the gesture is reserved for the father, as a sign of respect and recognition of authority. The gesture might also occur between friends: someone who has wronged his friend, and comes to him in contrition, will often kiss him upon the top of his head. Usually, having done so, the other party will have no choice but to show forgiveness.

4 – Dating and Getting Married

Translation

Why do you want to marry me, my love? It is cheaper if you buy yourself a [satellite] dish.

Culture

The girl in the cartoon is referring to the fact that because of satellite dishes, Arab viewers are now free to watch television broadcasts without any government censorship, which was not the case until recently. Television through satellite dishes can now include adult material, which was once completely prohibited in all kinds of Arab media. The girl (apparently not very keen on the man) is suggesting that he no longer has to bother with the expense of marriage in order to be exposed to sex, since he can simply watch adult material via a satellite dish.

☪ Arab men pride themselves on their sense of chivalry. Inheritors of a traditional view of women as hidden jewels, vulnerable creatures to be cherished, tended and protected, Arabs greatly value their role as protectors and providers. For example, despite their own personal desires, many Arab men will dissuade an eager girlfriend from physical involvement, for fear that it would ruin her dignity and reputation. Thus, in the cartoon, it is in his role as "protector" that the man reacts with such terrified surprise to his girlfriend's apparently brazen, dishonorable suggestion.

☪ In attempting to "Westernize" their appearance, the cartoon characters have fallen into a common trap of assuming all Western-style clothing is *necessarily* fashionable clothing. However, while "Western" in and of itself may be fashionable within some sectors of the Arab world, Western fashion is actually separated into a hierarchy of equally Western trends. Thus, the characters here are unwittingly wearing clothes associated, in America, with a rather brassy or cheap style. For example, who really wears leopard spandex? The man's well-gelled hair, aside from occasionally being a symbol of sleaziness, is unadvisable in hot Arab climates.

Speaking of Western styles of dress, sneakers have a surprisingly bad reputation within the Arab world. This is because, on their first introduction in the 1950s and 60s, sneakers were some of the cheapest, most basic footwear available. Because of this shared cultural memory, many Arab men find themselves very hesitant about wearing sneakers, unless they are committed to appearing Westernized. The hot climate also prevents sneakers from catching on culturally.

Translation

"The liar, the cheater. He wrote in an email he looked like the star of *Titanic*. It turns out he's the whole Titanic."

Language

The star of *Titanic* refers to Leonardo DiCaprio. Generally speaking, movie stars' names are well-known in the Arab world, but even a famous star's name may be regarded as difficult to pronounce, so he or she will be referred to by his or her most famous role. Other famous movie stars' names may not be pronounced correctly due to the way they are translitared on the movie posters and in the media, especially since there is no P or V in Arabic.

☪ Comparing someone to a large building or ship means that he or she is fat.[13]

Culture

In the Arab world, whenever a girl wishes to meet up with a male stranger (or near-stranger), the situation is fraught and potentially dangerous. So the meeting requires a lot of planning: she must concoct a suitable alibi for her family, and select an appropriate destination. This site will be far from the family home, so that no acquantances see her strolling with a man. To that end, the man and woman will not, usually, even stroll together—rather, to avoid watching, condemnatory eyes, they will walk a few

---

[13] See "22 — Begging," p.446.

strides apart from one another, maintaing the pretense that they are wholly unfamiliar with each other. (This will change by the time they reach their final location—usually, a heavily secluded area. For example, the girl in the cartoon has traveled to what is, in all likelihood, a faraway mall.)

Typically, when a girl goes to meet a male stranger, she will bring along a confidante for protection. In most cases, rather than a friend, the confidante is her sister: less judgmental and more empathetic than friends, a sister will often better understand the girl's situation, and encourage her (though still with modesty and restraint) where others might dissuade her. The practice doesn't stop at first meetings— even if the man in question is the woman's fiancé, the sister will still accompany the two of them out on a date. She'll give them space—but she'll always be there.

Abbaya

The abbaya originated in the Gulf region, but has become the one piece of clothing that all Arab women wear, regardless of where they are from. It was originally made as a practical garment to be thrown on top of whatever clothes a woman was wearing, so she could leave quickly or run a brief errand. They are now so elaborate and elegant that people wear them at special occasions as formal wear.

Women like it because it is conservative, comfortable, and cheap, compared with other countries' national attire. The abbaya is now the uniform of many Arab universities, especially Islamic ones. It gained widespread appreciation, since many Arabs went to work in the Gulf region and discovered how practical it was. When reverse immigration occurred, and Arab families came back from the Gulf, they brought this one piece of clothing with them and continued to wear it. Its practicality lies how easy it is to put on and that it can be worn with pants. It comes in many colors but most are black and all are dark. It is suitable for all age groups and women are seldom seen without one.

Customers for the abbaya are usually young women, followed by married women. Most prefer the Gulf abbaya, which is embroidered with simple decoration. Most in the Arab world are imported from Saudi Arabia and the UAE, but some from China. Several styles exist, but the most famous is called the Prado (referring a Toyota 4x4, sold in the U.S. as the Lexus GX470, and in the Middle East as the Toyota Prado— car models sold in the U.S. often have different names in the Middle East). This abbaya has an inside tie or fastener, so that the outside appears tie-less. Many female customers request abbayas that are decorated with crystals and beads or leather around the edges. Because of their growing popularity with children, there are now abbayas with Disney characters on them.

Translation

Title: Old-time caricature
The man to the aesthetically challenged woman: "I have no objection to committing American-style suicide—on the condition that you commit suicide first."

The humor here is that this man wants to get rid of his ugly companion by making her commit suicide before him.

Language

The "American-style" phrase is found in many areas of activity and it changes according to what's in the news and movies. It is associated largely with cars, accelerating from zero to a high speed is called "leaving the blocks American style," based on Hollywood car chases. "American-style exams" refers to multiple-choice tests or open-book exams. American in association with clothes and food, usually denotes speed, ease and freedon to choose.

Culture

This cartoon also illustrates the absence of certain forms of political correctness in the Arab media. Here, the man is making fun of his girlfriend for looking ugly, and also speaking flippantly of several American national tragedies.

Translation

Woman: "Listen, love, take this present and give it to your mother! It's Mother's Day, not Love Day!"

Man: "I know, love of my life. I brought a present for *el hajjah*. I also brought you a present because you are the mother of disgust, the mother of misery, and the mother of problems!"

Language

In Arabic, when a thing is described as the mother of something, it means that it exists on the largest scale possible, as when Saddam Hussein described the 1991 Gulf War as "the mother of all battles." When the man in this picture describes his female companion as the mother of disgust, problems, and misery, he states that she could not be more obnoxious.

Hajjah is the female version of *Hajj*, and is a title for a Muslim mother.

☪ For both Love Day (equivalent to Valentine's Day) and Mother's Day, as well as a variety of special occasions, flowers are one of the most popular gift items in America. In the Arab world, however, flowers are not such a common gift as in most of the West, for the simple reason that, due to the region's climate, flowers are not nearly abundant enough for use in everyday gift giving, so that something edible is preferred or artificial flowers that last.

Translation

Title: Breaking the eyebrows

Man: "See, my life, in order for our relationship to continue, you have to remove the eyebrows, I mean, the barriers that are between us."

Language

The words *eyebrows* and *barriers* are very similar in Arabic.

Culture

Having thick eyebrows or other body hair is considered unattractive. The women of a family tend to gather every few weeks to remove excesss hair on arms and legs by making a paste from lemon, sugar and water that is mixed together and simmered for long time before it turns into paste. This is spread on their arms and legs and other areas with uwanted hair and removed in one quick movement, taking with it all excess hair and keeping the area clean and smooth for long time – rather like waxing but without the fabric, with the added benefit that any left over paste can be eaten. Arab women believe that using razors thickens the hair and requires more frequent care than the sweet paste. Thread can also be used to remove fine hair around the lips and the eyebrows. At the barber's shop men may also ask for their facial hair to be tidied with thread.

Translation

Title: The Rising Percentage of Spinsters.

Angry woman: You know me, you don't know me. What matters is that you should marry me right now or I'll make sure you never get married.

Culture

In Arab cartoons, unattractive women are often the butt of the joke. Sometimes, when a man is in the process of wooing an Arab woman, he may be successful in convincing her that they should engage in physical intimacy by suggesting he intends to marry her. If the man then chooses to end the relationship after their intimacy, it will be devastating for the woman. She will try her best to make the man reconsider. Once she has exhausted her efforts and the man has not returned to her, she may rely on supernatural means to see him punished by God or the jinn for leaving her.

☪ Arab women can be very aggressive when pursuing a man for marriage. There is no such thing as a restraining order, and women may well go to such lengths as continually calling a man, showing up at his place of work or even his home. Far from viewing these women as "Bunny Boilers," as a Western man might, Arab men will often agree to marry a woman who pursues them so persistently. A woman may decide to pursue a man irrespective of his marital status; men are often naïve about relationships with women and in Islam a man does not have to divorce his wife in order to marry again. A powerful man can be seduced by a woman from any social background if she is strong-willed enough, however these relationships will often not last.

☪ To the chagrin of good girls, their looser sisters are the ones who usually get married first, even though the marriage market is very tight. Many Arab girls will delay wearing *hijab* until they are married, so that they can attract the interest of prospective suitors. Many Arabs see marriage as a business transaction—since love and marriage seldom go together… and the man like to see what he is buying.

Translation

Title: Happy Summer

"This scene is familiar on the Nile Corniche."

"What is wrong with this drawing?"

Culture

This is indeed a familiar scene on the Nile Corniche, especially in the evening hours, when couples engage in heavy flirtation, despite the women's hijabs. The caption asks what is wrong with this picture, suggesting that these women should be watching their behavior and not putting themselves in this type of situation while wearing the hijab. They are flirting while wearing hijab, and the rest of their clothes are not in keeping with the modesty that the *hijab* should imply.

These women are often criticized publicly by passers-by for their behavior, which is why their faces are turned away from the traffic. Usually the shouts will call on them to respect their *hijab* or say "Shame on you, hajjah," and so on.

☪ For a young man, rolling up the sleeves and unbuttoning the top button of a shirt is a sign of masculinity.

Translation

"Ok mother, I decided to marry this man. He is the only one who owns an apartment and a housemaid's visa."

[*N.B. In some Gulf countries, governments distribute labor visas to citizens in order for them to hire household help from overseas, but this is a long process.*]

Culture

Owning an apartment can be a determining factor for a suitor's request for marriage to be granted, making him an attactive choice. Having the maid's visa already means that his wife will be able to have help immediately.

Black Market for Household Help

In some rich Arab countries, the services of maids, housekeepers, chauffeurs, and security personnel are considered essential. Some household workers immigrate to these countries legally to work. Often, though, the workers are those who travel to countries like Saudi Arabia for al-Hijj or al-Umra and overstay their visas in search of jobs.

In some of these wealthier nations, because there is still a shortage of household workers, people will steal one another's maids, through the help of headhunting businesses that have been established to facilitate this process. Some citizens entice their neighbor's workers by offering to double their salaries if the workers agree to move over and work for them. Strict employment laws make this process very difficult, as you need the consent of the original employer to switch. There are brokers who specialize in bidding for the services of the help, approaching the household workers disguised as food delivery people, as to avoid detection by the employers of the household workers they are approaching. These brokers provide documents that would allow a household worker to switch employers without having to get the consent of the original employer. Sometimes wealthier people hire security personnel as a symbol of status, and not because there is a real security threat. Nevertheless, once hired, the security personnel will often create situations to show their employer how necessary and how strong they.

Translation

In dialogue box: Do you accept him as a husband?

Yes — No — Cancel Order

On laptop:
www.mazoon.com

Culture

The *mazoon*, the word between *www.* and *.com* in the cartoon is similar to a justice of the peace, and literally means, "permitted." He performs the marriage ceremonies for all couples.

The *mazoon* performs both marriages and divorces. Usually, he keeps a ledger with all of the information concerning the bride and groom that is necessary to carry out these ceremonies. While in America, vows are exchanged between the bride and the groom, in Arab countries, the groom and the bride's father formalize the contract. The bride herself may or may not be present, depending on the custom of the country. In this ceremony, the bride's father, acting as his daughter's agent, will repeat after the *mazoon* that he is offering his daughter in marriage. He then mentions her name, that she is a virgin and an adult, according to the rules of God's book, the sunnah, and the creed of the Islamic scholar (see below) that the family follows, and that a dowry has been agreed upon. The ceremony will be formalized with the hands of the groom, the father of the bride, and the *mazoon* held together under a handkerchief. The groom will then say that he accepts the man's daughter in marriage and that he acknowledges that the man is her agent. He will then repeat the same words that the father of the bride has said previously. At that point, the *mazoon* will congratulate both parties and the women present will ululate and offer sweet drinks.

When the *mazoon* performs a divorce, he will also try to work as a marriage counselor. Although divorce is considered *halal* (lawful in Islam), it is still considered a last resort, and the *mazoon* will thus do everything possible to reconcile husband and wife and resolve the differences between them before divorcing them.

Marriage in Arab culture is very traditional and ceremonial. In some traditional communities, the first time a husband sees his wife is on their wedding day. Where international influence is stronger, though, customs have changed, in some cases dramatically. Highly Westernized couples have even adopted a risqué wedding tradition whereby the groom removes his wife's garter in front of the wedding guests. Perhaps more significantly, in many places men and women are now able to date, though they would still not be able to live together until married. The Internet and Bluetooth have changed how men and women can interact. Men can send their phone numbers or email addresses via Bluetooth to women around them, and this could be the start of a relationship. In some poorer Arab countries, web sites have been established where older men can browse pictures and histories of young potential wives. After choosing a young wife, she is taken back to his country where she could end up falling in line behind his older wives after the initial excitement has waned.

In all Arab and Muslim countries, the *mazoon* has always been male, but for the first time in 2009, Egypt allowed a female *mazoon*, who got the position over nine male candidates.

☪ In the preceding section, there is mention of "the creed of the Islamic Scholar that the family follows," which refers to the differences of opinion among Muslims concerning some points of religion and law. These have given rise to four doctrinal schools, each of which, though, considers the other orthodox as to fundamental matters and derives its law and religion from the same four sources: the Qur'an, the traditions of Prophet, the concordance of his early disciples, and analogy. The four schools are the "Hanafi," "Shafi," "Maliki," and "Hanbali," each deriving its name from the respective scholar whose tenets they have adopted.

As noted above, some Arab grooms will not view their bride's face until the wedding day. This tradition has served as popular fodder for Arab comedies, which often invoke a familiar trope of a profoundly anticlimactic "reveal": the bride will remove her veil, only to reveal a cartoonishly unattractive mug. In such films or shows, these brides are usually given male names.

Translation

"You know what my ambitions are? To get married and instead of buying individual *bukhari* from a restaurant, buying two individual *bukhari*."

The man wants to get married so he can buy a meal called "individual *bukhari*" (a Saudi dish of rice and roast chicken) as two *bukhari*. The humor lies in the doubling of the "individual" portion — and ambition also usually refers to something slightly more substantial than the selection of chicken dishes.

Single men always associate marriage with better quality food, and this is one of the reasons they want to marry, since they they will be able to eat better than they currently do, whether because their wife-to-be is a good cook (an highly prized attribute) or because they will be exchanging visits with relatives and friends. Once they are married men, there will be a lot more invitations, as the social embargo against single men will have been lifted.

Groom's Breakfast in Sudan

Two traditional breakfasts occur in the days surrounding a wedding. The first and more elaborate occurs on the morning of the wedding and is followed by a second, the next day.

The wedding night is known as "the night of entrance," which may refer to the couple's entering into their marriage contract or physical consummation. The following morning the couple is offered a hearty, sumptuous breakfast to replenish the energy that has been expended, which is known by a variety of names, including "the matutinal breakfast," and is meant only for the couple.

The most elaborate of the breakfasts that occur on the morning prior to a wedding is the Sudanese version, called "the Groom's Breakfast," meant for the families of the newlyweds. This traditional Sudanese matrimonial custom often lasts for days. Planning commences at the time of the engagement, and the actual preparation of the breakfast takes a whole day, with the mother of the bride and the mother of the groom bringing the "carriage of food": the groom's mother brings the ingredients, the bride's mother creates. The groom's mother brings all traditional Sudanese delicacies: juices, spices, flour, oil, sugar, split peas, yellow lentils, dry ochre, fried lamb, and porridge with yogurt, and including a personal gift for the bride's mother. After finishing the breakfast preparation, the bride's mother will choose ten women to accompany her and the food to the groom's house. Upon arrival, the extra women will be assigned to a room where they can set up the breakfast. These women, however, will not leave the car until the groom's mother and siblings come to meet them, to uphold the pride and self-respect the bride and her family feel. There will be a joyous and euphoric atmosphere.

The groom's mother invites all relatives and friends to attend the ceremonial breakfast which commences at exactly ten o'clock in the morning on the day of the wedding. The breakfast arrives in a large car, ornately prepared and accompanied by traditional Sudanese ululation, and people sing praising the mother of the bride, the beauty of the bride, and the kindness of her family. The context is not completely serious, with those present teasing that the mother of the bride that she should set the breakfast up faster.

The Sudanese Groom's Breakfast business employs many people, involved in decorating the tableware, setting up the meal, and hiring out female chefs to help prepare the food in a mix of both traditional Arab and Sudanese cuisine. The beauty of decorations, their quantity, as well as the quality of the tableware is a reflection of the class and wealth of the mother and her family. Tradition allows wealthier families to flaunt their wealth by creating extensive Groom's Breakfasts, to the point that it must be brought in multiple cars containing enough to feed an entire neighborhood. Poorer families, on the other hand, may have to borrow or rent the tableware from neighbors so they can fulfill the request of a Groom's Breakfast by the groom's mother. The Breakfast can put financial strain on families, as each family wants to outdo the last one. The wealthier brides' families will leave gold bracelets at the bottom of the serving bowls, so the women serving will find them and keep them as presents.

A new trend is presenting morning tea before the Groom's Breakfast. Various teas, coffees, and cookies are presented to the bride's family at exactly six in the morning. Tradition dictates that the groom will present valuable presents to the women preparing the meal—ranging from gold coins, jewelry, tea or coffee sets, expensive perfumes made of sandalwood or, more recently, cell phones and money, to traditional Sudanese saris—made in Switzerland, as the Swiss versions are considered of higher quality. (Many traditional Arab clothes are now being made by large fashion houses, offering higher quality garments than those made locally.)

After finishing the Breakfast, some Sudanese families return the empty serving containers to the mother of the bride with boxes of fresh fruits, indicating that the food presented was very good and how proud they are of the bride's family and their generosity. The women will leave the house singing, praising the hospitality of the reception, as well as how fine the groom is. The Breakfast ends at exactly eleven in the morning, with the mother of the bride leaving to prepare food for the wedding, which is that evening.

Groom Mix

The Groom Mix is a concoction used as a sexual stimulant made of Yemeni honey and other natural ingredients. It is sold by religious people (these observant Muslims usually make money by selling Islamic perfume and books, the same way you see them in the street of New York City selling essence) and has proven results. Wives complain about its effect, annoyed by their over-stimulated husbands who pester them and show no regard for their preferences.

Arab Culture

Translation

"Chat"

"Then greeting"

"Then email"

"Then mobile"

"Then making a date"

"Then a date"

Culture

This cartoon represents the changing process of dating in Arab countries stemming from the Internet age. In the past, courtship followed a very specific well-known order: a look, then a smile, then a greeting, then a chat, then making a date, then a date.

In this and the following cartoons old-style Arabic language and customs are juxtaposed with their equivalent in the modern age, which the Arab reader finds funny.

Translation

Title: Distinguishing a camel from a female sheep in the provision of small talk and *chat*.

Right to left under the figures:

"Allowed." "Allowed." "Forbidden."

This cartoon is exceptionally funny for Arabs because of its title. It has a very strong background in Islamic literature. Hundreds of years ago, fatwahs were issued in books, and challenges that required such fatwahs were rare. The title of this cartoon is in the style of these fatwah books, where the first half rhymes with the second. These titles would always be very relevant to their times. The comedy here arises from the clash between first and second halves of the title—one traditional and the other contemporary.

Culture

This cartoon refers to a fatwah that was issued regarding chatting online. It allowed chats between the same gender, but not mixed gender communication.

☪ The widespread demand for fatwahs resulted in the multiplication of unqualified individuals ready to provide instant and sometimes ill-considered judgments on the minutiae of life. The scholars of earlier generations had been willing to say, "I don't know," which, according to a proverb, is in itself a fatwah, but also giving time to deliberate. The newer generation was taken up by programs on religious TV stations, the two feeding off each other, and producing fatwahs that have been criticized as incorrect and frivolous.

Translation

On screen: "Marriage.com"

Culture

In Arab countries nowadays, many things can be done online. Why not marriage?

Translation

Title: Birds of a feather flock together!

He says: I'm an important character, I'm not in a relationship, a businessman, living in Abdoun [a nice neighborhood], and now I am getting my master's degree.

The truth: Total loser, womanizer, good-for-nothing, and failed to pass his high school exam.

She says: I study at the University. I am cultured. I am spoiled. I am not in a relationship, and my father has lots of money.

The truth: She doesn't have a job and lives with her parents. She is a ditz, is in 1000 relationships, and her father is broke.

Language

When an Arab girl says that she is spoiled, it does not have the same negative connotations as in America. In Arabic, it means that she is loved and being taken care of, which is a desirable quality in a girl.

The connotations of many English and Arabic proverbs coincide, such as "Birds of a feather flock together." Common phrases that deal with camels or things from a desert environment, such as "the straw that breaks the camel's back," can usually be traced back to an origin in Arabic. The quotation from the Gospels, "It is easier for a camel to go through the eye of a needle, than for a rich man to enter into the kingdom of God" also appears in the Qur'an, but with a different meaning. Instead of relying on the imagery of the rich man, the Qur'an says, "To those who reject Our signs and treat them with arrogance, no opening will there be of the gates of heaven, nor will they enter the paradise, until the camel can pass through the eye of the needle: such is Our reward for those in sin."

Culture

There is a stigma associated with not passing the high school exam, identifying the person as a total loser; usually students will strive for very good grade in this exam and not passing it means the student is either not bright or doesn't care, both of which are not a good sign in a society that respects education.

Success in an exam is usually celebrated with a family party. In a large family, though, it is possible to have two children taking the same exam, and if one passes and the other fails there will be no celebration for the successful one, as sign of solidarity.

What Arabs brag about

Many factors affect the desirability or status of a person in Arab society, such as family background, education, fortune, address, and many more, all of which are important in impressing a potential mate or friend. How wealthy your family is, which school you go to, what part of the city you live in, whether you have traveled aboard, whether you have a close relative who lives abroad, where you work, how educated your family is, even whether you have a good-looking relative (for example with lighter skin or prettier hair), whether you own a car, a house or an apartment, whether you play musical instrument, whether you speak a foreign language — all these factors can determine whether you are a good catch or not, since almost all people in the Arab world do not engage in relationships for the sake of having a good time but for potential marriage.

Translation

"Would you like a raise in your salary?"

"And a fixed monthly income?"

"Quickly ask for her hand today."

On bag: "[female teacher]"

The balloon is phrased like the voice-over in a commercial, starting with the teasing questions about a problem and, in the final frame, offering the solution.

Culture

Arabs have traditionally preferred to marry women who will be housewives, and generally when a working woman marries, even if she is a doctor or engineer and has spent years studying, her husband, who may be well-educated too, will ask her to quit her job and "hang her certificate in the kitchen." There are two reasons for this: to remove the woman from a mixed-gender work environment and to guarantee the completion of household duties. Traditionally, the husband's salary is sufficient to support the family, but this is undergoing major changes. Inflation and a rise in consumerism now make a working woman the most desirable wife, but not all professions apply. Arabs of the Gulf prefer a teacher to an engineer or doctor because the latter two require excessive working hours. Teachers are able to make money while still fulfilling domestic duties. Female engineers and doctors are frowned upon. Engineering is too masculine of a field, and husbands fear the temptation such an environment provides their wife. A doctor is less desirable as a wife, as she will be interacting with partially clothed male patients. Jobs in the media, too, are not favored since the idea of being hired to perform, and potentially interact physically with men, is incompatible with Arab values. Overall, though, views of women have shifted. Beauty, ancestry, and culture were once paramount, while a woman's profession is now the most important factor, both so the man can boast of his wife's achievements and so he can be financially secure.

This also reflects a change in the concept of manhood. In the past, the Arab man would not consider himself complete unless he provided for his family without outside aid. He would not dare to ask his wife for financial help in the upkeep of the house. Arab men now have no qualms about asking for or borrowing money from their wives to help pay bills, loans, and tuition, as well as buying real estate that will be under the husband's name. This type of transaction is generally done without documentation, so the wife will be helpless in the case of divorce or separation. Usually in such situations, the husband compromises by giving the deeds to his children, so the wife is not completely lost.

In Praise of Older Women

Again, traditionally Arabs prefer to marry younger women. This does not refer to underage marriage, but, in general, a wife has been around three-quarters the age of her husband. This tradition is undergoing a major revision. Many young men now seek to marry successful, financially stable, older women to help guarantee their own economic well-being. By marrying older women, young men avoid the expense of a large wedding, as big ceremonies are generally reserved for a first marriage, and can also avoid paying the high price of a dowry (*mahr*). Older women have therefore become the goal of the more marriage-minded men, if they are seeking to improve their condition, and this is a significant trend. Older women are viewed as having more compassion than younger women, who are viewed as being overly superficial. Families still frown upon sons marrying older women, however, as they are concerned with older women's ability to produce offspring. Further, oriental men (how Arab men refer to themselves) hold to the concept of *qawama*, which is the man's custody over the woman as her provider and protector. The man must provide for her, but he also has the last word. By marrying a more experienced, older woman, this concept of *qawama* may be undermined as he may be dependent on and submissive to his wealthier wife, which is looked down upon in the culture.

Translation

Father to daughter: It's true that he's an educated young man, has a house, and is lawful. But I can't do anything about it, my daughter! You know you are betrothed to your cousin Daheem, God have mercy on him.

Language

Though most familiar in the West as a term to describe properly slaughtered and prepared meat, *halal* simply means "lawful," and can refer to anything or anyone that is proper according to the laws and traditions of Islam.

The father's, "I can't do anything about it," would be literally translated, "There is no trick in my hand."

A person's family can betroth him or her to another person when they are just five years old or even younger. The joke here is that the young woman is betrothed to her cousin, and her father will not let her marry anyone else — note the lock on his head — despite the fact that the cousin has died, as evidenced by the father's use of the phrase "God have mercy on his soul."

Marriage of First Cousins

Marriages between first cousins are not uncommon in many parts of the Arab world. Such couples continue to refer to one another as "cousin" because the indissoluble blood-tie is held in higher esteem than the contractual marriage bond. Such unions are regarded with favor as stronger than marriages that do not have the benefit of such deeper bonds, and unlike most couples who would marry only after extremely short and formalized courtship negotiations, cousins would have the opportunity to get to know one another as they grew up.

When a woman has been betrothed while she was still a child (to her cousin, for example), but the promise was not fulfilled for one reason or another, usually the person she was betrothed to will determine her *mahr*. The betrothal would be arranged by the family, but the reason for their not getting married could be a decision by either the man or the woman, once they are of age.

Translation

The Father: "My little daughter, what you're doing is not right. You turn down everyone who comes asking for your hand in marriage. If you think, by doing this, I'll let you get engaged to that guy who says he knows you from a website... even if you loved the sky and the earth, I wouldn't let you marry him! What are you saying? That last guy is a good man—and he has a Lexus!"

The girl: "I don't want to."

Language

From the extensive use of the Arabic letter "s" it is clear that the two characters in the cartoon are from Saudi Arabia.

☪ "If you love the sky and the earth" is a phrase unique to Gulf Arabic, and has analogs in the English "if hell freezes over" and "when pigs fly." Like these two English expressions, "if you love the sky and earth" is used to denote a patent impossibility, and the love is literal not abstract: just as fiery hell cannot ever chill, so a person cannot ever physically "love" the sky or the earth—i.e. he or she cannot hold all of earth in a single embrace, cannot sensibly kiss the sky. Thus, the father in the cartoon declares that even if such a ludicrous impossibility were achieved, he would still refuse to let his daughter and her Internet beau marry—employing exaggeration, essentially, to emphasize his opposition to their union.

Culture

Since a number of Arab countries strictly limit interactions between men and women, many young Arabs are turning to social networking sites such as Facebook, MySpace and Hi5 to meet members of the opposite sex. Older generations look down upon this practice with disapproval, as most marriages traditionally have been pre-arranged by the family members of the bride and groom. Therefore, should a young man approach a father, expressing interest in his daughter, the father will demand not, "Where do you know her from?" but rather, "How did you even get to know her?" — A reflection of just how extensively male-female interactions are regulated. Needless to say, such Internet-born unions have little to no chance of being sanctioned by the parents of those involved.

☪ In certain Arab societies, parents can force their choice of husband on their daughters through different means. In most cases, their daughter's opinion or taste does not count since "love will come after marriage." Though mothers tend, by and large, to be more sympathetic to their daughter's feelings in a marriage (having undergone the same ordeal in their time), even a loving father is apt to feel that his daughter's innocence and naïveté would be bound to lead her to make foolish choices if she had the freedom to do so.

Translation

Man: "My sister, I refused him because he seems very greedy for your inheritance. By God, my four wives and I pray day and night for you to find the right man. Anyway, you're still in the prime of youth… and death, I mean your whole life, is ahead of you."

☪ A certain look is associated with middle-aged, unmarried women deprived of sex or real intimacy for their whole lives, and applies across countries and races. They remain unmarried not through choice (as with a nun, for instance), and as the passage of years brings more disappointments the face seems to become grayer, broader at the cheekbones, and washed out.

Culture

In Islam, marriage will not be considered valid without having a guardian accept the union. The guardian has to be a male, often a father or brother, or any male relative in absence of the immediate family.

Women prevented from marrying

According to Islamic traditions, a woman needs the permission of her guardian to get married[14]. This guardian is usually her father, brother, or any male relative willing to step in. There is no hierarchy for

---

[14] Women need permission to do many things, see "9 — Women," p.214.

choosing such a guardian, it is simply who is close to the family. Traditions dictate that a guardian can force a woman to marry someone whom she does not like, or prevent her from marrying a suitable partner. A suitable man, in Islam, is one who is properly religious and conducts and behaves himself in a good manner. Quite often, the guardian will not permit the woman to marry her suitor. This prevention of marriage is called عضل *adl* in Arabic, and is generally invoked because the woman is reserved to marry one of her relatives, or the suitor is of another tribe or nationality. A father on his deathbed may tell his son, as a last request, to prevent his daughter from marrying anyone but her cousin. Frequently, marriage is prevented if a greedy father or brother desires the salary of the woman, and does not want to lose the income to her husband. Some fathers with employed daughters in Arab countries will take her entire salary to "save it for her." By her getting married, the father will not only lose the income, but she may ask for the saved money back, especially if her new husband hears of it. This is problematic, as the father will view any leftover money as his. It is, therefore, not unusual to find forty- or fifty-year-old women who have never been married because their guardian refuses to release them for marriage. Arab psychologists and sociologists are against this phenomenon and note that many girls will not complain about their father's conduct to a Sharia court, which can overturn the decision. The woman views this action as disobedient to her parents. The court, however, if consulted, will generally be able to convince the guardian to lift the ban on marriage.

☾ A strict and traditional Arab father will refuse a suitor if he knows that his daughter has met him before the suitor asks for her hand, let alone dated him, however briefly.

Translation

Title: Kinship

Single man: O my uncle, I'm not coming to say hello to you because the God-glorified month of Ramadan is approaching. I'm coming because yesterday I sent you a letter to wish you a blessed Ramadan and I want to know if it has arrived or not.

Language

Muslims glorify month of Ramadan and the day of Friday by attaching *af-fadīl*, outstanding, excellent or preëminent, and can also refer simply to "the preëminent month" or "day" as in the cartoon.

 *Ya 'ammee!* signifies "O my uncle!"

Culture

The younger man's kneeling posture is a sign of respect, since it is associated with prayer. The older man's posture shows total relaxation, from association with the way that the legs are rested after prayer.

In traditional Arab family-oriented cultures, single men are treated differently. Frequent visits of single men to other members of the family are not welcome, especially if this family has unmarried women. These visits will put restrictions on the freedom of the people living in the household, because they do not want their unmarried daughters and these single men to socialize; even if they are close relatives. In Arab countries, the social interactions of women, even in their houses, are very limited. In this cartoon, this single man is visiting his uncle just to make sure that the letter he sent to congratulate his uncle on the approach of Ramadan has been delivered. It is clear from the expression of the uncle that he is annoyed by the visit. In America, protective parents of a daughter would not be alarmed if her male cousin should visit frequently because cultural norms and taboos generally restrain romantic liaisons between first cousins. In many Arab countries, however, marriages between cousins are welcomed, because they strengthen family ties. Children are often promised in marriage even before their parents have married. For example, if a woman has great respect for her brother, she can promise to marry her future daughter to his future son. Because these arrangements are not uncommon, if a male relative has no prospect of marrying into a family that he frequently visits — perhaps because his education is not of an acceptable level (e.g. a family might want to their daughter to marry a doctor) — the family will be annoyed by his continued appearance.

Buck-teeth are often thought to show stupidity and rural slowness — much as in the West and with equally little real basis.

Translation

Right frame

Title: Thursday, the groom.

Thursday: I managed to see my earlobe, uncle, now let me marry your daughter.

Left frame

Title: Thursday, the groom.

Thursday: I managed to bring you a sparrow's milk, my uncle. You take care of the propane cylinder.

Language

The phrases "when you see your own earlobe" and "when you bring me sparrow milk" are used as ways of saying that something is impossible—like the conditions in the traditional English song *Scarborough Fair*. The father of the girl has set these impossible tasks, but the groom, called Thursday, has managed to achieve them, as in the tale of Cupid and Psyche.

The sparrow is a common bird throughout the Arab world. Some birds do produce crop milk, including pigeons and flamingos, a secretion from the lining of the crop with which the parents feed their young by regurgitation, but not sparrows.

 The cartoon suggests that a propane cylinder is as difficult to get as sparrow's milk.

Culture

"The girl is reserved" or "the girl is being talked about"

When a father does not like a potential suitor for his daughter, the most polite and efficient way to decline the request is to say "the girl is reserved," or "the girl is being talked about." The first statement generally means that the girl has been promised to her cousin. Usually the girl will not know that somebody has expressed interest in her, since it is not common for the father to tell her unless his relationship with his daughter is very strong. The phrase is used whether or not the daughter is actually reserved. As for "being talked about," it indicates other people are seriously interested in her and until the exact outcome of deliberations is known, the daughter's hand cannot be talked of with other parties. A persistent suitor knows the tradition and that these are simply polite ways of saying no, but he may ask the father if he may contact him at a later date, in case the situation has changed. The father tends to agree to this.

If a girl herself wants to decline an offer from someone who is interested in her, she can tell the man that she has been talked about. This can also used humorously to elicit laughter from friends, because it is such a cliché.

Power marriage

Marriage can be used for dynastic reasons, as with European royalty and aristocracy in the past, although in most cases the families have reached power relatively recently, while old families are no longer in control. Marriage strengthens the ties between powerful families, so that the president of an Arab country may offer his daughter in marriage (or consent to a request) to a influential figure, as in the case of Egypt's President Sadat whose daughter Jihan was married to Mahmoud, the son of Othman Ahmed Othman, a powerful contractor whose company built the High Dam at Aswan. This pattern was repeated when President Mubarak married his son Gamal to the daughter of Mahmoud el-Ggammal, another rich contractor.

As in these cases, most "power marriages" take place between the children of the government elite and wealthy business people. Their relationship has usually built up over years, as the businessman enables the implementation of government policy and the politician entrusts expensive contracts to the businessman. Marriage between their families then takes the relationship one stage further. This type of connection particularly benefits the businessman more obviously, indicating official backing and trust, and giving him access to other countries in the Arab world and even Europe if the politician is recognized and liked there.

As Arab women enter increasingly into professional fields, more and more Arab families are concerned that their highly skilled and educated daughters should not marry beneath them and take husbands who hold lesser qualifications and enjoy more constricted job prospects than they do. Doctors, dentists, and engineers, for example, enjoy extremely high-status in the Arab world, and the family of any woman who is pursuing one of those careers will be very eager that she marry a man in a similiarly exalted field. This pressure does not exist for men, given that the traditional expectation that a man would provide a household's main source of income.

Muslim traditions governing whom one is allowed to marry are complex and make use of the traditional definitions of familial propinquity that have been analyzed in the discussion of inheritance law. A central concern, of course, is that any children who might result from a match be brought up in the Islamic faith; as it would traditionally have been assumed that a father would dictate his children's religion, female Muslims, called *Muslim'eh*, are strictly enjoined from marrying any non-Muslim except in cases when physically compelled to do so.

Male Muslims, for their part are forbidden by the Qur'an (Chap. 4, v. 22, 23) and the sunnah from marrying their mothers or other ascendants and also their daughters or other descendants. Furthermore, a man's sister or half-sister; aunt, great-aunts, and so forth; and also nieces and her descendants are all forbidden. In addition to birth mothers, Islamic law recognizes the tie of foster mothers and wet-nurses. The *Hanafi* code forbids marriages with any woman from whom one has taken a drop of milk, whereas the *Shafi* code only bans marriages with women who suckled one five times in one's first two years of life. This connection by nursing, in fact, is considered as equivalent to a blood connection. The practice of polygamy, finally, adds some further complications: mothers-in-law; daughters of wives; former wives of one's father; former wives of one's son; and sister, aunts, or nieces of one's present wives are all forbidden. In slave-holding societies, Muslims were able to marry their own slaves without manumitting them, but they could not marry someone else's slave if they already had a free wife.

ـ لامؤاخذة يا أونكل.. ممكن أدفع نص المهر, و آخدها يومين في الأسبوع ؟

Translation

Man with teacup (the prospective groom): Excuse me, Uncle, can I pay half dowery and take her two days a week?

Language

The groom in this cartoon uses the English word, "Uncle," in his address to his soon-to-be father-in-law. Arabs sometimes use English words in their Arabic, but their pronounciation is, naturally, different, with one particularly noticeable difference being that words are pronounced more as they are spelled. The short "U" in "uncle," then, becomes a long "U" sound. Similarly, the first "o" in "Hollywood" becomes long, and the "oo" in pronounced as in the word "woo."

"Uncle" may be used in addressing a man of one's father's age as a term of respect.

Culture

This cartoon illustrates the important distinctions that Arab culture recognizes in posture and carriage depending on one's situation and status. The man in the suit may be showing brazen effrontery in his request to his prospective father-in-law, but his bearing, at least, is polite. Firstly, he keeps his legs politely closed; sitting with legs apart or—even more—crossed, is a posture of dominance that would be arrogantly inappropriate in this situation. He keeps his hands and arms to himself, and he leans forward, both enabling him to speak softly and showing rapt attention to what the other man says. The father of the bride, in contrast, can dominate the interview with his legs apart. Crossed-legs, as it happens, are rather rare in the Arab world and carry arrogant connotations.

The suitor in the suit is covered in attributes that, to an Arab reader, immediately mark him as a lover. Beyond his dapper appearance, his seductive, half-closed bedroom eyes, and especially his pencil-moustache are all common indicators of a romantic character. Many of these ideas and stereotypes, of course, can be traced to glamorous Hollywood leading men.

The Arab Wedding Night

The wedding night, in Arabic *leylet ed-dukhleh* (the Night of Entrance), for a newly married Arab bride and groom, could be considered the scariest night in their lives thus far, as it will be the first intimate encounter for both of them. Usually for women, their first source of knowledge for what to expect on their wedding night is from their mother, and sometimes an older sister who has already been married; it will be an older sister, because in Arab culture, the daughters must get married in birth order. The man usually gets his knowledge of the night from his equally ignorant peers, or sometimes a married man, who will explain what to expect. However, most men are reluctant to ask about what to expect, in order to keep up their reputation of having knowledge of what to do on their wedding night. Many youths will consult informational books that have been published on the subject, which will sometimes have pictures, and lead to more confusion than before. There are many restrictions placed on these books, however, so they are scarce.

This lack of foreknowledge leaves the young couple prey to swirling anxieties, half-formed expectations, and apprehension. Brides have been horrified with stories of the pains of penetration, and grooms are worked into nervous excitement, eager for marriage pleasures but bewildered as to what, exactly, he is supposed to do. Adding to the pressure, both families congregate outside the bridal chamber and wait for the consummation of the wedding, as it is the custom for the groom to present his new mother-in-law with a sheet or handkerchief of his wife's hymeneal blood as proof of her virginity, which handkerchief will then be celebrated and paraded by the jubilant family. Such enormous anxieties and expectations too often lead a man to adopt a rough manner in during this sensitive act, which can have a detrimental effect on the relationship between the couple for the rest of their marriage.

In some Arab countries, the father, uncle, and brother of the bride will often not attend the wedding, because they feel ashamed of the fact that their daughter, niece, or sister is going to be losing her virginity.

After an Arab couple gets married, as in America, they take a honeymoon. However, in Arabic, honeymoon is literally "honey month," and the newlyweds often take an entire month vacation following their wedding.

Requirements for marriage

In many Arab countries, couples who wish to marry must undergo a variety of medical tests, sometimes having to pay a small fee to do so. Some common tests include screening for H.I.V., hepatitis, liver disease, and drug use, along with an ultrasound of the woman's uterus and, recently, a sperm count for the man. This last requirement has been extremely controversial, as Arab culture objects strongly to masturbation, condemning it as "the secret habit." Otherwise, though, society is strongly in favor of the tests as a safeguard of the health of people entering into marriages. Indeed, fatwahs, or religious edicts, were issued to prohibit the marriage of persons infected with H.I.V. with those who are uninfected, and the tests help prevent such things from happening. Some lawmakers have raised objection to the tests on human rights grounds, arguing that they should be made optional, but the overwhelming support for the tests has kept them obligatory. In addition to society's broad support, the Arab states hope that, by means of these tests, they can ensure the health of the next generation.

If the tests results should be positive, the health office will contact the ill half of the match and advise him or her to withdraw discreetly from the marriage. If he or she refuses, then the office will contact the other member and his or her guardian or family, giving them the test results but requiring them to sign an agreement not to make their knowledge public.

The law requires that certification of having taken all these tests must be presented by a couple applying for their marriage license. In Islam, a verbal agreement and two witnesses is all that is needed to be married, but in order for the government to recognize the union and for the couple to enjoy all the benefits that recognition brings, then they must submit to the tests—and pass.

Masturbation and Sexual Purity

The traditional stance of learned sheikhs was very strongly against masturbation. Indeed, some even issued fatwahs likening the masturbatory act to having sexual congress with one's mother inside the Kaabah in terms of its sacrilegious vileness. Recently, however, opinion has softened on the matter. Though masturbation is still regarded with disfavor, many Arab authorities have issued revisionary fatwahs that advise Muslims that masturbation is to be regarded as a preferable alternative to fornication. This holds both for men and women, though unmarried women are further advised to take care that their masturbatory practice not deprive them of the signs of their virginity.

The discussion about masturbation's status under Islamic law has become substantial and widespread, especially among young Arab males and females. In fact, of all the topics on which Muslims desire a fatwah, the legality of masturbation surely the most widely demanded. The difficulty has arisen because, despite the fact that the Qur'an says nothing of masturbation itself, there is an explicit prohibition against the thinking of illicit, uncouth or lustful thoughts—which, of course, constitute a fundamental dimension of masturbation.

Vocal pitch

In America, men attempting to assert their masculinity employ a deeper voice, as this is what the culture dictates as manly and right. The same can be seen with women. Those trying to act in a feminine way rely on higher-pitched voices, since deeper could be viewed as manly and less refined. In Arab culture, the opposite is true. This phenomenon is rooted in Islam, which encourages women to use a more forceful way of talking and not to resort to the higher, airy voice seen as attractive in America. The reason for this is first mentioned in the Qur'an (Chap. 33, v. 32) as advice to the wives of the Prophet Muhammad, who were told not to speak in a manner that could be perceived as seductive. This seductive way is considered to indicate softer, higher-pitched voices, so women are not encouraged to use it, since a male listener could misconstrue her voice as inviting. You will see that Arab women have a tone of voice that seems monotonous when compared with their Western counterparts. Such a tone does not mean that an Arab woman is uninterested, it is simply the way she has been taught to speak.

On the other hand, men are not advised to speak in the assertive way that is seen as masculine in Western cultures. The ideal is a softer, calmer tone. They prefer not to raise their voice, especially if they do not need to, so that conversation involves steady voices. This, too, is rooted in the Qur'an (Chap. 31, v. 19), where God advises men to speak in a quieter voice, through the story of Luqman advising his son.

Younger Arabs, especially in metropolitan areas, are sometimes criticized for speaking so softly that they sound like women, as they replace emphatic letters with non-emphatic. They adopt this softer tone as a way of appearing more modern and attractive to women. Women, on the other hand, now often use a more forceful tone to project an aura of assertiveness, and to indicate that they are deserving of respect. Neither of these variations reflects sexual orientation.

Translation

"I have a simple question. Are you coming here to ask for my daughter's hand or to install a carport?"

Language

This cartoon is from Saudi Arabia where men can wear either white or checkered white and red headdress. Some Arab men consider wearing a large headdress a fashion statement, but the older Arab men disapprove of changing these traditional garments for fashion reasons.

Culture

The traditional Arab way of getting engaged involves making an appointment with the man of the house. The suitor must then go to visit them accompanied by his mother or father and express his interest in getting engaged to the girl. If the man of the house finds him suitable, he will put his hand in the suitor's hand and read the opening of the Qur'an. Usually the women on the girl's side of the family will express their joy by making *zagrouta*s (ululations). During this initial visit, the girl may not be present. In certain cultures, the girl can join the meeting. In some traditional Arab countries where the chances are slim of a man ever being able to meet a marriageable woman in normal circumstances, the introduction between them will happen through a professional matchmaker. The matchmaker is a woman you go to if you are looking for a husband or a wife for your child and have no other means to find other prospects. She is older with a lot of social connections in the community, and well trusted. Mothers are usually the ones to visit the matchmaker on behalf of their children and Arab women are eager to play the role of matchmaker. Any Western girl who visits this area of the world, will realize this fact once these women ask her if she is married and offer their help to find a husband if she is single. Now in the age of the Internet, traditional Arab matchmakers have expanded their business to the Web, using social networking sites like Facebook, and making matches between those interested in marriage from different countries.

☪ Those from the Arabian Gulf will often wear the lighter, white *guthra* during the summer months (cf. the man on the right in the cartoon), and the heavier, red-checkered *guthra* during the winter (cf. the man on the left).

Translation

Title: The way some girls think before marriage

Right to left:

At age 20, she says, "Nothing's wrong with him, except he has a big nose."

At age 25, she says, "Ah, he's got big lips."

At age 30, she says, "Nothing's wrong with him, but he's got big ears."

At age 40, she says, "Where is he?"

Culture

As in America, when a woman is still young and receives a lot of attention from men, she tends to be picky about who she will marry. As she grows older, however, and the attention decreases, she laments her lost opportunities. Generally speaking, in Arab countries, appearance does not play as large a role in deciding on a spouse as it does in America. In this age of rising Islamic fervor, many Arab girls consider the strength of their suitor's religious belief to be a more important factor than his looks.

It is lawful for Muslim men to marry Christian or Jewish women, but the offspring will follow the Islamic faith of their father and the wife will not inherit anything when the husband dies. It is not lawful, however, for Muslim women to marry anyone outside of the faith.

Translation

Title: Girls dreams

(1) From 17-24 years old

I will only marry someone who looks like Brad Pitt, has a Porsche Cayenne and a villa in Deir Ghbar. My wedding will be in Kempinski and my honeymoon in Thailand…etc.

(2) From 25-28 years old

I want to have someone who is financially comfortable. It doesn't matter if he's handsome, or if he has a Mitsubishi, and has an apartment in The Gardens. I will have my wedding at Swimming Sports City and my honeymoon in Sharm el-Sheikh [Egypt.] That's it.

(3) From 29-32 years old

(*Smoking*) I hope anyone will ask to marry me. A car is not a problem. It doesn't matter if our house is a rental, our wedding in a [modest] wedding hall and our honeymoon in Aqaba [a coastal town in the far south of Jordan]... As the proverb says, "A shadow of a man rather than a shadow of a wall." Just let him come.

(4) From 33-40 years old

I just need any man, even our retarded neighbor Atwa. Our wedding will be on the roof and I will live with his family. And I don't need a "tar-moon." I just need a groom, any groom. Wah wah wah.

In the third panel, the woman's pile of spent cigarettes clues the reader into the woman's growing anxiety that her chances for marriage are dwindling. She is, ironically, even further reducing her chances of marriage, because the stigma associated with smoking will limit the number of men who find her eligible.

Language

"Tar," *zift*, is used as a degrading substitute for any pleasant word. In Arabic, one might respond to the question "How are you?" by saying "Like tar" to mean terrible In the cartoon, the woman cheapens the word "honeymoon" by replacing "honey" with "tar" – "I don't need any damned honeymoon."

"A shadow of a man rather than a shadow of a wall," refers to the emotional and financial support that a man will provide. Even if he is not the perfect husband, he would be better than being alone in a room where the only shadow is that of wall.

In recent years there has been a joking variation of this last proverb: "Shadow of the Affairs rather than shadow of a man," referring to the Ministry of Social Affairs, which in richer Arab countries provides support for divorced women, in most cases more generously than husbands. This has led to a number of women seeking to provoke their husbands into divorce.

Culture

Criticism of picky girls is a theme in the male-dominated Arab media. These cartoons discourage young women from waiting for a perfect husband and potentially missing the marriage-train.

For a woman to live with her husband's family is usually purgatory, involving a testing of her limits and patience, and she will have no control and be required to help.

The mentally impaired are a fixture in many Arab neighborhoods. These people are often known and befriended by neighbors and trusted to do simple tasks in exchange for food or money.

Translation

Title: A spinster's wish

[*Clasping her hands and closing her eyes, in front of a 40th birthday cake*]: I don't want a groom, I just need a break from this awful name [i.e. spinster].

[*N.B. the frames and pictures on the wall – certificates, riding a horse, graduation – indicate that she is an educated, accomplished person.*]

Language

The word 'anis has the same negative connotations as its

English counterpart "spinster" and is disliked as much, which is why this woman wants to rid herself of it.

 Culture

The stigma associated with being unmaried is lessening, and many professional women would rather stay single though their family and friends will continue to introduce them to potential husbands. Women generally do not actively look for husbands,

The Rising Number of Unmarried Women

One of the reasons for the rise in the number of unmarried women is tribalism or clannishness, the tendency for Arab men to marry within their own tribe or clan. Families vary in how much or how strongly they observe this tradition, which is a form of bigotry on the part of the men, starting with the father, who passes his bias to his children. In an Arab family, when considering a prospective groom, the father has the final say. If the father is not present, the eldest brother (even if he is younger than the bride) will decide. The father can refuse any man who is not a member of his tribe or who has no blood connection, because there is no kinship or relationship. The clan and tribe can comprise thousands of people, and therefore differs from any Western association with in-breeding. Tribal roots are often traced back centuries to establish lineage to important historical or religious figures.

Because of these clannish tendencies, some women prefer to remain single, rather than marry their cousins or other relatives. Some families are very adamant about not taking a man out of their family, in the belief that the "stranger" will mistreat their daughter, and to preserve the continuation of the bloodline and lineage.

Sometimes the family will refuse a suitor because he is from a different area of the country. In the Arab world, where you live can have bearings on your marriage prospects. This can apply to regions or even neighborhoods, because different areas have long-standing reputations among the people of the country and sometimes beyond. Upper Egypt, for example, is considered to be populated by people of lesser intelligence and to marry someone from this area would be considered as marrying beneath one's station.

Sometimes a family will test the background of a suitor or any person with whom they want to associate closely by casually finding out what he calls a certain object, like a camel. The suitor's response will help the family identify the region that the suitor comes from and his social standing. This type of prejudice is adopted by children at a very early age and is used to determine friendships.

Some members of tribes will never marry a member of a second tribe if there is a past feud or quarrel with this tribe. The quarrel may date back ten years or more, but the animosity persists and makes all members of the other tribe off-limits. This practice dates back to the pre-Islamic era where association to tribes was of paramount importance.

☪ Being a smoker can have a negative impact on a person's marriageability, especially women, as can working in a mixed-gender environment.

Translation

Title: "The Pyramids of Giza."

Man holding rosary: "Haven't you gotten married? Do you want to get married?" (*Repeated three times*)

Woman in the middle: "Find yourself a [female] employee…her salary plus your salary…her family will help you…two rented rooms…furniture on credit…and step by step…step by step…step by step."

Woman on left: "By God, Mother, your mistake on my neck, there is nothing better than the protection. Just have the intention…just have the intention…just have the intention."

Man in doorway: "The meal of the groom."

☪ This is a scene repeated in households all over the Arab world. The family of a potential bride can find that it needs to have a sit-down meeting with a possible suitor attempting to convince him to marry their daughter.

☪ In American culture, circled eyes often indicate that someone is dazed or bewildered, which is not the case here. The eyes of the three characters are meant to show a focused, intense look at the young man, possibly hypnotic (also a possible meaning in an American cartoon).

Language

The blunt words of the father are an indication of his reluctance to participate in this conversation. The repetition of questions shows the pressure being put on him.

"Female employee," here means a woman in employment or with a job.

When the woman speaks of protection and having the intention, she is referring to the man's protecting himself from temptations outside the sanctity of marriage. In Arab-Islamic culture, if one has good intentions and sincerity, God can reward. Although there are instances of experiences not coming to fruition, the effort will be accepted and recognized. In comparison to American culture, one can still get points for trying.

The "groom's meal describes the cultural undertaking of the family sharing a meal with the groom, but can take on an alternate meaning. In the picture above, the two young men in the doorway proceed to poke fun at the young man with beads of sweat running down his face, to illustrate the compromising situation. Just as he is terrified to be in the room, the men refer to his fate as groom's food, or a literal translation, the eating of the groom.

The last woman's phrase here translated as "your mistake on my neck," is analogous to the English, "on my head be it." She expresses her confidence that her advice is sound and offers to be beheaded if it should prove otherwise.

Culture

One may ask how a young man may find himself in such a high pressure situation which holds such bearing over the rest of his life. He is no stranger to the family, and could be a visiting relative or friend of the family's son. These meetings are premeditated by the older members of the family, and in effect, they lie in wait until the potential suitor comes for a visit. By meeting with him like this, the family lets the man know that they like him and would consider him a good addition to the family. Although stressful, this situation is not decisively committal, and serves the man notice that if he has any intention to marry their daughter, the family supports him and accepts him.

☪ These meetings are not easy on the family and can be embarrassing because in Arab culture it is usually the woman who is sought out for marriage. The family will intervene like this when their daughter has not been successful in marrying herself, or when they feel that she is not capable of doing so. Because the market is very competitive for brides, the family has to overcome their shyness and not simply wait for a groom who may never come.

Usually the family will do something like this as a marketing tool for the daughter who has not had much success in marketing herself either through her beauty, prestigious job, or skin color. The family might also become worried as an unmarried daughter gets older (possibly as young as twenty-two) and completes her college degree. Once she is finished with college, they fear that she will not be involved in social settings as much and will not be seen by men.

As for the man, he does not have to have all the qualities that the woman must have, because by nature of being a man with a good education from a good family, he will be attractive to many families with single daughters. The most important thing in choosing a husband is his family background, the next is education.

☪ The most important thing for an Arab family is to find a husband for their daughter who is from a good family with good values and upbringing. Because of this, they usually avoid using matchmakers, as these professionals can often be fooled by single men of lower education, background, and wealth. The matchmaker will vouch for the man, even if he is not known to her (and all official matchmakers are women), and she will attempt to arrange the engagement so that she can receive fees from both the bachelor and the bride's family.

☪ Usually the father views this process as beneath him. He does not want to find himself in a position of "talking up "his beloved daughter to strangers. Usually the mother pressures the husband to do this because the father has a wider social circle, and due to his age and job, he has access to a dating pool of good quality. Usually the husband is reluctant to offer his daughter to friends and colleagues, and will often get angry with his wife. If the father's requests to marry his daughter are not accepted because a colleague is already engaged or something, it is highly embarrassing to the father. He will take out his anger on the mother and sometimes never try to do it again.

The brothers of these women also get put into strange situations. Sometimes the mother can/will intercept and talk to male friends of her sons. The sons will often get angry at this.

The mothers usually feel no shame for doing these things because they see it as securing future happiness for their daughters and ensuring cohesion among the family as a whole.

Translation

"Zaghrouta (Shrill of joy)"

Language

The sound of *zaghrouta* is written above in Arabic: *lou lou lou louyy*. (The plural of *zaghrouta* is *zaghareet*.) It is a high-pitched sound that Arab women make to mark their extreme happiness at any joyful event or news, such as the announcement of a wedding, during a wedding procession, or the news that someone has passed a crucial exam. It informs neighbors that you have something to celebrate and that something good has happened to you so that they can congratulate you in the future. If the neighbor is equally excited, they will make the *zaghrouta* too. Only women make this sound, never men, and not every woman is equally capable of producing a beautiful *zaghrouta*—the best are usually middle-aged. The sound is made by making the tongue go up and down as air is blown through.

Ululation expresses great devastation as well as great joy. It is used in mourning or grief to express resilience and fighting spirit, so it is common at funerals. There is also the mixed emotion of a noble death, where, for example, a mother who lost a son in war should not, according to the Qur'an, lament over his death, but express her joy at her child's destiny as a martyr, or *shaheed*, and that he is in paradise.

Culture

House of Occasions, *Dar al-Munasabat*

Arab people celebrate different occasions at many different places, including in their homes, at a hotel or at a "House of Occasions." Weddings and solemn gatherings like funerals will be held in homes, while only happy occasions will be celebrated in hotels. The House of Occasions, however, can house all kinds of gatherings.

Celebrations and gatherings at home are the most cost effective because there is no rental fee, and they offer variety too, as they may take place inside or outside, next to the house. If the celebration takes place inside the house, the host family will rent extra chairs to accommodate their guests and, depending on the occasion, they may hire a band to play music or a sheikh to recite verses from the Qur'an. The sheikh may be seen reciting verses at a funeral or at a wedding. Families can also rent large tents that they will then erect in the street. These tents, usually large enough to accommodate hundreds of people, are often an inconvenience to neighbors and drivers. The tents are often equipped with microphones and speakers standing outside to broadcast the event to the entire neighborhood, which is an added nuisance to people nearby.

If a family does not want to host an event in their home, they can rent a hall called a House of Occasions. This hall, sometimes within the grounds of a mosque, is similar to an American banquet hall. At the House of Occasions, for a fee, the mosque or a private hall's owners will supply the family with almost everything they need for the celebration: catering, chairs, decorative flowers, a photographer and a mazoon, the person charged with drawing up a marriage contract. A mazoon charges a minimum of fifty dollars and a small percentage of the mahr (bride gift), often around three percent. Houses of Occasions can range from the very upscale and elegant to the more basic and thrifty, depending on their location. Some are made to cater to certain groups of people such as police officers, doctors, engineers, members of a particular union, and so on, and priority is given to members of the group. The House of Occasions is often the best choice for many Arabs wanting to hold events, as it is relatively inexpensive and less trouble than holding an event in the home.

Rich Arab families will usually hold their weddings in large, five-star hotels, where large sums of money can buy them an elaborate ceremony and celebration. Holding a wedding in a hotel reflects the family's wealth. Funeral ceremonies can also be used to show a family's wealth. When a prestigious or very well-respected person dies, the family will most often choose to hold the funeral in the grounds of the grandest mosque available, so that many people can come and show their respect to the family and the deceased.

Some Arab families will choose to hold their weddings inside mosques, though only the formal part of the wedding will be celebrated here—there will be no music, only the groom signing the marriage contract with the bride's guardian. This is done to show respect to God and to ask Him to bless the marriage. After this initial part of the ceremony, they will move to a second location to hold the reception.

There are specific drinks that are associated with either happy or sad occasions. Sharbat is a very sweet, colorful drink that is served during happy occasions and celebrations. It is similar to a very strong juice from concentrate that is diluted with very cold water. This drink is passed around during weddings and is consumed during the celebratory ululation. On more solemn occasions, a drink made of very dark and bitter coffee is passed around in tiny cups.

☪ Light is a sign of celebration in the Arab world, and when celebrating wedding colorful lamps are hung-similar to Christmas lights but actual lamps outside the house, and the same thing is common during religious holidays when the minarets will be adorned with lights.

Light also used in standard greetings—the salutation "Morning of goodness" is answered "Morning of lights," and the same for the other times of day. More warmly, a person can be greeted "You light up..." with a place or on its own.

It is also used in names: *Nour* itself can be used for both men and women, while *Anwar*, meaning "has more light "or "brighter," is only for men. Light is also one of God's attributes.

Translation

First panel (on right)
Man: "Father, you passed the high school exam. One thousand congratulations. May God bestow good health on you. Quickly, quickly father, to the acceptance and registration."

Second panel
Title: Acceptance.
Woman: "I accept you as a husband according to the sunnah of Allah and his Prophet."

Third panel. **Title**: And Registration.

Mazoon: "Register, my daughter, your name and place of birth. And your signature. O bride."

Language

This cartoon plays on the words acceptance and registration, comparing the admittance into a university to accepting a suitable husband. Registration can refer to the process after accceptance, such as registering for classes at the university, and in the context of marriage, registering information with the Justice of Peace, or, *mazoon,* to begin a marriage contract.

As a symbolic number, a thousand is the preferred number of blessings, thanks, congratulations or positive wishes.

☪ As a term of endearment, a father can call his daughter "father" and mother can call her son "mother." The mazoon as a man of religion and an older man refers to the woman as his daughter, and could refer to the man as his son.

Culture

Most families will begin to entertain the idea of the daughter getting married following her secondary education. If there is no serious mention or offer of marriage by the end of her college education, deep concern will spread throughout the family, result in lower status for the girl and fewer friends, as her popularity wanes, so that exclusion might follow. In turn, the family will resort to extreme, often unusual measures.

Translation

Title: Days of *milka* [i.e. the period between the religious ceremony of marriage and the wedding celebration]
Husband to his wife: You have no shame, you're eating ice cream in front of me like you are used to it! You are divorced!

☪ The woman in this cartoon is wearing a piece of clothing known as a *burqu'*. This attire is distinct from the *barqa'a*. The former is traditional women's clothing in the Gulf that leaves the eyes visible to others, whereas the latter is a costume of Pakistani origin that only leaves a small slit for a woman to see through. The *burqu'* is fading from use and tends to be worn only by older women, but the *barqa'a* is gaining popularity throughout the Islamic world amongst particularly observant Muslim women.

☪ The loop in the man's right hand is an Islamic rosary which, despite sharing the name, has a different design—with thirty-three or ninety-nine beads—and is performed differently than rosaries in Christian traditions. Many Muslims are careful always to keep a rosary about their person so that they may occupy their free moments in praising God. Those unfamiliar with Islamic traditions may be disconcerted to see Muslims inaudibly moving their lips as they repeat praises of God while running their fingers over a rosary.

Language

"Used to it" is a catchphrase of the popular Arab comedian Addel Imam. It originated in Imam's play "A Witness Who Saw Nothing." During a police interrogation, the investigator asks Imam's character if the crime's victim—a single woman who lived by herself—was "used to" receiving guests. "She was always used to it," Imam replies, and then repeats the phrase "used to it" a number of times. In doing so, he uses a humorous, over-the-top lilt, which insinuates that the victim is not only used to receiving guests per se, but more specifically johns—thus implying that she is a prostitute.

The cartoon's humor is absurdist humor, entailing the seemingly senseless association of two vastly different concepts: in this case, ice-cream eating and prostitution. Thereby, the humor arises from the friction between the foreign concept (i.e. ice-cream eating) and the conceptual and associational framework into which it is incorporated (i.e. prostitution and its attendant mores—moral severity, illegality, etc.).

Culture

Arab and Muslim marriage traditions involve three stages: the engagement, the religious ceremony (which involves the writing of the marriage contract), and the public wedding celebration.

In countries in which the sealing of the contract is the happy result of a successful engagement period, that signing is known as the *katb al-kitab*. In certain conservative countries such as Saudi Arabia, though, the engagement period is elided. Consequently, the first opportunity for the couple to become familiar with one another comes after the marriage contract has already been signed, though crucially before the union is publicly affirmed. In these conservative countries, this period is known as the *milka*, and, though the couple uses this time to get to know one another and lay the foundation for their future life together, the couple must maintain a decorous distance.

If an Arab man decides in haste to leave his wife, he will use the phrase "You are divorced!" similar to the way one might use the phrase "You're fired!" This divorce is not legally binding. However, after a husband says this to his wife on three separate occasions, his wife has to marry someone else in order for him to get her back. This is a form of punishment for an Arab man who abuses his power, as his wife will consummate her new marriage with another man.[15]

It is a common custom for a man under such circumstances to hire a person to marry his ex-wife, on the condition that he will divorce her the next day so that he, the former husband, can marry her again. The wife, however, can withhold her consent, unless she is not of age, in which case, her father, or other lawful guardian, may marry her to whom he pleases. A poor man (generally a very ugly person, and often one who is blind) is usually chosen for this role and he is termed a *moHallil*. It is often the case that the man thus employed is so pleased with the woman he is introduced to on these terms, or with her riches, that he refuses to give her up and the law cannot compel him to divorce her, unless he acts unjustly towards her as her husband, which of course he takes good care not to do. This scenario is, of course, the basis of a good number of comedies, both in the cinema and on the stage, but it also happens in real life.

---

[15] Al-Qur'an, 002.229-230 (*Al-Baqara* [The Cow]).

☪ If a man finds that he has, in the heat of the moment, uttered the third expression of divorce and regrets it (as long as his wife also wants to stay married and there are no witnesses), the matter can be brushed under the carpet as a private matter that concerns no one else except the couple without recourse the law of remarriage.

Translation

Right panel: During the *milka* period, you talk and she listens.

Left panel: After the marriage, she talks and humanity hears.

Culture

In conservative Arab countries like Saudi Arabia, the only time a person can really become acquainted with his partner is during the *milka* period between the contracting of a marriage and its consummation. Saudi men have several different strategies for establishing the marriage dynamic during this period. Some men choose to woo their fiancees with sweet words and by bringing presents; others can choose to be very aggressive in order to assert his dominance. In the first picture, the man has chosen the former method of courtship. His fiancée plays coy as she has, no doubt, been advised. However, once they have become married, the wife lets go of her shyness and becomes the loud nagger she really is under the surface.

Translation

Title: Thursday the groom

The groom to his future father-in-law: Be a good man and lend me your suit for the wedding, O my uncle.

Culture

Arabs sometimes name their children after specific days of the week or months from the Islamic calendar. The days of the week that children can be named after are *Khamees* (Thursday) and *Gumaa* (Friday), and the months are Rajeb, Shaaban and Ramadan. However, such names are associated with rustic families, and in modern times these names have been used in films for humorous characters, so the names themselves now carry connotations of bumbling lack of sophistication. Adding to this groom's ridiculousness is the fact that Thursday is the traditional day for weddings to be held. Finally, the Arabic word *khamees* rhymes with the Arabic for groom, so it sounds something like Jake the Snake would in English.

☪ It is not uncommon for men to borrow suits from one another for special occasions, including their wedding, because most men do not own suits due of the extremely hot climate. This groom, though, goes far beyond the usual practice and violates all limits of good taste in asking his father-in-law-to-be. This is an egregious faux pas, as he ought to be trying to impress his bride's family, not impose upon them.

My name is Two Muhammads

When Arabs give names to their newborn children, the name is not only a way to identify the person. Arab names reflect a cultural, social, or political reality, and often they link the person to the period when they were born. Historically, Arabs give names to their sons and daughters according to the place and time, or to circumstances, as well as political situations, such as the rise of beloved leaders. They may be named after the name of a popular colonel or king, or a social figure, such as a famous actor or musician. Some people choose names to identify the child with a culture other than their own, or name them after something they admire in a different culture. Egyptians, for example, still give their sons pharaonic names, such as Nema, Habi, Thutmose, Nefertiti, Hatoun, and Tiba, though this will be more common amongst Coptic Christians than Muslims.

This naming system is not limited to individuals but extends to family names, as well. There are many families that used to be famous for certain occupations, or they have come from famous places. Neither may now be relevant—the family may no longer practice the occupation and the place may no longer exist—but the name remains. Saddam Hussein, for instance, had the name al-Tikriti, which is where his family was from.

Names also come from the environment. In the Arab countryside, where life tends to be slower and dependent on farming and waiting for the harvest, the names reflect the environment. Here are found the girl's names Hanneya (Felicity), Khadra (Green), Mabrouka (Blessed), and Marzouqa (a girl's name meaning "God always provides"). Boys might be Rizq (sustenance), Farag (relief [from worry or unpleasantness]), and Awad (reparation). This last name comes out of the belief of Muslims that everything comes from God, and that all that has been given can be taken away. If, then, a person manages to express no grief for a loss, God will compensate their loss or take note of their patience. Because life is so harsh in much of the region—a crop is not guaranteed when planted, a fortune can turn with the weather, loss is common—one is in God's hands; so, when anything good happens it is viewed as being God's reparation for the hard times.

Other names include dual forms: Muhammadain (Two Muhammads) or Awadain (Two Reparations). The reason varies, but the most prevalent is the miscarriage or death of a child, which leads the father to name the next child with a dual form, as the new child also replaces the one that was lost.

As for those Arabs who live in a Sahara ("desert" in Arabic) or are Bedouin, they will give their children names that relate to their way of life, such as the boys' names Fahd (Cheetah), as in the late king of Saudi Arabia, Saif (Sword), Qazafi's sons; or Saqer (Falcon; Arabs are fond of falconry). Girls will also have names derived from the desert environment, as in Badr (Full Moon), Mahr (Foal), or Maliha (Pretty).

Children may also be named after the first thing their father lays eyes on, which in a desert environment may include wild animals, such as Gazelle, Horse, or Fox.

Natural phenomena also feature such as Valley, Rain, Spring, Summer, Winter, Sun, Moon, Half-Moon, Star, Planet, Supernova, Earthquake, Comet, Thunder, and Lightning. Similarly names for flowers, trees, and plants have been used, including Rose, Flower, Jasmine, Branches, and Ear of wheat, as have animals and their sounds, Eagle or Giraffe as well as those already mentioned, and Chirping, Tweeting, or Cooing.

In regions where tribal warfare was common, names would reflect strength, to strike fear in the hearts of enemies and provide power for the person named: Lion and Rock, for example. The opposite was true when naming slaves, who would be given more tranquil, pleasant names, such as Sweet Basil, Ruby, Turquoise, and Camphor-tree. The rationale for strong, intimidating, and powerful names for children and soft, delicate names for slaves was a belief that the "children's names are for our enemies, and the slaves' names are for us."

The names of children from poorer neighborhoods tend to reflect their economic situation, where most hold blue-collar jobs or none, so names such as Ahtayat (Gifts), Ehsan (Donation), or Aziza (Dear) exist. The first two names reflect the population's familiarity with the alms or donations they live on and that receiving a child is seen as a gift or donation from God, since the new child brings both good fortune and, more pragmatically, money due to their ability to work. In a poorer neighborhood a family's station or education is far less important for a woman than physical beauty. Names, then, reflect these beliefs—so, a poorer family might name their daughter something that reflects the idea of beauty, such as Badr (Full Moon), Delal (Coquetry), or Gamalat (Beautiful, in the plural form, as Arabic adjectives show number).

Wealthier families now often name their children with Western or Turkish names, these latter recalling the former Ottoman elite. In the era of globalization and the Internet, this practice is spreading. Throughout the region, Arabs are giving their children the names of Western pop stars and actors, while Turkish names reflect the strong presence of Turkish programming in Arab television. You can now find names such as Susan, Brad, Nancy, or Nourhan and Rusha. To counterbalance this trend in names becoming Westernized, some families have begun drawing from earlier religious eras, using names that held important religious value, such as Amina, Lyla, Lubna, and Yousef.

As for those who live near the graves of well-known religious figures, names may be based on the dead figure, such as Umm Hashem (a daughter of the Prophet Muhammad, who is buried in Egypt) or Hussein (Muhammad's cousin).

Children are also named after the day or month on which they were born. Thursday (Khamees) and Friday (Gumah) are the most common names of this type, as both are considered blessed days. Also Ramadan and Sha'aban are common, as they are blessed months that guarantee the children blessings.

Arabs can also give male names to female children. If the father was hoping for a male child to carry on the family name, but receives a female child, he may give her a male name, though this is a practice generally found in poorer or less educated classes. Other names carry resignation to the will of God, with a hint of disappointment, such as the name Rida (Content) or Nihmedoh (We Thank Him [Anyway]).

Arabs can also give unpleasant names to their children to ward off the evil eye. If a family longed for a male child, and was able to produce only girls, when a boy is finally born, the family may give him a name such as Shahat (Beggar).

Emigration has also affected naming because of the movement of many families from poorer countries to wealthy, oil-rich ones. Families give names reflecting their new home, such as Suhail, Temeen, and Eiad, which are all Gulf names.

As in American names, gender ambiguity can exist in certain names; say with the English name Dana, Shawn or Taylor. Often such Arab names reflect natural features, Shames (Sun), Qamer (Moon), or Badr (Full Moon). In Arab culture, however, all things gender neutral are generally associated with the feminine, which is not considered positive for the men bearing such names.

Your name is your enemy

Your name can make or break your career. Many Arabs use their personal name first; followed by their father's name; and then their grandfather's name, which is often the family name. The concept of family name is so strong that it tends to come at the end of the name, and can tell others a lot about you. Countries such as the UAE or Kuwait, for example, have taken the tribal concept of living together in a desert, and translated it to the city. It is not, therefore, rare to see an entire neighborhood occupied by one family, or tribe. Your name, then, can tell others exactly where your family lives, an important concept in Arab culture. While in the West someone who has been harmed will go to the police or court, Arab culture dictates that the tribe will deal with such matters. So, by knowing your name, the person who is wronged knows where you are from and where to go to receive justice. In the same vein, if you act well, the person you helped will tell their family. In future dealings then, all members of the family will take your past good behavior into account. Favors done are mutual as a result, but not necessarily paid by the same individuals. Due to this, it is important to look good in the eyes of other families.

Upon starting a career, a boss's behavior towards an individual is based on family name. If a positive relationship exists between the boss's family and the employee's, he will be treated extremely well. If the relationship between families has been tarnished (such arguments can stretch back fifty years), the employee's future may be ruined. Both situations hurt an individual. If you are from a tribe friendly with the boss, you will learn little, as nothing is demanded and no skills acquired. If the families are on bad terms, there will be poor treatment with little hope of advancement and life will be difficult.

Translation

Title of both cartoons: Marriage from Abroad!

Culture

This cartoon portrays a very old Arab man with his new, young bride, who is taking money out of her groom's pocket. In the background, an X is drawn over the picture of his old wife.

Many wealthy men in the Gulf area (though not necessarily old) marry young foreigners—mostly from poor Arab countries such as Egypt, Morocco, and Algeria—who, in the eyes of the Gulf citizens, primarily want their money. Though the woman may be eager to make use of her new husband's fortune, many of these men pursue the foreign wives for reasons of economy: a poor woman from a poor country will expect a far smaller dowry than would a prosperous daughter of his own land. With this smaller investment, these men feel, unfortunately, more free to abuse the new wife and quickly divorce her. When the husband does not divorce her, the young wife becomes a virtual slave to the man, his old wife, and his children. Usually when a woman is a second wife, the old wife enjoys seniority over her; even if the husband shows a preference for the younger woman, this dynamic does not last very long, and the power of the first wife will prevail.

Native-Foreigner Marriages

Recently, due to a confluence of circumstances, the incidence of marriage between native citizens of Arab countries and foreign nationals—both foreign Arabs and those of other ethnicities entirely—has increased dramatically. In 2008, for example, the Saudi Arabian government recognized 2,769 cases of Saudi men marrying foreign women, and 1,635 cases of Saudi women marrying foreign men. That same year, Egypt saw 621 cases of native women marrying foreign men. The highest incidence of native-foreigner marriages within the Arab world belongs, in fact, to Saudi Arabia, followed by the UAE, Bahrain, Qatar, Egypt and Oman—in that order.

In response to this recent upswing, more culturally conservative countries like Saudi Arabia and the UAE have sought to enact preventative, countervailing measures, while countries like Egypt have taken steps to ensure the safety of Egyptian citizens presently married or engaged to foreigners. In what follows, we will exam the various restrictions, regulations and attitudes attendant to the issue of native-foreigner marriage in the three countries mentioned above (that is, Saudi Arabia, the UAE and Egypt).

To begin with, we cannot speak of marriage between native citizens and non-Arab foreign nationals within the Arab world—a considerable can of worms in its own right—without first recalling, however briefly, Arab attitudes toward foreigners in general. And we have seen, thus far, the welter of urgent dilemmas arising from illegal aliens, naturalization movements, international corporate investments and, finally, the alternately encouraged and condemned influx of Western cultural media and mores. By now, it is clear that this occasional Arab antipathy toward foreigners is not, in fact, an antipathy toward foreigners *per se* — a thriving tourist industry is always an appreciable boon — but rather toward the multiplicity of non-traditional, non-Islamic cultural practices and traditions they inevitably bear with them.

This aversion to non-Arab foreign nationals should be understood as historically conditioned, the unfortunate outcome of years of oppression, exploitation and collusion. Finally, the decades of European imperial rule gave way to a Pan-Arab movement that, in reaction to the long history of foreign violence and corruption, severed ties with the international community. During this era (from the 1950s to the mid 1970s, roughly), foreigners, while entertained and encouraged as tourists, were viewed with suspicion and hostility if they tried to more meaningfully insinuate themselves into a local community. Thus, those close with such foreigners were accused of espionage and treason and, accordingly, ostracized from the community. These hostilities were exacerbated by an Arab tendency toward conspiracy thinking: forged in furnace of the very real tragedies visited upon the Arab people through very real conspiracies, the prevalence of "conspiracy thinking" led some to see elaborate machinations where only innocuous friendships existed.

As mere acquaintances between foreigners and natives were scrutinized so acutely for so many years, one can begin to imagine how problematic a situation the foreigner-native marriage could actually prove. And if that were not enough, such marriages face yet another, more traditional hurdle, this time deriving from ancient Islamic tradition. One hadith (or saying of the Prophet Muhammad) declares that a person should only marry his or her equal. "Equal," in this case, is understood to assume four different forms: first, that the persons be of the same faith; second, that the persons be of the same social status; third, that the persons be of the same economic status; and fourth, that the persons possess the same intellectual aptitude. (The cartoon of the plug is titled "Unsuitability," and shows a man putting a 110-volt plug, as used in North America, into a 220-volt outlet, as used in the Arab world and Europe.)

Taken together, these diverse conditions quite ably explain why the vast majority of native-foreigner marriages within the Arab world involve, specifically, foreign *Arabs*. Yet, even when both bride and bridegroom are fully Arab, the various "equality" parameters, as well as a host of national hang-ups, have made it such that native-foreigner marriages are nonetheless much belabored by bureaucratic red-tape and discriminatory, government-sanctioned restrictions. The Westerner might find this strange, as he expects this sort of social strife to arise from ultimately ethnic, and not class or national, issues.

Saudi Arabia

In Saudi Arabia, a number of people are categorically prohibited from marrying foreigners. Generally, this prohibition is intended to cover all those responsible, in whatever capacity, for Saudi national security, and includes: those in the upper echelons of government, including ministers and deputies; those in the judicial system, from judges to bailiffs and notary publics (the one prominent exception being lawyers); all courtiers; all state department employees; all military personnel, from generals to privates, and including military and national guard hospital staffers; all customs officials; and all those who study abroad.

The restrictions pertaining to male citizens who wish to marry foreigners are different from those pertaining to female citizens. (There is, in fact, a deplorable misogyny evident in the core of these marriages policies.) Nonetheless, they possess all the distinct hallmarks of bureaucratic lavishness. A Saudi, male full citizen is permitted to marry a foreign national if and only if: (1) he is between the ages of thirty-five and seventy; OR (2) he is a widower or divorcee (that is, completely so—he cannot be a widower or divorcee with still one or two extant wives) of any age; OR (3) the foreign national in question is his immediate relative (say, a cousin), and he is between the ages of thirty and seventy; OR (4) he is disabled, chronically ill or otherwise handicapped.

Meanwhile, a Saudi, female full citizen is permitted to marry a foreign national if and only if: (1) the foreign national is a practicing Muslim; AND (2) her guardian (e.g. her father, uncle or brother, etc.) consents to the union; AND (3) her employer consents to the union; AND (4) she is over twenty-five years of age; OR (5) the foreign national in question is her immediate relative (say, a cousin), and she is over twenty-one years of age.

Accordingly, the two (separate) native-foreigner marriage application processes follow upon predictable courses. A man must supply the government with: proof of employment, a birth certificate, a state ID and/or a state family ID, a letter from his employer stating his position and income, and a full medical report stating his fitness for marriage. If necessary, he must also include proof of past marriage or completed divorce, or his last wife's death certificate. A woman, on the other hand, must provide: a birth certificate, a state ID and/or a state family ID, proof of her guardian's consent, proof of her employer's consent, and a full medical report. Finally, both men and women must complete elaborate written applications, which require them to provide: information—religious, national, professional etc.—about their (hopefully) soon-to-be spouse, and also an explanation of why, precisely, the applicant wishes to wed his or her intended.

We must now address the question of exactly who this "intended" is. As previously mentioned, the majority of "foreigners" in native-foreign pairings are foreign Arabs. In the case of Saudi Arabian males, the foreign paramour will often violate any (or all) of the equality constraints—including, crucially, religion. However, such foreign paramours will consistently do so in a "downward" fashion. In other words, if they *do* violate any equality constraints, these foreign lovers will normally be of a *lower* social, economic or intellectual status than their grooms-to-be. And this is what makes the case of many of the Saudi women currently involved in native-foreigner marriages so unique: increasingly, wealthy, well-educated and socially influential Saudi women—in particular, doctors and academics—are marrying foreign, less educated, blue-collar laborers. Among this set, the most popular sort are Egyptian men, followed, in order, by men from Lebanon, Jordan and, finally, Palestine. Often, the groom will begin as a worker at her family's estate—for example, as her personal chauffeur—and in this way grow close to his future bride. (Recall, too, that such domestic employer-employee interaction is one of the few condoned, largely unscrutinized male-female relationships possible within Saudi Arabia.) The Saudi Arabian public is, on the whole, displeased with this new trend in native-foreigner marriages. As to the bride—she might have one (or more) of the many numerous and equally viable reasons for marrying a less well-to-do foreigner: for example, romantic love; or the fact that, due their divergent cultural backgrounds, such foreign men typically afford women much more liberty than do Saudi men; or finally, the woman's desire to have the marriage contract in her, rather than her husband's, hand.

Aside from the elaborate marriage requirements, the Saudi government employs other, more oblique (but no less perfidious) means of curtailing the incidence of native-foreigner unions. The most potent such weapon is Saudi Arabia's curt, vastly stringent citizenship requirements. For example, suppose that a Saudi man is wedded to a foreign wife, their children—even if they are born and reared exclusively within Saudi Arabia—will not be recognized as legal citizens. Rather, they must instead apply for citizenship, a hazardous roll-of-the-dice that will bring luck to numerous sons but a pitiably slim number of daughters. And in the citizenship application process, the luck of those born to a native mother and foreign father is, expectedly, worse still.

Citizenship brings with it a number of crucial benefits, both legal and social. For one, although technically native to Saudi Arabia, the daughter of a foreign parent will nonetheless be considered a foreigner, and thus be barred from marriage (to a proper Saudi citizen) up to the age of twenty-five. In addition, those who are "native" only in fact, and not in law, will encounter nigh-insurmountable difficulties in acquiring a job commensurate with their level of education.

In addition to citizenship requirements, the Saudi government will also mobilize inheritance law as a deterrent to native-foreigner marriages. To that end, non-Muslim women are forbidden any spousal inheritance whatsoever. Meanwhile, the inheritance rights of Muslim foreigners, while not wholly stripped, are substantially limited. It is important to note that inheritance restrictions affect not only the spouse, but extend to the children as well: as legally regarded "foreigners," their rights are thereby in jeopardy.

Finally, in order to stop such unions, Saudi officials will also attempt to persuade, manipulate and intimidate the families of the bride and the bridegroom. It is not uncommon for tireless, dedicated minor magistrates to spend hours reasoning with the guardian of the bride, attempting to dissuade him from signing the marriage contract. And if the father does not consent to the contract, the *mazoon* is, in most traditions, not permitted to marry the betrothed. And that is to say nothing of legal, state-recognition, which is separate from (albeit, contingent upon) the union's consecration by the *mazoon*. (In fact, approving guardians will schedule the *mazoon* for as soon as possible—that is, far before legal recognition is achieved—in order to make public the nature of the ostensibly strange, frequent male visitor, and thereby dispel any rumor and speculation.)

So what is one to do if, in that most dire of situations, the bride's guardian will not condone the union (and, thus, the *mazoon* will not consecrate the union, and the state will not legally recognize the union)? Some particularly enterprising native-foreigner pairs have done the following:

Step 1: Visit a *mazoon* from a different tradition. Not all traditions require that the guardian sign off on the marriage. Acquire the consent of a *mazoon* from such a tradition, and thereby consecrate the marriage in the eyes of God.

Step 2: Travel to the groom's country. There, have the bride take the groom to court, citing his failure to provide support (a key condition of any marriage contract). He, of course, will be in on the ruse. When the court requests proof of marriage, she will claim that she lost the marriage certificate. Thus, the court will inquire after the groom, and ask whether or not he is, indeed, her husband. Hiding his eagerness, he will admit that yes, yes he is. The court will speedily find in the bride's favor, ruling that the groom must support her, his wife. Tada! In a mightily roundabout fashion, they have gotten a country to recognize their marriage legally!

Step 3: Return to Saudi Arabia with the *mazoon*-consecrated marriage contract and the foreign court's recognition of the marriage. Use this to lobby Saudi Arabia to recognize the marriage.

Of course, by no means is success guaranteed. However, if the present book leads any man to explore Arab culture more deeply, and if, in his consequent travels throughout the region, he should fall deeply in love with a nice Saudi girl—well, should worse come to worst, he will have an idea of what to do.

United Arab Emirates

The U.A.E., like Saudi Arabia, labors strenuously to discourage native-foreigner marriages. In this endeavor, the government's primary weapon is citizenship requirements. In 2008, the state issued an official decree ruling that any woman who weds a foreigner without governmental permission will be unceremoniously stripped of her citizenship. In the case of those that do receive such permission, the foreign beau—and resulting children—will not, under any circumstance, *ever* be granted U.A.E. citizenship. Finally, in the case of divorce, the U.A.E. will not financially support native divorcees, as they would have divorcees wedded to U.A.E. citizens.

In addition to legal ramifications, there are social ramifications as well. The people of U.A.E. are a deeply proud bunch, keen to preserve their own purity of heritage. Thus, the populace is divided between roughly seventeen families, which also partially determine districting (i.e. families live together in sizeable family-dominated sectors). If a member of a family marries a foreigner, the rest of the families will effectively ostracize all relatives of this minor domestic traitor, refusing to intermarry with them.

It should be noted that, unlike Saudi Arabia, an U.A.E. citizenship is a fortune-making proposition: the government regularly provides its citizens with lavish, exorbitant handouts.

Curiously, 41% of marriages within the country end in divorce. However, only 24% of native-foreigner marriages in the U.A.E. end in divorce.

Egypt

Recently, Egyptian assemblywoman Ibtesam Habib submitted legislation to the Proposals and Complaints Committee of the People's Assembly that, if ratified, would substantially alter Egyptian marriage policies. Overall, her intent is to protect Egypt and its citizens—particularly its female citizens—against the numerous possibly deleterious ramifications of native-foreigner marriages.

First, it would require that the foreigner's government "consent" to the marriage. This would take the form of official documentation. She argues that such consent would necessitate the government to conduct a general investigation in the intended groom's background, thus mitigating the potential for fraud or altogether worse ills. In addition, the foreign government would have to "record" the fact of the marriage officially, thus expediting and facilitating any future judicial proceedings against the groom-to-be.

Second, if the foreigner is more than twenty years her senior, he would have to deposit 200,000 pounds in his bride's name into an Egyptian bank account. On a related point, the law would require that the bridegroom attend the contract-signing ceremony in person. These two provisions are intended to combat the increasingly common trend wherein wealthy foreign men send aids to scout and "marry" Egyptian woman. More often than not, such women—treated, essentially, as mail-order brides—are subjected to harsh servitude once they arrive at the homes of their new husbands. Sadly, once the marriage has been legalized, it is not uncommon for the husband to harass, cajole, threaten and abuse his wife into returning to him the initial 200,000-pound deposit.

Tying the Knot (Loosely) with a Tourist

In countries like Morroco, Egypt and Tunisia where tourism contributes significantly to the economy, native men will travel to coastal cities for the purpose of finding tourists to marry. These marriages, referred to in Arabic as "clean sex tourism" are usually marriages of convenience, and can be more easily dissolved than others. In fact, it is quite common to find an Arab man who has been married seven times in one year.

The reasons for why Arab men try to marry tourists vary. There is a strong desire on the part of young Arab men to go to foreign countries where there may be more opportunities for work, and this desire drives these men to want to meet foreign women in the hopes that marrying a foreigner will help them gain entry into another country.

A considerable number of female tourists in these countries are middle-aged professional, Western women who have intentions of engaging intimately with younger Arab men. The young men, however, will not engage in these types of relationships with Western women without marrying them first as there are religious and legal restrictions, in addition to privileges that provide incentive for couples to be married. Legally, an unmarried couple cannot book a hotel room. Once married to a native, a tourist may enjoy the cheaper hotel rooms and apartments.

The problem of terrorism also encourages men to marry tourists in coastal cities. In popular tourist destinations where the risk of terrorist activity is higher, police are suspicious of Arab people who are native to the country but not to the tourist areas. Men who are married to tourists will say that they are married to a foreigner to avoid interrogation.

Sometimes women from other countries want to marry Arab men so that they can live and work in those countries. These women often come from Eastern European countries. The demand for female entertainers—belly dancers or performing artists—in nightclubs and hotels with a Western look is very high. In order to be allowed to work in an Arab country, however, foreigners must obtain a work visa, and marrying native is the easiest way to do so. Not only does marriage increase the likelihood of obtaining a visa quickly, it actually does more to ensure a foreign woman's employment. The Arab Belly Dancer's Union restricts the amount of foreign women in their ranks, and gives preference to those who have married and live with natives in order to protect the jobs of their own union members. The requirements of such marriages are so minimal and can be met so easily, that a woman can walk down the street and find a man, who may already have all the paperwork and witnesses ready.

The desire to marry foreign tourists is not just a trend among Arab men. Arab women will also seek foreign partners. They too will travel to foreign cities where they will attempt to convince a man to convert to Islam— Muslim women cannot marry outside of their religion—and marry him in order to obtain permission to work in these areas.

Fifteen thousand cases of marriages of convenience occurred in 2005. This increasing trend is thought to be threatening the social fabric of these small cities. Small, conservative cities are now being populated by foreigners.

Marriages of convenience can present legal problems for Arab countries. Sometimes, foreign women, unhappy with their lives in the Arab countries, will leave with the children of their marriage to return to their home countries without the husband's knowledge. Some Arab governments refuse to address these issues, because tourism is a big part of their national income (Morrocco, for example aims to attract more than ten million tourists in the year 2010). However, the lack of resolution regarding these matters may bring trouble. In 2007, an Egyptian man held a group of German tourists against their will, in order to pressure the German State Department to return his children to him after they were taken to Germany by his former German wife.

Translation

Title: Since the cost of *East Asian* labor has risen, there is now permission for laborers to be brought in from Eastern Europe.

Culture

In oil-rich Arab countries, domestic help is often provided by foreigners. Many problems are associated with this trend due to cultural, religious, and language differences. Traditionally, most of these workers came from Southeast Asia. But as the demand for domestic help rose, their prices also rose. As a result, families began to hire people from Eastern Europe. The women from these countries are very attractive, making the wives of these households jealous. In this cartoon, the husband, who would never be seen doing chores, will gladly help this Eastern European maid. This makes his wife jealous.

Translation

Title on right: Lebanese flirting:
Lebanese Suitor: You see how big the moon is, I love you that much.

Title on left: Our flirting:
Saudi Suitor: I swear to God, I will step on the belly of anyone who mentions your name on his tongue.

Culture

Arabs view the Lebanese as more romantic and more modern than most other Arabs. This cartoon illustrates how gentle and delicate

their flirting is compared to the flirting in other Arab countries. Lebanon has always been a more fertile, modern and Western-influenced country in contrast to the harsh natural conditions in these newly oil-rich.

Arabs and the Moon

The moon looms large in the Arab imagination. From the distant past when, the Qur'an teaches, Abraham was lured towards lunar worship before God brought him to monotheism, it has drawn on the minds of the Arab peoples, haunted their culture, and been their guiding companion in the desert. The cool light of the moon makes a welcome change from the harsh, desert sun, and many ancient poems extol the beauty of its light. Today the moon maintains its cherished place and is used, as in the cartoon above, as a by-word for beauty, and its monthly cycles are the basis for the Hijjra, the sacred calendar of Islam.

One of the most prominent appearances of the moon in modern Arab culture is the use of the crescent as the symbol of Islam. The ancient affection for the symbol flowered into the current association with Islam in 72 AH, when the crescent was incorporated into the decoration of the Dome of the Rock, and was cemented a few years later when it was chosen for the coinage of the rising Islamic empire. Wherever Islam spread, so too did the crescent symbol, appearing over and over again in mosques and other decoration. For centuries, it has been proudly displayed on flags and banners, and today, it appears on many Arab national flags.

Hijjra

The Hijjra was an epochal moment in the history of Islam. The term refers to the period during which the Prophet and his early band of adherents fled from the persecution of the dominant Quraysh tribe in their home at Mecca to the freedom and safety of Medina (then known as Yathrib). It is considered as the beginning of the Islamic period and as such, its date (622 CE) is used to begin the Muslim calendar. English-speaking scholarship typically renders the term with a bald literalism into "migration," but recent criticism prefers to honor the similar significance and similar circumstances to the Israelites' escape from captivity by offering "Exodus" as a fairer translation.

4 — Dating and Getting Married

Translation

Title: What is alloted and allocated.

Language

The first term in Arabic is *qismat*, the origin of the English word "kismet," and means literally "division" or "lot." The second *naseeb* is very similar, meaning "portion" or "allocation." Nowadays they are always used together, with the meaning of "fate" or "destiny."

The Qur'an speaks of *qismat*, God's division of *rizq*, livelihood or sustenance, among his worshipers, and this *rizq* is said to be in the sky. These men therefore are the alloted portion that comes from the sky — even though to a Western viewer it may look like an interpretation of the hit song *It's Raining Men*.

Naseeb on its own usually has more negative connotations and is used to show resignation to fate or failure, but also as an excuse for not having tried hard.

Kismet is used in English as an exotic alternative for "fate" or "destiny," in the context of resignation to something beyond one's control. It has been argued that the dying words of the British admiral, Lord Nelson, which are usually given as "Kiss me, Hardy," were in fact a recognition that he was fated to die at Trafalgar: "Kismet, Hardy." Others date the word's first use in English to later in the nineteenth century.

Culture

The term *qismat we-naseeb* generally refers to the fact that nothing should be desired too much, as the individual is ignorant of where true harm and benefit lie, while God knows, so that being deprived by fate of what seems good, may in fact be beneficial. It is used first and foremost to refer to marriage, deriving from the tradition of arranged marriage—the partner has been alloted since the beginning and it is not for the individual to choose according to preference—so that the phrase "marriage is fate (*qismat we-naseeb*)" has become proverbial.

5 – Family Life

Translation

Husband to wife:
"One fourth of my salary is going to the kids' notebooks and half is going to private tutoring… That means I won't be able to spend any money on you, *Tafida* (wife's name)! You are divorced!"

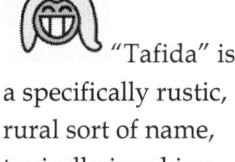 "Tafida" is a specifically rustic, rural sort of name, typically invoking thoughts of simpletons or bumpkins. In addition, the Arab reader would understand a "Tafida" to be a particularly submissive, traditional and devoted wife.

Culture

Many Arab households keep track of their spending by writing down their expenses every night and put a portion of their money aside for savings. The importance of saving is instilled in Arabs from childhood, when they are given savings booklets in schools by bank or post office representatives (the post office also acts as a bank in Arab countries).

☪ Back-to-school season is even more stressful in Arab countries than it is in America, because the average number of children in an Arab family is four. The divorce rate in Arab countries usually spikes during this period. There are many expenses associated with going back to school in Arab countries that are much more onerous than in America. The biggest expense of educating a child in an Arab country is private tutoring, especially if the family has children in one of the three important certification years (the sixth, ninth, and twelfth years). Even if a student is very bright, he or she still needs private tutoring because of the complexity of the subjects and the ambiguity of the government-issued textbooks. Still, the Arab education system is deficient, because it continues to rely on the memorization of facts instead of the development of logical thinking.

☪A man can divorce his wife simply by saying, "I divorce you." He can change his mind later and reunite with his wife. This process cannot be repeated more than two times. After the third time, the husband cannot take his wife back; she must marry someone else and consummate her marriage with him in order for the first husband to remarry the wife again. If a man seriously wants to divorce his wife, he can say "I divorce you three times," and his divorce will be considered final.

☪Today, some choose to inform their wives of their intentions to divorce via text message. However, a fatwah has declared this practice invalid, holding that the object of the enunciation—i.e. the wife—must physically hear the statement, and not merely read it, for it to be binding.

In many Arab countries, a woman's guardian, either her brother or her father, had to have given permission in order for the woman to be allowed to marry her suitor legally. There have been changes in the law to allow a woman to marry the person of her choosing, regardless of her guardian's preference. Now, the only time a guardian has the right to refuse a woman's marriage is if, according to Islamic law, the marriage between the couple would be considered illegal.[16]

Translation

Newspaper: Over budget

Woman: "They saying they allow organ transplants."

Man (looking at "blue pills").

Language

The word for "over" or "overshooting" is the same as that for "inability" or "incapability" which together with the word "sexual" is the common term for impotence. The word for "organ" or "member" is commonly applied to the penis.

Culture

For a long time, an Arab woman could not legally file for divorce from her husband and expect a swift outcome except in the instance of impotence.

Impotence is a very potent reason to ask for divorce for fear of the woman being tempted. Generally, women can file for divorce without the grounds of their husband's impotence, but in those instances, her case may linger in court for years. When a woman files for divorce outside of the accepted reason of

---

[16] See "4 — Dating and Getting Married," page 83.

impotence, the husband can retaliate by demanding that she return to him and live in what is called the House of Obedience. There he provides her the minimum amount of food and shelter until their case has been settled. Now, Arab countries have begun to enact new laws that are making it easier for women to divorce their husbands. In 2000, Egypt was the first Arab country to enact laws that allowed women to get divorced for any reason, but on the condition that she gives the man a sum of money that he and his lawyer determine. Unscrupulous lawyers, who the husband may hire, will demand that she return all the wedding expenses, presents and may even demand a second sum in exchange for not contesting the woman's request to divorce. Immediately after the enactment of this law, 5000 cases went to court from women requesting divorce from their husbands. Bahrain, the most recent country to enact laws allowing women to divorce, has given just a few provisions allowing women to vote. First, a woman is allowed to petition for divorce if her husband does not provide for her. Second, a woman is allowed to file for divorce if her husband is continually absent from their home. Third, if at the time of signing the original marriage contract the husband is forbidden from taking a second wife, and the husband violates this provision, the woman has grounds for divorce.

[N.B. These two couples are mismatched. It is a depiction of how you can't always get what you want, and that whatever you have you want the other thing.]

Culture

When it comes to happiness and satisfaction with life, based on such factors as health, wealth and access to education, a 2010 survey found that the happiest part of the Arab world the United Arab Emirates, followed by Kuwait, Qatar, Bahrain, Jordan, Saudi Arabia. Libya came seventh, followed by Lebanon, Algeria, and Tunisia. Eleventh was Yemen, followed by Palestine, Iraq, Egypt, with Syria occupying the fifteenth place and Sudan last place.

Arabs love Mercedes cars and consider them status symbol as shown in this cartoon.

Despite the cartoon making fun of modern day attitudes, most Arab women are unmaterialistic. This stems from a religious frame of mind that places reward in the afterlife, emphasizing patience and acceptance of the will of God as among the highest virtues. Even the countries whose wealth derives from oil still retain strong features of the simpler, more austere desert culture of their forefathers, and this is most evident in a preference for traditional and unfussy food and clothes, which suits the environment better.

Translation

On left, walking at the front: Female teacher
Walking behind: Homemaker

Culture

As the main earner the teacher has earned the right to walk in front of her husband.
Note also the gait of confidence that is associated with the person walking in front.
In Arab culture, men usually hold a superior role, acting as the breadwinner, supporting as well as protecting his family and, in common custom, walk in front of women.
The role of a school teacher is known to be prestigious, and the woman brings income to the household with the ability to spend adequate time at home with her family as well.

Translation

Piece of information: It is known that the lioness is the one who will most often chase prey and hunt, while the male lion shares with her in the meal.

Language

In some countries the word *labwa*, lioness, can be very derogatory, indicating a sexually insatiable woman. The context of the cartoon makes it unlikely that this meaning is intended.

Culture

While the concept of the stay-at-home husband is rare in the Arab world, it is possible among professional couples. The scarcity of eligible men often results in men "marrying up" to a more highly paid woman. Arab women are generally not viewed as stingy, and are willing to support their underachieving husbands for both traditional and religious reasons. They gladly help out for the sake of the children.

Translation

Title: The Pluralist

Language

The Arabic word, *mowaddid*, is untranslatable. Its root is the word for "number" and it means someone who has more than one of anything. It is a very new word that has become current and is used to refer to a polygamist, a man with more than one wife.

 Note that the man's feet are trying to take him toward his new wife, while his head tells him to go to his old wife — suggesting a conflict between desire and reason or heart and head.

Culture

This man is a lucky person. The grand staircase indicates a big house with space for two wives (multiple wives will usually have their own houses). Polygamy was in the decline in the Arab world during most of the last century, but has recently shown an upward trend again. The reasons are complex, but boils down to too few men who are able to get married, whether because of economics, migration or an increase in the number of men who do not see the need to get married. There are therefore many women who face the possibility of not finding a husband, which is potentially difficult for society, and this has led to resurgence in plural marriages. This has brought other problems in its wake, so that there are now calls for support organizations and groups to study the situation and to offer counseling the men, to help cope with the demands of this special lifestyle — in terms of finance, emotional and physical energy, endurance, and patience. They are asking the state to provide structural support that will offer practical help and advice.

Arabs believe that there is divine wisdom in allowing multiple wives, that it is fundamentally allowed by all the Religions of the Book, and that the wife in a polygamous marriage is better off than a single wife. The reason for this is that the woman will know the days when her husband will be with her in advance, so that the rest of the time is her own to decide how she spends.

"Polygamy is the Solution"

"Polygamy is the solution" is a slogan that many people, both men and women, are convinced is the way to mitigate the problems of women who are still looking for a husband at an older age. One of the alternatives, for them to marry foreigners, is extremely hard for their brothers or cousins to accept and disheartens them.[17] They also aim make it unnecessary for women to go out looking to meet men, as this risks offending both Islamic standards and provoking God's wrath on society — with the breakdown of the family and the withdrawal of God's *rizq*, blessing or grace. They look at how they used to live, in far simpler conditions and relative poverty, and see how much God has given them and do not want to risk forfeiting His bounty.

Many people think that polygamy, usually meaning only a second wife rather than more, is an excellent solution for men to be fair to both wives, and many men think of polygamy as a way to find sexual satisfaction, and will brag about how many wives they have. Arab women who are divorced will generally seek to remarry, as often as necessary, because of the stigma attached to divorced status. Many others, however, believe that polygamy is not feasible in the modern world, when the man is out of the house for long periods and unable to deal with one wife, let alone two, and that it is unfair to the first wife, who would normally have gone into marriage expecting to be the sole wife, and has done nothing to deserve sharing her husband.

Translation

Husband: "School expenses, Ramadan expenses. Broke."

Culture

Since Arab men are the sole breadwinners in their households, many are kept up at night worrying about making ends meet.
The school calendar imposes extraordinary financial burdens during the summer vacation and the back-to-school season. The main periods of expense on the religious calendar are Ramadan and Eid. Great financial hardship falls on families when the two calendars coincide. Each of these seasons has its own expenses that can stretch any family's means. Vacation, of course, implies traveling, and is followed by back-to-school,

---

[17] Brothers are the closest male relatives to their sisters, and therefore most protective toward them, while cousins are both relatives and, potentially, suitors, and may well have grown up with the possibility of marriage to the woman, so that even if marriage is no longer considered or neither of them wants it, he will feel a special tenderness, so that her choice to go beyond her own nationality is a kind of defeat that is taken personally.

which requires supplies and clothes; Ramadan entails money spent on food and finishes with the Eid, which requires food, travel to family, presents, and charity.

During the month of Ramadan, families adhere strictly to cultural expectations. First, the house is prepared for the holiday with a full cleaning, and decorations to create a festive environment. Part of the Eid tradition includes buying new clothes and shoes for children. In America, people may give money in lieu of gifts, but it is generally more common for close friends and relatives to buy gifts. In contrast, it is traditional for an Arab man to give a gift of money (*eiddya*) to his children, parents, and his wife. With constantly rising in prices, a family's budget can be swallowed by the month of Ramadan. In addition to Ramadan, Arab families must prepare for the celebration of Eid, and many families suffer financially in order to live up to the expectation associated with Eid al-Fitr, the expense of which can equal three months' salary! If these coincide with back-to-school shopping, the combo of three major shopping events can be a killer (the summer vacation can always be reined in).

People scrimp and save in anticipation for the festival in order to splurge during Ramadan and Eid, going so far as to borrow money. It is not unusual for a month's salary to be gone within the first five days of Ramadan. Some workplaces will advance a month's salary prior to the festival, to be paid back afterwards. Women may resort to selling their jewelry to buy Ramadan necessities.

The start of school usually involves a number of children, and all schools have uniforms — children of poorer families may have few other clothes to wear and can be seen wearing uniform at weekends and holidays.

Translation

Title: "When your son comes to manhood..."

Man smoking sheesha: O God, this is your son Mahjoub, as God has willed. Man, it is unbelievable how this generation grows, the good thing about it is that you take him as friend.

Father: I am not taking him as friend or anything, honestly. I'm scared of him.

Language

"As God has willed" and "If God wills": *Ma sha' Allah* **and** *In sha' Allah*

In this cartoon, the man admires the build of his friend's son by saying "as God has willed." It is considered improper for a person to express his admiration of anyone, such as someone's son or daughter, whether for looks or accomplishments, or indeed for anything that is not his own property, by a simple compliment such as "How pretty!" or "You have a good-looking son!" The most appropriate expression in such cases is *ma sha' Allah*, "What God willed [has come to pass]" or "As God has willed," which implies both admiration and submission to, or approval of, the will of God. Otherwise, the man may think that his friend envies his son his good health or good looks and he would be alarmed. While *ma sha' Allah* looks to what God has wrought, *in sha' Allah* is used when looking to the future, "If God wills," "As God shall will," or "God willing," showing the believer's recognition that, whatever he may say about the future, he knows that only God knows what will actually come to pass. So any statement about the future is usually qualified by this submission to God's providence.

The tattoo on the younger man's forearm reads: "If your father gets old, he will take you as a friend." The son is using his father's desire to be a friend to get money from him.

Culture

There is an Arabic proverb that most parents still follow in raising their children: "Until seven, teach them; the next seven years, beat them; the next seven years, befriend them." Another proverb is similar, saying "When your son comes to manhood [about 14], befriend him." This aim of befriending one's children as they grew older worked well for a long time and was a deliberate way of easing a son into more responsibility. A father would go out with his son, and if he was self-employed would give his son a role in the running of his business, a situation that also started to relieve the father of some responsibilities—a storekeeper would train his son up in his business, and a taxi-driver would let his son drive the cab, and in some cases make the son a partner or include his name in the business title. Whatever his job, the father would generally take his son with him for work-related socializing, and when the boy was free during long vacations might take him on business trips. He would be proud to introduce his son to his friends and associates, while the boy would be eager to spend time with his father and to visit new places. Any contacts would be important potential connections for the future, easing the young man's entry into the world of work. This was a relatively trouble-free process in most cases, with both father and son approaching the process with enthusiasm. A key element was the prestige that the father enjoyed within the family structure, so that spending time with him was a privilege, and he was regarded as an important source of education for life. Recently, in the last fifteen years perhaps, the process has started to break down as the son rejects his father's overtures of friendship. There are two main causes: firstly, the father's former prestige has diminished, as mothers work and show less respect to their husbands; secondly, the son feels that he knows more than the father does and that the father's knowledge is irrelevant in the information age. Linked to this is physical strength, since fathers used generally to be stronger and heavier than their teenage sons, whereas a young man is now likely to be more muscular than his father, because of changes in lifestyle and growing interest in working out.

If the son got into trouble with the law, this would have major consequences for his family. Their reputation would suffer, affecting the father's business and the sisters' marriage prospects, and society's blame would fall on the parents for not being able to raise their children properly.

Translation

Sign: Hospital

Doctor: "You won't receive the boy until you pay the bills and the fines that you owe."

Culture

There have been instances in which private hospitals withhold a newborn from the parents until all of their maternity care bills are paid. Hospitals can go to extremes in collecting their fees either by forcing the father to write a check before delivering the infant or by withholding his passport or the child until the bill is settled. This practice, however, is illegal, so if the parents complain and cause the authorities intervene, the hospital will claim that it is caring for the child, keeping it under close observation, because of health problems.

Many types of hospitals exist in Arab countries. The lowest tier is made up of government-run hospitals, which charge next to nothing for treatment, but leave much to be desired in the quality of patient care. Most doctors must undergo their residency periods in this kind of hospital prior to graduation; as a result, government-run facilities serve as training grounds for new doctors. However, there are more expensive hospitals that rival the best American institutions and carry similarly high price tags. At this type of hospital, if the patient does not have the insurance to pay his bill, collection methods may be extreme.

Arab names

All Arab names have meanings and in Arab culture, the father usually chooses the name for a newborn son and the mother usually chooses the name for a newborn daughter. The most common Arab names are Muhammad for male babies and Amel for female babies; Muhammad means "praiseworthy," and Amel means "hope."

Boys are often named after the Prophet (Muhammad , Ahmad, or Mustafa), and that name's overwhelming popularity can be attributed not only to the enormous respect that people have for the Prophet himself, but also to the belief that God will reward parents who so name their son. Following in popularity are the names of members of the Prophet's family (Ali, Hasan, Hussein, etc.), his close companions (Omar, Osman, Amr, etc.), or some prophets and patriarchs of early times (Ibraheem [Abraham], IsHak [Isaac], Ismaeel [Ishmael], Yaakoob [Jacob], Moosa [Moses], Daood [David], Suleyman [Solomon], etc.). Boys can also receive names meaning "Servant of God," "Servant of the Compassionate," "Servant of the Capable/Powerful," etc. (Abd-Allah, Abd-El-Rahman, Abd-El-Kadir).

Girls are mostly named after the wives or daughters of the Prophet or other members of his family (Khadeegeh, Aisheh, Amneh, Fatmeh, and Zeyneb). Girls also can be given names that mean "beloved," "blessed," "precious," etc. (MaH-boobeh, Mah-brookeh, Nefeeseh, etc.). They could also be named after a name of a flower or of some other pleasing object.

In some Arab countries, many girls' names have nicknames that are used as a sign of affection. Some examples are Khaddoogeh for Khadeegeh, Eiyoosheh for Aisheh, Ammooneh for Amneh, Fattoomeh for Fatmeh, Zennoobeh for Zeyneb, and Neffooseh for Nefeeseh.

First Names:

Arabic first names can fall into several categories and can change over the course of one's life. Some of the categories are:

Names derived from one's own child (usually indicating parentage of the first-born son)

Paternal name

- Abu Bakr = Father of Bakr
- Abu Hassan = Father of Hassan

Maternal name

- Umm Kalthoum (a famous Egyptian singer) = Mother of Kalthoum
- Umm Ahmad = Mother of Ahmad

Names from conjugated verbs (very common)

- Ahmad = I praise
- Yazid = he increases

Names from participles of verbs (very common)

- Adil = just; fair
- Mahmoud = praised
- Muhammad = the one who is praised; praiseworthy

Phrasal Names

- Saladin (Salaah ad-din) = righteousness of the religion
- Aladdin ('alaa ad-din) = nobility of the religion
- Abdallah (abd Allah) = servant of God

Names that are adjectives

- Karim = generous
- Saaid = happy
- Latifa = Nice
- Sharif = noble

Arabs also use names of the months in the Islamic calendar or days of the week as names for their children. A person could be called Shaaban (the month before Ramadan) or Ramadan, or Khamees (Thursday) or Jumaa (Friday).

Paternal and maternal names could also be used in what is known in Arabic as *kunya*.

Paternal names are the most common form of Arabic name (at least in modern times). Children (male and female) take the first name of their father. Many times the '*ibn*' (son of) and '*bint*' (daughter of) is left out.

Examples:

Karim Ahmad would be a child whose name is Karim and whose father's first name is Ahmad.

Boutros Boutros Ghali (former Secretary-General of the UN) was actually named after his grandfather, Boutros Ghali. But most of the time, if you ever see an Arab with the same two first names he was named after his father. This is the Arab equivalent of the senior-junior system used in America where a child is named after his father (i.e. George Bush Sr., George Bush Jr.).

Last Names

Arabic last names are not passed on in the same way as they are in Western countries. Most of the time, a child's middle name is the father's first name and a child's last name is the paternal grandfather's name. From parent to child, people are usually distinguished by one or more last names, of the following kinds:

- ❖ Relationship to parents/ancestors— Son of Ahmad, Ibn-Ahmad; etc.
- ❖ Honor or distinction— the Light of the Religion, Noor-El-Dean; the Tall, El-Taweel; etc.
- ❖ Birthplace or hometown— of the town of Rasheed, El-Rasheedee; etc.
- ❖ Country— the Egyptian, El Masry; the Saudi, El Saudi; etc.
- ❖ Family, sect, trade or occupation— the dyer, *el-Sabbagh*; the merchant, *el-Tagir*; the jeweler, *gohargee*; the bespoke gold and silversmith, *saigh*; the seller of hardware, *khurdagee*; the seller of copper wares, *naHas*; the tailor, *kheiyat*; the darner, *reffa*; the fine, ornamental needle worker and maker of silk lace, *Habbak*; the maker of silk cords, etc., '*akkad*; the maker of pipes, *shibukshee*; the druggist, candle-seller and perfumier, '*attar*; the tobacconist, *dakhakhinee*; the fruitier, *fakihanee*; the seller of dried fruits, *nukalee*; the seller of sherbet, *sharbetlee*; the seller of oil as well as of butter, cheese, honey, etc., *zeiyat*; the greengrocer, *khudaree*; the butcher, *gezzar*; the baker (who also rents space in his oven to families without their own for baking or roasting dishes), *farran*. E.g., Omar al-Khayyam—famous poet and author of the *Rubaiyat*, (Omar the Tentmaker); Said al-Haddad (Said the Blacksmith)

Each kind of last name is now generally placed after the first name.

How Do You Spell That?

The spelling of Arab names, such as Muhammad, like all transliterations, comes from replacing the Arabic script with what is deemed to be its closest Latin equivalent. Aside from that, there are many versions of the same name, depending on where the family is from and variations in pronunciation.

Alias (kunya/kenya)

Kenya in its basic form applies to a parent: it is the way of calling him or her by the name of his or her oldest son (such as saying, "father of so-and-so" or "mother of so-and-so"), a tradition usually followed in Arab countries, and is applied as a prefix to one's name. So, if your name was Ahmed, and you named your son Ali, your new nickname/alias is Abu Ali.

This way of assuming names or aliases is called in Arabic *kenya* (colloquial) or *kunya* (formal). Sometimes *kenya* proves a tricky problem in traveling, surveillance, and international monitoring: many people who, lacking the relevant documentation to begin with, also go by an alias twice or thrice-removed from their given name, can serve as severe hassle and impediment to easy monitoring in airports and other venues.

With *kenya*, a similar problem can arise domestically. In some Arab countries, where new digital technologies of organization and record-keeping are quickly taking hold, the widespread use of *kenya*s has given rise to a unique difficult. Citizens who, in the light of increased monitoring by the police (especially after 9/11), wish to acquire official documentation of their citizenship, are finding that, due to the popularity of their *kenya*s, they cannot discover anyone who can testify as to their legally given name—cannot, in fact, discover anyone who even knows it! The problem does not end there: sometimes, their fathers went exclusively by *kenya*s, and also their father's fathers, and so on and so forth.

Abu literally means "father of," but sometimes Abu—or Ibn or Bin ("son of")—is used to indicate that a relationship, connection, or familiarity with the name that follows that is not necessarily a father or son relationship. For example, Abu Dhabi translates as "Father of the Antelope," the Arabic name for the Sphinx at Giza is *Abu Al-howel,* or "Father of Horrors," and the famous temple at Abu Simbel derives its name from Sunbul or spikenard, an aromatic unguent popular in ancient times.

The *kenya* is also sometimes used metaphorically rather than literally. A modern example would be the Moro Islamist group Abu Sayyaf operating in Southern Philippines (Mindanao). The word *sayyaf* means "swordsmith," so "Father of the Swordsmith" signifies the group's belligerent charter

In colloquial Arabic, someone or something that has a quality can be described as *abu* or "father of" that quality. For example, a person might be father of generosity (*karum*), of understanding (*fahm*), of ignorance (*gahl*). Furthermore, in some countries double-decker buses or trains are "father of two levels," pickled white eggplant is "father of vinegar," and a jacket showing two prominent pockets might be "father of two pockets." Things may also be described as sons of a quality: a funny man and skilled comedian might be known as "son of a joke" (*ibn no-kta*). Women can also have *kenya*s: *Umm* means "mother of," and *bint* means "daughter of." These, too, can be used of objects or qualities: a centipede, for example, is "mother of forty-four legs." Both "son of" and "daughter of" are also frequently used in insults, as one thereby abuses another's parentage. The practice is much the same as English insults like "son-of-a-bitch" and "whoreson," though Arabic encompasses a wider variety that might be insultingly cited as parents.

☪In Arabic, most Arabic male names can be converted to their female compliment by adding the letter "*taa-marbouta*" to the names' end. In addition, the use of a name's female equivalent is sometimes used as an insult, particularly for foreign leaders—for example, Egyptian president Hosni Mubarak will be called "Hosnia Mubaraka."

Western names

Many Arabs choose to give western names to their children. Most of the people who give their children these western names are Christian Arabs who want to distance themselves from the Arab and Islamic culture. There is a long history of Christian Arab migration to the West, as they sought to seek out lands where they would be able to practice their religion without stigma or discrimination, and many contemporary Christian Arabs entertain high hopes of joining their relatives and moving west. The process, too, is much simpler for them that it is for the majority of Arabs because western embassies recognize their plight as minorities and give them special consideration. Given this expectation that their children may well live in the West, Christian Arab parents give their children Western names in the hope that they will thereby mitigate the negativity Westerners sometimes feel towards those with more standard Arab names. George, Albert, Michael, and Alexander are the most popular western names given to Arab boys, while Suzanne and Mary are the most popular western names given to Arab girls.

Neutral names

When, as a student, Egyptian novelist and Nobel laureate Naguib Mahfouz asked to study in France, the Egyptian government rejected his application. Mahfouz is a Muslim, but those vetting him had assumed, on the basis of his name "Naguib," that he was a Christian. The two Christian students already accepted into the program were more than enough, and they did not wish to admit any more. In the Arab world, this is a familiar story. Upon first meeting, strangers will often inquire as to one another's first names; if this information is insufficient for determining whether or not the person is a Muslim or a Christian, they will thus request surnames as well. In order to avoid discrimination, Coptic Arabs—the oldest Christian sect in the world and—for many years shied from giving their children Christian names. Instead, they opted for neutral names—names that are not distinctly Christian or Muslim. However, as Copts gain increasing clout abroad, Coptic Arabs become more emboldened, and now regularly equip their children with Christian names such as Luka, Shinouda, Gerges and Mina.

☪ There are some names in the Arab world that one would never find in the West. The most striking of these is "Hitler," which is common now among Arab men in their seventies. Before WWII, Egypt lay ailing under the severe, exploitive and oppressive scepter of British rule. Accordingly, when the Nazis began to wage war on British powers, Egyptians rejoiced. Hitler pledged that, should the Axis prove victorious, Egyptians would be liberated from the English and granted self-sovereignty. Many Arabs at the time viewed Hitler as a great hope for the Arab people, and named their children in his honor. Today, the most notable Hitler is Hitler Tantawi, the chairman of Egypt's Administrative Control Authority (ACA), a state body that specializes in corruption cases.

☪ It is not unusual to call your new-born son after a weapon. An Egyptian named his son "Sam 6," which referred to an anti-aircraft rocket that was used so successfully in the October 1973 war against the Israeli airforce.

Arabs' Respect for their Names

Names with references to God (such as Abdullah), the Prophet Muhammad, or any other prophet (such as Yusef, Joseph; or Isa, Jesus) are treated differently by Arabs, who show great respect upon writing or calling them out. For example, if one is in the bathroom, which is considered an unclean place, an Arab will not call for one with the name Abdullah since it has God as part of it, and it would be improper to call God's name in an unclean place. A potter named Muhammad or Abdullah will not sign their works, as the pot will be placed in fire and it would disrespectful to put such names through fire. People with these names will not be cursed by other Muslim Arabs, out of respect for what the name denotes, so people will refrain from cursing or unpleasantly describing such people. Those with such names will also not have them written on urine samples, or other unclean substances, from the hospital.

Translation

Title: The 6th sense.

Wife: "You are not thinking about the *misyar*. Are you?"

Husband: "I wish I knew how she knows."

Culture

In Sunni Muslim culture, the standard form of marriage may be varied into the *nikah misyar*, or "travelers' marriage." Such alliances are carried out using the normal contractual procedure, but the wife voluntarily agrees to waive a number of the rights that would, in a standard marriage, be due to her, such as the right to live with her husband, have housing provided, have an equal division of nights among wives in polygamous arrangements, and enjoy maintenance money, or *nafaqa*. In a *nikah misyar*, couples live separately as they did before marriage but visit each other when able and enjoy each other's company in a *halal* manner. Such arrangements can be useful for couples unable to establish a new household, but they are not considered valid by Shiaa Muslims, who consider them *haram*.

☪ Marriage in some Arab countries is getting so expensive that, with incomes are under pressure from rising unemployment, the prospect of marriage for most young men and women is becoming a remote possibility. By choosing one of the less formal types of marriage, they can get married and forego what makes marriage prohibitively expensive. Different authorities have different opinions on the legality of these types of marriage in Islam.

Translation

Son: "Why doesn't Mickey Mouse have kids?"

Father: "Because he married Minnie Mouse in a *misyar*-style marriage."

Culture

Though its legal status in Islam remains uncertain, it is agreed that *misyar* marriage is better than succumbing to temptation with a man or woman who is not lawful, *halal*. Arabs might resort to *misyar* marriage when they are abroad as tourists or if they away from home for an extended period of time for work or study, for fear of temptation.

Translation

The wife to her husband: "You won't be able to close your eyes"

Culture

Siesta

Because of the weather, Most Arabs begin the workday very early, and end around two in the afternoon. Lunch, the largest meal of the day, is usually taken around three, after the workers or students have come home. After lunch, most people nap, as a means of a escaping the oppressive heat and

as a means of recovering from the exhaustion from the very taxing public transportation. Public transportation is very crowded, so much so that it often too hard to reach the doors to exit a bus and people exit through the windows! This assuredly drains the passengers' energy. Because of all this, napping is very important to Arabs. When the head of the family has gone for his nap, it behooves the rest of the family to do their best not to disturb his sleep. In this cartoon, the wife has placed the washing machine next to her husband's bed because she does not want him to sleep.

This practice of napping in the afternoon goes back thousands of years. In classical Arabic, there is a word *qailula*, which refers to the time during the afternoon when people nap. Napping is so much a part of the Arab culture that the word *qailula* can even be found in the Qur'an (Chap. 7, v. 04)

During the napping time, the rhythm of life slows down significantly. The streets are deserted, and people are very careful not to disturb one another. Residents rarely call or visit during this time of the day.

After napping, some men go to meet their friends at the coffee shop, where they smoke and socialize. Students wake up and begin their homework. Dinner is a usually taken later in the evening, and it is often light and consists of the same foods as breakfast, as Arabs do not like to go to sleep after eating a very heavy meal.

Translation

On right: "Husband in front of the people"

On left: "Husband inside the house"

Culture

This cartoon depicts a man who appears to assume two completely dissimilar gender roles in varied

environments. He assumes a masculine façade while outside of his house as indicated by his leonine appearance. However, at home and out of the public's sight, he transforms into a pregnant rabbit. Timid rabbits are referred to in Arabic much as chickens are in American speech, and this cowardly and cowed man has taken on traditionally feminine characteristics, such as his feminine wardrobe, his stereotypically feminine domestic tasks, and his pregnancy. What is especially striking about this cartoon is the fact that he is pregnant. While a man can assume the more traditional feminine gender role of a housekeeper and nurturer, he is seldom depicted as having reproductive capabilities. This could be interpreted as him having not only assumed femininity mentally but completely embodying it physically.

Translation

Title: Relatives' questions according to age

"From infancy to nursing: Boy or girl?"

"From nursing to school: Is he good or a troublemaker?"

"Through school to university: Literature or Science?"

"Stage of Marriage life: Pregnant or not yet?"

Culture

Because the Arab family unit is very close, Arab relatives ask many questions of their family members (more extensively than in America). A frequent question young women are asked when traveling in the Middle East will regard their marital status. If the woman says that she is not married or engaged (has a boyfriend), they will offer to find her a husband.

The third question, "Literature or Science," has a particularly heavy weight in the Arab world. Beginning around 11th grade, Arab students must decide which course of study they wish to pursue ("literature" encompasses the fields familiar in the West as the humanities), and the divide quickly becomes unbridgeable. The students take separate classes and will not even apply to universities specializing in another field. This forces a student to decide relatively early, in what direction he wants his life to go. Practically minded Arabs attach a certain stigma to literature as the lesser of the two options, for there as everywhere, a course of study that leads directly to a job is more financially prudent than studies that lead one to be expert in a field with few career applications.

Translation

Wife to husband: "O cheater, I'm not staying with you one more day! You flirt with the housekeeper on the roof, have her wear jeans, and eat meat *(specific type of meat for that area cooked with yogurt)*. I saw both of you on **Google Earth**."

This is another cartoon that makes fun of older people and modern technology. It is humorous that an old, traditional Arab woman would catch her husband cheating on her using Google Earth. Another funny aspect of this cartoon is that this traditional old woman is packing a very stylish, Western-style T-shirt to wear after leaving her husband

Culture

Demanding satisfaction

If a married couple has a fight then it is common for the woman to leave, to go and stay with her family for a while, generally between two weeks and two months, although the amount of time she intends to be away is not established before she leaves. Unlike in America an Arab wife will leave the children with the husband so that he has the responsibility of looking after them on his own, and can learn to appreciate all she does. Usually the argument will be resolved upon the husband giving his wife a *radawa*, which comes from the root for "to satisfy, please, content" and means something like "a satisfaction." *Radawa* is a sum of money (or an expensive gift) made as a present from the man to his wife. Unlike American women,

Arab women do not want flowers (they wilt). In Saudi Arabia this satisfaction will often be worth more than $5000.

A husband that cares about his wife will give her some time on her own before calling her, taking her out for a meal and giving her the *radawa*. If a husband doesn't care much the reaction would range between telling the wife to stay away until she calms down to telling her to call when she's ready to be picked up, for a woman this kind of talk makes her feel unloved. If a woman leaves too often, a husband who starts out being very concerned about it would become less affected as it happened more frequently. A husband who really does not care might threaten leaving the wife with her family and not go to pick her up.

Some women think the man should leave the marital home because the home is the woman's place. Who leaves is usually established early on, for a woman who does not have family, or the inclination to travel if her family lives far away, the husband will be the one who has to leave and go to a hotel, staying away until his wife calls. Arab women usually do not like to leave their house and stay with their family and would do it only as a last resort. Arab men do not like their wife leaving; he would be concerned that their relationship problems would be broadcast to all her family and friends. Arab men are very private, especially about their marriages.

☪ Traditional Arab women can either wear full *niqab*, which covers the whole face except a slit over the eyes, or else they can wear a piece of cloth—Arab-style *burqa'a*—like this woman, that covers half of the face. The *niqab* is worn by very strict Muslims, whereas the other way of dressing is traditional within the culture and is not associated with Islam. If a Muslim woman wants to cover her face, she will generally turn to the *niqab*, instead of using a separate piece of cloth like the one worn by this woman. As in America, Arab women have the ability to pack up and leave their husbands, but in a domestic dispute, the husband will usually be the one to leave. This does vary by age: when the couple is young, the woman will be more likely to leave, because she can return to the house of her parents or her siblings, while when the couple is older, the man often leaves.

☪ Domestic violence in the Arab world, despite popular belief, is not rampant, but shouting and yelling are. Most of the time, the worst weapon a couple has against each other is the silent treatment, especially if they are elderly. As in America, after several days pass and nerves calm down, the husband and wife begin to speak to each other again. This type of argument occurs between both married couples and siblings. In most cases, in a domestic dispute in the married life of a young couple, the woman has the advantage over her husband in that she can call her immediate family and friends to support her.

☪ In the cartoon, the woman is wearing a covering for her face in addition to the "hijab." Though this is not always the case, some women are so adamant about keeping their faces covered, that they choose not to remove their covering at home with their husbands despite being allowed to do so.

☪ In America, there are many more nannies and babysitters than there are housekeepers, but in Arab countries, the opposite is true. Accordingly, whereas in America it is something of a cliché for men to flirt or even have an affair with a babysitter or nanny, the cartoon shows that in the Arab world, housekeepers are the proverbial prey of adultery-minded men. The Arab men, in this, may be thought of as getting the worse end of the deal, for while, in America, babysitters and nannies are usually students or younger women with many desirable qualities, Arab housekeepers are usually resigned to being housekeepers for their working lives and are apt to be older and with less ambitious fire. Most often, the Arab housekeepers are in their line of work, because they have no other options, while American babysitters often choose to be babysitters while pursuing their primary careers.

Translation

Title: Old-time caricature
Woman: "Your sign is Pisces. May I know what romantic adventures you'll have next week?"

In Arabic, the Zodiac sign of Pisces is called the whale. The humor of this cartoon is that the wife is suspicious of her husband because his horoscope predicts that he will have a romantic adventure.

Not all newpapers in the Arab world will publish horoscopes, since in Islam only God knows what the future holds. The horoscope is, however, very brief, usually only a line as opposed to the little paragraph of Western newspapers.

Culture

Arab women are jealous and keep a very close eye on their husband until they are satisfied that there is no danger of his wandering. Women are traditionally jealous—their husbands have greater freedom and the women do not usually know what their husbands do outside the home. They however have a lot invested in the marriage, which has usually involved a significant commitment of time to prepare for, as well as emotional energy in learning to adapt to their husband and his demands. Anything that endangers the marriage therefore threatens that investment, and this is, of course, far greater if there are children. It is also a woman's religious duty to keep her husband to the right path and stop him straying, and she may also fear that if she feels neglected, she herself might be tempted to stray. No woman, especially a professional, wants the prospect of being a second wife, while divorce brings a significant fall in status and makes a woman sexual vulnerable—more available in the eyes of the men around her—and there is no no market for older divorcées, so she is likely to be alone.

Most Arabs are strong believers the supernatural and, when they have access, will eagerly read their horoscope, particularly women. Treating a horoscope's hint of "romance" as evidence illustrates the old saying that women lack brain and religion: brain for thinking that their husband will cheat on them and religion for believeing the horoscope which is contrary to Islam.

Translation

Title: Astrologers lie even if they say the truth.

[*Clockwise from top left*]

Scorpio — Taking care of your fashion will give you an irresistible attraction. Many friends and relatives will try to avoid you without a clear reason.

Leo — The Leo enjoys a strong and overwhelming personality and she imposes respect and domination over everybody.

Taurus — Your dream of achieving quick wealth will become possible. You only need a lot of patience. *On the desk*: Corporation. Interest yield from 60% to 100%

Aries — Your romantic relations will flourish and grow considerably, but will result in unbearable financial loss. *Pile of cards*: Prepaid phone cards.

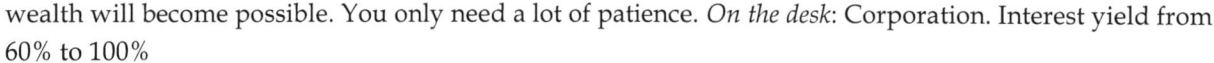 Each of these cartoons has a darker humor to it. The Scorpio woman is fairly obvious, since scorpions are types for unpleasant qualities, such as treachery. Rather than being the dominant male described by the horoscope, the man (shown to be a Leo by his mane), is ridden by his termagant wife. Arabic culture has a very low opinion of bulls' mental capacity, and the Taurus in the picture lives down to his reputation; he is holding a bag full of money and is about to get swindled by a pyramid scheme, also called in the U.S., a Ponzi scheme, the only type that usually offers this level of return. The patience the cartoon mentions is the decades waiting for the government to prosecute and hand out the investors' funds. Although Americans often think of rowdy rams butting heads, to the Arab way of thinking he never loses the meekness of a young lamb, hence his depiction here as meek and besotted. His panel mentions "unbearable financial loss," which refers to the numerous phone cards that a lover will have to go through to talk to their loved one.

Language

"Astrologers lie even if they say the truth" is a hadith that advises Muslims against believing in astrology. The hadith says that if you believe it your prayers will not be accepted for forty days, since only God knows what is in the future. Starting the cartoon with that hadith is indication that readers should not believe in it and just take it for the humor.

Translation

Wife to husband reading Mickey Mouse magazine: "My mother always envied me because of your political awareness."

Culture

Traditionally, Arab women are not very connected to the outside world, and Arab men are more aware of world affairs. Women are not interested in finding information on their own, so their only source of information is from their husband, who will tell them what has happened in the world when he gets home. Gradually women are changing and, with the help of the Internet, younger women are becoming more involved and interested in world affairs and politics, and no longer only rely on the men for their information.

Mickey Mouse has long been the number-one magazine for Arab children, retaining the top position despite the introduction of other magazines. American cartoons (e.g. Superman, Batman, Mickey Mouse, etc) have been around for a long period of time. Reading Mickey Mouse magazine indicates that the man is not particularly well read and does not deserve the envy of this woman's mother.

Envy

The word envy carries a lot more weight in the Arabic language than its English counterpart. In Arab culture, envy does not simply refer to coveting another's circumstance or possessions and may also refer to having a grudge. This is because envy is mentioned in the Qur'an as a valid reason for concern. If a person feels as though he is being envied by someone because of any material possessions, he is to recite a special surah from the Qur'an (Chap. 113), which only has five verses and opens: "I seek refuge with the Lord of the daybreak." This should ward off any envious negativity.

People who are not familiar with Arab culture should be careful about praising or complimenting too emphatically any item that an Arab has, for such admiration can be taken negatively. Rather than saying "thank you" for the compliment, as the speaker might expect, he will be wary that the speaker is envious. Often times the Arab person will make a gift of an item that they think is coveted as a precaution against the evils of the other person's envy, which may extend far beyond that item.

There are ways to compliment someone without creating concern about envy. When admiring another person's item, the compliment should be accompanied by the words *ma sha'Allah*, "as God has willed." This way the person who is complimented will not be worried that the person is envious of his belongings. If a person giving a compliment does use *ma sha'Allah*, the person receiving the compliment will prompt him with

"Praise the Prophet," and the admirer should then say "God's peace and prayer be upon him," so that any ill effects of envy are thwarted. These phrases are ways of invoking divine protection against negative influences, slightly superstitious and almost automatic, but they also indicate the speaker's awareness of the potential problems. By using "*ma sha'Allah*" the speaker indicates "I know that you may think I am envious, but be assured I am not," while with "Praise the Prophet" the person is inviting the admirer to confirm that he or she is not envious, which they will confirm with "God's peace and prayer be upon him" — an automatic response for any Muslim.

There is another way Arabs counteract the ill effects of envy. When someone feels as though their child or their property has been envied, they will fumigate the object of this envy. If what is envied is a person, then right before sunset you are to cut a small piece of his or her clothing, place a little salt, coriander seed and alum on it, and then burn it. Then circle the head of the person with the smoke coming from the piece of burning cloth. When the fire is out and the cloth has been reduced to ashes, then the child is to be sprinkled with the ashes.

If you suspect that someone envies you, in order to find out who it may be, you should carry out the following ritual. Right before sunset, take a piece of alum, place it on burning coals, and leave it on the burning coals until it begins bubbling. While the alum is burning, recite the opening and last three chapters of the Qur'an. When the alum stops bubbling, smoke will escape from it, and this smoke should resemble the appearance of the envious person. Then take the alum and pound it into powder, and put it into food and give the food to a black dog to eat.

Charms

A *Hejab* is a charm worn to protect someone from the evils that may befall him. The verb *hajaba* itself means to protect or to hide, and one of its derivations, the word *hijab* is used to refer to the headscarves women wear to cover their hair. *Hejab* charms are used for protecting the wearer from diseases, evil enchantments, evil eyes and any kind of ill. Often these *Hejab*s are enclosed small copies of the *mos-haf* or verses from the Qur'an written onto a small scroll and encased in gold or silver and worn around the neck. The chapters from the Qur'an most commonly used in the *Hejab* are chapters 6, 18, 36, 44, 55, 67, 78, known as the "Protection Surahs" and are put to paper to be given to loved ones to protect them from the devil, evil jinn and any other objects of fear. Arab mothers often give to their children the verse that reads, "The preservation of both is no burden unto Him. He is the High, the Great." Another common verse reads, "God is the best protector, and He is the most merciful to those who show mercy" among others. Other *Hejab* commonly found are the 99 names of Allah, which is expected to bring about good fortune for the person wearing it. *Hejab* are also used to bless homes.

There are various things that are regarded in the same light as written charms, such as dust from the tomb of the Prophet, water from the sacred well of Zemzem in the precinct of Mecca, and pieces of the black brocade covering of the Kaabah. The water of Zemzem is much valued for the purpose of sprinkling upon grave-clothes. Every year, on the first day of the Eid al-AdHa, which immediately follows the pilgrimage, a new covering is hung upon the Kaabah. The old one is cut up and the greater part of it is sold to the pilgrims.

Some Arabs like to hang worn-out shoes from the back bumper of their cars for fear envy. For example, if you have a new, expensive car, Arabs believe that if you hang worn shoes from the back bumper (the older and more ragged the better) they will ward off envy by associating the car with something completely worthless. This has nothing to do with concern for theft, but rather with disrupting feelings of envy, which may be felt by someone who looks at the car. Absolute value is not important—a donkey-cart is valuable in the eyes of its owner and, if he fears it may trigger envy, it will need an old shoe, though in this case it will not be a human shoe, but an old horseshoe as it is a cart.

Translation

Doctor: O Protector! Now I know the reason for your impotence.

Sign on wall: Dr. "Sexually Aroused, Worshiper/Slave of the Mighty" / Impotence Treatment

Language

In Islam, God has 99 attributes, with each given a specific name. A Muslim calling on Him, then, has a very great deal more ability to be specific in his invocation, suiting it to the attribute that meets his need; in a way, this is vaguely analagous to a Christian's ability to pray to the patron saint of a particular endeavor. "The Protector" to whom the doctor in the cartoon calls is, as the name implies, an attribute of God in His role the shielder of the faithful from unpleasant or harmful influence. This is the first thing that an Arab says on seeing a disaster or accident.

Arabic speakers are generally more attuned to the meanings of names than one tends to be in English, and names can be used to humorous effect in fiction, as in this cartoon. The doctor's name, given in the frame on his wall, carries a number of ribald *double entendres*. The doctor's first name, Baheeg, can mean "wonderful" or "charming," but it also has the slang meaning of "I get sexually aroused." His last name, Abd'elqawi, means the slave or worshiper of the Mighty, Powerful, or Vigorous, a name which can certainly be taken in multiple ways—especially for a doctor treating impotence. The man's face, worn, with a large nose and pronounced chin, as well as the bow tie, all suggest low libido to the Arab viewer.

Publications about sex in the Arab world

Publications of all kinds about sex, even academic materials, are banned in most of the Arab world. Adult magazines are confiscated from any travelers bringing them into a country where such materials are banned. Since the introduction of the Internet, the banning of these publications has been less effectual than in the past, as people have gone online to find adult materials. While ruling Iraq, Saddam Hussein founded a "Faith Campaign," where he disposed of all sex books and magazines, even academic ones, from school libraries and Iraqi organizations, pushing Islamization. He also confiscated many novels, including those by the Egyptian writer Naguib Mahfouz and the Lebanese writer Nazar Qabany. After the fall of Saddam and Baghdad in 2003, the underground market in sex publications flourished.

Arab people were among the first to write about sex. One of the most famous Arab writers to write about this topic was Maddany, (614 CE–704 CE) who was born in Basra, Iraq. He wrote about topics that concerned the people of his time, especially sex, in the context of Islam. Some of his most famous works include: *He Who Married a Set of Sisters*; *He Who Married the Daughter of His Wife*; *Sexual Positions*; *Those You Can Marry*; *Who You Hate to be in a Relationship With*; *Women Who Imitate Men* and *The Book of Homosexuals*.

Sexual relationships in the Arab world

Discussion of the topic of sex in the Arab world was taboo for a very long time. Many people suffered silently because of public ignorance on the topic. Many women were unable to enjoy intimacy because of male dominance within sexual relationships. One of the most pressing issues for Arab men and women regarding sex is what Arabs call "tying," or the inability of the man to perform on his wedding night. Arab men may encounter performance anxiety on this night, as it is usually an Arab man's first sexual encounter and there are so many expectations about the first intimate experience. For a long time, Arabs relied on magicians to cure them of this problem, not realizing that it is an underlying psychological rather than physiological problem.

Translation

Title: In the pharmacy

Outside counter: "Blue pill, please."

Shouting: "One package of Viagra for Abu Marzouk, Hanafy."

The humor here is that the pharmacist is shouting out something that the customer has asked for discreetly, and also that he is shouting in the manner of a coffee-shop waiter passing on an order. In Saudi Arabia, the Egyptians have a virtual monopoly on running private pharmacies, and the humor of the cartoon is in the way the pharmacist shouts his customer's order, the same way Egyptian waiters shout orders in the caféshops of Egypt.

Culture

People use Viagra in Arab countries as much as they do in America. However, there it conceived of primarily as an extra boost to young vigor, rather than as a cure for aged impotence.

Translation

Title: Life of a retiree

Bellowing man: Mother of Mubarak, I smell smoke and who opened the door? Did you turn off the fence light and where is the coffee?

Language

Arab retirees are considered to be objects of pity. The Arabic word by which they are referred, "مت قاعد" is a portmanteau that, in English, would be something like, "DiedSitting."

Culture

The age of retirement is 60 years old for most Arab employees. Because an Arab often will not take care of his health as carefully as his western counterparts might, by the time he reaches that age he will probably be in dire need of retirement. This relatively early retirement does not necessarily bring hardship. In Arab countries, the government is typically the largest employer. Accordingly, many retirees can look forward to government pensions and need not suffer a decline in their standards of living. Incidentally, the United Arab Emirates' high standard of living has caused its people to outshine the generally subpar mortality rates of the Arab world, with life expectancies of 78.7 years for men and 81.5 years for women.

As anywhere, though, a husband who retires can severely disrupt the lives of his wife and kids. In this cartoon, he is just sitting, drinking tea, ordering people around and sticking his nose into their affairs. He calls for his wife (he addresses her as, "Mother of Mubarak" not as an oath, but simply because their eldest son is named Mubarak (an address by reference to eldest son is a traditional mark of respect), tells her to mind her cooking, and generally meddles in all the household's affairs.

All Arab houses have fences—more walls in fact—to maintain their privacy. The climate means that people often sit outside or keep the windows open, so the fences are important, and they will usually have lights on them to illuminate the sidewalk outside for their guests or maybe even strangers, and these will be turned off late at night or when they go to bed. Children are rather less concerned about privacy and may use the lights to play in the street after dark.

When guests are expected, the lights will be turned on in all the rooms that are going to be used to welcome them and as a sign of celebration. Most lights and chandeliers have two tiers, and for family normally only one is used, but for guests both will be turned on. Low lighting and candles may seem more inviting to a Westerner, but would be seen as insulting by an Arab, indicating that the hosts want to go to bed. A restaurant that wants to be successful will need to be brightly lit if it is catering to Arabs — those with a more international or Westernized clientele may prefer ambient lighting.

Translation

Girl: "Father, what is that? Since you retired I can't swim, I can't change my clothes. He's peeping at me all the time."

Rabbit: "This is the problem when old people retire."

Language

When a young person is scared or surprised their first reaction will often be to call "Father" or, more commonly, "Mother." "Mother" indicates more that you want comfort, whereas "Father" is a call for protection and tells any threatening presence that your father is nearby to deal with it.

"Shayib" means "gray person" and is the usual word for older people if they are behaving inappropriately for their age, such as dressing too young or flirting with young girls. It is not a negative word, but tends to be used in contexts of reproval.

Culture

The majority of retired people spend their time in coffee shops, going to mosques, taking care of household chores, praying, and preparing themselves for their end. The old man in this cartoon who is spying on his neighbor is not in the majority.

The rabbit's comment about "old people" retiring refers to a distinction between standard retirement and early retirement, which is relatively common in the Arab world. Early retirement, at any age after fifty, may be a choice, feeling that the extra money earned is not worth the sacrifice, but may also be imposed, especially if a boss feels that his position is threatened by a particular employee.

Translation

Title: The wait

Culture

Despite the fact that in some conservative cultures women cover all of their bodies, they still pay great attention to what is visible, particularly make up and manicure.

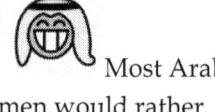 Most Arab men would rather have root-canal work than go out with their wives or sisters. One of the reasons is "the wait": waiting for them to get ready to go out, and then waiting at the end of a visit while they say goodbye. Many Westerners may be under the impression that wearing an abbaya, a woman would take less time getting ready than her American or European counterpart, and that the jokes about women keeping their husbands waiting to go out would therefore not apply. This is not the case. And the goodbyes at the end of a meeting may well last longer than the visit—after declaring that they are leaving, the chat goes on and then moves outside, and the man might get as far as his car while his wife continues talking, then as the conversation continues, they may move back inside to be more comfortable and even find that it is so late that they need to spend the night (most visiting is with relatives, so that this is perfectly feasible).

Translation

Woman to her mother: "I'm not upset that he divorced me. I'm upset that my birthday is next week and I missed out on the present!"

Language

The Arabic term *Hamah* means "in-law," as in "mother-in-law," and is derived from the verb that means "to protect," *Hama*. Traditionally, men were eager for their mothers to reside with them and take an active part in overseeing their wife's behavior, making a mother the "protector" of the family's honor.

Culture

Social festivities, particularly birthdays, weddings, Eid or celebrations for passing an exam, are important opportunities to give presents. Presents are a vital part of the social economy, opening up channels of communication in a special way, and can only be offered on a suitable occasion: a birthday present can be used to ask for forgiveness from someone for a slight or offence—and virtually oblige the person to give it; an gift for Eid or for a person's birthday may be the only tactful way to give some money to a friend or relative who needs it. The woman here is not just materialistically thinking of her missed present, though that is the joke—but the birthday might also offer an opportunity for reconciliation or making a fresh start.

Women are very close to their mothers. Mothers represent wisdom and provide advice. Daughters often confide in their mothers about every aspect of their life with their husband, even their sex life. The house of a mother is often a refuge for a daughter that is abused by or fighting with her husband.

On the other hand, the relationship between the mother and the husband is not as close and loving. Simply because the mother will take the side of her daughter regardless if her daughter is right or wrong. Mothers will often be a source of grief for her daughter's husband, as she is always embarrassing him and pointing out problems with how he is treating her daughter. Many Arab comedy films have been made about the relationship between a husband and his mother-in-law. There are even actresses who specialize in portraying mothers-in-law in these films. Some mothers will even live the rest of their lives in their daughter's households, to the dismay of the son-in-law. The mother will also have a very strong relationship with her grandchildren. The mother-in-law will also step in and help raise the grandchildren while their mother is working or busy with other things. Both mothers of the wife and husband often have an uneasy relationship because they favor their child in the relationship.

Divorced people, especially women, are looked down upon in Arab culture, because society considers them failures in marriage. Arab women treat divorced women as a potential threat—divorced women will not be invited over to their houses as often or included in groups. Generally speaking, a divorced woman is treated differently in Arab society, because she no longer has the family restrictions that are represented by a husband. Similar treatment can also be applied to divorced men.

Alimony payments are not as strictly enforced in the Arab world as they are in America. Arab courts do not have the same resources or power to enforce these laws. While, in America, wages can be garnished, the driver's license can be suspended, and other similar measures can be taken, these tools are not at the disposal of Arab divorce courts.

How to Deal with the Protector

The mother-in-law—the husband's mother in particular—has a bad reputation. It is so bad that the ideal man for an Arab girl is a man whose mother has died, or whose mother lives in a different city. Movies help perpetuate this reputation so that many women go into marriage with trepidation and a heightened sense of caution toward meeting their future mother-in-law. Women feel that the mother will be watching too attentively and interfere in their affairs. There are many books in Arab culture about how to deal with a mother-in-law. Usually they suggest befriending or taking her as a second mother. Their reputation is so pervasive that it is very hard for mothers-in-law to be seen otherwise.

Arab Culture

Translation

Man: Shall we go to the sea or shopping?
Woman: Whatever you like.
Man: Okay, let's go to the sea.
Woman: No, shopping.
Man: Let's go shopping.
Woman: No, the sea.
Man: Okay, the sea.
Woman: No, shopping.

Culture

This cartoon shows that the woman and the man cannot agree on where to go, and are always contradicting each other by saying the opposite of what their partner is saying. Many Arab men view their wives as difficult to satisfy and to get along with. Arab men typically prefer to spend time with their friends at coffee shops, unlike America where a couple may be best friends and do everything together. In Arab culture, a man has the opportunities to travel and explore life, while the woman does not have these opportunities and stays at home with a very limited social life. Men do not look at women as an equal partner because they feel that women have not experienced life as they have. Therefore, women are looked at to be less intelligent and have less common sense than men because of their lack of experience in life.

Translation

"Before marriage"

"After marriage"

Culture

For many Arab men, the first encounter with sex is on their wedding night. Before being married, the men, who have been eagerly awaiting their wedding night, are in active pursuit of their wives. After marriage, however, they may lose interest in their wives, and, as this cartoon suggests, it is the women who are in pursuit of their husbands. This is not always the case, and women too are known to lose interest in their husbands.

Translation

"This is what happens when you believe those commercials on Satellite TV about herbs!"

Culture

Arab medical tradition places great emphasis on the medicinal value of herbs and plants, and to this day, Arabs maintain a great faith in their ability to cure conditions that

western-style treatments cannot. With the introduction of satellite TV stations, advertisements for these herbs became widespread, with very little control over the advertising's veracity. Consumer reports where the products are tested are almost non-existent in Arab countries. Therefore, people can fall victim to false advertising.

Herbal medicine

"Spice-dealer's prescription," *Wasfit al-Attar*, is the name Arabs give to homeopathic medicine. Spice dealers are everywhere in Arab cities. It is very hard to find a neighborhood without one. Their goods are usually stored in burlap bags, set on the ground, with the tops rolled down to present their contents. All the sacks set out like this contain dry goods, such as lentils or pulses, soap, spices, and anything else that doesn't easily spoil. It is also the place where many Arab women like to get their unconventional medicines. Customers here tend to be female, and they usually use the advice of the spice dealers to help with their cosmetic or medical needs. Arab women are always looking for methods to tighten skin, lose weight, and soften hair (like silk), or enlarge their breasts, lips, or thighs, out of fear that their husband will take another wife. Spice dealers usually view this type of business as very lucrative and will provide their customers with a wide selection of remedies for these cosmetic and medical needs. Many view the dealers as a complete encyclopedia of what a woman needs, so he can volunteer his services, prescribing cosmetic treatments or pills with beneficial medical effects. The conventional wisdom among Arabs is still that what they buy from spice dealers can be effective, but they recommend not buying anything powdered: you should buy the raw material and grind it yourself. Women usually resort to these types of treatments through word of mouth. Arabic newspapers often publish reports of people who get extremely sick after trying such medicines and recommend that people use the conventional medicines found in pharmacies.

☪ Arab advertising generally is restricted to touting the virtues of the product it is selling and cannot — even obliquely — refer to competitors' product

☪ Known by a variety of names worldwide, opuntia, Indian fig, Barbery fig, the pear cactus or prickly pear — in Arabic, *teen shoukey*, which translates literally as "thorny fig" — is widely popular throughout the Arab world. Indigenous to the Middle East, the poor woman in the cartoon has sprouted a pear cactus from the crown of her head.

Throughout the Arab world, vendors of prickly pears transport their products with the aid of large wooden carts. When he is open for business, the prickly-pear salesman will lay out his fruits upon the cart's top: to one side will be those that he has already peeled, on the other, those that he has yet to skin. Preparing a prickly pear is an involved process, and requires the vendor to don two thick gloves that, to a certain degree, protect him against the fruit's sharp, very painful spikes. He must then slice the fruit in a prescribed, very specific fashion, after which he will cover it with ice, so that it cools. If you glimpse a vendor when he is without customers, he will very likely be at work with a pair tweezers, removing the thorns that have become embedded in his hand despite the protective gloves.

☪ The extensive knowledge of materials and skill with chemical mixing that are essential to the spice dealer's trade has also made them useful to terrorists wishing to devise explosives. Accordingly, spice dealers have lately come under strict scrutiny and regulation from the authorities.

☪ Haggling over prices is widespread in Arab markets and can make buying and selling a tiresome processes to those unaccustomed to such modes of bargaining. When a shopkeeper is asked the price of any of his goods, he generally demands more than he expects to receive; the customer declares the price exorbitant, and offers about half or two-thirds of the sum first-named; the price thus bidden is, of course, rejected: but the shopkeeper lowers his demand; and then the customer, in his turn, bids somewhat higher than before: thus they usually go on until they meet about half-way between the sum first demanded and that first offered, and so the bargain is concluded.

If one of the hagglers becomes entrenched at a price the other finds unacceptable, a useful tactic is temporarily to drop the matter and strike up a friendly conversation. After some amiable conversation, the formerly intransigent bargainer may feel more warmly and be willing to adjust his price further.

Translation

Title: New invention... distributors wanted.

Language

The sound of snoring—that is, the harsh and porcine grunt itself and not the word that represents it—can be used in the Arab world as an extreme and vulgar insult.

Culture

Arab women are similar to American women in that they may be annoyed with sleeping with a man, because they are fighting, or perhaps he is snoring. In Islam, sometimes the husband will not sleep in the same bed as his wife as a form of punishment that is mandated in the Qur'an for a wife disobeying her husband.

House of Obedience, *Bayt al-Ta'a*

Most Arab women, finding problems with their husbands, return to their parents' home with their children. If a husband is the vengeful type, he will leave his wife and children at her parents' home without providing for them for as long as he desires. The husband will then demand that the wife go to what is called the House of Obedience. This house does not have the amenities that she once enjoyed while living in her home with her husband, and is equipped with only the bare necessities needed to survive. After receiving the order to go to the House of Obedience, the woman has seven days to move. If a woman ignores her husband's initial demand to enter the house of obedience, the husband will file a motion in court. If she still refuses to go the house of Obedience, the husband can take judgment against her for violation of marital duties and will divorce her and she forfeits any possible marriage settlement, including child support. When the court has become involved, a judge and a clerk will go and survey the house to make sure it has the same description and quality of living as described by the husband in his motion. The house of obedience will correspond to the economic status of the husband, as the house's furnishing must be owned by the husband and not the wife. The location must be away from both the wife and her husband's families. Many human rights organizations regard this House of Obedience as a prison cell without bars and advocate that these countries ought to abolish personal status laws (laws that regulate marital relations) and move these cases to civil courts.

Translation

Title: Engagement and marriage

Wife: "Father of Masoud, talk to me the way you used to during our engagement."

Husband: "I'm not going to say anything more than 'go to sleep'."

Culture

An Arab man usually has difficulty sweet-talking his wife, since to do so would be perceived as weakness, so

many women go through married live without hearing "I love you," and the last time they hear it will probably be on the first day of their marriage. He is no longer courting her, his general love-making is likely to be awkward anyway, and he is in a position of control, so does not need to take her feelings into account. Life is often hard, leading to a generally gruff style, and a husband may think that a harder demeanor will protect him from excessive demands, both emotional and financial. The woman herself may stop making an effort once she is safely married and do little to invite compliments. However, Arab women's exposure to foreign TV and the Internet have heightened their sense of lack of romance in their life, as they see dramas with a Western husband kissing his wife goodbye, bringing flowers, holding her hand and smiling, engaging in intellectual conversation, taking her out to dinner.

In Arab countries, the process of courting is different. The engagement period begins immediately, because "dating" as it is understood in the West is not acceptable. A man can only call to a woman after she has become engaged to him. After the engagement, both the woman and the man will wear an engagement ring on the ring finger of the right hand. The woman will wear a gold ring with the name of her fiancé inscribed on the inside of her ring. The man will wear a silver (if he is following the "sunnah") ring with the name of his fiancée inscribed on the inside of his ring.

Although women are generally advised to push for a short engagement lest couples split or fiancés' attentions wander, the complexities and expense of marriage can force engagements to linger for several years. The engagement period is the only chance that a future husband and wife have to become acquainted with one another before marriage, and so the male is allowed to go to the home of the female for a partially supervised visit, usually on Thursdays. Upon his arrival, a male relative will receive the suitor in the salon. That male relative will then be joined by the mother, who will offer the suitor a drink. Later, the engaged woman will come down very nicely dressed and in full make up to join the party for small talk. During the first visit, the couple will be supervised by a member of the woman's family, but over time, the amount of supervision will decrease. Sometimes the family will allow the suitor to take the young woman out, but in these instances, the couple will be accompanied by a male relative or one of the engaged woman's sisters. It is very important that the female remain as conservative as possible when she is alone with her suitor. It is not considered favorable to hold the man's hand or kiss him, lest he question the woman's chastity.

It is very important for the woman's family to make a good impression upon the suitor, since the dynamics of the relationships during an engagement are such that the suitor has the upper hand. Every family wants their daughter to be married, and will do anything to impress a suitor if he is considered a good catch. The family will always present themselves at their best when the suitor is coming to meet their daughter, and any family members who may make an unfavorable impression upon the suitor are kept away from the salon. Plenty of gifts are exchanged, and invitations to have lunch or dinner are extended from the woman's family to the suitor's family.

The engagement period is often a very tense one because the suitor may break the engagement at any time. Such a breaking of the engagement presents a problem for the woman, because it may reduce her desirability for any potential new suitors if they discover that she has been engaged in the past. This may also erode the woman's self-esteem, as well as exhaust the family's resources.

During the engagement, the couple will also begin preparing for their married life. They will begin searching for a home, buying furniture and useful equipment for their living space. During this time, the groom may leave to work in an oil rich country in order to make money to accommodate their expenses.

☪ It is not uncommon to see men who become engaged to women with no intention of marrying them in an attempt to enjoy the benefits that come with engagement. Once they have had their fill, they can break the engagement with no consequence or concern for their reputations.

☪ It is ironic that Arabs now have difficulties courting their wives, since the poetry of former centuries indicates that historically they were among the most romantic of men.

Translation

Love is…

making him feel comfortable!

Culture

The "Love is…" cartoons were created by an artist in New Zealand but have been syndicated worldwide, and many Arab newspapers have continued to publish this type of cartoon, adapted to reflect Arab culture. Back in the 1950s and the 60s, the actions of the woman in the picture would not have been uncommon: a woman then often waited for her husband to come home, took off his shoes, brought him a basin to soak his feet, and ensured that no one disturbed him, and so on. Circumstances have changed, and now women work and no longer have the time to perform these tasks for their husbands, indeed they would look down on any woman who did this for her husband.

The cartoons probably show little about real love, but do convey some of the dynamics of married life.

Translation

Top: Man after marriage

Bottom: Woman after marriage

Culture

Most Arab men and women do not experience sex until marriage, so when they do experiment and start to enjoy sex, they wonder what it would be like with another partner. In our society, men and women typically date before marriage, so they are not put in this situation after marriage, because they have already experienced it as a teenager or young adult. In order for a girl to get married in Arab culture, her father has to attest that his daughter is a virgin during the marriage contract process. Arab men can make a large amount of money if they find out after marrying a girl that she is not a virgin. In rural areas, the tradition of dancing in the street with a blanket that is stained with blood from the new wife proves that she was a virgin and that the marriage has been consummated—both causes for celebration.

As for the woman, marriage is her ticket to fulfill her fantasies, and obtain freedom from her family. They are no longer looking over her and controlling what she is doing. In an Arab family, every family member works to ensure that the girl stays a virgin and keeps a good reputation so she is worthy to be married to a suitable husband.

In the cartoon, it is shown that the man has wandering eyes after marriage, as the idea of sex is not scary for him now as it was before marriage. The woman is more likely to not be as reserved as before marriage, and express her feelings.

Translation

Title: Whenever you give a woman love, she asks for more
Woman: "Please give me today's share of love."

Culture

Arab men are not the most romantic men in the world and many do not take women's feelings into consideration, because they grow up in an environment that lauds toughness and masculinity. For these reasons, men view being sensitive and showing love to their mate as a contradictory emotion. Outside his house, a man may seem jovial, while inside his house, a man may seem stern; this is because he wants to show that he is in charge. When a member of the household sees a father with his friends, they will be very amused, because they will often never see that jovial side of him. Arab society for a long time discouraged

men from showing any sign of sensitivity to their household, because the father in many households in the disciplinary figure. These rules do not apply uniformly to all households in the Arab world, and recently, the image of the stern faced father has been changing, for to economic and social reasons, Arab women are now joining the workforce and are no longer as financially dependent on men as they were before.

Arab children are more independent now than they were before. One factor in this greater independence is that the father may be absent, for instance if he finds work in an oil-rich country, leaving them in the care of their mother. This makes the children more responsible for their behavior, since their father is not always around, and makes them grow up more quickly. In addition, the spread of the Internet and satellite television has introduced new concepts of how families in other countries interact among themselves.

Translation

Title: Why do men lie?
Woman to man: "Please, may God grant you a long life. Lie to me."
Cat: "ha ha ha!"

Culture

In the archetypal Arab marriage, the men consider that their wives make unreasonable demands on them, expecting them to neglect their duties as sons and brothers, to ignore their friends and social responsibilities, and, in effect, to disregard their religious obligations. Wives are said to resent anything that takes their husband's time or resources away from themselves, the home and the family. The husband's relationship with his family is usually the major source of grievance, especially any financial help he may give them. Women are also jealous and on the look out for any potential sign of their husband's eye wandering, so that men are careful about what they tell their wives.

Anything that might provoke an argument is to be avoided, because an argument is never civil and will quickly get out of hand, inevitably involving children, family, and even neighbors, which will be a source of real embarrassment and minor scandal.

In order to avoid this, men have to lie, which is the quickest and safest way to defuse a potentially dangerous situation. The men therefore blame their wives for making them lie.

Translation

"Divorce me, divorce me, divorce me…"
Translation:
"Take care of me, look at me, feel me, love me."

Culture

If a woman feels that an argument has reached an impasse, and feels sure of her marriage, she may, as in the cartoon, repeat the phrase "divorce me" as a challenge and form of seduction with reverse psychology. The situation is more common in the early years of marriage, while the couple is still learning about each other, and is frequently shown in film and on television, usually with a passionate, young wife, who wants to assure herself of her husband's love, and it is followed by kisses from her husband, signs of tenderness and maybe make-up sex.

The woman who tests her husband in this way or uses similar threats, such as leaving for her mother's house, must, however, be very careful. If she chooses her moment wrongly, the husband holds all the cards.

☪ The Arab laws surrounding divorce are highly involved and remarkable for the disparity between the positions of men and women. When a man divorces his wife (which he does merely by saying, "You are divorced," or "I divorce you"), he pays her a portion of her dowry (generally one-third), which he had kept back from the beginning of the marriage, to be paid on this occasion, or at his death; and she takes away with her the furniture and other goods which she brought at her marriage. He may thus put her away from mere dislike and without assigning any reason. A woman, on the other hand, cannot separate herself from her husband against his will, unless there is some considerable fault on his part, as cruel treatment, or neglect. Even then, application to the court is generally necessary to compel the man to divorce her; and she forfeits the above-mentioned remnant of the dowry.

It is possible for a man to divorce his wife twice and each time take her back without any ceremony and, indeed, without her consent. Upon a third divorce, or upon a "triple divorce" conveyed in one sentence, he cannot take her back again until she has been married and divorced by another husband, who must have consummated his marriage with her. The first and second divorce, if made without any mutual agreement for a compensation from the woman, or a pecuniary sacrifice on her part, is termed *talak reg'ee* (revocable divorce); because the husband may take back his wife, without her consent, during the period of her *eddeh* (which will be explained below), but not after, unless with her consent and by a new contract. If he divorce her the first or second time for a compensation—she perhaps requesting, "Divorce me for what thou owest me," or "hast of mine" (that is, of the dowry, furniture, etc.)—or for an additional sum, he cannot take her again but by her own consent and by a new contract. This is a *talak baïn* (irrevocable divorce),

The *eddeh* is the period during which a divorced woman or a widow must wait before marrying again; unless pregnant; the *eddeh* is three lunar periods (i.e. three months) for a divorcée and four months and ten days for a widow. In either case, if the woman is pregnant, the *eddeh* terminates upon delivery. However, a woman divorced while pregnant, though she may make a new contract of marriage immediately after giving birth, must wait forty days longer before she can complete her marriage by receiving her husband. A man who divorces his wife is under obligation to maintain her—be it in his own house, in that of her parents, or elsewhere—during the period of her *eddeh*, but he must cease to live with her as her husband from the commencement of that period.

A divorced woman who has a son younger than two years old may retain him until he has attained that age. Further, under the law of the *Shafi*, she may be compelled to do so, and the law of the *Maliki* may compel her until the boy has reached puberty. The *Hanafi* law, though, limits the period during which the boy should remain under her care to seven years. Once again, the law is different for females: a divorced wife may retain her daughter until she reaches nine years of age or the period of puberty. If a man should divorce his wife before the consummation of marriage, he must pay her half the sum which he has promised to give her as a dowry, or, if he has promised no dowry, he must pay her the half of the smallest compensation allowed by law, which has been above mentioned, and she may marry again immediately.

When a wife refuses to obey to lawful commands of her husband, he may, and generally does, take her or two witnesses (witness, incidentally, must always be Muslims in accusations against persons of the same faith) against her to court, to render a complaint against her; if the case be proved, a certificate is written declaring the woman *nashiz*, or recalcitrance against her husband. This process is termed "writing a woman *nashiz*." Such a ruling exempts her husband from the obligations to lodge, clothe, and maintain her. He is not, however, obliged to divorce her; by refusing to do this, he may prevent her marrying another man as long as he lives. This clearly functions as a strong inducement for the wife to pledge subsequent obedience, and in the case of such a pledge, he must either take her back and maintain her or divorce her. A wife may also declare herself in court to be *nashiz* and unwilling to live with her husband, though her she would be dependant, in such an event, upon her parents or other relations for support. In this case, the husband generally persists, from mere spite, in refusing to divorce her.

Translation

Arrow: His wife

Wife: "This is someone who makes your life miserable, takes all of your money and lets you see the stars at the height of the noon. Guess who?"

Language

This cartoon introduces another Arabic expression. When you tell someone, "I'll make you see the stars at the height of noon," it means that you will beat them up or generally cause pain, not necessarily physical. This is comparable to the expression in English, "I'll make you see stars."

Rather than simply putting hands over someone's eyes from behind and saying "Guess who?" the Arab form involves giving a clue, usually involving something one has done—though not as negative as in this case.

Culture

Depicting wives as giving grief to their husbands is a common theme in Arab cartoons and the media, as is seen throughout this chapter. This is not a source of resentment or complaint from women in the Arab world and is treated largely as humor and even true to life. In many ways, it resembles some of the sexist humor that was common in America and Europe until relatively recently, where wives were often portrayed as waiting for their errant husbands, criticizing and constantly nagging them. In addition, the humor reflected some reality, but also created some and also created myths that audiences accepted even if they saw no real evidence in their own lives.

Translation

Title: Sit Sousa (The hard-of-hearing woman)
Housekeeper: "There's a leak in the gas cylinder.
Old Lady: "What are you saying? America spies on China?

Language

Sit means *lady* in Arabic. *Sit Sousa* appears in different Egyptian cartoons. In Arabic, the sentences "There's a leak in the gas cylinder" and "America spies on China" sound very similar to a hearing-impaired person.

Sousa means a woodworm in Arabic and it is unusual name to give a lady, and would indicate various unpleasant qualities. It could denote a person who brings havoc, someone who is plotting, or a home-wrecker.

Culture

In some Arab households, natural gas comes from cylindrical tanks instead of a gas line. The gas cylinders are handled without great care and can sometimes crack, producing a leak and a potential explosion. Leaks can lead to people inhaling gas and dying in their sleep and gas explosions are one of the most common causes of household accidents, though the explosion itself is usually relatively limited since the spaces are ventilated.

Both upper and middle class homes in rich Arabic countries often employ the services of a live-in maid. Their situations and living conditions vary widely, ranging from mature and dignified women to uncared-for farm girls of ten.   These latter are generally brought to their employer by their impoverished families who cannot afford to support them, and their lives are filled with drudgery and harsh conditions, sometimes even being forced to sleep on the kitchen floor. These children do not even keep their own wages, as they go to their family instead. The conditions for adult maids, again, vary, though they at least keep their own earnings. The issue of domestic service in the Arab world will be examined more fully in the second volume of this book.

☪ In Arab countries, the cat enjoys unchallenged predominance as the household pet of choice. This love of cats has deep roots in Arab culture; one of Muhammad's nearest followers earned the nick-name Abu Hurairah (Father of a Kitten) for his fondness for felines, a rare creature in the Arabian Peninsula at that time. Modern pet owners appreciate cats' cleanliness and ease of maintenance, frugally feeding them with otherwise unusable table leftovers or letting them earn their keep as pest controllers.

Cats' great rival in the West, dogs, are largely scorned and feared; those few who do keep dogs mark themselves out for social isolation, as most people will avoid visiting a dog-owning household. Part of this comes from the fact that the touch of the dog's wet nose is enough to invalidate any ritual cleanness. Indeed, most Arabs find nothing adorable in any dog—and pigs, incidentally, even less. With society at large so little fond of dogs, the Animal Control authorities have scope for rather more drastic means that in most places in the West. To combat the endemic problem of packs of stray dogs, Arab dog "catchers" carry rifles and live ammunition, and any unlicensed dog is liable to be rounded up and killed. The animals killed by the Animal Control are used to feed zoo animals.

☪ In many Arab households, radio is still the main source of entertainment especially among old people, where they can listen to it while engaging in other activities—the large unit shown in the cartoon is an old radio, and it is not uncommon to find well-maintained radios that are still in use after many decades. Most of the time they will use it to listen to the Qur'an, and every country will have a channel dedicated to recitation of the Qur'an, which will often form the background in stores and shops as well. Arab like to start their days by listening to the quran,

Translation

"Listen, woman [*mara*], it is true that the way to a man's heart is through his stomach, but that shouldn't keep you from brushing your hair!"

Language

"*Mara*" is a derogatory term for a woman.

Culture

Arabs by and large prize home cooking, and it is expected that an Arab housewife will be able to prepare good, thrifty meals from scratch, often even to the point of raising and butchering animals. A good Arab mother will therefore take great pains to pass on to her daughters her kitchen expertise in anticipation of the day when they rise to take charge of households of their own.

The saying that the way to a man's heart is through his stomach is exactly the same in Arabic as in English. There are many sayings and proverbs in Arab culture that deal with family life and the relationship between men and women. There are more sayings about Arab family life than American family life because Arab life is more complex; after all, Arab men are allowed up to four wives—each of whom is likely to have her own children—and the extended family is far more intimate than even the American nuclear family. For example, there is a proverb that a husband with two wives is "a groom every night," referring humorously to his capacity, should he chose, always to sleep with a different woman from yesterday. The saying for a woman marrying someone for his money would be: "Those who marry a monkey for his money will find that the money will be gone and the monkey will still be a monkey."

Some people neglect their appearance after being married for a while, but generally speaking, Arab men don't mind because that would make her less attractive to other men, and the most important thing for the average Arab man is that his wife dress conservatively.

Most Arab women will not be seen by anyone other than immediate relatives when they are home, as visitors and the women themselves are aware of the importance of privacy. Children like their mother and father to be at their best at all times so they are not embarrassed by the way they look and can introduce them to their friends.

☪ Chicken and rice is considered the finest dish that an average Arab family can serve to its guests, or that a wife can prepare for her husband. It is a simple dish, consisting only of plain white rice and lightly fried or boiled chicken. In the cartoon, the characters are dining in bed. In Arab households, the bed is not only used for sleeping, but also for any number of activities, such as eating, reading, lounging, and studying.

Translation

Husband: "Why don't you wear something like that for me?"

Wife: "Why don't you brush your teeth for me?"

[N.B. In many houses there will be a photograph of the husband and wife, or just the husband, on the wall, usually taken during the early years of their marriage.]

 The cartoon makes fun of the man's lack of self-awareness, including his bad breath and unclipped toe-nails. This is not common in real life, but not unknown, and many Arab women are critical of the approach to appearance and hygiene of the men that they come into contact with — husband, brother, sons, chauffeur etc.

Culture

Arab Hygiene

Both men and women are particularly hygienic for religious reasons, since the Qur'an advises people to purify themselves regularly. Muslim Arabs have to perform ablutions to be in a state of religious purity, in order for them to pray, read the Qur'an, visit a mosque, or perform religious tasks. Arab standards of hygiene are stricter and more rigorous than Western standards. Before and after Arabs eat, they must wash their mouths and their hands. After using the toilet, Arabs will wash their bottom area with water. After an Arab man urinates, he makes sure to wash himself carefully. When he has finished urinating, he will walk to the sink making certain that no drops of urine touch his clothing, and use water to wash the tip of his penis ensuring its cleanliness. This is important because if even a single drop of urine remains, he will be considered impure and must change his clothes before he can pray.

Even if an Arab is purified and has performed an ablution, he or she must also make sure that their clothes are pure and properly clean. If a man experiences involuntary nocturnal ejaculation during his sleep, he must immediately change his clothes and shower in order to be considered pure enough to pray. Many Arabs will use a *loofah* in the shower to clean their bodies, as the desert environment calls for extra attention to be given to the cleaning process since it is very hard on the skin. A shower does not count as ablution, because ablution requires a statement of intention and specific rituals that include gargling. A shower can count as ablution, so long as a person includes the statement of intention and all of the proper rituals. If water is not available, ablutions can be performed using sand from the desert, or dust. In such cases, it is not unusual to see an Arab person forcefully hitting his mattress or couch in order to create dust that he will use in an ablution.

Most Arab men do not grow beards but those who follow the sunnah do, cropping the moustache but letting the beard grow as much as possible. This is a relatively recent phenomenon—Islamic scholars prior to the eighties were almost all clean-shaven. Wearing a beard commands respect from others, and Arab men never color their beards, as a grey beard commands more respect than a black beard, because the grey signifies wisdom.

Nowadays, many Arab women use the same cosmetics that Western women do, but some women still hold to the tradition of using cosmetic products made from natural resources. For example, the women of the household will come together to make a paste from water, sugar and lemon, boil it gently, and then use it to remove all of their body hair. Arab women rub their feet with pumice stone to be rid of calluses. Strict Muslim Arab women never use nail polish, because the polish will cover their nails, and the water from the ablution will not be able to touch their nails directly, rendering them not completely clean or pure for prayer. Very few Muslim Arab women will color their hair, for the same reasons.

☪Arabs do not pay as much attention to their dental hygiene as people do in America. Floss does not exist in some Arab countries, and some Arabs, mostly in rural areas, may not brush their teeth with a tooth brush on a regular basis; they may, however, use something called *swak/miswak* which is a teeth cleaning twig from a tree with anti-microbial properties, prescribed by sunnah.

Translation

Woman: He's very cheap, Mother, you have to help me divorce him. Do you believe he doesn't want to change the car that he bought for me last month?!

Culture

Mocking the rich and their unreasonable behavior, along with showing compassion for the poor, is possibly a relic of the Socialist era and reflects attitudes that still pervade Arab countries. The majority of the Arab population is poor or comes from a poor background and those in power like to send the message to the rest of society that "they feel their pain." Even if they are in secret enjoying lives of wealth, the elite does not usually flaunt it for a number of

reasons: to avoid envy, unrest (if they are politicians) or taxation. Many Arab countries still reserve a large number of seats in their parliaments for those who designated as "laborers and farmers'

Translation

Man: "Divorce is a dangerous social disease and epidemic of society."

Woman: "Do you know who's sitting behind me? That's the wife he divorced last month."

Culture

There are various forms of marriage that are less than "full" and the ease with which such marriages can be entered into and then left has meant that a good number of men over the course of, for example, ten years may have married as many as twenty or more wives, and that by the time they reach middle age women may have been wives to a dozen or more men in succession. A man who does this does not have to be rich: he may choose a beautiful young widow or divorcée from among the women of the poorer classes who will consent to become his wife for a small dowry and, when he divorces her, he need not give her more than double that sum to maintain her during her ensuing *eddeh*. Such conduct is, however, generally regarded as disgraceful and few parents in the middle or upper classes will allow their daughter to marry a man who has already divorced many times.

6 — The Big Problem of Obesity

Translation

On Right: "Before marriage...like a branch of a Maringa tree."

On Left: "After marriage...like the trunk of a palm tree."

In Arabic, when you liken a woman to a branch of a Maringa tree, it means that her physique is thin. When you liken her to the trunk of a tree, it means that she is fat.

Culture

Up until recently, Arab men favored full figured women. Thin women would do anything to gain weight in order to get married. Lately, things have changed: the taste has started to lean towards thin women.

Skinny girls have traditionally done whatever they can to gain weight. Psychological disorders of compulsive weight-loss such as anorexia are virtually unknown in the Arab world. Historically, since the Ottoman Empire and even before, men in the Middle East as a whole have preferred heavy-set women. They have looked towards heavy-set women as being taken care of by a prosperous family—fat being a sign of a life of affluence and leisure and skinniness signifying a hard life and poverty. Along with a generous frame, an ideal beauty would have fair skin, a further sign of a leisured life spent indoors, away from the tanning sun. In addition, a full figure was taken as a sign of fertility and suitability for childbearing.

A brief survey of Western art will quickly reveal that similar tastes reigned for much of history, for much the same reason. However, Western tastes have altered over the past century and skinny body types have become the general ideal. With the recent globalization of pop culture, western ideals have been gaining influence in Arab countries, and tastes are beginning to shift there too, but women who conform to western notions of skinniness are considered unhealthily thin. Such a woman visiting her traditional Arab friends and family may well find herself being actively fattened to restore her to what they perceive as a healthy figure.

In addition to Western cultural pressure, many Arab governments and other official health authorities have encouraged people to lose weight to combat the adverse effects of obesity, just as governments around the world have. Arab cuisine's reliance on clarified butter, in particular, has become the target of the government's concern. Fattening foods, though, are a deeply ingrained part of traditional Arab food culture. Every special occasion in Arab culture is marked with special foods: for example, *Qataif*, a popular dessert of Turkish origin, is special to Ramadan and is not to be found during the rest of the year;

and the *Eid* festivities is celebrated with extraordinarily heavy baked cookies and especially heavy meat stew.

Still, Arab men tend to prefer a fuller figure than is typical in the West. Arabs who come to America are doubly shocked by the extreme skinniness valorized by Western beauty ideals on the one hand, and by the extreme obesity generated by Americans' love of processed foods. The traditional Arab farming practices, though they have undergone some changes in recent decades, place much more emphasis on natural processes and small production, in contrast to Western, industrialized farming—the current Western fashion for organic farming is simply the traditional, standard method in the Arab world. Furthermore, Arab farming practices produce leaner animals. The American habit of breeding fat animals and then being forced to trim the fat from the meat before consumption was, until a few decades ago, unknown to the Arab world.

As satellite media and the Internet hasten the Americanization of Arab culture and western farming practices make inroads, the Arab tastes in food, beauty—and everything else—are in the process of undergoing major changes.

In an arranged marriage—the most common type of marriage in the Arab world—it is the mother who selects a bride for her son. Almost universally, these mothers are loath to choose a girl who is too lean or skinny. Aspiring brides (and their families) are aware of this, and seek to "flesh-out" too-slim girls with pillows and padding. Accordingly, the groom's mother will attempt, as inconspicuously as she can, to inspect these brides-to-be for anything unnatural—taking every chance she can to hug, stroke, grasp, squeeze and brush against these girls when she meets them.

What is the biggest obstacle to women driving?

Right frame: "Before Marriage"- *Left frame*: "After Marriage"

Translation

[*Both drinks are labeled:* Diet]

Culture

Arab families—and especially Gulf families—usually dine from one giant, centrally set platter. The platter will hold the main course, which typically consists of rice, chicken or meat, and stew or vegetables—if and only if the vegetables were cooked with the meat.

☪ In some Arab countries, especially the Gulf countries, people enjoy sitting on the floor while they eat instead of using tables and chairs. Some people use very low tables, called *tublya*, which can be reached while sitting on the floor.

In Arab countries, the most important meal of the day is lunch, which is eaten around one – four P.M. Visitors are expected to bring a gift of food if invited for a meal in Arab household. You will also take part in the preparing and serving of the meal. You will be offered more food than you can eat, and you should leave some food on the plate after you are finished, as it shows you are full and satisfied. In some Arab countries, using your fingers to eat is favored over using a knife and fork. Spoons are used for soup or rice or other foods cannot be eaten with the fingers. After eating, it is not unusual for the hostess and female guests to fight over who will do the dishes, while the men sit and wait for tea or coffee.

☪ It is sometimes said that Arabs prefer to eat from one plate, but this is not quite true. Eating from a single plate is very traditional for a number of reasons: Firstly, when people are poor they are less likely to have plenty of crockery, and when eating from the same plate, the spoon is usually replaced by a piece of bread to avoid contaminating the whole plate. Secondly, there is a particular etiquette, which means that people will end up eating less, which is an important consideration if there is not so much food to go round. Thirdly, God is said to bless smaller quantities, and by sharing the meal, God's blessing will make it more satisfying. Fourthly, many people do not eat their main meal at home, so that, although the meal will be cooked at home, it will be taken to the work place where it will probably be shared, so that a single dish is the most practical way of transport. Fifthly, the Arab host wants to offer his guest more than he can eat, and this may only be possible by showing the food for the whole company on one dish. Finally, the traditional way of killing an enemy was by poison, so that sharing food was a way of reassuring guests that the food was safe. The etiquette is based on advice of the Prophet to eat with right hand and to eat only what is closest to you. It is also considered polite not to be the last person eating, so that most people will eat quickly and stop quite early to avoid being the last. This etiquette ensures a certain fairness and that eaters will probably stop before they would otherwise, while the Prophet's comments show that the tradition goes back beyond Islam.

As these reasons indicate, though, eating from one plate is rooted in not having much food to go around and involves a fairly elaborate etiquette, so that eating from separate plates is a sign of greater prosperity and is more relaxed, and the diner is less like to finish his or her meal feeling hungry. Most people therefore prefer it, if it is possible.

Translation

On the box: Pizza
On the paper: Diet

Language

The Arabic word for diet is "regime," taken from the French.

Translation

"Before marriage"
"After marriage"

Culture

It is noticeable in the Arab world that men lose weight, sometimes dramatically, later in their marriage, while the opposite occurs for women. If an Arab man is asked why this happens he will claim depression suppresses his appetite. Married men may have many health complications — high blood pressure, diabetes — while most women will not be subject to such disease, as they are able to vent their stress to relatives and children. When men have gripes they will keep them to themselves to maintain dignity. Like the West, women tend to outlive their husbands, sometimes by a long time.

Usually fat people who are made fun of are married, with overweight single people off limits.

A sure-fire way to get a laugh from an Arab audience is to show a fat woman with an extremely skinny husband.

Translation

Title: Old-Time caricature
Man: "The school textbook is mistaken; not all dinosaurs are extinct."

Language

This is another cartoon that pokes fun at fat people by referring to this fat woman as a dinosaur. In English, calling someone a dinosaur implies that they are old, but in Arabic, this name implies that they are big or fat. The contrast between a skinny husband and a fat wife is common material for Arabic cartoons

Translation

Title: Let's forget
Scrawled upon dresser, from right to left: "Star of Arabs"; "Only you, Diana"
"How is the diet going with you?"
"I quit since I saw that you admired Diana Karazon so much."

Culture

In her right hand, the lapsed-dieter wife bears what, in the West, is known as a Turkish coffee pot, or a *cezve*. In the

Arab world, the implement is employed in scenarios very similar to that depicted in the cartoon: a woman will use the cezve to brew her husband his after-work cup of coffee, which she'll bring to him on a tray as he lounges in bed, watching TV, browsing the newspaper or enjoying a cigarette.

The coffee ("*kahweh*"- This is the name of the beverage) is made very strong, and without sugar or milk. The coffee-cup (which is called *fingan*) is small, generally holding not quite an ounce and a half of liquid. It is of porcelain. In preparing the coffee, the water is first made to boil, the coffee (freshly roasted and pounded) is then put in, and stirred, after which the pot is again placed on the fire, once or twice, until the coffee begins to simmer, when it is taken off, and its contents are poured out into the cups while the surface is yet creamy. Arabs are excessively fond of pure and strong coffee thus prepared, and very seldom add sugar to it (though some do so when they are unwell), and never milk or cream; but a little cardamom-seed is often added to it.

☪ In Arab homes there are always two sets of cutlery, one is for the family's personal use, while the more expensive set is reserved for guests.

☪ Diana Karazon is a Jordanian pop music sensation. After bursting onto the scene with her victory in the Arab "Pop Idol," Karazon did gain a sizeable amount of weight—thus, the wife's implication that, in adoring Diana, he therefore also adores generously voluptuous, euphemistically "big-boned" women.

Translation

Ratio and proportionality

🧔 The couple on the left is shopping for a piece of clothing that is evidently stylish, colorful and expensive. A Western reader might find some humor in the idea of the woman poring over clothes when she is totally covered, but this would not seem at all strange or incongruous to an Arab reader, for whom the humor lies in the mismatch of husband and wife, and the man's sticker shock.

Culture

The phrase *nisba wa tanasub* (ratio and proportionality) comes from the title of a classic work of Arabic geometry by Ahmed Ibn Yusuf (d. 912 CE) and the cartoon uses it to make fun of the incongruities shown by these couples.

The Arab love of symmetry, balance and matching goes far beyond just artistic considerations and affects their general approach to life, so that the person you marry must match you, while the clothes you wear should match each other. Arabs pay great attention to coordinating their items of dress, and Arab men will put thought into details of their outfit that might be considered fussy or effeminate by Western men. Such attention to detail extends to cars, houses, decoration in general, in a style that can seem kitsch to Western eyes.

Translation

Rising inflation in Saudi Arabia

Language

The world inflation also means enlargement or exapansion in Arabic.

Culture

Traditionally Arab men have been slim, walking everywhere, with little meat in the diet, and what there is very lean. With the introduction of fast food, greater wealth leading to a diet with more meat, fat and rice, less physical activity, driving rather than walking and a generally sedentary lifestyle, men have started to become significantly fatter. The same factors affect women to a large extent, though if a woman wants to lose weight her husband is likely to tell her to do more chores around the house.

7 — Domestic Violence

Translation

Headlines: "British study: Marriage to two women increases men's lifespan by 12%."

Culture

The wife here is taking preemptive action at the possibility of her husband's taking a second wife. A fellow-wife is called *dorrah*, and their squabbles are proverbial and often talked about. Indeed the root of the word *dorrah* means damage or harm.

It is perhaps natural to assume that when two wives share the affection and attentions of the same man, they will not always be on friendly terms with each other. Islam therefore enjoins a husband who has two or more wives to be strictly impartial to them in every respect,[18] but compliance with its dictates in this matter is rare.

☪ Domestic violence can turn deadly very quickly in Arab countries because many Arabs are stubborn, proud, and have short fuses. Instead of pacifying the situation, Arabs will usually irritate their partner to a point of no return. Unlike men, women generally will not resort to lethal force until they are pushed that little bit further.

The victims of domestic violence are generally the focus of the blame, with judges being asked to consider what provoked the killer to pull the trigger or use whatever form of deadly force came to hand. In all cases, there is a tendency to consider the circumstances of the crime as a whole, rather than focusing exclusively on the act of murder, and to view them in the light of tradition and religion. In certain countries such as Egypt, women have less respect for their husbands[19] and the stereotypical wife is more demanding and less submissive than in some other countries. Wives may deliberately goad their husbands, daring to use a deadly weapon, humiliating them in front of peers, or physically assaulting them. Arab men are still Arab men and hold their dignity high, and when this is impugned they can

---

[18] "Ye are never able to be fair and just as between women, even if it is your ardent desire: But turn not away (from a woman) altogether, so as to leave her (as it were) hanging (in the air). If ye come to a friendly understanding, and practice self-restraint, Allah is Oft-forgiving, Most Merciful." Al-Qur'an, 004.129 (*An-Nisa* [The Women]).

[19] See the last cartoon in "2 — Social Life," p.52.

quickly lose their temper and commit a crime. Many of these situations occur because neither party will back down and results in a crime of passion rather than a premeditated murder. They are most often started by suspicions of infidelity: either of extramarital affairs or a desire to marry another woman.

☪ Arabs have vastly different relationships to guns depending on where they live. In metropolitan and suburban areas such as that in the cartoon, having gun in the house is not at all prevalent. It is difficult to obtain a gun license, to do so one must be over 21, have a clean criminal record, own property, and provide proof that one is seriously threatened. Therefore, most of those who legaly can have guns are people like jewelery store owners, bank tellers, and money-exchange bureau workers who fear robbery, business people carrying large somes of money who fear mugging, farmers who must be able to defend their livestock from rustling or from predators, or celebrities in fear of assault from crazed fans. Police, understandably, are allowed permits without such close scrutiny. Furthermore, one must account for live ammunition that one buys and permits must be renewed every year. Given the barren environment of much of the Arab world, people applying for a gun for "hunting" are widely ridiculed and suspected. Amongst the reasons why a license might be revoked, beyond falling short of the necessary requirements, are: being caught at a wedding with a gun (this policy is meant to stamp out the hideously dangerous practice of firing into the air at the start of a wedding procession); entering a casino, bar, or nightclub with a gun (to prevent people using them in alcohol fueled rages; being diagnosed with a serious mental disorder (for obvious reasons).

Once the gun is procured though, gun safety is generally lax by western standards; rather than locked gun cabinets, it is generally thought sufficient to hide a gun under a cloth in a closet. Such precautions clearly were inadequate for the husband in the cartoon. Though both men and women who meet the necessary standard can acquire a gun, the historical means by which women commit murder tend towards means like rat poison and kitchen knifes.

There are cases when someone can lose his license to carry a gun, in Syria you lose it if you file for bankruptcy

How wives handle a mistress or, in most cases, a second wife

In Arab culture, Arab women handle their husband's infidelity in a particular way. Arab men do not cheat on their wives as often as men in other cultures do. They are restricted by religious beliefs that consider infidelity one of the biggest sins. The Qur'an requires that when one party accuses another party of adultery, the accuser must be able to provide four witnesses to corroborate these claims. If the accuser cannot corroborate his claims with witnesses, then he will receive a punishment of eighty lashes and he will be forever unable to give testimony that is considered valid by the authorities.

Some adulterers turn themselves over to the authorities, admitting their own adulteries in an attempt to be punished on Earth in order to avoid God's more severe punishment in the hereafter. You may hear about the stoning of women who commit adultery taking place in Muslim countries because it is the designated punishment for adultery in the Qur'an. This is not completely accurate. In the Qur'an, the punishment for adultery is one hundred lashes witnessed by believers. In fact, all punishments described in the Qur'an must be witnessed by believers, in order to deter future transgressions. Once someone has been found to have committed adultery, that person is only able to marry others who have also committed adultery.

Divorce is allowed in Islam, as is having more than one wife. So if a man feels a need to have a relationship outside marriage, usually he will think about the religious consequences of his act. There is a lawful and Islamic way for him to have another woman in his life and, in the meantime, he should not expose himself to God's wrath: since it is not socially acceptable to have another woman while you are married, he can satisfy his needs by marrying that woman. The first wife may or may not approve of his second marriage and she has a right, based on the grounds of his marrying another woman, to ask for a divorce. If she does not know about his second marriage and then finds out, her reaction will be similar to that of a Western woman in an established marriage who discovers her husband has been unfaithful. With an Arab woman, the only difference is that she has little recourse since her husband's action is technically lawful. After Arab women find their husband has married another wife or committed adultery, they typically seek help from their family, including staying with their parents. Children involved in a domestic dispute usually take the side of the mother if they are old enough to understand. This is because Arab children are typically closer to their mother because fathers are seen as disciplinary, and are not home as much as mothers are.

☪ Though Islamic law holds that men in polygamous arrangements should treat their wives equally, in practice one wife generally holds a preferred status and is known as "the great lady." These women hold authority over their rivals and outwardly, at least, are respected and honored by their rivals. Married men negotiating further marriages often find that protective fathers or their prospective brides will demand assurances that earlier wives will either be made subordinate to the new or divorced, but generally the first wife is the one who holds the primary position. Fellow-wives, known as *durrah*s, naturally tend to come into conflict with one another, and men of sufficient means typically try to provide each of their wives with either individual households or at least suites of rooms that may be separated and function independently from those of the other wives.

"Great lady" status is not fixed, and men may often alter the position held by their wives. An enticing new wife may often displace her rivals for a time, but in the long run kind and dutiful wives are more likely to maintain a lasting hold on the place of honor than are their beautiful but tempestuous rivals. One notable exception to this general rule is when a long-favored and loving wife is unable to produce children and a rival bears her husband heirs, as in the example of Abraham's relationship with his original chief wife Sarah and Hagar. The man in such a situation often finds that his love for his children elevates their mother to the chief position amongst his wives, whatever the women's personal virtues.

☪ It is not very unusual for an Arab wife to look for a second wife for her husband. The most common reason for doing so is the discovery of her own infertility when her husband wants a child. Another reason would involve a wife gravely insulting her husband such that he loses his dignity among his peers or social circle; the search for a second wife would then serve as a pre-emptive action (i.e. to avoid divorce) in which her family would also cover all of the expenses associated with obtaining the second wife, including the dowry. The wife's family would be held accountable and blamed for the wife's actions, rather than she alone. Finding a second wife would be an indication of the wife's repentance, an apology, and a means for her husband to regain the dignity he had lost.

Translation

Title: Sudden inspection.
On the bag: "First aid."

☪ Arab women usually adopt an assertive and determined persona when investigating what they suspect to be their husband's infidelity. Accusations would be flying in a "shoot first, ask questions later" manner, and the men, even if innocent, will feel accordingly intimidated. This is the one arena in which Arab women take on a completely different attitude.

☪ The broom is the preferred disciplinary tool of Arab households. Arab women will threaten to break the broom handle on the head of misbehaving children.

Culture

Arab women are very aggressive in investigating any potential spousal infidelity, and because of the infiltration of cell phones and other electronic devices, these would logically be the first place to look for any suspicious emails or numbers. Other websites such as facebook are also a good place for the suspicious to visit for clues. So many divorces have occurred due to facebook infidelity that a fatwah was issued to prohibit muslims from using it (not to engage in adulterous behavior; since that is already prohibited).

☪ The Indonesian maid in the background is a fixture in many Gulf Arab households, because Indonesia is the only poor Muslim nation in Southeast Asia, and they are preferred workers because of their mild manners and religious backgrounds.

Usually a wily maid will play on both sides of such disputes, instigating her female employer and confirming her suspicions while also doing the same with the man, showing sympathy toward the unfair treatment he is receiving from his wife. The maid often will also be the first person a wife will question regarding her husband's behavior and whether or not she noticed anything untoward. Playing such a role can be lucrative for the maid since half of a warring couple will obtain his or her information about the other half from her; of course she will be amply compensated, but this role requires the maid to be highly circumspect, as eventually both parties will reconcile and could blame the whole episode on the maid.

☪ In many Arab households, pictures of the man of the house are prominently framed and display on the wall as this husband's picture above (in better times), since Islam does not permit the depiction of certain subjects. This being the case, portraits of the family will usually decorate the walls instead of paintings or statues.

Let's imagine that the woman above found damaging evidence in her husband's blackberry or flip camera, the following cartoon shows how a woman in a similar situation might react.

Translation

Title: Lewinsky-Clinton in Jordan

Screaming woman [reacting to her husband's infidelity]: "You liar! You cheater! You father of earrings! Go to her! Go to her! Divorce me!"

Man with belt in his hand [her husband]: "Woman! Enough already! Behave yourself! You scandalize us because of someone who is a home wrecker and liar."

Man with gun [brother of the screaming woman]: "By God, even if you are the mayor, I will drag you to the police station and court!"

Man with beanie [to brother of home-wrecker]: "Yes, a home-wrecker and a liar. Shoot her and don't make the situation worse."

Child calling downstairs: "Muhammad, come upstairs and take a look at what's going on!"

☪ The cinder block held by the bald man is commonly to be found in fights, as is the belt which the husband wields. Guns, though frequently brandished during a dispute, are infrequently fired, so the crowd is unlikely to be fazed.

Language

The wife calls her cheating husband a "father of ear-rings," which has the same connotation as "skirt-chaser."

"Even if you are the mayor, I will drag you to the police station and court" indicates that the wife's brother will instigate the divorce process, even if her husband is well-connected.

"Sousa" is a woodworm; in other words, a home-wrecker.

Culture

A domestic dispute in the Arab world may be no less chaotic and public than an American political sex scandal. A woman with a significant greivance, particularly in the lower- and middle-class, will quarrel loudly with her husband, which attracts the attention of family and neighbors, who participate in the fight by restraining and attempting to pacify the angry spouses and vengeful brothers-in-law. Actual violence is uncommon, but the threat is always present. A husband will do his best to keep his wife quiet, even to the point of beating her, in order to avoid public confrontation and humiliation. The fight can go on for hours, and usually ends when one of the quarrelers is taken away to the house of a brother or neighbor.

☪ The woman holding her face in her hands is hiding her face out of shame—her parents' fight might compromise her family's reputation. Arab people prefer to handle family issues in private and maintain a composed public image. Because the community is close-knit, word of a public dispute is guaranteed to spread to people who haven't witnessed it.

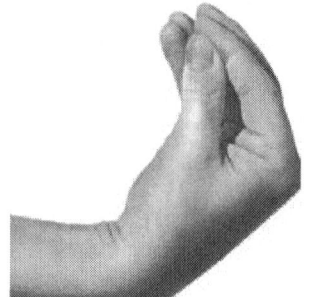

Hand gestures in disputes

Notice that the wife is throwing out her arms, her index fingers pointing outwards, in the middle of a traditional gesture of distraught women. A woman might make this motion, accompanied by a scream or lamentation, upon hearing the shocking news of infidelity or a death in the family.

Meanwhile, both the husband and the wife's brother have threateningly formed a circle between their thumbs and index fingers, with the three remaining fingers extended.

In the foreground, the bald man raises a single finger, another threatening hand gesture, while the man in the beanie restraining him has brought the tips of all the fingers on his right hand together.

☪ Two of these handgestures are seen both in Arab and American culture.

The first gesture (*upper right*) is similar to an Italian gesture, involving bringing the fingers together at their tips, but rather than "weighing" the hand up and down, the Arab version rocks from the wrist in slow motion. This indicates "Calm down" or "Wait and see what I'll do."

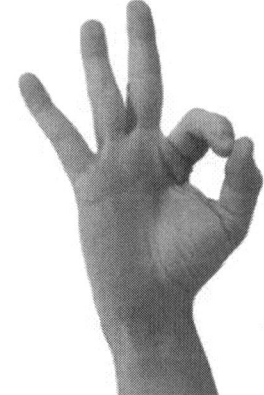

The other looks like what Americans think of as "A-OK" (*lower right*). The forefinger and thumb form a circle while the other fingers stick out. The Arab version is formed the same way, but involves a rocking of the hand, as if shaking your finger at someone. Its meaning is similarly "Wait until I get my hands on you" and is more threatening.

☪A related sign, with a closed fist moving backward and forward, while the opposite hand holds the wrist, has similar meaning to the American "F— you" (where an "upper-cut" movement with one arm while the other moves into the crook of the elbow) or the raised middle finger,

Culture

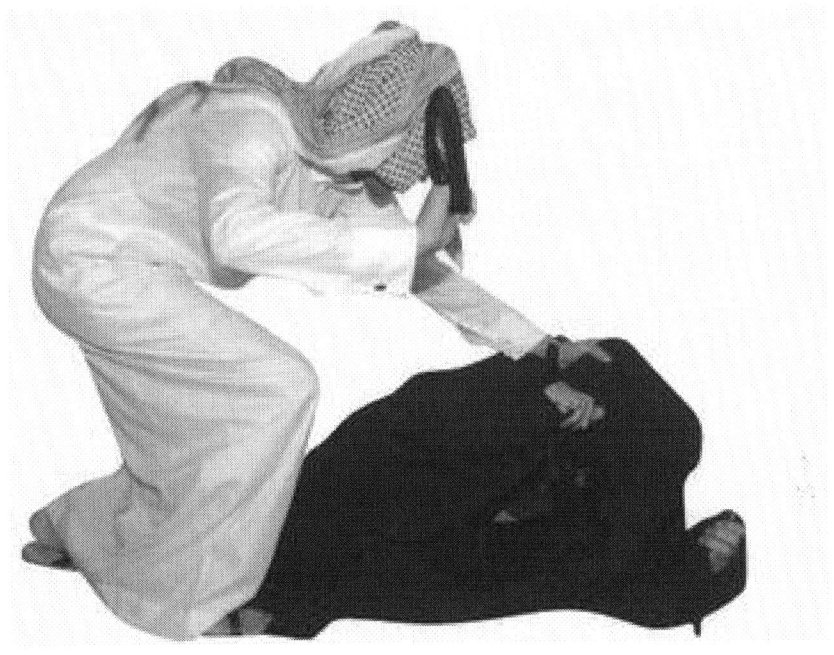

Domestic violence is a common issue, and the reactions it generates sadly are sometimes extreme. Sometimes husbands justify violence against their wives through a misinterpretation of a verse in the Qur'an: "As to those women on whose part ye fear disloyalty and ill-conduct, admonish them (first), (Next), refuse to share their beds, (And last) beat them (lightly); but if they return to obedience, seek not against them Means (of annoyance): For Allah is Most High, great (above you all). (Chapter 4, verse 34).

Beating is most likely to be directed toward the wife. Sisters and mothers are seldom victims of domestic violence.

An Arab will not hit someone with a shoe, preferring to use a more flexible instrument such as a sandal or flip-flop—which also has a clear sound though not especially painful, although the wife might react as though it were. In extreme circumstances a husband may physically attack his wife with a wooden bathroom sandal, which is very insulting symbolically as well as painful. A man who beats his wife, and the wife herself, are usually young and often uneducated; beatings would occur in the early years of the marriage, as age confers respect. This practice is contingent upon the wife's reaction to the first beating. If she does not object physicallyand draw boundaries, it is likely that her husband will feel little compunction against beating her. Conversely, if she responds more pugnaciously, he may be more averse to relying on physical violence. Beatings are typically short-lived, as people will usually interfere and separate the couple, after which a reconciliation will ensue. As the women are fairly well-covered and not brutally stricken, there are rarely serious injuries.

Between old husbands and wives, financial disagreements are a leading cause of domestic violence.

Translation

On TV: "Breaking News"

"Hurricane Gunu"

Culture

Arab men can be intimidated by their wives as much as men anywhere else.

 For many Arabs, the only place that they will see attractive women is on TV, which is why their standard for beauty can seem to be less demanding than in the West.

Culture

Some think that Arab women as put upon. This is not the case for the majority. The truth is that they are very vocal especially to any hints of their husband's infidelity. Most Arab wives are very suspicious of their husband spending time in front of their computer, having read in the news about men cheating. While this wife prepares to attack her lovestruck husband, the wife in the second cartoon has already logged her husband out of his love-chat.

☪ The Internet has a bad reputation in the Arab world, and many attribute society's ills to it, seeing it as a source of temptation and even cheating. Governments view it negatively too, though usually because they can no longer control people's access to information.

Translation

(*From right to left*)
"With the first wife"
"With the second wife"

Culture

Having a second wife in the Arab world is like having a trophy wife in the West. After a man has established himself financially and his wife's looks have faded, he may decide to marry a younger and often prettier wife.

Translation

Title: Domestic Violence
On boxing ring: "The houses of some."

Culture

Though it is undeniable that domestic violence occurs in many Arab households, its place should not be exaggerated; it is generally accepted that abuse is wrong, but there are few concerted efforts to control or reduce it at a national level. Much of the violence is perpetrated by husbands on their wives, but women—or the brothers of a young woman acting against their sister's husband—can also be the abusers and children are frequently the victims. Most often, male heads of households are the abusers in their role as the enforcers of discipline; male sons and hired female servants are next most likely to inflict physical punishment. Some prevalent forms of physical abuse include cudgeling, hair-pulling, and branding with cooking utensils (referred to as "ironing with cutlery"). Verbal abuse can include a variety of execrations and threats, particularly directed by parents against daughters. Girls might be threatened with being taken out of school to do maid's duty and save the expense of maintaining a servant, abused as unworthy even of their share of the family's meals, or disparaged for having been born female. Sexual abuse by fathers against daughters, however, is virtually unknown.

Children can be punished for a variety of reasons, as in all countries, but most prominent in Arab countries include inattention or disrespect to elders, failure to study, excessive television-watching, meddling in parents' belongings, disruptive play, and noise-making while the father is trying to sleep. Siblings do not usually fight while they are still living in their parents' house, but sometimes disputes will occur over inheritance. Generally speaking, Arab family ties are very strong, and due to religious beliefs, children will give great respect to their parents; occasionally grown sons have been known, whether alone or in collaboration with their mothers, to abuse their aging fathers, but crimes committed by a child towards his parents, are very strongly looked down upon and the subject of media coverage throughout the Arab country.

7 — Domestic Violence

Translation

On the sign: "STOP."

[N.B. In all Arab countries, the traffic signs are the same shapes as those in the United States, not like the circular sign in this cartoon.]

Translation

Man lying down: "In other words, I can throw you out on the streets and disown you. I'm not your father and I don't know you, BUT I will create mechanisms to lessen your suffering."

[N.B. The object next to the baby bottle is a disciplinary device.]

Culture

This cartoon plays on the way some Arab governments treat their people by considering them burdens and their desire to abandon its people while creating measures that barely meet their minimum needs.

In Arab countries, it is not uncommon to see a family of limited means with a large number of children. In this cartoon, the man does not even have a mattress to sleep on, but he has five children. Family planning was tried, unsuccessfully, in many Arab countries because contraception and other means of preventing unwanted pregnancies run counter to the values of their culture and religion. Culturally, for many, the more children a family had, especially boys, the more clout that family would have. It is very important to perpetuate the family name. Within a poorer household, more children mean for more workers, and greater sources of income for the whole family. Religiously, people rely on God to help provide for their families, citing the Qur'an's warning that they should not kill live children out of fear of poverty, because God would provide sustenance for both the parents and their children. This may be a misunderstanding of the verse, however, for the promise does not necessarily encourage people to continue having children they are not entirely able to afford. There was a fatwah issued that advised people against using contraception, and other religious leaders discouraged family planning, suggesting that such practices go against the will of God. Large families are even seen as a positive good for Islam; Muslims believe that Muhammad will take pride in the number of faithful Muslims who populate, have populated, and will populate the earth and having big families gives him an ever greater number of which to boast on Judgment Day. Beyond these urging of devotion, of course, baser urgings contribute, too, to population growth; poorer families have little access to entertainment outside of the home, and the only source of entertainment is the time spent with spouses. This may also lead to unwanted pregnancies, especially when these poorer families are not using contraceptives.

In a large country like Egypt, the population increases by about a million each year, as explained both the custom of families who choose to have large numbers of children and the lack of adequate family planning for those who don't. This explosion in the population has led to the fairly new phenomenon of Street Children. These are children who cannot be taken care of by their families and whose families have cast them away as a result. Often these children can be found begging, stealing, and engaging in other illegal activities instead of being in school and learning.

The Chinese practice of limiting each family to one child was considered but ruled out for religious reasons.

☪ The device, in the picture, with the handle and two prongs is used to hold a child's feet together so that the parent can hit the soles of their feet when the child is being punished.

☪ The latitude given to parents in their children's discipline can be unfortunately taken advantage of, with, for example, an addict father forcing his children to beg to support his expensive habits.

Translation

"If I swear to you from today until tomorrow that the fire was from an electrical short circuit, you won't believe me."

Culture

Burning a meal would be justifiable reason for domestic violence, especially among the poorer classes. For poorer people a meal can represent quite a lot of money, and almost all cooking is done in the home. If the husband does not like a meal or is very angry, he can use the food as a gesture either throwing it in in the garbage or out in the street.

☪ Often times, corrupt government employees hide evidence of their misappropriation of goods by intentionally setting the storage place for such goods on fire,

claiming that those fires are the result of electrical short circuiting, in an attempt to account for the loss without being found out. Because of the lack of forensic experts to determine the real cause of these fires, these ploys are often successful. There are set times during the year when governments will take inventory of their goods, and it is during this time that the amount of fires will increase. This season is referred to as "The Season of Short Circuit Fires." In this cartoon, the housewife who is obviously responsible for burning their meal blames her inattentiveness to the food on an electrical short circuit fire in order to escape the anger of her husband.

Translation

The oval face shape of the woman in the last cartoon is characteristic of Egyptian women, whereas the pear-shaped face of the woman in this cartoon is more common in Saudi Arabia.

Culture

This cartoon shows the imprint of a hand on a woman's mouth who has been slapped for excessive talking.

☪ In Arab culture there is a phenomenon of the males being taciturn after many years of marriage when in the presence of their wives and other couples. At the beginning of a marriage, the man would speak much more in these same circumstances. Arabs have the proverb "If talk were of silver, silence is of gold," and in general Arab society values taciturnity in women. However, women start to be talkative and outspoken at a point during their marriages, and the ratio of talk to silence by a man and woman gradually reverses as a young couple ages.

Translation

Title: It happens these days

From outside the panel: Would you like to eat something, my beloved?

Gentleman: Give me an orange.

Voice off (as orange hits his face): Take it!

Language

"It happens these days" means "believe it or not," since whatever is referred to never happened in the old days, usually indicating a change for the worse.

Culture

This cartoon records the change in gender roles and expectations playing out within Arab households under the influence of the West and the women's movement. Whereas a husband would once have expected to be waited on dutifully by a meek and subservient wife, the woman heard (but not shown) in this cartoon has clearly had enough of being told to fetch things and is in a rebellious mood.

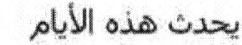

Translation

Title: She who loves her husband also loves his cat.

Culture

This woman is taking her revenge of her husband out on his cat. The cat is the favored animal in an Arab household, while dogs are not as favored.

Cruelty to animals is widespread in the Arab world. Only some Arab countries have animal welfare organizations like our Humane Society or ASPCA, and those organizations that do exist have only a limited effect. Many Arab streets are crowded with donkeys, horses, and mules pulling heavy carts for merchants and farmers.

The mistreatment of these animals is made plain by the open wounds on their backs and legs, and the flies that follow them. Poor young children are often seen mistreating animals in the streets. As pointed out earlier in the book, the Egyptian Zoo lost its membership to the International Association of Zoos because of mistreatment of zoo animals.

7 — Domestic Violence

Translation
Groom: My favorite painting

Culture
Some advice Arab men receive on their wedding night or their first day of marriage is to establish "who's the boss" (assert his dominance). In this cartoon, the groom shows his bride a picture of a Stone Age couple and implies that this is how he foresees their lifestyle. Some Arab husbands slaughter a cat on the wedding night in front of their wives to assert their position.

The slaughtering of the cat is a thing of the past, but the idea is still around and mentioned in jest, including in a humorous songs.

Translation
Title: The assault on servants
Large woman: Don't let her stay one more minute in the house. Send her packing immediately, and don't pay her salary. She saw me [powerless/humble] and weak. She threatened that she would show me the stars at noon. oh my nose, oh my cheek, oh my molars, oh!

For an Arab reader the funny part of this cartoon is the woman describing herself as [powerless/humble] and weak while she is fat, big, and strong.

Culture
Many maids in Arab countries suffer physical abuse from their employers, and these women, generally immigrants from Southeast Asia or Africa, have few means to protect themselves. Occasionally, an exceptionally scandalous incident will prompt maids' home countries to prevent their citizens from

taking domestic service jobs in a country, but the income is sorely missed by the impoverished girls of such countries and the bans are much resented and rarely effective. Governments can do their own economies great harm by such bans; according to recent figures, immigrant maids send around 1 1/3 billion USD annually from Saudi Arabia home to Indonesia. Therefore, countries increasingly elect to protect their citizens not with draconian bans but rather by negotiating for basic legal protections. For example, Indonesian maids now have the legal right, in Saudi Arabia, to a private cell phone with which they can call for help and are visited by embassy officials whose task it is to ensure that their living conditions are humane.

The numbers of women involved is enormous: in 2009, 240,000 women entered Saudi Arabia from Indonesia alone, and there are over one million foreign maids now working in the country. Arabs themselves are often conflicted about the growing popularity of hired help, and many men, especially, can rejoice when maids are barred from immigrating. Though they enjoy the luxury of a maid's service, maids are also resented for encouraging Arab wives to sit lazily around the house and grow fat. Also, maids are widely mistrusted, being assumed to be the dregs of the country they left. For each incident of violence against maids, employers are keen to point out thefts, abuses, and other wrongdoings committed by maids.

In this cartoon titled, "Men Snatcher," a jealous first wife throttles a woman who has been trying, literally, to net her husband. For some women approaching what they perceive as the end of their marriageable years, it is preferable to be a man's second wife that to live as a spinster. For them, polygamy is the solution to the scarcity of eligible bachelors. The cartoon is set in a shopping mall because even in a country as conservative as Saudi Arabia, it is still considered acceptable for an unaccompanied lady to go there, making it a good environment for a manhunt.

Translation

Title: Old-time Caricature: Husband Killings
Man: "We have been married for twenty-five years, which means that the statute of limitations has expired."

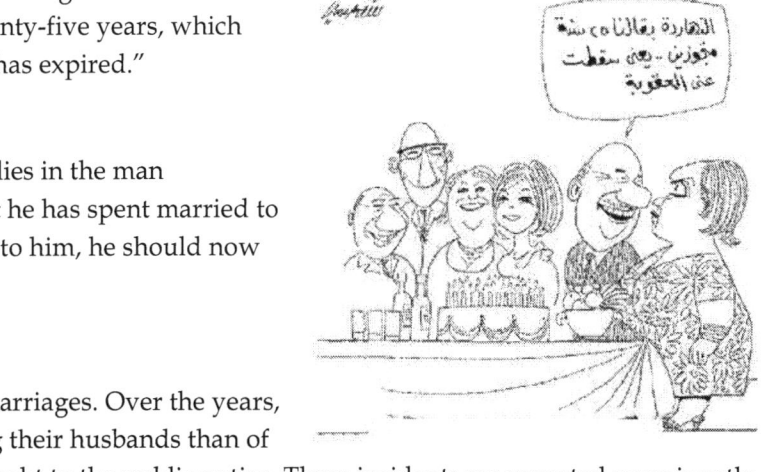

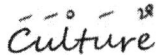 In this cartoon, the humor lies in the man comparing the twenty-five years that he has spent married to his wife to a punishment. According to him, he should now be relieved of this burden.

Culture

Many people are unhappy in their marriages. Over the years, many more incidents of wives killing their husbands than of husbands killing their wives are brought to the public notice. These incidents are reported prominently by the Arab media. When Arab women resort to violence, it is often gruesome and extreme. If they are seeking to end a long cycle of abuse, they often have to make sure that they do kill their husband, and may have relatively limited means at their disposal, but they will have time to plan. Some wives even gain notoriety for their unique murder methods, earning the sobriquet of their murder weapon or method, e.g., Saneya Anbouba or "gas-cylinder" Saneya.

8 – Underage Marriage

Translation

Shadow of man counting cash, with finger on mouth: "Hush"

Girl: "Father, where am I going? Amusement park?"

Paper in hand: "Marriage certificate"

Under title: "8 years old"

Culture

Many fathers are willing to give away their daughters in marriage as a business transaction, taking money for their blessing, rather than behaving as a proud and devoted parent. Although some fathers will take money for their daughters, because of low socio-economic status or the need to pay off debt, many are purely avaricious, intending to use the money for their own selfish purposes, such as buying a car. It is possible for other family members to voice their disapproval of an underage marriage, but the father of an underage daughter who is engaged has the power to veto the rest of the family — his word is final. One way in which family members might express their disapproval more proactively is by informing authorities that can check into the legality of the marriage and the consent of the young daughter. If the marriage is legal and the child expresses her consent to the suspicious authorities (which can be tacit), the marriage will take place, the underage daughter will be wed, and the father will be paid for his blessing.

It is not uncommon for wealthy Arab men to venture into poorer communities in other Arab countries and seek out families willing to offer their young daughters as wives for money. As opposed to the

United States, in some Arab countries there is no minimum age at which a girl can marry. Many wealthy sheikhs take advantage of these lax regulations and marry young, unknowing and unsuspecting girls.

Underage Marriage

There is no minimum age for marriage in Islam, however most states, following Western practice — or bowing to Western pressure — have enacted laws that set a minimum age which is usually around 18.

Underage marriage is a not wide-spread occurrence in many Arab countries, as Arab society may once have been tolerant of underage marriage on the basis of religion. The source of their acceptance is the story of Prophet Muhammad marrying Aisha ("the Mother of the Believers") when she was nine years old and he was fifty-three, though this story cannot be verified. Pedophelia is considered to be a very serious crime in the Arab world, one punishable by execution. Pedophiles have used marriage as a means of engaging in relationship with girls, sometimes offering large sums of money to poor families for permission to marry their daughters. This problem is exacerbated by, depending on the country, a very low minimum age for marriage or even the absence of a minimum age altogether.

Arab governments are doing their best to intervene in situations like these. There is a push to educate people about the harm of underage marriage by stressing the immorality of such practices as well as the biological damage sexual relations can cause the young girls. In cases of underage marriage, courts will annul marriages or grant divorces to the young women. In a widely publicized case in 2009, an eight year old Yemeni girl was granted a divorce after two months of marriage to a twenty-eight year old man. Because of the absence of clear laws prohibiting the marriage of underage girls, a court in Saudi Arabia refused to annul a marriage of an eight year old girl and a 60 year old man. This prompted the Saudi Arabian Department of Justice to start the process of creating proper legislation on the issue. Often times, underage marriage occurs with the consent of the young girl's family. Now, the government is trying to amend this by requiring, in addition to the approval of the girl's family, the permission of a judge and approval of a medical team affirming that the girl is fit for marriage.

Female Infanticide

Generally, Arab society prefers a male child to a female child. In pre-Islamic Arabia, husbands would bury their newborn females alive, which prompted the Qur'an to address this phenomenon in a very concise but very moving verse. It says, "And God will ask the female infant who had been buried alive ("*mau'udda*") for what wrongdoing was she killed." Nowadays, this practice is long gone. However, there is still a preference for male over female children and, instead of killing a female child, the husband divorces his wife. Tens of thousands of women are divorced annually simply because they have given birth to a female child, though many hide this fact by claiming financial hardship as the reason for filing for divorce.

☪ In some countries in the Arab world, mothers may prefer to have a female child, in the belief that raising a female child would prove easier than raising a male child.

Translation

Title: Underage Marriage

Culture

Many Arab countries, when debating a law that deals with the age limit for girls to marry, must satisfy two parties: feminists and champions of human rights, on the one hand, and Islamic conservatives on the other. Their differences are irreconcilable. When a law, in Jordan, was issued allowing the marriage of girls who are fifteen, the decision was received differently by both parties. The conservatives called it a blessing and legal in Islam, while the female rights activists called it rape. Arab legislators try to walk a thin line to satisfy both sides, but many Arab countries are very conservative and lean towards the side of religious conservatives, seeing nothing wrong with fifteen-year-olds getting married. The law stipulates certain conditions that must be met for a girl who is only fifteen to marry. There must be some special circumstance creating an exception or a need to be married. The exception claimed is that the girl was engaged in an unlawful relationship, resulting in pregnancy out of wedlock, which would relegate a person to lifelong misery in most Arab countries. The condition by which she must marry is if she is raped and becomes pregnant. Then, she must marry her rapist. Rights' activists, naturally, object to this, saying that instead of punishing the rapist you condemn the girl to a life of rape. Proponents of this law point to Sharia law, as it allows women to marry before eighteen as long as they are well developed and mature. Those who are religious dislike the Western tradition of giving women freedom of movement, travel, moving away from family, sexual freedom and abortion, and marrying without the consent of immediate family. They believe that these allowances erode family values.

Translation

Woman: "The girl will be 15 years old tomorrow. What do you think we should give her for her birthday?"

Man: "A groom."

Culture

Fathers are so eager to marry their daughters off as soon as they are old enough to be married. The wives maintain guardianship of their daughters until a certain age, and then guardianship is transferred to the father. Because of some instances wherein daughters have been

married while still underage without the consent of their mothers because of their father's eagerness to marry the daughter off, and thus certain Arab governments have considered enacting laws that leave guardianship of a daughter to her mother until she has reached maturity.

Often, the father's incentive is monetary: especially for poorer families, the prospect of a substantial dowry is an enticing opportunity. (In addition, the daughter's marriage will make it such that the father has one less mouth to feed.) This is not say that rich father's are not likewise eager: in the case of the rich, the monetary incentive may still be present, but it will be of altogether more oblique sort — for example, marrying one's daughter off to a important and profitable business partner.

However, the *mazoon* is a possible impediment to the success of one's plot to marry off one's underage daughter. Thus, it is not uncommon for eager father to present the *mazoon* with a different girl entirely, and claim that *she* - i.e. the older girl – is the one getting married — when in reality, of course, the bride-to-be is the underage girl.

Translation

A man plus a woman of roughly equal age = Unsuitable

An older man plus a young girl = Suitable

The background shows a court ledger

[N.B. the drops from the old man's mouth indicate that he is coughing.]

Culture

A Saudi judge invalidated a marriage between two adults on the grounds that they are not suitable for each other, and in another case, the court affirmed the suitability of a marriage between an adult and a child. The grounds of the first verdict were based on the parties originating from different tribes while the two subjects of the second verdict were from the same tribe. The most important factor in determining the suitability of a marriage is the respective social standing of the two parties. In the aforementioned cases, the marriage between the two adults was deemed unsuitable because one came from a more privileged social environment, whereas the marriage between the older man and the young girl featured families and persons of more comparable social ranking. The first marriage was invalidated by the court because the bride's brothers petitioned to annul the marriage on the grounds of the unsuitability of the man and woman. This can be compared to incidences in the West in which an elderly, wealthy parent is to marry a younger person of more modest means, though the concerns are not purely financial, as even a pairing between a nouveau riche and an established family would be discouraged. In such an instance as here in America, a family member may ask the court to invalidate a marriage on the grounds that it is unsuitable, asserting that one of the persons is not in his or her right mind, thereby protecting their inheritance and preventing any untoward acquisition of the family's resources. Translated into American terms, a marriage between, say, a Boston Brahmin and an illegal immigrant migrant worker could be declared unsuitable, whereas one between the children of two Congressmen would be considered suitable. To a sizable group of Arabs, an older man is respected for his age and is regarded as a blessing to society for his wisdom and experience, so he will generally not be criticized for his actions, including marriage to a young girl.

For those who seek change, nothing is more effective in bringing about reform than the attention of the Western media, which can have far more and more rapid effect than years of local campaigning—witness reform on female circumcision, women drivers and underage marriage. And those who oppose such change denounce the Western media for the same reason.

The group most exasperated by underage marriage is unmarried Arab women who cannot find husbands while older men marry younger girls. However, even males take issue with these incidences of older men marrying younger girls, as older men tend to be wealthier and more able to afford marrying multiple women, which adversely affects the pool of potential wives for younger, less affluent males. People are upset with the judges' verdicts, failing to see any logic behind the permitting of marriages of such lopsided maturity. While the validity of the law is widely acknowledged, people question why it is that an unmarried woman of advancing age may not be allowed to find a mate outside of the tribe when necessary.

Many people in the Arab world trace the burgeoning incidences of older men taking younger wives to the development of Viagra, which has maintained sexually vigor in adult males well into ages formerly thought to be provinces of physical decrepitude.

Cultural change

Like Islam, Christianity has no explicit teaching about a minimum age, and so the youngest age at which a person, specifically a girl, can be married has varied greatly over the years and according to country and culture. The royal families and great dynasties of Europe of the Middle Ages and Renaissance would betroth children still in their infancy, and a girl was regarded as marriageable once she had reached puberty—in *Romeo and Juliet* Shakespeare has Lady Capulet tell Juliet, "I was your mother much upon these years that you are now a maid" and the play tells us that Juliet is still only thirteen. In many ways, this can be seen as a response to a significantly shorter lifespan and the higher probability of complications in childbirth. The idea of a minimum age came to Europe along with cultural change and economic development, and similarly is coming to the Arab world, rather later.

9 — Women

Translation

Title: Saudi Women and Driving

Culture

Saudi women live under enormous legal restrictions and the movement for women's rights in Saudi Arabia is still in its very early stages. The first women did not start being admitted to higher education until 1960; their dress is still strictly controlled and, as this cartoon shows, they are not officially permitted to drive, though there are rural areas where necessity forces the authorities to wink at such restrictions. With political power firmly in the hands of the monarchy and women legally confined within tight social barriers, there is little scope for the kind of campaign of public protests and argument that the British and American suffragettes employed to such effect. Every suggestion that women's rights might be expanded is howled down by hordes of conservative men who quite conveniently find that their convictions about how a moral and faithful society ought to be run enable them to continue to keep the female half of the population subjugated.

☪ The reader should not infer that Saudi Arabia is the Arab country that most oppressive toward women. In fact, Yemeni women face the severest hardships, including strict limitations on their freedom of movement outside of the house, and also on their education. This situation can partly be explained by the constant domestic skirmishes between the Yemeni government and Al-Qaeda affiliates, who are slowly increasing their grip upon the society. Arab women enjoy the highest degree of freedom in Tunisia, followed by Morocco, Algeria and Lebanon.

Translation

In this cartoon we see a Saudi woman watching as a car key is dangled in front of her. The key is being handed to a dirty male hand, labeled "chauffeur."

Many women are so exasperated by the hygiene of their chauffeur that they try to buy them perfume and clothes, thinking that having a dirty chauffeur reflects badly on them, but to little or no avail.

Second on the worst-dressed list are the husbands who, when at home, wear only underwear and a singlet or wife-beater, which many women find a little gross or slobby—the men defend themselves by saying that the oppressive heat they have to endure outside means that they like to cool off inside by wearing the bare minimum.

Culture

The chauffeur is the most important servant in the Gulf household because he is the only person other than the husband who can drive the wives and daughters. But many accidents and incidents occur with these men, usually immigrants, that have made Saudi society seriously consider allowing females to drive. These incidents have ranged from sexual harassment of young female students by the school bus driver to abductions of passengers by cab drivers. These kinds of incidents roiled the conservative Saudi society which is not used to these types of behavior.

The majority of people are in favor of women having the right to drive. They insist that it is unsafe to allow a non-family member to have so much access and control over young females, especially when that person's background is unknown. As corporal punishment is not considered child abuse in Arab nations, these children are very reserved and even fearful about causing any form of disruption, and supporters of women's right to drive suggest that most children would never report any incident of harassment or mistreatment to their parents. The fear is that this could lead to severe damage to the child for years, and by extension, that the system protects the perpetrators.

In 2010, a Saudi cleric issued a fatwah that for a woman to avoid "illegal seclusion" with her driver, she should breastfeed him, thus making him related to her by the bond of wet-nursing (a recognized category of relationship). Women jumped on this fatwah, starting a campaign "Either you let us drive or we breastfeed the foreigners!" The whole situation is generally regarded as ridiculous—and humorous.

The argument in favor of maintaining the ban thrives on men's fear of infidelity that might result from the freedom granted by allowing women the right to drive. Another argument is that, given the situation of multiple wives and daughters, the number of automobiles on the road would possibly quadruple, thereby creating a traffic nightmare. A popular argument against women driving points to the fact that they are already openly harassed as passengers. This is shown in the next cartoon, where we see men gawking at a fully covered woman who is being driven in a car. This situation is not confined to Saudi Arabia but occurs throughout the Arab world. Elsewhere in the region, when women get behind the wheel, male drivers will aggressively harass them, flirting from their cars and even following them.

Staring

Staring at women is an endemic problem among Arab men, even when the women are totally covered. The starer will look at the way she walks and her body shape to create an image of what is under her *abbaya*, both what she is wearing, her age, and social status. Women are used to this and have learned how to deal with it. Walking with a husband or brother does not protect a woman from the stares of passing men. While the staring is by no means acceptable to the woman's company, they can do little but ignore it. Even men who are with their wives will stare at other women.

The roots of staring are in the culture, which is male-dominated and has for a long time limited the movement of women. As women have gained more freedom and can be seen in public, the new situation has proven to be something of a shock to men, since there is still a general lack of interaction, creating a certain amount of emotional deprivation and sexual repression. The challenges of getting married, constant stimulation from television and the way that women are generally secluded, all do little to help the situation and as a result sexual desire becomes bottled up. There are women who do encourage the staring by walking a certain way or putting their names on the abbaya (being covered completely makes identifying women difficult).

Interestingly, more loosely dressed women are less subject to stares than the modestly dressed (you want what you cannot have…or see). This means Westerners tend to be safer from the gawking and that when Arab men visit the West they curtail the habit.

There are three types of starers. The first enjoys staring, does not try to hide it and looks with curiosity. The opposite of this is the shy one, who only steals abashed glances, and he is followed by the Believer — the good Muslim who doesn't look twice, as he believes that he should avert his gaze, but only after a first look. Women do try to brush this off, but there are times where a man glances too long and is reproved by the woman. Men's point of view is that they bring it upon themselves, due to their dress, despite the fact that they are fully clothed and sometimes only have eyes visible.

Shopping centers and stoplights prove to be the primary areas where women are subjected to this, as they are in greatest contact with men here. Some malls have reacted by prohibiting the entrance of young men.

The phenomenon is clearest at traffic lights, however, as in this cartoon, where women feel the glare of the attention from the men around when they are with their chauffeur. Some become so annoyed that they ask the driver to take the license number of the cars of those who are staring. Women advise each other to memorize the number of the moral, or religious, police and other police patrols so that they can call them. The religious police (the Commission for the Promotion of Virtue and Prevention of Vice) will generally stop the car they have been notified about, usually occupied by young men, and talk to the occupants for up to three hours, so all passers-by can see them. The police attempt to convince them of the immorality of their actions and delay them as a type of punishment. A simple phone call will trigger this process, and all calls are responded to. Still, most women simply ignore the situation, and it is only the few who become truly annoyed that call the police.

Men usually have excuses for their behavior, or delude themselves into thinking that the most covered are the most attractive. Women wearing the *abbaya* with the inside tie, which fits to the form more, an open or colored *abbaya*, those wearing high heels, make-up, perfume, or hazel contact lenses are the main objects of scrutiny. Even something as small as uncovered hands can prompt stares.

☪ Another argument against women drivers concerns their situation and safety in the event of an accident. When Arabs get into accidents, the drivers usually get out of the car and exchange insults which can lead to physical violence. The reason for this is because, unlike in America where it is mandatory, most Arab drivers do not carry insurance and any damages are the responsibility of the driver. In most cases the police are not involved at the scene of the accident, and this raises concerns regarding the welfare of female drivers. Because many Arabs perceive women to be bad drivers, it is argued that a woman involved in an accident will immediately be considered at fault in a situation and that her negligence caused it.

☪ Change has already begun for Saudi Arabia. In most suburbs and villages, women now enjoy relaxed restrictions on their freedom to drive and they have proved themselves very capable and responsible. Given the success of these local changes, the Saudi government does not have to look far for evidence supporting a woman's right to drive and eventually restrictions should be removed throughout the country.

Those who advocate female driving use the example of women driving in the countryside as proof that they could, if given the chance, drive; however, opponents counter this claim by pointing out that there is a difference between driving in the desert and the kind required in the city. They also point to the personalities of women behind the wheel in the two environments. Bedouin women, from the desert, are serious, mature women who perform a job for their family or tribe by going to buy animal feed or transporting water. For city women, on the other hand, there is no clear task they are fulfilling, and there is concern over harassment by men in surrounding cars, which is not a feature of driving in the desert or territory inhabited by the same family or tribe. The advocates for women driving do point out that women used to drive the modes of transportation available in the Prophet Muhammad's day. Opponents are quick to dismiss this as being a different time with different kinds of people.

☪ Men also argue against allowing women to drive, saying that they would be driving men's cars and not their own, since, without a job, most of them don't have the resources to buy one, and that, as bad drivers, the women will smash the cars up with the cost of repairs or higher insurance falling on the man.

Translation

Title: Learning to drive away from the eyes of snoops

Culture

Many Arab countries lack driving schools, and some others have them but do not permit women to attend. Women therefore rely on friends or relatives to give them clandestine driving lessons, sometimes in isolated spots in the desert as in this cartoon. Of course, unprofessional instruction, nerves about violating the law, and lack of regular roads make this a dangerous practice, and women can be in danger of ending their instruction like this, in a nasty smash-up.

The entire process of licensing drivers can seem disorganized when compared with the standards that prevail in much of the West. Road tests are administered to some, but the well-connected can obviate that step and be awarded a license untested. Perhaps paradoxically, many Arab drivers are highly skilled, as, given the chaos that prevails on many Arab roadways with the prevalent disregard for traffic laws; one cannot slip into the inattentive torpor or distraction that is the cause of so many crashes in the West.

☪ in the background is The Kingdom Center also called *Burj Al-Mamlaka* is a supertall skyscraper located in the city of Riyadh, Saudi Arabia. It is the tallest skyscraper in Saudi Arabia and the 45th tallest building in the world with a height 1,020 ft.

Translation

Title: "The Woman Driving the Car."

Wife: "How wonderful! [O peace!] I can visit my girlfriends, go to the malls, cruise around, go to coffee shops, etc, etc, etc."

Husband: "How wonderful! [O peace!] She can take the kids to school, do the household shopping, visit [the relatives/friends in] the hospital and I can take a breeeeeeak."

Culture

Arab men are burned out because of the ban on women drivers. They have to do everything by themselves. They have to run errands, take the kids to school, etc. If they have a car they have to do the work of two people. Many husbands can't wait for the day when their wives can drive, so that they can take some of this burden off them. In this cartoon, the woman's dreams of driving revolve around recreational activities, and this could be a problem for the husband because things might not change as much as he hopes.

Translation

Man at desk, sleeve: "Owner of Office Contracting [Foreign Workers]."

On computer screen: "Do you agree that women have a right to drive cars? Yes/No." [*Arrow points to No*]

Top folder: "Requests for contracted [foreign] drivers."

Middle folder: "Requests for contracted [foreign] maids."

Bottom folder: "Requests for contracted [foreign] housekeepers."

Culture

The parties involved in preventing women from driving—including religious conservatives, liberals, young people, government officials, husbands, and women—have different rationales and reasons for their stance. One of the parties is depicted in this cartoon: the owner of an office that brings foreign laborers into the country for household help, such as chauffeurs and drivers, maids and housekeepers. It's in his best interest to keep the ban on women drivers in place so he can keep bringing foreign drivers into the country and make money from commissions.

☪ In many cartoons you will see people with either a mug or thermos with the tag of a tea-bag hanging from the rim. Arabs will always have a cup of tea present with them in the office or house. Also notice that the man is smoking, which is allowed in many offices.

Translation

Title: The Hidden Jewel

[*N.B. The cartoon depicts a woman selling clothes on the sidewalk.*]

Language

The Arabic adjective *maknooneh* means "hidden," "well-kept," or "cherished."

☪ When writing a letter to an Arab woman, the traditional and formally respectful form of address is, "*es-sitt el-masooneh wa-l-Jóharah el-meknooneh*" ("The guarded lady and hidden jewel").

Culture

This cartoon highlights an irony of the government of Saudi Arabia's attitude towards and restrictions on women. The underlying premise of the policy on women is to keep them relegated to the domestic realm, away from public view. In Saudi parlance, they are to be "well-kept jewels," treasured at home but hidden from others. To this end, Saudi women are heavily restricted in their economic possibilities, forcing them to be dependent on men for their livelihood: they are unable to drive, as has been seen, and, as this cartoon illustrates, they are also unable to rent permanent store space. As, in practice, many families are unable to survive without the commercial efforts of women, all this law actually achieves is forcing women to labor in the heat outdoors as street vendors. Many Saudis who are more progressive are appalled at the humiliating and punishing treatment of their country's so-called "jewels": how, they argue, can a nation that so prizes its women force them to labor in the sun while permitting immigrants to operate nicely air-conditioned shops of all descriptions?

Translation

Title: "The Arab Woman"

On short list: "Religiously unlawful."

On long list: "Socially unlawful."

Culture

The source of many cultural restrictions on women is not religion but society. The restrictions on women that are not sanctioned by Islam include the following: freedom to drive, freedom to travel alone, and the freedom

to reveal her face in public. Socially imposed restrictions are far more abundant than the restrictions instituted by Islam, and women's freedoms therefore vary from country to country.

Translation

Woman: "My rights."

[N.B.: the symbols in the lower right hand corner of the cartoon's panels are the Arabic signs for the numerals "1" and "2," respectively.]

Culture

Arab women are working hard to change this situation, but they live in a male-dominated society, so changes are occurring slowly.

To many Muslim men, "freedom" is a euphemism for immorality, caused by Western influences on the lifestyles of Muslim women. Where Muslim women may perceive the ability to drive, to vote, to travel without permission, as liberties they are denied, Muslim men perceive these same acts and desires as a Western

conspiracy to undermine their traditions and beliefs. Conservative opinion holds that women who, before being aware of Western culture, were once respected and respectful have degenerated into Westernized women who live independently, engage in promiscuous sex, and indulge in alcohol.

Translation

Man to wall: Do you understand?

Wall: Yes, of course.

Man to woman: Do you understand?

Woman: No!

Language

This cartoon is another example of a set phrase that exists in both American and Arab culture: talking to a brick wall.

Culture

In many Arab cartoons, wives are depicted as stubborn and in an unfavorable light. The woman here is less responsive and understanding than a brick wall. Such obstinacy is only associated with wives, not mothers, sisters or single women. There are few societies that esteem mothers as highly as Arab culture, and few probably that are as positive toward sisters.

Translation

Wife: "Do you believe that my car tires squeal in 3rd gear?

Husband: "The car is automatic. And squeal in 3rd gear? Aah, O my belly."

Culture

Arab women are often shown as being mechanically challenged, as they also are in Western comedy. The depiction of women in cartoons and in the media in general, with the exception of poetry and songs, is often harsh. As with the obstinacy above, it is mostly wives who are depicted in an unfavorable light in Arab media, and while mothers are always depicted with respect, the same treatment does not extend to the mother-in-law, who is often depicted as the main source of grief and problems for the spouse.

Translation

Book title: Women's Rights

Reclining woman: Sweep the house, wash the laundry, cook the food, change the children's clothes, and demand my rights from society.

Culture

This cartoon depicts a rich Arab woman who relies on her maids from Southeast Asia to run her household and even to ask society for her rights.

The cartoon also exposes the ironic hypocrisy that lurks behind the efforts of middle-class and affluent people to gain human rights even as they oppress the workers. The rich woman hopes to gain recognition as a competent and worthy member of society but remains blind to the humanity of the servant whom she orders about. Though her book may call for universal "Women's Rights" (its title), for her this is narrowed into a far less stirring movement for the rights of well-off, native-born, women of leisure.

☪ Domestic service can be a challenging calling in any society, but some practices are particularly common in Arab countries that make the lives of maids particularly arduous. A number of Gulf Arab women supplement their household's income by operating market stalls or running similar small businesses. Many such women require their maids not only to perform their household duties, but additionally to serve as shopkeepers in the markets. As these maids are generally hired from immigrant populations, many do not speak Arabic, but the simple transactions, facilitated with posted prices, can be carried out without much communication between the customers and the women minding the stall.

Culture

Wealthy Arab women are especially fashionable and, given the restrictions on dress, in order to scream "fashion" they will focus on shoes, make-up and accessories. Bags are very succinct way of demonstrating both wealth and taste, and much like

their Western counterparts, many have adopted the trend of carrying very large ones. This cartoon shows a woman with a bag that has is excessively large, and she leaves it to her maid to help her carry it.

Though their dress is not so prescribed as women's, men in the Gulf tend to wear a uniform of *jallabaya* that does not allow much self-expression, and they will also use accessories—particularly cars and Rolexes as their status symbols. Men also carry large bags, though with towels, soap and sandals, so that they can clean themselves and perform the necessary ablutions before prayer.

Translation

[The man threatens his wife with a gun and lays into her with misogynistic tirade of the proverbial faults of women in general.]

Man:
You are [derogatory term for a woman], (lacking brain and religion), (and created from a crooked rib) and (your cunning is formidable), and your name is (hareem), (you'll

grieve me to the grave), (and your death would be an act of kindness), (and if your sister died, your honor is preserved), (and the little girl is affliction) (and spoiling of the girl will shame you) (and his daughter died because his intentions were good) (and the beautiful girl is half a disaster) (and ask their advice, and do the opposite) (and even if she reaches Mars, she'll still end up cooking) (and give her up for marriage and take a break from the worry) **after all that, you still need me to have mercy on you and forgive you!**

Language

All the sayings in parentheses are traditional Arabic sayings: some proverbs, some *hadiths*, and some verses modified from the Qur'an. The man begins his invective by addressing the woman as *mara*. This abbreviation of the proper Arabic word for woman, *Imra'a*, is often used by working-class Arab men to belittle women.

The man then quotes a popular Arabic saying of obscure origin that holds that women lack both intelligence and religious fervor and should therefore be ignored and expected to fall to folly. These shortcomings, to the extent that they are true, can be attributed to the lack of emphasis on women's education in many parts of the Arab world and the religious prohibition against women engaging in religious activities during their period.

Though the story does not feature in the Qur'an, Islamic tradition holds to the story that Eve, known in Islam as Hawa, was created from Adam's rib. However, the tale goes further and asserts that the rib in question was crooked, which imperfection was passed on to Hawa, rendering her and all womankind inherently inferior.

The accusation that the woman's cunning is formidable is an almost direct quotation from the Qur'an. There, it is a general assertion about women in general, inspired by the calumnies uttered by Potiphar's wife against Joseph.

"*Hareem*," which is the term both for the place and the occupants of the secluded women's portion of a traditional Arab household, has by extension become a term for women and things relating to them. The term is redolent of things hidden from view and kept private, so in the cartoon, the man is obliterating the individual identity of the woman.

Male Arabs are typically very protective of the honor of their female relatives. A man worries for their welfare from his first awareness of familial responsibility until his, or their, death.

To a traditional male Arab viewpoint, women represent temptation and danger, luring one to moral sliding oneself and potentially engaging one in violent conflicts with other men. Therefore, a woman's death can be construed as a general moral good. By killing the woman, the man in the cartoon thinks he does himself and the world an act of kindness, removing a source of discord and dissolution. In a similar way, a sister's death, no matter what her character, relieves a brother of worry and responsibility.

Again, fathers would often feel ill-disposed to exposing their honor to the risk of having a daughter, so it was the fate of many infant girls to be killed.

The next proverb warns against spoiling women with excessive tenderness or indulgence. Strict discipline is recommended so that one's wives and daughters are careful of their, and one's own, honor.

As in many of the proverbs, the man's exclamation about good intentions hinges on the idea that female relatives are a liability. God is posited to reward a man with a good heart by granting him the favor of his daughters' death, so that they may not live to shame him.

A beautiful woman in a family is "half a disaster," be she a daughter, sister, or even wife. She will be the focus of men's attentions and lusts and pose a constant challenge for one who is interested in his honor. One should even be wary of taking a beautiful woman as a wife, tempting one always to ponder what her past entanglements may have been.

Men are warned to do the opposite of what women advise because women are thought to be mentally and religiously deficient and also prone to use what intelligence they do have to promote their own, crafty ends.

The proverb about women going to Mars but ending up cooking means that no matter how extraordinary her accomplishments may be, the proper and destined place for a woman is in the kitchen.

Finally, the man quotes a proverb that advises fathers and brothers to find a husband for any women in the family as quickly as possible, thereby becoming free from the burden of primary responsibility for her behavior.

Culture

The cartoon is an extreme representation of the traditional low standing of women in Arab culture. The strict separation of the genders only served to heighten male anxiety over the virtue of their female relatives and to inspire them to enforce ever stricter control. By piling so many derogatory proverbs and opinions into this one cartoon, the image reflects a growing sense amongst educated Arabs that such traditional attitudes are out-dated and in need of humane revision.

Culture

The Arabic media used not to discuss women's issues, but the cartoons on these two pages indicate that the tide is changing and as they criticize the place of women and girls in society.

the boy / the girl

girl / boy

Some manners and customs

[artist's signature]

Similarity of age

Women's Rights

Domestic Violence: Every action has an equal and opposite reaction [*glove*] Pressure

"It takes you an hour to get me coffee"

Employment [*straight road*] Marriage Full Education

"Dear, it's your life and your future. You are the one who is getting married, not me. Let me know what you decide!"

Translation

Sign: International Trips Departure Hall

Top: In the hall

Bottom: In the airplane

Culture

The people from conservative countries, like Saudi Arabia and the Gulf States, must dress and act in certain ways to obey the laws of their society. Certain people abandon these ways of dressing and acting when they leave and travel internationally. For example, alcohol is prohibited in Saudi Arabia, so the first thing some Saudis will do upon arriving at the airport of a country where alcohol can be purchased legally, such as Egypt, is buy some. It is not unusual to see the whole stock of alcoholic beverages in duty free shops at some airports being emptied within minutes of the arrival of Saudi airplanes.

Similar behavior applies to the women of these countries, as portrayed in this cartoon. When preparing to leave their country, they are all dressed conservatively making sure to obey their society's law, but as soon as they are on the airplane they discard their traditional clothing in favor of Western clothes, which is often more revealing. This behavior is not limited to the ordinary citizen, but extends to even the highest reaches of society. They too have to maintain a certain level of decorum while in their home country, but when they traveling there is not the same pressure to maintain this behavior.

Translation

Title: Riyadh-Paris

Pilot Speaking: Dear passengers, a while ago we passed out of Saudi airspace, the ladies can now take off their abbayas…Happy trip and thanks.

Culture

The fact that travelling women will often remove their abbayas *en route* is well known and is sometimes mocked in the Saudi press. However, if any other country's media published a similar cartoon, the Saudis would regard it as insulting and might consider boycotting the country where the cartoon was published. This boycott would include stopping vacation-travel to that country, causing the country to lose millions of dollars. This is why many countries are very aware of the sensitivity of their Arab tourists, and will try not to insult them in any way. Sometimes wealthy Arabs commit crimes in other countries and are not prosecuted because those countries fear being boycotted by other rich Arab tourists. One such example is that of a Saudi man who went drag-racing on the airport road in Cairo and lost control of his vehicle, crashing into a space occupied by pedestrians and killing several people. His departure from Egypt was facilitated quickly and quietly due to his status as a rich Arab tourist, and as a result, he was able to escape prosecution. This sort of courtesy, however, is not always extended in return. If a tourist from a poor country breaks the law in a rich Arab country, he will be punished and chastised in their media.

Translation

Right: The Arab girl's clothes in her country.

Left: The Arab girl's clothes outside her country (except those whom God has mercy on).

Language

In Arabic when you say "except those whom God has mercy on," it means those who will not perform an act that may trigger the wrath of God, or an act that God may consider a sin.

Culture

Who is allowed to sell lingerie?

In many Arab countries, the gender of a salesperson is a factor in what items they are allowed to sell, and it is usually the government that decides which genders are allowed to sell what items. In recent years, there has been a debate in conservative Arab countries on who should be allowed to sell women's lingerie, sleepwear, cosmetics and toiletry items. This is not a concern in countries like Egypt and Lebanon, but in conservative countries, like Saudi Arabia, it has grown to be a widespread issue, that has resulted in clashes between the government, businessmen and religious authorities. The Saudi government, for example, wanted to restrict sales of these specific women's items to Saudi women only. This constituted a problem for the business owners, since the majority of salespeople are foreign men and hiring of saleswomen takes a considerable amount of time, since the women need to be found and trained, as they do not usually work in this trade. This restriction is not limited to stores, but to anyone who is selling lingerie, even street vendors, and penalties for not complying with the new law are imposed, such as closing down and suspending the vendor's license to sell. According to the law, no men are allowed in any store that sells these women's items and the areas where they are sold must be enclosed, so that no one from the outside may see in. The Saudi religious authorities prohibit women from trying on any piece of clothing before it is purchased. In Saudi Arabia, a woman must purchase the clothes, and try them on at home, and then if they do not fit, the woman may return or exchange the item for something that fits.

In many Arab countries, the American way of shopping does not exist. Instead of being allowed to walk into a store and select your purchase before you go to the checkout, a salesman must get the items for you, no matter how small or large it may be. This type of shopping is rooted in the belief that one should not trust the customer. There are some Western-style malls in the Arab world, but the prices are higher than they would be in normal Arab stores. Large department stores are often owned by the government, so the salesmen are often government employees and are not held to a very high standard of customer service, since they are difficult to dismiss. While in America almost everything you buy can be returned or exchanged, in the Arab world, almost nothing can be.

Translation

"Your *hijab* is crazy, Zizi. It matches your hair color."

Language

There are two basic forms of nicknames: those based upon the formula "*abu*…" and "*Umm* …," known as "*kenya*," and those which play around with the syllables of the given name, called "*dala'*," literally "pampering/spoiling name." In the cartoon, a form like "Zizi" indicates a Westernized attitude (see below) as much as the woman's clothes.

Culture

Nicknames using *abu*, "father of," and *Umm* , "mother of," provide a

simple alternative way of referring to a man or woman, using one of their children's names, while "*ibn*" and "*bint*," "son of" and "daughter of," refer to the parents. Mainly in the case of men, this formula can then be adapted to include any physical feature, so that he can be referred to as "Father or a bald spot" or "Father of glasses." A famous singer, who only had one arm, is known exclusively by the sobriquet "Father of the arm." In the case of "*ibn*" or "*bint*" the attribution is often more general—"*ibn al-Harrah*" or "*bint al-Harrah*," "son or daughter of the alley," is a phrase that refers to someone with strong roots in a "neighborhood, while a number of insults are also based on this form, such as "son of a dog.

Nicknames based upon the syllables of the first name do not follow any fixed pattern but, as with Western names, there are standard forms, and they often involve using the vowel sound "ou" or repetition of a consonant/syllable. For example, Ahmed is usually Hamada, or Mido; Tarek is Rou'a; Khalid, Khalouda; Mustafa, Soufa, Fou'a or Fafa; Ibrahim, Bibo; Walid, Welwel. Women's names are not bandied around with such abandon, but nicknames of course apply within a family and among friends, for instance: Ayesha, Ayousha; Fatimah, Fatoumah or Fifi; Zeinab, Zanouba or Zizi; Hala, Loula and so on. The form along the lines of "Fatoumah" or "Zanouba" is perceived as more Arab and traditional than "Fifi" or "Zizi," and a woman who wants to be Westernized might well resent or dislike the first form. This is probably because these forms derive originally from French nicknames. Anwar al-Sadat's wife, Jihaan, was known mockingly as Gigi, indicating her Westernized habits and tendencies.

The same is true to some extent of men's nicknames, where "Mido," with sounds that are readily pronounceable in a Western context, may seem trendier than "Hamada," with the distinctively Arabic hard "H" at the beginning.

Translation

"Do you have heels that are a little higher?"

Culture

As mentioned in reference to bags, shoes are one of the items of clothing that allow a woman to demonstrate her sense of fashion.

Cartoons often make fun of women's fashion, especially extremes of style or make-up, and men generally find high-heeled shoes pointless.

Much like their Western counterparts, Arab women's indecisiveness when shopping is something of a cliché.

Arab shoe stores are particularly extravagant in their displays and shiny, clean appearance—which sometimes draws criticism that frivolous items are given such display while for food, where hygiene is important, the display is often dirty or poorly maintained.

The shop attendant in the cartoon is a foreigner and, though there have been movements to restrict those selling women's items to Saudi women (see above), in general foreign, non-Arab men are largely trusted in these roles—probably more than Arab men would be, and definitely more than local Saudi or Gulf men. This is because they are seen as having had enough exposure to women, both culturally while growing up and in their general lifestyle that they do not represent the same pent-up danger that Arab men would.

Men's and women's stores are, of course, separate.

☪ Maintaining the shine of shoes is difficult due to the desert environment of most Arab countries. Egypt for example is very dirty and dusty, whereas Saudi streets are typically less dirty. But the desert environment can wreak havoc with any type of clothing. Coming to America is a shock for Arabs because at the end of the day, they do not have to shine their shoes or wash their clothes as they do every day at home. Shoe-shines are everywhere in Arab countries, as there is high demand for their services, though in some areas they are illegal, and are often subject to arrest.

Weather in most of the Arab world is so hot that some will wear their shirts straight from the wash knowing that it will dry in a few minutes

Translation

On right: "Before leaving the house"

On left: "After leaving the house"

Under title: Women, fully clothed yet naked, coy, and their heads lean over like a camel's hump.

Culture

This cartoon is a play on an unauthenticated saying of Prophet Muhammad. This saying likens the head of a superficial woman to the leaning hump of a camel. The hump is made of stored fat, which the camel can live off when food is unavailable, and a leaning hump is a sign of an underfed camel.

☪ Although the woman on the left may appear to be completely covered, the bright decorations on the abbaya, as well as the sandals and lipstick, go against the spirit of modesty, because they draw attention to themselves.

Translation

Next to the burger:
Double Inflated Hijab

Rabbit: You all know about the double burger. But do you know about the double inflated (hijab)?

Culture

A new trend among teenagers in Kuwait and the United Arab Emirates is wearing hijabs that have been "inflated." The making of Islamic clothing fashionable is often criticized, as it contradicts its very purpose, and this style of *hijab* is heavily criticized in the Gulf media.

By wearing their *hijab* inflated, women are trying to show that they have long, thick, beautiful hair without having to show it. Long hair is considered very beautiful in these countries. In order to give the appearance of an inflated hijab, the young women pile their hair in ponytails and beehive styles, and wear their hijabs on top of them. The same style, sported by a doctor or nurse (to judge from the folder with a crescent and her white coat), makes the young boy think of Marge Simpson in the cartoon below.

Translation

Heading: The Raised Up Hijab

Man: This, Allah save you, is one of the benefits of having a sunroof in the girls' car.

Language

"*Allah save you,*" *Allah yesalemak*, is used in different contexts which depend on the country. Generally the name of God is used, but the second part of greeting will usually have some appropriateness to the context, and this greeting is generally used in a situation that is associated with some danger, risk or jeopardy. Here the man is saying it to the other man simply as a good wish while talking to him, and uses it partly because of the danger or risk involved in driving a car.

In other countries it is used exclusively to say welcome back ("Thanks be to Allah for your safe return"), since travel has historically been tiresome and dangerous.

Culture

The "girls' car" usually refers to a smaller car that in men's opinion is easy to drive and manuever, but that they would never consider driving themselves.

Translation

A woman uses six animals in her life.

[*Clockwise from top left:*] a shoe made of snakeskin — a jacket made of bull skin (leather) — the fur of a fox — a coat made of bearskin — a bag made of crocodile skin — and the sheep that bought her all these things.

Language

In Arabic, when someone is referred to as a sheep, he is being called a fool.[20]

Culture

This cartoon lampoons the man who listens too much to his wife and buys her whatever she wants.

☪ While a Western man will be happy to repeat his wife's opinion or to say that he has to do something because of her, an Arab man will find this to be an emasculated position, and while Westerners may regard women as generally more moral than men, the situation is the exact opposite in the Arab world.

---

[20] The same applies to goats, see "1 — Sagging and Swagging," p. 13.

Translation

(Clockwise from top right)

Tricks some girls do these days

Shave off their eyebrows!! →

So she can draw them the way she likes!! →

The scandal is what happens when she draws one but forgets the second one!! →

Or rain starts to fall and the eyebrows melt!! →

Or if she wants to perform ablutions (sorry, that's a mistake) these types don't pray!!!!

Girl: "Why do people look at me like that? I know I'm beautiful but not that much."

Bottom title: By the way, this story is true and not fiction. Yesterday I saw a girl with one eyebrow and the second one had run.

Culture

Some Arab men are of the opinion that some Arab girls use too much make-up to little good effect. In Islam, wearing make-up is looked down upon, heavy make-up being prohibited. That, combined with the fact that many women have been brought up to cover their faces, means that when they decide to reveal their faces and make themselves up, they are inexperienced and have had little practice – and hot weather can be cruel to certain styles of make-up. The men say that, at the worst, they look like clowns.

Women will usually only make themselves up for special occasions, such as meeting a potential suitor or attending a wedding. Any make-up will have to be removed as part of the ablutions prior to prayer – which means constant re-application, though, as the cartoon implies, since heavy make-up is already unIslamic, this may not be a major concern.

Translation

Title: New female TV anchor on her way to the studio

On the trailer: Make-up

Bottom: Vroom

Translation

Title: Women's Soccer

[*N. B. The stadium advertisements promote manicures, hair styling, and other female-focused products. Notice the stands filled with women, some carrying a sign reading: "Capt. Mazna / #15."*]

Language

Arab women dislike being called *hareem*, but in Arabic this word is used to denote something that is set aside or exclusively made for women, such as women's clothes or in this cartoon women's soccer. Women consider the term derogatory and a throwback to the days when the *hareem*, or the women of the house, has distinct apartments allotted to them, where no males are allowed to enter, except the head of the family, and certain other near relations and children (both place and people were designated as the *hareem*).

Hareem has its root in "prohibited, taboo," and is the origin of the word in English, spelt both "harem" and "harem." The Arabic term *haram*, meaning "unlawful, forbidden [in Islam]," comes from the same root, but is a different word and should not be confused.

Culture

This cartoon ridicules women's soccer. Arabs consider soccer to be a very manly sport and tend to play it with a roughness and physicality that does not lend itself to their conception of femininity. The notion of women playing soccer, then, seems preposterous, which indeed it is if women are fully covered in the long, constricting robes shown here. The cartoon highlights the incongruity with the woman fixing her make-up in a hand mirror just outside the penalty box.

As absurd as the cartoon argues that women playing soccer is, women's sport has recently been making inroads in the Arab world. Indeed, multi-national sportswear brands such as Adidas and Nike now make sportswear designed to permit Muslim women to move and play sports while preserving their modesty.

Phys. Ed. in Arab Girls' Schools

In the Arab world, the vast majority of middle schools and high schools are separated by gender and, in most girls' schools, physical education is either severely limited or essentially non-existent. Some countries—most notably, Saudi Arabia—have prohibited female phys. ed. entirely, citing its considerable potential to cause illicit temptation in witnesses, instructors and passers-by. Those countries that do allow gym class in girls' schools typically restrict phys. ed. to one session per week and require that, rather than athletic garb, the students wear *hijabs*. Such countries do often offer a variety of popular sports, such as volleyball, basketball and soccer.

However, this situation has garnered significant attention in light of a recent development: in the Arab world, like in America, there is an alarming increase in the incidence of obesity and diabetes among children and young adults. The vast majority of Arab youths spend their leisure time in front of the television, while only a small portion occupies their free hours with exercising, playing sports, or going to the gym.

Predictably, this obesity predicament—particularly as it pertains to young women—has been exacerbated by the many limitations placed upon girls' phys. ed. Some Arab pundits accuse Islamists in the Saudi education ministry of harming girls' health through unnecessary restrictions. Others claim that the weather is to blame: as most government schools lack the necessary indoor facilities, gym class must be held outside; however, the weather can easily prove prohibitive—especially if the participants are attired in *hijabs*.

Finally, one proposed solution would have school-aged girls take up the duties of housekeeper within their own homes. Housekeepers are ubiquitous throughout Saudi society. If the girls would assume their responsibilities, the argument goes, not only would the families save money, but the girls might also lose some weight, and get into better, healthier shape.

It is worth noting that such a proposal does intend the brashly dismissive, misogynistic connotations that the Westerner would surely perceive in it.

Translation

Inscription on boy's jalabya: 'The Guardian'

Folder under woman's arm: 'Official document' or 'application'

Language

The boy's label, *waliy al-amr*, literally means the man in charge of affairs, or guardian.

Mu'āmala refers to a legal document that requires a signature from a government official.

Culture

Waliy al-amr refers to a legal guardian or the authorized agent of a female. In the case of an upcoming wedding, he assists the bride in drafting a marriage contract. The *waliy al-amr* can also function as the guardian of a child, or as depicted in this cartoon, be responsible for a female member of his family. In Islam the term refers to a ruler who must be obeyed and revered by the rest of the Muslim population.

In Arab countries women of all ages are required to have the consent of or be accompanied by a male relative in order for them to travel or to process official documents. This male relative is typically her husband, but is often a father, brother, or uncle in the case of widowed or unmarried women. In many cases, the son is considered next in line to act as a woman's *walīy al-amr* if he meets a certain age requirement.

 Even Arabs find it ridiculous that a small child should be regarded as his mother's guardian.

Translation
Title: Official ending to discussions between the man and the woman.
On tape: Lacking brains and religion

Culture

There is a famous saying in Arabic that women lack brains and religion, which means that they are less intelligent and adhere to religion less than men. In this cartoon, it is implied that whenever a woman expresses an opinion that a man does not agree with, regardless of the subject, whether it be religious or worldly, he will not consider it because the woman either lacks religion or is not smart enough.

☪ By now, the reader will have doubtless noticed the surfeit of Arab cartoons that vilify, demean and ridicule women. These cartoons reveal that Arab misogyny, like all forms of bigotry, is rife with internal contradictions — harboring, within its core, the logic of its own negation. Thus, women are mocked as uncoordinated, accident-prone and physically weak — and yet, at the same time, presumed strong enough to sit long hours at outdoor shops, having been banned from managing more comfortable, leisurely indoor stores; strong enough to walk long distances, having been prohibited from driving cars; and strong enough to endure long bouts of physical brutality, having incurred the wrath of a vengeful husband. Likewise, women are portrayed as obese grotesques, fat, filthy things that nag and moan unendingly—and yet, at the same time, regarded as so sexually potent, so easily, irrepressibly capable of inspiring such profound lust that, sometimes, they are veiled from head to toe.

The truth of the matter is that, in the last two generations, matters have grown far worse—and far more urgent—for Arab women. Prior to World War II, Arab feminist movements were growing in both size and influence, battling for what they perceived to be the natural, God-given rights that had been denied women by Arab rulers. For example, the much-venerated Egyptian feminist Huda Shaarawi—who led the first "female" political protest, in 1919, against British occupation—successfully founded the Egyptian Feminist Union (EFU) in 1923—the same year that she famously removed her veil from her face. Later an adjunct of The International Woman Suffrage Alliance, the EFU was the fount of modern Egyptian feminism, and paved the way for a variety of diverse and radical feminist organizations.

Despite its early successes, feminism within the Arab world wields increasingly less power and appeal—a trend that, to a certain extent, correlates with the reemergence of a fundamentalist Islamic mentality. Yet, it is important to make the point that the Qur'an itself says little of gender relations. It does, however, briefly elaborate the primary distinctions between men and women. Men are declared to be, however slightly, superior to women. Crucially though, this superiority lacks a foundation in ontology, and instead arises out of the era's necessary social relations: men have the capacity to provide, to serve as breadwinners, while women do not. This privilege is considered an exceptional privilege, a distinction of merit, and thus accounts for the disparity between the genders. The Qur'an states that for testimony, "get two witnesses, out of your own men, and if there are not two men, then a man and two women, such as ye choose, for witnesses, so that if one of them errs, the other can remind her," indicating that it is women's memory that is regarded as weak.[21] In other words, when it is said that, for definitive proof of guilt, an accuser is required to provide, say, four witnesses, this means only four *male* witnesses, but eight female witnesses.

That said, the more vitriolic misogyny, characteristic of contemporary discourse, has no basis in the Qur'an. Rather, we must look here to the current proliferation of Salifism, a movement that regards the personages, ways and mores of the early Muslim community to be the necessary exemplars for contemporary life and society. Thus, much of the fodder for modern-day Arab misogyny (in particular, that spouted by extremist groups like the outlawed Muslim Brotherhood) derives from centuries-old texts—commonly called "heritage books"—authored by the ostensibly pious men of yesteryear.

We shall first examine the relevant hadith. Unlike the Qur'an, Islamic traditions holds that the hadith, in their transmission down through the ages, have been vulnerable to redaction and textual tampering. Thus, the devout, right-minded Muslim will take their message with a grain of salt, and become dubious of any hadith that contradicts the Qur'an. There are, however, a considerable number of misogynistic hadith. They are curious in that, unlike the cartoons' predominant tropes—e.g. women as foolish, women as clumsy, women as harshly annoying, etc.—the hadith, rather than demean and ridicule women, vilify them instead. The earliest is attributed to the Prophet's cousin, Ali. It instructs, "Beware a woman's counsel—it will lead always to disaster." Likewise, a saying attributed to Ibn el Juse, a prominent Salafi doctrinal scholar, declares: "Whenever God sends a prophet, the devil hopes to destroy him with a woman." Indeed, numerous other hadith link women to the devil. We learn that the devil has called woman his "confidante," his "arrow that never misses its mark," and his "messenger in [his] time of

---

[21] Al-Qur'an, 002.282 (*Al-Baqara* [The Cow]).

need." "Woman," he says, "you are half of my army." Of course, the second half of the army is not comprised of human men, but rather of demons.

In the Christian tradition, any attempt to vilify women typically derives its *raison d'être* from the Fall: seduced by the duplicitous servant, Eve brashly disobeys God's command, resulting in banishment from Eden and the basis for original sin. In the Qur'an, however, Eve does not occupy a unique position of culpability: rather, Adam and Eve are concurrently seduced, and blame is jointly shared between them. Nonetheless, some Islamic traditions, as indicated by the first hadith, place a considerable emphasis upon woman's role as temptation and distraction vis-à-vis God's prophets. To this day, "Tempting the Pious with Evil Women," by ancient scholar Ismail bin Nasser al-Salahi (also known as "Ibn al-Qitaa"), is still widely read and cited by Islamic fundamentalists. In the text, al-Salahi examines instances of the temptation referred to in the title. This specific scenario is, in fact, more common in Islam than in the Judeo-Christian tradition, and can be observed in the story of Nuh, or "Noah," his wife, a non-believer, drowned in the Great Flood; in the story of Lut, or "Lot," his wife, also a non-believer, died in the destruction of Sodom (similar but not quite the same); and in the story of Yusuf, or "Joseph," the wife of his master attempted, quite strenuously, to seduce him and, when she failed, tried to frame him for assault (as in Genesis).

(By the same token, however, a number of the tales of temptation present in the Biblical tradition are absent from the Qur'an. In the Islamic tradition, then, King David never commits adultery with Bathsheba, and King Solomon is never led astray by the affections of pagan seductresses.)

Another set of sayings from the early Islamic era criticize women as ungodly—ungodly not from maliciousness, necessarily, but rather through stupidity and ignorance. A hadith attributed to Umar Ibn Khattab advises that one should always say "no" to women, because saying "yes" to their requests will invariably harm them. A similar proverb instructs: "consult with women, and do precisely the opposite of their counsel." "Let women neither write nor reside in high-up place," reads another. If they are permitted to write, they might conduct inappropriate correspondences and if they are permitted to live in high-up places—say, the a sixth-floor apartment—they might witness something they ought not see: something corrupting, harmful or, worse still, something suggestive.

Strangely, the most vituperative teachings against women come from poets, not scholars. One saying is attributed to famed Umayyad poet, Jarīr Ibn Aīyah Ibn al-Khaafā (popularly known simply as Jarīr). The story goes that, upon hearing a woman reciting poetry, he declared: "If ever a chicken crows like a rooster, slaughter it." The thrust, of course, is that poetry—and really, literacy itself—is a man's domain, and ought to remain out of the reach of women. What, then, should women take up? Another poet, al-Salmi, provides the following answer: "Why should women practice writing, governance and oratory? These are the pursuits of men, not women. Rather, all we can give women is the chance to spend the night in severe ritual impurity." In this case, "severe ritual impurity" refers, more likely than not, to semen. Finally, the introduction to *1001 Arabian Nights* contains the following versified counsel:

> "Rely not on women,
> Trust not to their hearts,
> whose joys and whose sorrows
> are hung to their parts!
> Lying love they will swear thee
> whence guile ne'er departs.
> Take Yusuf for sample,

> 'Ware sleights and 'ware smarts!
> Iblis ousted Adam
> (See ye not?) thro' their arts."

Today, these texts and sayings are still taught, uncritically, in many Arab schools. In some countries, in reaction to the allegedly misogynistic content of many school textbooks (written, as they were, by traditionalist Muslim males), the writing of texts for girls' schools has been handed over to female authors. Despite these recent advances, Arab education still enables the proliferation of certain attitudes and practices that lead to the vilification and degradation of Arab women. A case in point is the following excerpt, drawn from a pre-Islamic Bedouin text that, to this day, enjoys enormous popularity, as well as confidence among teachers and schoolchildren. In "A Bedouin's Advice to Her Daughter on Her Wedding Night," the author, Umama bint al-Harith, instructs her daughter in the secrets to a successful marriage. "Submit to him with contentment," "listen well to him and obey," "never let his eyes fall on something ugly—be it in your appearance or your behavior": such injunctions, taken from the text in question, appear to counsel a complete submissiveness on the part of the wife. The prospective wife should also be sure to align her pleasures and displeasures with her husband—for otherwise, she is told, she will not be happy.

"Advice to Her Daughter" is often read, then, as epitomizing the logic behind the oppressive and anachronistic treatment of Arab women. A wife's duty is not merely to her husband: rather, through fulfilling her wifely responsibilities, a woman fulfills her duties to God. In this way, the prospect of piousness is interjected into the husband-wife relationship, and employed as a retroactive justification for the wife's comprehensive subservience to her husband—and, thus, the lowly status of women in some fundamentalist thinking. It can be argued, however, that this understanding constitutes a misreading—or, better yet, an incomplete reading—of "Advice." By virtue of its error, it reveals to us that the core of misogyny is not in the texts of the past, but in the prejudices of the present. "Be a slave to him," al-Harish declares at the outset, "and he will be a slave to you." If it is a woman's godly duty to serve her husband, then it is also a husband's godly duty to serve his wife. So too, therefore, must the man "submit to her with contentment," and "listen well to her and obey."

10 — Arab Leaders

Translation

[Translating from the top left]

The man on cell phone (Amir of Kuwait H.H. Sheikh Sabah Al-Ahmed Al-Jaber Al-Sabah): This brawl constitutes a threat to security. You have to have an American base here in the League!

Man waving "V for Victory": Beep! Beep! Qazafi!

Voice from below the table, by the man with "V for Victory": That's the way to do it!

Man with clenched fist: Give it to him!

Man whispering in dark suit (Egyptian President Muhammad Hosni Mubarak): Sharm el Sheikh, it's not suitable for conferences. Next time, we'll do it in a slaughter house.

Man waving scimitar (Saudi King Abdullah Bin Abdul Aziz): "The horses, the night, and the desert recognize me, as do the sword, the spear, the paper, and the pen" Let me at 'em!

Man in robes with curly hair (Libyan President Muamar Qazafi): We Africans don't respond to Arabs like you!

Man separating King Abdullah and Qazafi (Syrian President Bashar al-Assad): What made me leave my house today?

Small man hanging on King Abdullah (Yemeni President Ali Abdullah Saleh): Take it easy, Hajj; would you like a piece of qat to chill you out? [Qat is made of plant leaves and is chewed every day by most Yemeni men – and some women – for its mild narcotic effect.]

Man waving fist at bottom: Go easy on the man!

The Palestinian dejectedly slumping from the room bears a paper reading: Form Number 6

Form Number 6

Form Number 6 is a form that employees are legally required to sign upon leaving a job. Signing the form confirms that the employer has given the employee everything they are owed. Because of the significance of this form, and the possible consequences of an employee not signing the form for any reason, employers will often ask that employees sign the form before they start their job as opposed to when they leave.

In the cartoon, a Palestinian is shown leaving a room with Form 6 in his hand, as behind him the Arab leaders are depicted fighting and shouting. The fact that the Palestinian is leaving with Form 6 suggests that the Arab leaders believe that they have done everything they have to do and they no longer owe him anything. The Palestinian is in tears, which suggests he is unhappy about the deal.

Language

King Abdullah recites a verse from a very famous poem by the reknowned Abu al-Taib Moutanabi. The poem is the exultant cry of a hero who has mastered all the arts cherished in pre-Islamic times; he wins glory both as a warrior and as a poet, mastering sword and pen. It was written in a very elegant classical Arabic, but the king spoils the effect by following the quotation with the rough, colloquial, "Let me at 'em!"

Culture

This cartoon refers to the summit meeting of the Arab League in Cairo in March 2009. We find, front and center, Libyan President Muammar Qazafi and Saudi King Abdullah – Qazafi's brazenness, it would seem, has angered the sword-wielding King. While the actual summit did not devolve into antic violence, Qazafi did rile the King with a few pointed, boastfully delivered words: a casual, nonplussed Qazafi slouched beneath and unkempt mop of hair and broad sunglasses interrupted the Qatari Amir to inform Abdullah that, among other things, he was a "British puppet" and an "American ally." He continued: "I am an international leader, the dean of the Arab rulers, the king of kings of Africa and the imam of Muslims, and my international status does not allow me to descend to a lower level." During that conference, the leaders were also divided as to which Palestinian faction to support – FataH or Hamas.

As is clearly shown by this cartoon, Arabs have some trouble getting along.

There are twenty-two countries in the Arab world; twelve in Asia and ten in Africa. Some Arab countries feel closer to certain countries, in culture and language, than they do to other countries and are thus separated into specific blocks or regions. For example, Algeria, Morocco, and Tunisia form the Arab Maghreb region; they are all located in Northwest Africa, have the same dialect, and have similar historical backgrounds. Another region is the Gulf Countries, which consists of Kuwait, Saudi Arabia, the United Arab Emirates, Oman, Qatar and Bahrain. Egypt and the Sudan, formerly one country, make up a third region; while Syria, Jordan, Lebanon and Palestine constitute another region known as Al-Sham. The remaining seven Arab countries, such as Libya, Somalia, and Yemen (formerly North and South Yemen, or "The Happy Yemen") do not have any strong ties connecting them and stand on their own. On the surface, it may seem that all Arabs get along, but when the relationships are examined more closely, one can find many examples of hatred and disagreement among them. Even though two countries may be in the same region, there is still a possibility that there exists some internal hatred between them. Rivalries flourish, despite the fact that Arab countries are related by factors such as religion, language and similar cultures.

Arabs carry a great many assumptions and preconceptions about their various nationalities, with history, cultural influence, and economic prosperity shaping how each nation's citizens are viewed by the rest. Broadly speaking, wealthy nations with a developed, Western-style infrastructure are highly thought-of: Saudi Arabians, Kuwaitis, and citizens of the Gulf States all enjoy high-status among Arabs for this reason. However, the fact that so much of this prosperity is newly won oil wealth can feed a degree of resentful disparagement, as Arabs' long memories recall the days when these were nations of poor Bedouins. In contrast, Lebanon is respected for its high degree of development both now and historically, despite the fact that it has not attained such dizzy prosperity; its cosmopolitanism and sophistication have earned it, in some circles, the soubriquet "The Switzerland of the East." Libya, for its part, enjoys enormous wealth but very little prestige, as its isolation and the peculiar political stranglehold of al-Qazafi keep the strangely stunted exception that proves the rule. Jordan, Algeria, Tunisia, Egypt, Morocco, Syria, and pre-invasion Iraq had a significant degree of respect in recognition of past prosperity and influence, but as, in recent decades, stagnation and decline afflicted each for various reasons, and so each has lost prestige. Lacking wealth, lacking cultural influence, and lacking international clout, Yemen, the Sudan, Mauritania, and Comoros are often thought of as the least of the Arab nations, their people living backward lives with few prospects for improvement.

Almost all Arabs hold some hatred or dislike, rooted in jealousy, towards Egyptians. This is because Egypt used to be the cultural, political, and economic center of the Arab world. As other countries have recently overtaken Egypt in economic development, the wider Arab community has derived great satisfaction from mocking Egyptians for their poverty, characterizing Egypt as a land reduced to fava bean-eating, bread lines, and chronic deprivation. Egyptians, for their part, retort that if they have fallen behind their newly rich neighbors, it is because Egypt, since 1948, has dedicated its resources to the defense of Arab lands, fighting three major wars and engaging in interminable minor conflicts.

Egypt also receives criticism from the opponents of modernization, being held up by conservatives as a model for a society in which international contacts have debased traditional values of religion and family. The serious-minded majority in most Arab countries denigrate what they see as the frivolity of Egyptian culture, denigrating Egypt as an irreverent land of dancing and joking. Even the dialect of the Egyptians — which Egyptian pop culture and media have spread throughout the Arab world, and can be used fluently by most Arabs — is argued by these conservatives to be a uniquely egregious corruption of classical Arabic, in stark contrast to the relatively benign demotic spoken in other Arab countries. In many Arab nations, Egyptians immigrants are blamed for anything that ails their society, and are singled out for any mistake that any Egyptian may make. Egyptians, in turn, do not like to refer to themselves as Arab. Whenever an Egyptian person is called an Arab, they will often state that they are not Arab, but instead descendants of the Pharaohs. Once the Egyptian power started to dwindle, other countries began to become more powerful and to play larger roles on international fronts. Most of the Arab countries, however, will deny wanting to take a larger role and will state that all Arab countries want to work together on the pressing issues. Egyptians, for their part, are convinced that Pan-Arabism has resulted in the wasting of many resources and that Egypt was not given due recognition by the rest of the Arab world.

Arabs countries have no shortage of grievances and prejudices against one another. Arab leaders are notoriously temperamental with one another, and their personal squabbles are played out in their respective countries' media, with each population being whipped up to vilify and degrade the other. These heated international disputes flair up noticeable particularly during sporting events, when fans show disrespect during the opponents' national anthem or even fall to fighting. Arabs' strong sense of the welfare of the Arab world as a whole can actually serve to divide countries, as for example, Jordan's normalization of relations with Israel has led to Jordan's being reviled as cowardly and treacherous. Some examples of hatred within the Arab world are that Kuwaitis dislike Saudis; Syrians dislike the Lebanese; Algerians dislike Moroccans; and Jordanians dislike Palestinians. Libyans also have strong distaste towards all other Arabs and think that the other Arab countries are the main reason why the Arab world is lagging behind the rest of the world in development. Saudis are distrustful of Arabs as well, because they believe that Arabs are envious of Saudi wealth, and therefore hire Asians to work for them. There is also the well-known friction between Kuwait and Iraq that culminated in the Iraqi invasion of Kuwait.

Of course, not all rifts amongst Arabs pit whole nations against one another. The populations of Arab countries contain many cultural divisions, and mutual suspicions and oppressions are rife. Stereotyping and unequal treatment is facilitated by Arab governments' love of bureaucracy, as details such as a person's religion will be printed on official identification documents. Adherents of minority religions are thus easily identified and routinely discriminated against. The urbanized population, too, look down upon people from the desert, and a Bedouin background is a great social handicap; the people from the south of Yemen and of the Sudan suffer particularly egregious oppression for this reason. The degree to which such divisions within a country are officially sanctioned varies, but it can reach surprising extremes. Kuwaiti citizenship comes in a variety of classes, with pride of place being given to those who applied for citizenship at Kuwait's founding. Fewer government services and fewer opportunities are available as the degree of officially recognized citizenship diminishes. This iniquity was challenged by the fidelity of low-class citizens to the state during Iraq's invasion, and the sentiment for reforming these rules is strong; but reforms are not yet complete.

Whenever an Arab country achieves something substantial — for example, victory in a war or in an international soccer match — it is celebrated throughout the Arab world as an Arab achievement. However, whenever an Arab country fails in some regard, the failure is discussed as the country's own, and not recognized as an "Arab" failure.

Beep Beep

When an Arab drives by a celebration such as a wedding, he will honk his car's horn in a specific rhythm as a salute to the bride and groom. He will also honk in celebration if he should pass a wedding procession. Wedding processions in the Arab world are raucous affairs (and weddings are the primary occasion of family processions, Western-style funeral processions being rare). A boisterous crowd of shouting, singing, ululating and gun-discharging (though the guns are fired into the air, stray bullets have caused more than one wedding-day tragedy where this custom is practiced) friends and relatives brings the happy couple to the site of their marriage. One other common occasion for horn-honking is in support of a favorite sports team. It is to this usage that the cartoon refers, as the man cheers al-Qazafi as if he were a favored boxer, rooting for him amongst the melée.

Make no mistake: the Arab world agrees with the global assessment of al-Qazafi as an insane, and potentially dangerous, fool.

Translation

Title: "Thanks for the only thing that makes the Arab street follow the Arab summit."
On the Podium: "The Brother Speech"

Language

"The Brother Speech" refers to Muamar al-Qazafi's preference to be addressed as "Brother." Most Arab presidents like to be called "Brother" to encourage the belief that they are of the people, emphasizing the contrast between modern-day Arab politics and the former colonial rule by foreigners. Throughout the Arab world, familial titles ("brother," "sister," "uncle," etc.) are often used between people as sign of respect and endearment. For example, women are often called "Sister" in public, by both men and other women, as a sign of respect for their privacy and modesty. This practice is reinforced by the Qur'an, 49:10, which says, "The believers are but brothers, so make settlement between your brothers. And fear Allah that you may receive mercy."

Arab Leaders' Way of Dressing

Some Arab political leaders will alternate between wearing their traditional, national garments (most Arab countries possess a traditional style of dress) and Western-style business attire. Why this variation in dress? An Arab leader's dress is an index of his confidence and security, both at home and abroad. Thus, King Abdullah of Jordan—whose legitimacy is doubted domestically and internationally—will wear Jordanian clothes when at home, and Western clothes when interacting with the international community. This tendency to accommodate himself to his environment betrays a fundamental vulnerability in his political base. On the other hand, a secure, firm ruler like King Abdullah of Saudi Arabia—who is certain in the enduring power of his domestic regime, as well as the regime's status abroad—will never be seen in Western business attire, and attends functions with foreign dignitaries in classical Saudi clothing. Other Janus-dressed politicians include the king of Morocco, the Yemeni president and the Sudanese president. An important exception is the president of Egypt, where the "traditional" style of dress has essentially become Western business dress.

King Hassan, King of Morocco (r. 1961-1999), generally wore European fashion, such as business suits; however, during Ramadan, he would wear traditional Moroccan dress while giving sermons at gatherings called Majales Hassanya, meaning Hassan's assemblies. He was also known to ride an Arabian horse on the morning of the Eids where people would shake and kiss his hand, as they regard him as the Amir al-Mu'minin, or Prince of the Believers.

Gamal Abdel Nasser, President of Egypt until his death (1956-1970), wore a variety of clothing because of his military background. During the first years of the revolution he wore a uniform worn by military officers of the time, taking its design from British Army khaki and brown shoes. Afterwards, he changed to civilian clothing, wearing long ties with small knots. He would often wear a vest, and on occasion, wear short-sleeved shirts.

Anwar el-Sadat, president of Egypt (1970- 1981), was considered one of the ten best dressed presidents in the world by the German magazine Stern. He favored wearing dark suits, and in the first years of his presidency, he imitated his predecessor Nasser by wearing sunglasses. He was also known for smoking a pipe, and was very particular about his clothing. He wore military clothing that was designed for him in Germany or England and would often wear a bullet-proof vest, although security personnel had trouble convincing him to wear one all the time (to the extent that they would talk to his wife about it). He often refused, and the day he was assassinated was one such day. He was fond of having his picture taken while standing in his elegant suits, smoking pipes, and holding his famous pharaonic baton. Sadat also wore a sash, of the kind also worn by Egyptian judges, with his military uniform, and decreed it part of the presidential uniform. Sadat also sought the help of American image consultants, since he succeeded a president with a great charisma, loved in both Egypt and other African, non-aligned and Communist countries. The consultant advised him to appear with his wife, which his predecessor never did—she dressed in elegant suits and often used the title of first lady. He was also told to be photographed with his dog so as to appear an animal lover—but showing lack of sensitivity to the Arabs' dislike of dogs. He also wore jalabayas and abbayas and sat on the floor with the farmers of his village, Meet Abu al-Kum. He was also very open about his personal life, allowing cameras to enter his house, and to the shock of Egyptians, a photograph of him in his undershirt, shaving, appeared on the front page of Akhbar al-Youm—again on the advice of image consultants. Regular interviews were granted to Himmat Mustafa, the Barbara Walters of Egypt at this time, when he would wear his abbaya, sit cross-legged at his village home which he maintained as a getaway, similar to the way the second President Bush maintained his Crawford ranch, and talked about his life, allowing any question. This was funny for Egyptians who were not accustomed to seeing a president in such domestic circumstances.

Hosni Mubarak, president of Egypt following the assassination of Sadat (1981-present), was very careful to wear suits in all seasons, which seems excessive to most Arabs, owing to the heat. His ties were made of subtle colors, and, at the beginning of his presidency, he sometimes wore half-sleeved summer suits when visiting various sites. During the presidential race of 2005, Mubarak began a new look, suitable to his campaign. His slogan, "Mubarak… leadership and path to the future," saw him wearing more youthful clothing to counter perceptions of his age. In contrast to Sadat, he avoids military uniform, the ironic result of his far more solid military career and the fact that he feels no need to emphasize these credentials.

Ali Abdullah Saleh, the current President of Yemen, who assumed that position in 1990, dresses in Western style when visiting such countries, but when attending international gatherings, such as UN summits, he will wear traditional Yemeni clothing.

Muamar al-Qazafi, the president of Libya since a coup in 1969, began his career wearing formal military attire, with a large formal military cap and sunglasses. Al-Qazafi also wears traditional silk robes with black and white stripes and a large abbaya made of wool. On numerous occasions he has worn shirts and hats with pictures of African leaders, especially Gamal Abdel Nasser, the late president of Egypt. Al-Qazafi is also known to travel with a she-camel, so he can always be supplied with milk. He also travels with a tent, where he prefers to stay. He is very particular in the colors of his clothing, which must be derived from African colors. He does not generally smoke, but will when attending Arab summits, where he spends his time watching the smoke coming from his cigarettes as others make speeches. In the past he wore bolder oranges, purples, but in more recent years he has preferred clothes that originate from Libyan folklore, with a hint of traditional African myth. He also likes clothing with the African continent drawn on it or a map of the world.

Saddam Hussein, the former president of Iraq, from 1979 until 2003, wore olive green military uniforms from the beginning of the Iran-Iraq war and would rarely deviate from this dress. In the 70s he would wear elegant Western clothes, but in the mid-80s he began to wear unusual clothes with designs that have no relation to traditional Arab clothing, looking more like cowboy gear. He would also wear the latest Italian fashion, along with traditional Bedouin clothes and blue industrial overalls, the traditional clothes of Iraqi blue-collar workers, in an attempt to bond with the Bedouins and workers, groups which tend to be large and hold enough power to threaten or further his strength. He was formerly a very elegant dresser, choosing his clothes himself, often by internationally renowned designers, such as Pierre Cardin, and all imported in large quantities, so that he would select what he wanted and destroy the rest. When he was upset his clothes would reflect his mood. He used a relaxing mask to reduce the wrinkles on his face, and he would dye his hair regularly. Most Arab leaders dye their hair, so that eighty-year-old leaders have hair that is jet black and without a single gray hair.

Yasser Arafat, who in 1958 founded Al-FataH with his friends and died in 2004, is famous for wearing the Palestinian kufiya, also known as the Arafat kufiya, a headdress, and is the only one of his colleagues to have worn it. It was so well identified with him that when Ismail Haniyeh, a leader of Hamas, returned from al-Hijj wearing it, he was criticized as trying to copy Arafat. Those around him stated that he wore it only because he had shaved his head while performing al-Hijj and it was cold when he returned. There are two colors for the kufiya, checkered black and white and checkered red and white. The black and white, called al-Kufiya al-fatahwaya, meaning the kufiya worn by the FataH people, is worn by those in the FataH movement. The red one is usually worn by people of the leftist Palestinian groups, specifically the Popular Front for the Liberation of Palestine and the Democratic Front for the Liberation of Palestine.

Hafez al-Assad was the president of Syria for three decades, beginning in 1971, until his death in 2000. He had a military background and would almost always wear military fatigues, starting with the October War of 1973. In the final days of his presidency, he wore civilian Western clothing.

Bashar al-Assad, the son of Hafez, successor, and current president of Syria, always wears formal Western clothing and sometimes appears with his wife Asma who dresses equally elegantly.

King Abdullah II of Jordan (r. 1999-present), the son of King Hussein, prefers to wear royal attire in addition to black suits. He also wears the jersey of the Jordan national soccer team, and attends all the games that his national team plays.

Queen Rania al-Abdullah of Jordan, wife of King Abdullah, is the most fashionable first lady in the Arab world, and one of the most fashionable women in the world. She won the title of "Most Elegant Woman of 2003" from Hello! magazine, over Nicole Kidman, Catherine Zeta-Jones, and Jennifer Aniston.

The favorite color of late King of Jordan, Hussein bin Talal (r. 1952-1999), was blue, and he wore both military and civilian clothing. He preferred wearing a blue blazer and light- colored slacks when wearing civilian clothes, or lighter colored clothing more suitable for young people.

Arab citizens like to joke about the fashion-pursuits of their leaders. One popular joke about the nattily and trendily dressed President Sadat has his wife coming home one day to find him setting the house on fire. "Anwar!" she screamed, "What are you doing?" "I'm trying to get a fireman's uniform to wear today!"

In Arab culture there is a distinction between the clothing that young people and older people wear. This concept in the U.S. applies more to women, while there is a certain amount of homogeneity between ages for Arab women. The greater difference is among men, as they can wear what they like, and there is a large distinction between the clothing of the old and young. King Hussein sometimes dressed in this younger style. Younger men's clothing will most likely be lighter in color. Older people may wear summer suits, comprising pants and a short-sleeved jacket. They also wear sandals, which younger people will not—the opposite of the U.S.

Gulf Dress

The favorite *iqal*, the distinctive headband worn with either a shemagh or gutra underneath, is made of goat hair. It is very thin and can be folded over easily, so as to fit the circumference of the head firmly. Two long tassels often hang from the back. Gulf princes always wear an *iqal*, favoring black goat wool. Under the *iqal*, the head may be covered with a gutra made of soft, white fabric, able to flow in the breeze, or a shemagh, made of heavier, strong fabric with a design. Emir Isa ibn Salman al-Khalifa, the late Emir of Bahrain (1961-1999), was famous for wearing an *iqal*. Citizens of Kuwait, Saudi Arabia, and Sharqa, a part of the United Arab Emirates, were the first to wear *iqal*, as it had once been limited to kings and amirs.

A jilbab is a long, loose-fitting garment worn by Arab men and woman, with different cuts and colors depending on gender. It is a favorite garment for Gulf princes and kings. People of the Emirates refer to it as a kandura, while people in Kuwait call it a dish dasha and prefer it without a collar. Saudis and Qataris, on the other hand, wear kanduras with collars.

Beshoot is also a common Arab garment, a cloak or long robe that is worn on top of a jilbab. The design depends on social status, with royalty employing a distinctive style, with two bands or stripes on the front that can be buttoned together with a single button, while the average beshoot is tied together with a cord. The garment originates from designs worn by the cavalry of ruling Gulf families. The royal families of the Gulf use different garments for religious festivals and weddings, which are often designed by African tailors. Some Arab countries have begun paying attention to the importance of the heritage of their dress, as many tailors are old and the art is in danger of being lost. As a result, some colleges are opening departments that focus on the history and technique of traditional Gulf attire so as to preserve the craft.

Translation

Title: The Catalogue of Royal Disguises

Subtitle: Dear Official, expect to see him very near, at . . .

At the Ministry of Information [reporting as if newsanchor]: Yaser abu Hilala, Algazira, Amman.

At the Office of Immigrant Labor [speaking in Egyptian dialect]: Why is that mister? — by God! we are down on our luck.

In the Jouida Prison [he poses as a prisoner on Cell Block D]

In the Ministry of Social Development: Brother, we have been without our allotment for two months.

In the Social Security Department [speaking as an elderly man]: I forgot my Social Security Number; please help me my daughter.

In D'Urara bin Azur High School

In the Ministry of Tourism [note that he asks for help in English]

In the Ministry of Dedication: Peace be upon you, brother.

Language

Arabic has great resources for recording the sound of a voice, allowing qualities of the speaker's individual delivery and sound to be conveyed. The old man, for example, speaks the letter "s" as "sh," a standard indicator of old age.

☪ The cartoon second from the left on the top uses an Egyptian phrase, said by those who are down on their luck when they face a situation that needs compassion, and also uses a title *Baih*, which Egytians use in addressing their superiors. The clothes are also those associated with Egyptian farmers, so the cartoon implies that those seeking work in Jordan are likely to be Egyptian. In the cartoon on the bottom right, the king is wearing the outfit worn by Islamists and Islamic scholars.

Culture

The above cartoon depicts King Abdullah of Jordan going "undercover" in various guises. He is noted for disguising himself and mingling throughout the country in order to investigate what it is like to be one of his common subjects. This way, his governing can be informed by first-hand experience, rather than only reports filtered by ministers and aides. This kind of ruse is a common motif in legend and history, with one popular Arab model being the third caliph, Umar ibn al-Khattab (586? CE – 644 CE), who traveled throughout his empire to ensure that his subjects had enough food and water. Many Arabs have a great fondness of historical legends of this sort, and this is a fertile vein for Arab leaders to counteract the popular assumption of governmental apathy and to establish that they genuinely care for their people.

The gesture is not simply one of pure benevolence, of course. Saddam Hussein made such trips during the Iran-Iraq War, visiting common citizens and inquiring into their conditions, and for any leader, it is surely at least partially a publicity stunt to be seen to go to these lengths. However cynically one might view the public reporting of "surprise" visits, though, it can be argued that much of their effectiveness comes not from the visit themselves but from the fear the visits inspire in officials.

Translation

Al Assad:

~~President of the Republic~~

King of the Jungle

Language

"Assad" means "lion," hence the king of the jungle.

Culture

Here one country makes fun of another country's leader, something that is usually sanctioned at the highest levels and appears in the government-run press. This phenomenon reached its height during the 1960s, between President Nasser of Egypt and King Faisal of Saudi Arabia, until they made up their differences at the Khartoum Summit in 1967.

Translation

"Which clan are you from?"
"Which militia are you from?"

Culture

In-fighting within Arab countries often obscures the larger issues of the region. In this cartoon, the small boy tugging at the foot of one of the men is representative of the Palestinian Resistance, the cause which has been forgotten by the men who are too concerned with who they are fighting in their own countries. The infighting between Arab nations has been problematic for the Palestinian cause because third party mediators are reluctant to mediate between Israel and Palestine if there is unrest in Palestine itself, and other Arab nations cannot interfere when they are using resources to resolve issues on the home front.

Translation

Words on dumpster: The S~~u~~mmit Garbage Conference

[*N.B. The Arabic words for "summit" and "garbage" are similar. Only two letters differentiate the two.*]

Culture

Since gaining independence, whenever most Arab countries encounter a situation of urgency, they convene a summit. These summits were formerly the source of great hopes for many Arab people. However, for a number of different reasons, the promises of action are never fulfilled, and these summits have only produced recommendations, condemnations, and suggestions. Arab people have lost faith in the ability of their leaders to set aside their differences in order to reach a mutual decision or respond forcibly to a crisis. The idea of a summit has become a laughing matter for many Arabs, who consider it a waste of time that only serves to deepen disagreements among Arabs. Decisions made at these summits are widely disregarded in the international community.

Arab people have given many unflattering names to the various political summits between Arab leaders. For example, in addition to "garbage summits," people have also used the phrase "throat summits," referring to the perceived lack of productive results and overabundance of empty talk. The cartoon below, titled "The Arab Summit" illustrates this sentiment.

Why Arabs lost hope in Arab summits

The Arab League was established in 1945 under the direction of British colonial authorities, a gesture intended to assuage and accommodate rising nationalist sentiments within the Arab world. The Arab countries would soon be free of Western oversight, went the underlying logic, and therefore required an organized, cooperative means of exerting influence upon the international community. The League's charter, however, did little more than found the entity by name: in particular, no regularized convocation was scheduled—or even mandated. Thus,

the first genuine Arab League summit was not convened until January, 1964, when Egypt's then-president Gamal Abdel Nasser invited Arab leaders to Cairo in order to discuss the Pan-Arab policy toward Israel. The decisions reached in this and the following summit largely precipitated the 1967 war with Israeli: the agreed-upon venture to re-route the river Jordan—and thereby deprive Israel of its water source—has been cited by Israel as one of the primary reasons for their eventual military campaign. After the disaster of the war, it was the Arab League that issued the famous "three no's": no negotiation with Israel, no treaty with Israel, no recognition of Israel. (Apropos of hydro-political maneuvering, it is worth mentioning that, first, the Arab League saw its re-routing policy as a response to similar actions on the part of the Israelis; and that, secondly, since its

occupation of the Golan Heights, Israel has had near-total command over the Jordan River's water, and both Jordanians and Palestinians have complained of urgently needed water being withheld and hoarded by Israel authorities.) After the 1967 war, Arab League summits were sporadically convened, often in response to some looming threat or urgent calamity—for example, the first and second Gulf Wars. (Note: in the Arab world, the "First Gulf War" refers to what, in the West, is better known as the "Iran-Iraq War," while the "Second Gulf War" refers to what Westerners know as the "First Gulf War," which included Operation Desert Storm. Operation Iraqi Freedom, accordingly, is known to Arabs as the Third Gulf War.)

In 2000, Arab leaders determined that Arab League summits were to be held annually, at a regularly scheduled date. To this news, Arab citizens reacted with great hope: the 1990s had been a rough decade, to put it mildly, and the prospect of a newly streamlined, coordinated Arab political entity seemed a promise of better things to come. Whence, then, the eventual dismissal of such summits, as evinced by the above cartoon. The tide of optimism began to dissipate in the wake of the 2002 summit, in Beirut.

There, Saudi Arabia had introduced the Arab Peace Initiative, a comprehensive plan to bring peace to Middle East: in exchange for a return of lands won in the 1967 War, the establishment of a Palestinian state, and a just and humane resolution to the Palestinian refugee crisis, Arab leaders unanimously pledged to recognize, and fully normalize relations with, the state of Israel. Israel responded by launching an attack on Palestinian Authority headquarters in the West Bank, an event that Arabs worldwide took as an act of aggression, dismissal and hostility—a nigh-explicit declaration of Israel's unwillingness to assume peaceful, cooperative relations with the rest of the region. This, unto itself, did not diminish Arab faith in the League's summits; rather, this loss of faith came about through the lack of an adequate Arab League response. Indeed, as tensions with Israel mounted, and America intruded heavily into regional politics via its occupation of Iraq, the already tenuous relationships between Arab leaders began to further crumble. The regularizing of the summits had made one thing clear: the inability of Arab leaders to cooperate with one another did not result from a scarcity of dialogue (which was the cited rationale behind making the summits annual), but rather from the *way* in which they did dialogue with one another. In other words, a combination of historical events and cultural mores prevented Arab leaders from easily trusting, and collaborating with, one another: and, importantly, the League's charter provided no clear form for this dialogue, no innovative means of facilitating it and causing it to become productive.

The absence of an adequate reaction to the Israeli war in Lebanon further undermined public confidence in the annual summits. Since the introduction of Saudi Arabia's stalled peace initiative, the Arab League has, arguably, accomplished little of substantial note, often devolving into the antics that characterized the previous cartoon.

Translation

"Arab weapons of mass destruction."

Culture

This cartoon refers partially to Saddam Hussein's claim to possess weapons of mass destruction. The claim, of course, proved empty. Nonetheless, word of his boasts reached American ears, and they were used as one of the primary justifications for the U.S. invasion of Iraq.

In reality, Hussein was merely bluffing: in a later interview, he explained that he had pretended that Iraq possessed nuclear

weaponry in order to deter Iran from invading or attacking.

☪ Empty words are not for Arab politicians alone, and many of the characteristics of Arab rulers are those of their people too, who are prone to exaggeration or embellishment, while empty threats and promises are often rampant in Arab speech. Even God found the habit ingrained and tiresome, warning in the Qur'an that boasting of untrue things would bring down his wrath.

Translation

On the building: Arab League

Above the microphone: The Arab Deterrence Weapon.

[N.B. the Arab headdress on top of the truck.]

Culture

Arab people perceive the response of the Arab League to any crisis as just talk without action, as are most Arab rulers' responses. This frustrates Arabs because they see their governments not standing up for the country, just talking about doing so.

The Peoples of the Arab World at Conflict

The relationships between Arab rulers, princes, kings, and presidents are mercurial at best, a fact which affects the relationship between their peoples. Generally speaking, Arabs have been taught to look at what unifies them: the common religion and language, and they have the same appearance. This sentiment is a strong influence most of the time, but when the relationships sour between Arab nations, it is usually with deadly consequences. For example, during the Iran-Iraq war (1980-1988), when the Iraqi men were off fighting, Egyptian migrants took the place of the fighting Iraqis in the workforce and kept their country running, with thousand of Egyptians going to Iraq every day. When the war ended, however, instead of showing gratitude for those people who took their place, the returning soldiers slaughtered the Egyptian workers mercilessly, either out of jealousy or a desire to be rid of the Egyptians quickly in order to regain their positions at work. Egyptians refer to this as the Flying Coffins, because flights to Egypt from Iraq were laden with the bodies of Egyptians who had died under suspicious circumstances. This maltreatment of the Egyptians is what prompted President Mubarak of Egypt to join the war against Iraq when the country first invaded Kuwait in 1990. Other Arabs complain about mistreatment when they travel to work in oil-rich Arab countries that often have a slavery-like system of granting work visas to migrant employees. In return, rich Arab people from these countries complain of being taken advantage of when they travel to tourist destinations because of their wealth. Palestinians have complained bitterly about the sporadic closings of the crossings between Gaza and Egypt especially at times when the Palestinians are in dire need of aid from the Egyptian side. More recently, Sudanese refugees were treated poorly and even were killed when they sought refuge in some Arab countries.

Even with these instances in mind, it is necessary to point out that there is no deeply entrenched animosity between Arabs, as an important part of the culture and religion is forgiveness. And the ties that bind people together, those being the shared religion and language, are much stronger than anything else.

Translation

Above Poster: An American movie disrespects Anwar Al-Sadat

Al Sadat (on Phone): Don't stay quiet towards them, Jihan.

Newspaper: Mrs. Jihan Al-Sadat discusses her new book in Washington.

[N.B. In the movie I Love You, Man, one of the main characters names his dog after Anwar Al-Sadat because he says that the dog looks just like Al-Sadat.]

Culture

The naming of a dog after former Egyptian president Anwar al-Sadat in the American film *I Love You, Man* gave rise to mixed emotions in many Egyptians, including Sadat's own family. Feeling that the scene defamed her father's character and defiled both his reputation and that of Egypt, Sadat's daughter, supported by other members of her family, filed formal complaints and announced their intention to sue the movie's Hollywood producers and writers. The family asked that the movie be banned from Egyptian movie theaters and that the American embassy issue a formal apology. It is not only insensitive Hollywood moguls who cause such offense; in 2008, relations between Iran and Egypt soured markedly after Iran produced *Assassination of a Pharaoh*, praising the assassins of President al-Sadat.

In an Arab country, if a movie portrays religion, the country and its history, or a revered figure in an unfavorable light, then that movie most likely will be banned or, if possible, the offending scenes will be cut. A highly offensive foreign movie can have grave diplomatic repercussions, even to the point of the severing of diplomatic ties. Arabs are inclined to take such insults very much to heart because in the Arab world, the expectation is that all media products are government-sponsored and endorsed; they do not differentiate between the government and the media. Arabs naturally find the west's freedom of expression difficult to understand, as it is so far outside their experience.

As the world has become more aware of Arab and Muslim sensibilities in these matters, some filmmakers have begun to self-censor to avoid controversies. Roland Emmerich, modern Hollywood master of the disaster movie, destroyed landmarks around the globe in his 2009 picture about the end of the world, *2012*. In his original vision for the movie, the Kaabah was to be included amongst the locations shown obliterated, but his co-writer's fear of a fatwah dissuaded him, and the scene was never shot.

In attempting artificially to foster a glorious public image, Arab leaders do not restrain themselves merely to censoring media. Self-aggrandizement is a positive passion for many; and one noticeable outlet for the impulse is the self-bestowal of elaborate sobriquets. al-Sadat, for example, devised and promulgated the titles "The Faithful Leader" and "The Hero of War and Peace" for himself, and he was commonly known as such during his period in office. The former title was in reference to his devotion (the genuineness of which is evidenced by his recognizable prayer bump shown in the cartoon—along with his ever-present pipe), and the latter referred to his military success and subsequent settlement with Israel. These were no casual appellations, either; he was officially honored as the "Hero of War and Peace" on stamps while he was still serving (Arab presidents do not observe the nice distinctions that keep current heads-of-state off stamps in American-style democracies, nor must they yield to ceremonial heads-of-state as in constitutional monarchies like the United Kingdom).

Modern leaders maintain the tradition of carefully managing the titles by which they are known. Sometimes, this manifests itself in benignly casting themselves as a patriarch by being known in reference to their firstborn son; the King of Saudi Arabia is widely known as Abu Moutab, and Nasser, the late President of Egypt, was referred to as Abu Khalid. More grandiosely, some leaders choose to shower themselves with exalted titles. Libya's al-Qazafi is well-known internationally for the superfluity of his titles, including: "Dean of Arab Leaders," "Imam of the Muslims," and, impressively, "King of African Kings."

Translation

Title: "The craziness in the price of meat"

Man: O peace, if you bleat and grow a dock, you would be honey, Ahntara.

Language

To say that something "would be honey" if it had some attribute means that that attribute would make it perfect.

A dock is the lump of fat at the rump of a sheep. Arab animals are typically much leaner than American cooks would be used to, and accordingly the Arab world prizes highly such fatty portions.

The phrase "*Ya Salaam*" (O peace) is a commonly used interjection that has many meanings. "Ya Salaam" can mean "How beautiful!" "How sad!" or "How wonderful!" It can be used to express anger, frustration, and disbelief. The phrase is also an expression of elation and is often said upon hearing a good song or a pleasant recitation of the Qur'an. "O peace! If..." (*Ya Salaam, lau...*), as in the cartoon, can even be used to indicate wishful thinking. Because this phrase connotes so many different emotions, it is important to convey one's intent with the proper tone of voice so as to avoid misunderstandings.

Culture

This cartoon throws a new perspective on the ire of Mr. Sadat in the previous cartoon over the naming of *I Love You, Man*'s dog. Ahntara is a revered figure from the distant history of the Arab people, but as this cartoon indicates, it is also a common pet name. These pet owners are commemorating the hero through their name-choice, not denigrating him, proving that naming a pet after someone is not necessarily a slur. The spirit in which the gesture is made makes all the difference: a bold and faithful dog being named the name of a bold and faithful leader of his people does honor to the dog and respectful homage to the hero; a scrunched-faced puppy named after a recently deceased political figure because of a supposed resemblance is less flattering to both parties.

Translation

Title: Mummification is an ancient Egyptian custom.

Mummy: Minister

Culture

This cartoon could refer to the fact that some Arab government officials remain in power for a long amount of time—sometimes just changing their positions in government.

In many Arab countries, it is dangerous and sometimes unlawful to criticize a sitting president in the media. Cartoon writers criticize the people around him instead of criticizing him directly. In this cartoon, the writer could be criticizing the president for staying in power by referring to the long tenure of his minister. Direct criticism of leaders is strictly controlled by the leaders themselves and so tends to avoid those failings and misbehaviors that are the actual causes of embarrassment and scandal.

☪ While the rest of the world is fascinated by ancient Egyptian history and the pharaohs, Muslim Egyptians and, to a larger extent, all Arabs are in awe not merely of the beauty and genius of the ancient culture but also of the might of the God that could bring low so powerful a civilization. This comes from the Qur'an, where God puts a curse on the ancient Egyptians for not believing in Him or the signs He sends through his prophets. The Qur'an relates the story of the Pharaoh who asks his advisor Haman to build him a tower, so that he can climb to the top and get a glimpse of this God that the Prophet Moses believes in.

Translation

Title: With apologies to the song

Under chair: "Chair in People's Assembly"

"You tell me to go away, I won't go away. You're going to call someone to tell me to go away but I won't go away."

Culture

Some elected officials for the People's Assembly like their positions so much that it is difficult to remove them. The electorate usually concludes that they are either making such a good living from bribery and corruption that they don't want to leave, or that they have done something that they do not want revealed and which they are able to keep the lid on as long as they remain in power and use their immunity—which can only be removed by their colleagues in the same legislative body.

While Western politicians usually try to win voters with policies that address the problems facing their society, some Arab candidates make more obvious appeals—for instance, offering between 1,000 and 3,000 Egyptian pounds per vote in the advertisements that appear on the street, either in a lump sum or by installments. Others will offer such blandishments as 3 kilos of meat, or 2 cans of tomatoes, or lunch at a restaurant, or trips for Hajj and Umra, or distribute gift bags containing two cans of fava beans, a bottle of oil and butter. Once they have honored this promise, the voters will not feel that they have any right to expect further action.

Translation

Sign: Department of Motor Vehicles

Man in yellow: "Congrats, Mr. President, here is your license. You'll see that the car needs an oil change, air in the tires, and a full tank of gas to complete your journey."

Culture

This cartoon deals with the reelection of Mubarak as president of Egypt. In this cartoon, the person issuing the new driver's license (to lead the country on a new path after election) tells Mubarak that much has to change (except for Mubarak). This situation is indicative of the system of governance in many Arab countries. This particular cartoon appeared in a government-controlled newspaper. Realizing that people need change, the artist advocates changes only in policy, but not in leadership.

Translation

Title: NO to inheritance.

[N.B. The "No" is the big x holding the Egyptian flag. The image depicts the son of long-standing Egyptian president Hosni Mubarak.]

Culture

Many Egyptians believe when President Mubarak dies, his son Gamal Mubarak will take over the presidency. Mubarak and his son

repeatedly deny this rumor. Because Mubarak has refused to appoint a vice president, he delegates all of his duties to Gamal Mubarak, who is covered extensively by the media. However, after Obama's 2009 speech in Cairo, media coverage of Gamal has lessened, which could be the result of talks between

Obama and Mubarak regarding Mubarak's successor, the media's preoccupation with Gamal, and media focus on other presidential hopefuls.

The Bush administration opposed the succession of Mubarak by his son, but the Obama administration has showed no qualms about this possibility. This shift may be due to the number of issues facing the Obama administration on foreign fronts, such as Afghanistan, Pakistan, and Iran, in which the United States needs all the help that it can get.

Translation

We, the Arab kings, look with concern to the " widespread phenomena of the inheritance of presidents of republics, which makes us think seriously about holding democratic royal "elections.

Culture

In some Arab Republics, upon the death of an elected leader, his son will take over presidency after wining a fixed election. This has occurred in Syria, and the process is underway in both Egypt and Libya. This cartoon, commenting on the monarchic tradition that seems to be developing despite what should be a republican style of government, depicts an Arab king taking exception to those presidents imitating the royal process of succession. Therefore, he suggests that monarchies distinguish themselves from these imitators by holding actual democratic elections.

Inheritance

Unlike the Judeo-Christian inheritance law of assigning a double portion to the first-born son, general Muslim principles deny such exclusive privileges. In most cases it is common for a female to receive a share equal to half of that given to a male of the same degree of relationship to the deceased. One third of a person's property may be bequeathed, but not a larger portion unless he or she has no legal heir. Without the consent of all the other heirs, no portion is given to a legal heir, unless it is a wife or husband. The children inherit the deceased's whole property, or what remains of it after payment of legacies, debts, and other formalities. The share of a male is double the share of a female. If the only heirs are two or more females, they inherit together two-thirds by the law of the Qur'an. If the only child is a female, she inherits, by the same law, half. The remaining third or half is also assigned to the daughters or daughter, by a law of the sunnah, which applies to other cases as well, if there be no other legal heir. In the case of a child, son's child, or parents of the deceased remain, the parents inherit one-sixth. If the father of the aforementioned children dies, his share is given to his own father, and in the case of women, her share is given to her mother. If the deceased have left no children or son's children, the mother gets one-third of the property, or of what remains after deducting the share of the wife (or wives) or husband. The residual goes to the father, unless the deceased has left two or more brothers or sisters, in which case the mother inherits one-sixth and the father collects the residual. The siblings receive nothing if a father or any ascendant in the male line outlives the deceased in question. According to the 12th verse of chapter IV of the Qur'an, if the deceased leave behind no children and his parents are his heirs, then the mother receives a third. If he has siblings, the mother receives a sixth. It can be inferred that the mother's share is diminished while the father's is increased due to the existence of surviving half-siblings. In the passing of a woman, a man inherits half of what remains of her property after the payment of her legacies and so forth if no children or son's children remain. One-fourth is the share given to the wife, or wives combined, if the recently deceased husband leaves behind no child or son's child, but one-eighth is given to any such descendents if they are in fact involved. In the Qur'an these laws are found in chapter 4, verses 12-15 and 176. If the only remaining sibling of the deceased is a sister, she inherits half. If a deceased woman had no children and a single brother remains after her death, he would inherit all of her property. If she is survived by a son her brother would receive nothing, but if the surviving child in question were instead female, the deceased's brother would inherit what remains after deducting the daughter's share. If a deceased man is survived by two or more sisters and no brothers, the sisters inherit two-thirds, but if one or more brothers and one or more sisters remain they inherit the entirety of the deceased's property. The share of the brothers would be double that of the sisters. If only half-siblings through the father's side are involved, they would receive his whole property. No distinction is made between the child of a wife and one who was born to a slave and her master if the master acknowledges the child as his own. A child regarded as a bastard would inherit exclusively from his mother and vice versa. When there is no legal heir or legatee, the property is received by the government treasury. The property of the deceased is nominally divided into twenty-fourths (*keerats*), and the share of each son or other heir is said to be such *keerats*. The law is remarkably lenient towards debtors. The Qur'an states "If there be any [debtor] under the difficulty [of paying his debt], let [his creditor] wait till it be easy [for him to do it]; but if ye remit it as alms, it will be better for you." According to the chapter in which this scripture derives, any Muslim who accrues a debt is expected to write a statement of it and be attested by two men, or a man and two women, of his own faith. He is imprisoned if the debt is not paid, but is liberated upon establishing insolvency. If able, he may be compelled to work for the discharge of his debt.

Half is for five: the husband, the daughter, son's daughter, sister, or half-sister through the father's line.

One-fourth is for two: the husband or wife.

One-eighth is for one: the wife or wives

Two-third is for four: the daughter, the sons and daughters, sistser, or half-sister through the father.

One-third is for two: the mother and the mother's children

One-sixth is for seven: the father, grandfather, grandmother, mother, the mother's son, the son's daughter, or the half-sister through the father's line.

Translation

"Enough"

[*N.B. This cartoon refers to Mubarak, the president of Egypt, who has ruled for a long time.*]

Culture

To Egyptians, the Sphinx is a symbol of silence. Mubarak's presidency for 29 years is too long that even the Sphinx is saying, "Enough."

☪ Enough is the unofficial moniker of the Egyptian Movement for Change a grassroots coalition which draws it support from across Egypt's political spectrum to oppose President Hosni Mubarak's presidency and the possibility he may seek to transfer power directly to his son Gamal.

While it first came to public attention in the summer of 2004, and achieved a much greater profile during the 2005 constitutional referendum and presidential election campaigns, it has recently lost momentum, suffering from internal dissent, leadership change, and a more general frustration at the apparent inability of Egypt's political opposition to force the pace of reform.

Culture

The sphinx bears the face of Mubarak, the president of Egypt, who is said to have control over the elections (by holding the ballot box).

President Muhammad Hosni Mubarak of Egypt has been in power for twenty-eight years and it seems that the only way that he will leave the Presidential palace is in a hearse. The only person who is really qualified to take over his position is his son, who has been assigned many of his father's duties. Other people who could assume the presidency would need to learn the necessary skills on the job, because they would have no prior experience. The strongest opposition to his grip on power came from the Bush administration when they demonstrated their dissatisfaction with his long tenure by reducing their aid to Egypt and forcing Mubarak to hold elections for the presidency against an opposition leader under indictment by the government. Of course, Mubarak won the election by a large margin. Furthermore, Mubarak was treated poorly on his official visit to Washington and, as a result, did not visit the United States for the five years prior to Obama's inauguration. Obama attempted to mend fences with the Egyptian president but referred to leaders like him in his inauguration speech by saying, "To those who cling to power through corruption and deceit and the silencing of dissent, know that you are on the wrong side of history, but that we will extend a hand if you are willing to unclench your fist." Other leaders like Mubarak exist in the Arab world: Gaddafi has ruled Libya for over forty years.

Egyptians recognize that the Mubarak regime has allowed them the broadest freedom of expression since 1952. A common opinion is that if an Egyptian cannot express his opinion in the Mubarak era, he will never be able to express it. A similar saying existed during the period of Sadat, who initiated the trend of opening the country to the West by lifting trade barriers; under Sadat, the saying claimed that if an Egyptian could not make money during that era, he would never be able to make money.

Translation

This large question mark has the face of Mubarak imposed within it, with the caption "Who will come after Mubarak?"

Language

The question mark in Arabic should face the right since the language is written from right to left.

Translation

Panel 1 title: In the Past

Man: O God, guide our rulers to what pleases and satisfies You.

Panel 2 title: In the Present

Man: O God, don't reproach us for what the foolish among us have done.

Panel 3 title: Soon

Man: O God, make note of who they are, annihilate them, and don't leave any!!

Language

The English "prayer" can translate to two Arabic words. *Salat* is formalized worship including organized standing, kneeling, and prostration. *Doaa* is supplication, as shown in the cartoon. Muslims can use two different languages in their *doaa*. This learned man is using the classical form of Arabic in his supplication. One is perfectly able to use colloquial Arabic, but the classical form is preferred in *doaa*. The *salat*, of course, must be conducted in classical Arabic, as it largely consists of quotation from the Qur'an

A *doaa* can either ask God to bestow a benefit on someone — including oneself —, or it can ask God to bring someone harm. If one's *doaa* takes the latter, ill-wishing form, then one must be sure that one is asking not merely for personal revenge but rather for true justice.

Culture

Praying for leaders

It is incumbent upon Muslims to pray for the wisdom and righteousness of their rulers, and traditionally, the rulers would be, in fact, holy and just. Though the modern rulers themselves would no doubt disagree, it is generally held that the high

standards set in former times are no longer adhered to by the current leaders of Arab states, and Muslims are faced with a conumndrum of how to pray for them. Irrelgious and incompentent leaders become the target of the harm-wishing form of *doaa*. Of course, this practice is restricted largely to home worship, though, a public prayer leaders (imams) are not permitted, as government employees, to make such open critizicms. Indeed, a *doaa* directed against the nation's leader is a jailable offence.

☪ A common trope within American popular punditry and political analysis is an (apparently affected) incomprehension at Arabs' unwillingness to "do something" about their long-tenured rulers. Despite the seemingly perpetual strife and turmoil plaguing the region, there is a remarkable stability with regard to Arab political regimes: for example, Egyptian president Hosni Mubarak has been in office since 1981, while Libyan leader Muamar al-Qazafi has held power since 1969. Whence this political longevity? And whence this (perceived) Arab reluctance to combat such flagrantly anti-democratic institutions, so distasteful to the Western mentality? Oppressive security measures do, of course, play a role: organized intelligence and enforcement agencies, such as the *mukhabarat* and the police, contribute to the rigidly maintained, politically opportune stasis that characterizes the region. But power has more than sheer physical force at its disposal, and the furtive, quiet sway of ideological machinations exercises a remarkable effect upon the minds of the citizenry. To wit: the primary means of ensuring regime-stability is not the hulking threat of the enforcement agency, but rather the subtle exploitation of religious loyalties.

From an early age, children are indoctrinated in the political teachings of the *Qur'an* and early Islam. "O ye who believe," reads surah 4, *ayah* 59, "Obey Allah, and obey the Messenger, and those charged with authority among you." Since the death of the Prophet, those invested with religious and political power are known as either *Amir al-mu'mini* ("the Prince of the Believers") or *imam al-muslimeen* ("the Leader of the Muslims). If such a public figure should exist, his enunciations would bear the unimpeachable stamp of divine ordinance, and all Muslims would be subject to their commands. A just and wise ruler, he is to be obeyed unswervingly. Dissent may be voiced—but quietly, and with the utmost restraint. And, as mentioned above, one is required to pray for his health and wellbeing—and, at the same time, expressly prohibited from praying *against* him, spreading rumors that slander his good name, and staging armed revolt. To this general writ, the sole exception is a case in which the leader commands his citizenry to sin: for example, in legalizing of prostitution, homosexuality or alcohol.

Now, these undemocratic, nigh-endless regimes arise when a given leader declares himself the *Amir al-mu'mini* or the *imam al-muslimeen*—which, of course, is the case in nearly all of the countries in question. Thus, schoolchildren are taught extensively about their duty to serve and honor their national leader—no matter what he does (short, again, of ordering a sin). If one takes issue with a policy or piece of legislation, one is advised to pray that the ruler come to his senses, as it were, and re-acquire divine, guiding wisdom. In this way, many Arabs identify as synonymous their duties as citizens and their duties as God's servants. As a result, Arab political regimes stretch on for what are, in the democratized West, unheard of amounts of time.

Translation

"And when the newspaper wrote that Mr. Nazeef said that people who pray against the government will tomorrow pray for it, Sheikh Hamza had diarrhea and ran away from the hamlet. And he hid the black rosary he uses to pray against the government inside the mattress, in the house of his father-in-law. And he sends you a letter saying that he loves the government like everyone else and the one who forgives is the generous one, and may God make it full of life."

[N.B. The tall man in this cartoon is Nazeef, the prime minister of Egypt. The small man is identifiable as a farmer by his clothes and by the bundle, which is special to farm laborers, who use their large kerchiefs to cover their heads, wipe away sweat and carry food.]

Language

The small man ends with a saying that is used to ask for someone's mercy and understanding for a fault: "He who forgives is the generous one." The second phrase, "May God make it [your house] full of life," is used by those asking for charity, who pray for your house to prosper and have plenty of activity — so that your wealth will make the gift seem trifling and you may also give again..

The sheikh of this small village has taken as a threat — you'll be beaten to change your mind — a comment that was meant as a promise — what we do will win over our critics. This makes him panic (saying that someone has diarrhea is exactly equivalent to the English expression about shitting oneself) and overreact, hiding his rosary as if it could be taken as evidence. However, official threats are often veiled in subtle language, so his reaction may not be quite so strange.

Translation

Saddam Hussein: "By the way, I request the end of service reward (severance pay)."

Culture

There were cartoons and caricatures about Saddam Hussein's trial in the Arab media. However, it was generally regarded as too serious a subject for satire and the majority of Arabs regard his death as martyrdom.

Strictly according to the Qur'an, the title of martyr is given only to the unpaid soldier killed in a war for the defense of the faith. However, general opinion has expanded the definition over the centuries to encompass anyone who is killed through no fault of his own. Under this common, loose interpretation, anyone from plague or murder victims to persons drowned in boating accidents or smashed in car crashes can be deemed a martyr.

☪ Islamic tradition holds that it is a Muslim's sacred duty to take arms against aggressive enemies of Islam. One who fights without fee in such a conflict is promised the rewards of a martyr. Modern groups that have used this belief to recruit people for violent acts against non-belligerent states or civilian populations have misapplied and misinterpreted this tradition, for the Qur'an offers no sanction for unprovoked attacks. The widespread belief in the West that the martyr is promised seventy-two virgins in paradise has no basis in the Qur'an and is never mentioned in Arab countries.

☪ Many Arab capitals host an annual commemoratation of Saddam Hussein's death. Thousands of people attend, from ordinary citizens to the leaders and members of labor unions. Typically such events include symposia, poetry recitals and speeches, which celebrate Hussein's various accomplishments and discuss his murder at the hands of an alleged Israeli-American-Iranian conspiracy. To this end, speakers typically caution against the dangers of American Zionist aggression, and emphasize the threat of Iranian attempts at regional domination. Often one of Saddam's relatives—usually his daughter, Raghda, who lives in Jordan—will phone into the event, thanking participants for their remembrance and good wishes.

التليفزيون العراقي: و الآن موعدنا مع خطاب الرئيس المفدّى صدّام..ثم فيلم تسجيلي عن حياة القائد العظيم صدّام..ثم نشرة إخبارية عن آخر أخبار الزعيم صدّام..ثم فاصل موسيقي و أغنية صدّام يا صدّام......

Translation

The Iraqi TV Announcer: And now it's time for the speech of our dearest President Saddam... Then a documentary about the life of the great leader Saddam... Then a newscast about the latest news of the leader Saddam... And then a musical interlude and the song, "Saddam, O Saddam."

Culture

One of the striking features of autocracies is the ubiquitousness of images and news about the national leader. The streets are full of statues of him; in offices, his towering portraits glower down; broadcasts are filled with eulogies trumpeting his achievements. Public buildings and public infrastructure such as schools, hospitals, bridges, and roads are all likely to be named after the leader and display his image. Many a schoolchild may walk along the Leader's road to the Leader's school and start the morning singing a song in praise of the Leader's supposed glory. Every government act is announced as being undertaken at his instruction to alleviate the suffering of the poor and improve the lives of his people.

Of course, these have been the tactics of dictators as long as the technology has existed to effect them: the Caesars printed their faces on the coinage and disseminated sculptures around the Empire. The modern form now seen in Arab countries, though, was first attempted by Egypt's President Nasser. The illusion was dispelled for Egyptians in 1967 when Egypt was defeated in the Six Days' War, but the fashion was set for the other autocracies.

Translation

If you are looking for good faith and sincerity, in our *mehbash* [coffee grinder] there is a heritage that tailors clothes for loyalty, as if its heart is Jordan and its breath is Saltian [from the city of Salt].

[N.B.: King Abdullah of Jordan in the frame of the sunglasses.]

Language

In every Arab country the city where the leader was born or to which he traces his roots, is where he has his natural base and most fervent supporters. Tikrit showed particularly strong allegiance to Saddam Hussein, and he showed it great favor, not least as a potential haven in time of trouble. Salt is renowned for its dedication to the King.

The phrase concerning "tailoring clothes for" something is slightly convoluted, but indicates the ability to show others how something should be done, so here the memories or heritage embodied by the *mehbash* are implicitly perfect since they would be able to clothe perfect Jordanian loyalty adequately.

It is common to see advertisements such as this that laud the ruler of Arab countries and how much people love them. They are most prevalent in Syria and Jordan.

Though the ad's actual expression may seem far-fetched and contorted, it relies on the same elements as advertisements that seek to emphasize a deep-rooted tradition and authenticity, drawing on the customer's patriotism and love of national heritage. Selling something that is old-fashioned and well-known to its audience risks the boredom, so it is sold by association.

Translation

Man: "Of course he got the death penalty. He was despotic and tyrannical."

Culture

Some tyrant husbands treat their wives as if they were servants and don't see the fault in this type of behavior. This cartoon plays on how this husband reacts to the execution of a tyrannical and despotic person (Saddam Hussein) and doesn't see this very quality in himself for ordering his wife to wash his feet.

☪ For this reason many believe dictatorship is the way to govern Arabs because inside each one is a dictator. To some extent the rulers' oppressive behavior creates a pattern of oppression within the population, normalizing oppressive behavior toward each other, and this can in itself become part of a vicious circle, fostering further tyranny in the governing class.

Translation

Saddam Hussein to the judge during his trial: "I don't like your talk. If you don't straighten up I'll execute you."

Culture

Saddam Hussein, Tariq Aziz and the other Iraqi leaders put on trial were a source of pride to the Arab world for their deportment and defiant behavior toward the courts, which they did not recognize as legitimate.

Translation

Title: Saddam's Eid sacrificial lamb.
Above the door: Slaughter House
Sheep: "Are you new in the neighborhood?"

Culture

An Iraqi court tried Saddam Hussein on war crimes charges and sentenced him to death. He was hanged in December 2006. The execution was met with outrage because it

coincided with the first day of Eid al-AdHa (the Festivity of Sacrifice), a day on which sheep are often sacrificed. It was very humiliating for Arabs and many considered him to be a martyr.

11 – Terrorists

Translation

Terrorist/Announcer: And now, dear Jihadists, the time has come for our quiz show program: "Slaughter to Win." After that, our cooking program—with Chef Osama bin Laden—and today's dish is: "The Bomb Site." And after that, our program about fatwahs, and today's episode is about, "The Butchery Doctrine." And please turn off the TV because it is forbidden [*in Islam*] to start with!

Language

The dish referred to as, "The Bomb Site," is an  actual dish: *mansaf* (منسف). It is the national dish of Jordan and is made of lamb, aged yogurt, and rice. The name is humorous: the food is piled high and it is so delicious that people attack it with gusto, so that it is rapidly flattened.

Culture

As one would expect, the videotaped messages from suicide bombers and terrorist leaders are coveted "scoops" for Arab news organizations, and they draw significant ratings. Many in the Arab world are uncomfortable, however, with the practice of broadcasting these messages to the general public. They feel that terrorists should not be given the chance to present their socially disruptive arguments and attempt to sway viewers to their ideologies; tapes that might be taken as pure news by liberal, secular, or Western audiences might—untranslated and unmediated—be dangerously persuasive to those sympathetic to the terrorists' cause or win new sympathy with their clever propagandistic editing. Furthermore, many fear that the tapes carry covert messages to scattered terrorist cells.

☪ The Internet and private circulation are usually the only ways for cartoons dealing with terrorism to be distributed in the Arab world, as the mainstream Arabic media usually avoids them. Besides the obvious questions of taste that would arise from treating irreverently such a serious topic, cartoonists have to worry about becoming themselves the target of terrorist violence. The phrase "to spill blood" does not have the same meaning in Arabic that it does in English. In Arabic, one "spills the blood" of someone when one announces that that person should be killed by anyone associated or sympathetic with the people who issue the fatwah or decree. Thus, a living person may have his blood spilt, if he is under such a threat of death; indeed, if the threat is rescinded, that person may find his blood, suddenly, unspilt.

☪There has been a burgeoning of religious broadcasting channels via satellite, Islamic and Christian, both of which have had a role in fomenting religious intolerance. The Islamic channels have been the conduit for the issuing of religious fatwahs, usually by fanatics from an educated background but without religious credentials. These fatwahs have been discredited and widely ridiculed by the mainstream media for their absurdity—for example, one broadcaster proclaimed that growing a beard, considered a sunnah, would increase sexual potency; another stated that barbers should be banned, for shaving beards; another that if a man sits on a chair that has been sat on by a woman it cancels any religious purity, so he will have to undertake ritual ablutions before any religious activity. Some declare that sickness should be treated with "Prophetic Medicine," herbal medicine from the Prophet's time, and Qur'anic verses, and advocate using religion to exorcise possession by jinns. If these channels are criticized elsewhere on television, the producer or announcer may be met with death threats either sent personally or to public web-sites. As for the Christian channels, most aim to make Muslims question their faith, casting doubt on the Qur'an and and finding contradictions in the Hadith.

The channels are often not fully accredited and fall outside normal government regulations and broadcast guidelines, and once they come to the attention of the authorities, they are either called upon to put their affairs in order or are shut down. Many governments have started to crack down on these channels, as the absurdity of the fatwahs discredits religion and has real social impact on the population.

Translation

Terrorist: In response to the killing of the innocents in Iraq . . . we will take revenge . . . by killing innocents in Iraq!

[N.B. *The kneeling figure is dressed in orange in the original, and is clearly a Westerner, as the cartoon refers to the kidnapping and execution of Nick Berg, an American contractor in Iraq.*]

Culture

Terrorists' preference for beheading with a sword as the method for carrying out their executions springs from an Islamic form of punishment known as *qisas*, or retribution. *Qisas* is meant not only to be a punishment for the

person subjected to it, but it is also a deterrent for potential criminals, which is why the filming and broadcast of the executions is central to the terrorists' aims. Their employment of this method is a perversion of the legal executions still practiced in Saudi Arabia and Iraq.

The persistence of public beheading as a form of legal execution is one of the most jarring aspects of the Arab world to Western sensibilities, and it is important that one come to grips with it. Indeed, the Saudi government often encourages British and American expatriate workers (though only workers, as casual tourists are not permitted in the country) to witness the process of execution by beheading so that the facts, grim as they are, may dispel the lurid fancies that the concept raises in Western minds. Beheading is, in truth, a fairly common form of execution in Saudi Arabia: 35 people were beheaded in 2004 and 83 in 2005. Though the bloody spectacle might at first seem a medieval barbarity, to one accustomed to the culture a swift, sure beheading seems a humane alternative to the baroque array of execution methods practiced in the United States.

According to Sharia law, the sentence of beheading can be passed only for certain crimes, including the crimes of rape, murder, apostasy, armed robbery, and a second conviction for drug dealing. In such cases, execution is held to be a just reparation for the harm done to innocent members of the community. Where the victim is clearly identifiable—primarily in the cases of rape and murder—the law further allows and encourages the victim or the victim's family to grant mercy to the offender, to give up their right to retribution (in Arabic, seeking blood). This reprieve might be granted after the convict offers a hefty payment in compensation for his offense, but it can also be granted to impecunious criminals from pure forgiveness and mercy. Such a sparing of a criminal's life is termed "saving a neck," a phrase which carries a far more literal meaning in Arabic than in English. Prisoners' families may make appeals to the king or a prominent prince, and if he finds the prisoner deserving, he adds his authority to the suit; few families of victims would be able to reject such an august call for mercy, and those who relent are treated to lavish, royal generosity. In Saudi Arabia, in the special case that the victim is foreign but the culprit Saudi, the king will take it upon himself to intervene, and do whatever he can to spare the life of the Saudi criminal. In addition to his formidable political clout, he wields significant religious authority as well: the Saudi king holds the title "The Custodian of the Two Holy Nobles," an honor bestowed for his lavish financial support of the Kaabah and the Holy Mosque where the Prophet Muhammad is buried. In the case of the king's intervention, forgiveness can be a lucrative venture—the king receives those who forgive murderers at his personal estate, where a small service is held in honor of the visitor's benevolence. "We decided upon forgiveness," declares the visitor, "by God's guidance." This is followed by a recitation of a poem (usually celebrating the wisdom of the king and the compassion of the honoree) and the official signing of forgiveness-related legal documents. The king closes the ceremony, commending the wisdom of those who forgive such killers. In the above picture, the Yemeni brother of a murder victim, who forgave his Saudi killer, is greeted by the Saudi king. Such meetings are often headline news.

The procedures around the execution encourage such a sparing of life, as a special committee applies to the victim's family on the day of execution to relinquish their rights to the offender's death, as does the executioner himself in the moments before sentence is carried out. The prisoner too, of course, pleads before he is blindfolded, the hope for this salvation carrying him through the last moments of his life. Unsurprisingly, families generally wish the execution to proceed, but the executioner gives them every opportunity to change their minds, even swinging his sword in an "X" before making the fatal blow to give them more time to relent. Often, an experienced executioner will be able to tell at sight whether a family is disposed to "save the convict's neck." Recognizing the families' overwhelming emotions at this moment and the likelihood that they will be unable to speak, a simple raising of the hand is enough to signify their forgiveness. Should mercy be granted, the spectators praise them and God, crying exultantly, "God is the most Great," and praying that the family may go to Heaven in recognition of their benevolent decision.

That crowd, so startlingly in contrast to the modern American practice of execution, is vital to the function and purpose of the beheading. An execution is meant not only to punish him whose crime has been an attack against society, but also to discourage in the strongest possible way any others who might even think about committing such a crime. Thousands of people gather for executions, which are held in heavily populated neighborhoods to encourage attendance. Though for some the grisly spectacle proves too much and they panic or even faint in revulsion, many in the crowd clap and whistle enthusiastically in support of this visceral evidence of the strength of the laws. In this modern era, people even take and swap pictures of the proceedings.

Though executions are widely publicized to encourage these large crowds, the prisoner himself is kept in ignorance until the early morning of the appointed day, frequently a Friday, the Muslim Sabbath day. Men and women are treated in much the same way, the major differences being that a woman arrives to the place of execution in a hijab, is accorded more space until immediately before her death, and is typically offered more solace by the warden, who will recite from the Qur'an to solace her. The prisoner in all cases is woken early without explanation, bundled into a car, and brought to a prominent square after the main prayers, *salat al-jumaa,* at which people will already have assembled in great numbers. Some 200 policemen will already be in the square when the prisoner arrives to control the crowd and guard against any attempts by the convict's family to disrupt the execution. They will have cordoned an area 30mx30m around the site of the execution itself. Upon arrival, the prisoner is bound with his hands behind his back and blindfolded by the escort who brought him from prison. Then, he is taken to the center of the square, where he is sat on the ground facing al-*Qibleh,* the direction of the Kaabah towards which Muslims face when praying. Though the disorientation and physical distress from his shock and apprehension may make him appear to the public to be under sedation, the condemned is not anesthetized.

Meeting him at the place of execution, a sheikh recites appropriate verses from the Qur'an. For example, in a case of murder he might relate the procedure to the above-mentioned concept of *qisas,* or public punishment-as-deterrent: "And here for you, through legal retribution, [there will be a saving of] life, O you [people] of understanding, that you may become righteous" (2:179) (in other words, the taking of the murderer's life by the state will serve in the long run to save lives because of the number of potential murderers who will be dissuaded from violent ways by the retributive spectacle). Following the reading, a representative of the court (formerly the sentencing judge himself, though no longer) recites the particulars of the crime, thus reaffirming before the assembled onlookers the justice of what they are about to witness. The executioner himself then instructs the condemned to repeat the *shahada,* or the basic Muslim declaration of faith in the oneness of God and Muhammad's status as his Prophet and the prisoner may even prostrate himself. It is at this point that the appeals are made to the family to relent and grant a reprieve. The condemned, meanwhile, will be pleading, praying, confessing, gibbering, or waiting in silence, as he is inclined. If the execution is to go ahead, then the executioner removes his sword from its sheath and approaches the prisoner so that his sword hand is towards him. A sharp prick in the side makes the condemned person double over in pain, exposing the neck and facilitating a clean cut. With one quick, powerful blow, sentence is carried out. A doctor confirms the time of death, and the body is taken for burial. In punishing crimes of vicious enormity, the punishment is intensified with a form of execution known as Censure Killing (*taazear*), in which more than one stroke is used to draw out the criminal's pain, but usually, executioners take great pride in being able to sever a head in one stroke.

The executioner's profession is highly specialized, and frequently, it passes from father to son, with executioners bringing their young boys to observe their work and become accustomed to the procedure. A man who performs these beheadings is known by the term *sayéf*, which means swordsmith, thus differentiating him from executioners in countries that do not use beheading. The term harkens back to the days when the executioner would also be a skilled artisan who made his own blades; though this is no longer the case, the honorable term is retained. These *sayéf*s are a highly respected and elite group; there are only seven in all of Saudi Arabia. According with the highly public nature of beheadings and the large popular support for them, no stigma attaches to *sayéf*s; instead, they are honored as strong supporters of the law and civic order. With so few *sayéf*s, they must travel a great deal, hurrying around the country with three days' notice to their next assignment, never learning the name of whom they are to execute until it is announced in the public square. The government proudly honors these professionals, supporting them and providing funds for the *sayéf*s to buy their very expensive swords, which can range from 33,000 to 70,000 Saudi Riyals and usually are imported from Egypt or India. The only exception to this general admiration comes, naturally, from the families of the condemned prisoners, and to ward against threats from them the government offers the *sayéf*s thorough, round-the-clock protection, though they frequently waive this protection in the confident belief that God will protect them for fulfilling His will. The execution is the expression of God's law, so the executioner is a quasi-religious figure. The entire execution, in fact, can be seen as a religious act, and as such, the executioner must put himself in a state of ritual purity, as if he were going to mosque, praying two *rakah* before leaving his home to perform the execution.

The training for *sayéf*s is long and arduous. Those who are not born into the profession typically come to it through work as a jailer or prison escort. First, one must become inured to the brutal facts of the process simply through close observation of executions. This is known as psychological or practical training, and eventually encompasses assisting with the executions and even carrying the severed head. The other part of an executioner's education, the theoretical training, encompasses becoming proficient in the various techniques of beheading. *Sayéf* also study to sever hands and feet using a sharp, knife-like instrument, as these punishments are mandated for lesser crimes (in these cases, the prisoner is given anesthesia). Executioners also must practice the use of firearms, for on occasion guns are used instead of swords to execute criminals. Finally, a trainee will be able to stand ready to carry out sentence should the *sayéf* not, for some reason, be able to fulfill his duty. All this preparation helps to mitigate the extreme anxiety that an executioner will feel the first time he is called upon to do his job, an anxiety springing both from the nature of the deed and the fact that it is witnessed by so many thousands of people. Having executed the criminal, though, the *sayéf* can be proud and at peace, confident that what he has done was mandated by God. After performing the execution, the executioner wipes his sword clean and places it back in its sheath. Then, accompanied by his guards, he returns home, where his wife will wash his clothes, in case they are stained by blood, and he can sterilize his sword in preparation for the next execution.

☪ In criticizing capital punishment, opponents of the practice will often cite execution's ineffectiveness as a deterrent. Islamic capital punishment parries this objection through its eminently public nature: there is no question that, in Islamic practice, the execution of criminals is meant chiefly as a deterrent. So, whereas an execution in, say, Texas will admit a small, often hand-selected audience, the Islamic execution will be performed in a public square, staged for all to see.

The Qur'an

Islamic tradition holds that the text of the Qur'an is the direct word of God, transmitted to the Prophet Muhammad by the angel Gabriel over a 23-year period in the early 7th century C.E. The Qur'an itself, as a text, is considered the central miracle of the Islamic faith, a well-spring that is ever-demonstrating the tradition's truth to new generations. Before the Qur'an, God's prophets established their validity through the performance of miracles: so Ibrahim passed unscathed through a great conflagration, Moses turned scepters into serpents and sent plagues upon Egypt, and Jesus raised the dead. Islamic tradition notes that these miraculous works were directly available only to those present to see them. So, as the eye-witnesses passed on and new generations took their place, inevitably these miracles were lost to time, and people began to disbelieve them. Moreover, even those who witnessed such miracles often tried to explain them away, appealing to magic, for example, or optical illusion. But through the existence of a miracle that is also a reproducible, widely available text, Islam avoids precisely this problem—for, should they be interested, anyone may go and encounter the miracle, the Qur'an, for him or herself.

The question arises as to why, exactly, the Qur'an is considered miraculous. Muslims claim that the Qur'an exhibits a scientific acumen and linguistic sophistication all but unavailable to the community that first possessed it—unavailable, especially, to the Prophet Muhammad, who was widely known to be illiterate. As to the former point, Islam has won Western converts through the text's perceived references to contemporary scientific learning, such as modern cosmology's Big Bang theory. As to the latter, it is important to note that the text of the Qur'an is admired not only for its religious significance, but also for its considerable esthetic qualities. The text displays a high level of linguistic complexity, polish and sophistication: for instance, Arabic poetry values rhyme highly, and some 85% of the Qur'an verses sustain rhyme schemes. The Qur'an itself is confident in its own unsurpassable eloquence, and challenges both humans and jinns to compose verse of comparable truth, force and beauty.

In this way, the Qur'an possesses the unique ability to re-constitute itself as a new miracle to each subsequent generation: for example, earlier generations viewed its miraculous dimension as its linguistic sophistication, while modern-day converts, acquainted with contemporary scientific findings, have found miraculous the Qur'an's otherwise inexplicable presentation of such material within its centuries-old pages.

Cast in an elegant classical Arabic, the Qur'an is comprised of roughly 6,500 verses, or *ayahs*, which are arranged into 114 chapters, or surahs. Surahs vary widely in length, ranging anywhere from the formidable 286-verse *Surat al-Baqarah* ("The Cow") to the *Surat al-Kawthar* ("The Abundance") and the *Surat al-Nasr* ("The Victory"), each of which contains only three verses.

The language of the Qur'an has become the standard form of classical Arabic, and the Qur'an is the principle reason why the Arabic language still lives on today. Without it, the Arab world may have suffered a linguistic fate much like that of Latin in Europe, where a small collection of countries with a shared cultural heritage all speak substantially different idioms.

Those who memorize the Qur'an, as well as those whose voices lend themselves to beautiful recitations of the text, are revered in their respective societies. To this end, when Barack Obama appointed an envoy to the Middle East, he chose a *hafiz*, or someone who memorizes the Qur'an.

The supplicant must perform a variety of rituals before he may read from the Qur'an. He must be properly clean, for example, and perform prescribed ablutions. The audience, meanwhile, must listen with an ample and appropriate reverence.

Due to its ostensibly divine origin, many Muslims resist attempts at translation, and place a high premium on encountering the Qur'an in its original language. Consequently, proficiency in classical Arabic has become a central focus of Arab education. Nonetheless, translations do proliferate. Over fifty English-language translations exist, the earliest being the 1649 effort of Alexander Ross, followed by George Sale's 1734 translation.

Above, it was mentioned that Qur'an alludes to a number of modern scientific discoveries unknown to 7th-century Arabia. A few examples are as follows: surah 51 ("The Winnowing Wind), *ayah* 47 is said to mention the continual expansion of the universe, a mainstay of general relativity theory; surah 16 ("The Bees"), to the instantaneous collapse of the universe, akin to cosmology's Big Crunch theory; and finally, in its assertion that, like clouds, the mountains of the earth are in constant motion, surah 88 ("Ants") refers to the earth's motion through space and the shifting tectonic plates that comprise the earth's crust.

Sharia Law

The purpose of Islamic Sharia law is the protection of the *five necessities*. According to the Islamic faith, the five necessities are those virtues enshrined by God as of cardinal importance to human existence. These consist in: religion, human life, progeny, private property, and the intellect. Thus, the realms demarcated by each necessity are adjudicated by a set of relevant Sharia laws. In general, each set of laws both prohibits the abuse of the respective necessity, and explicates the conditions of its propagation and enrichment. Despite its origin in the Islamic faith, Sharia law purports to apply to non-Muslims as well.

Sharia laws pertaining to the first necessity, religion, treat the varieties of heterodoxy (e.g. sorcery, witchcraft, apostasy, etc.), enumerating the punishments commensurate to each form of heresy, as well as defining explicitly the nature and conditions of each heresy. This set of laws also lays down the rules that govern the jihad, whether it is achieved at the risk of one's life and or with one's money.

Sharia law pertaining to the second necessity, human life, adjudicates cases of premeditated murder, suicide and manslaughter.

Sharia law pertaining to the third necessity, progeny, encourages the perpetuation of the species. Thus, this set of laws governs the realm of matrimony as well. And, while striving to make marriage appealing and fruitful, it therefore also treats issues of adultery and infidelity. To this end, it attempts to curtail and limit the various situations that render adultery a possibility. These include: illegal seclusion, when a man is alone, unwatched, with a woman foreign to him; excessive, unmonitored mixing of the sexes; the wearing of excessive make-up; the traveling of women without a guardian. This set of laws also enjoins men to cultivate self-discipline when confronted with lust-baiting temptations—for example, to avert one's eyes upon encountering an immodest woman.

Sharia law pertaining to the fourth necessity, private property, regulates both the exchange of goods and the protection of property. Thus, it ensures one will only earn one's money legally, and not spend one's money on illegal goods and commodities. Additionally, this set contains laws governing theft, and outlaws the use of Western money.

Sharia law pertaining to the fifth necessity, the intellect, defines and prohibits both material and intellectual objects that possess the potential to harm the intellect. The first category includes consciousness-altering substances such as drugs and alcohol. The second category includes ostensibly noxious, destructive ideas, such as the paradigm of Darwinian evolution, which leads one to doubt the miracle of human creation.

Qisas, Diya and Afw

In Islamic law, crimes divide into two categories: those that result in bodily harm to the victim, and those that do not. The first category consists in premeditated murder, semi-premeditated murder, manslaughter and mutilation, while the second category spans the gamut from adultery down to petty theft. The practices of *qisas* and *diya*, briefly explicated in the preceding section, are invoked only in cases of the first category. In what follows, we commence with an examination of premeditated murder under Islamic law; then, marshalling what we've set forth, we will proceed onto a more lengthy discussion of these complicated, long-standing practices.

Premeditated Murder in Islamic Law

When a person commits premeditated murder, there arise three separate claims upon his or her life. The first is held by God Himself, whose claim derives from the culprit's decision to flout His explicit prohibition of the act. The second is held by the actual murder victim: it is believed that, at the Final Judgment, the victim may choose to strip the killer of the killer's good deeds; in this way, the victim will acquire the killer's accumulated good "karma" and count it as his own. (He may take as much or as little as he sees fit.) Finally, in this last, most earthly case (and, thus, the case most relevant to the present discussion), the third claim is held by the *waliy ad-dam* ("avengers of the blood"). Typically, the *waliy ad-dam* are synonymous with the victim's family — "family," in this case, referring to all those relatives who, in accordance with Islamic law, are regarded as inheritors of the deceased.

Thus, the *waliy ad-dam*, invested with the right to retribution, hold the killer's fate within their hands. They may select one of three courses of action: *qisas* ("retribution"), *diya* ("bloodwite"), or *afw* ("forgiveness").

In the situation of murder, then, the victim's natural, earthly right to retributive justice is re-distributed among his surviving family members. In order to enact *qisas*, the family's decision must be unanimous. That is, the forgiveness of any one family member will render *qisas* unavailable as an option. This "veto" clause arises from the plain severity of *qisas* in the case of murder. *Qisas*, as we will shortly discover, is the essence of retributive justice, an elaborate science derived from Hammurabi's Code; thus, the *qisas* for premeditated murder is, not surprisingly, execution.

If, in this fashion, *qisas* is vetoed, the family may choose either *diya* or *afw*. *Afw* is fairly straightforward, a blanket absolution for the culprit's wrongdoing. *Diya*, however, is vastly more complicated. In essence, it is an attempt to comprehensively monetize the human life and body, such that, rather than an eye for an eye, implicated parties can engage in the far more humane exchange of an eye for the monetary equivalent of an eye. Or, more accurately, an eye for an eye's-value-in-camels. The *diya* for premeditated murder is 100 camels (or, frequently, the present monetary value of 100 camels); all other *diyas* are measured as percentages of the murder *diya*. The murder *diya* will be distributed amongst family members in accordance with the Islamic rules of inheritance.

☪ It is important to note that, if the victim possessed any underage children at the time of his death, the family must wait until the children have come of age in order to make their decision as to *qisas, diya* or *afw*.

In the case of both semi-premeditated murder and manslaughter, the *qisas* is not applicable. Semi-premeditated murder refers to the accidental death of a victim in the course of an intentional physical altercation—e.g. one intends to punch one's colleague, but does not intend for one's colleague, in the immediate recoil, to fatally collide with the corner bookshelf. Manslaughter, meanwhile, refers to a wholly accidental or unintended killing. In the case of the semi-premeditated killing, in addition to paying a *diya*, the culprit must also do penance. Penance consists in emancipating one of his Muslim slaves. If no Muslim slave exists, the penitent must rather fast for two consecutive months. In the case of manslaughter, only the payment of the *diya* is necessary. Of course, in either situation, *afw* is a viable alternative as well.

These are not the only circumstances under which *qisas* is inapplicable. In what follows, we shall undertake a more thorough investigation of the practice.

Qisas

In all situations wherein *qisas* is a valid form of punishment (to wit, those that do harm to a victim), a number of constraints must also have been met. Firstly, the perpetrator must be a rational mind. This excludes young children (who have not yet developed the moral compass necessary to discriminate right from wrong), the criminally insane, and sleepwalkers (i.e. those who committed their crime while within a state of somnambulism). Secondly, the crime must have occurred between equals: thus, a master's murder of his slave, or a Muslim's murder of a Christian, are not applicable (of course, in both situations, the reverse is also true). Finally, and in extension of the second constraint, *qisas* in cases of mutilation must involve equal, and equally healthy, limbs. For example, if the culprit severed the right hand of the victim, and the victim decides upon *qisas*, the culprit's right hand must also be severed. If he does not possess a right hand, his left hand will not be severed (this is also because the resultant disparity—i.e. the culprit's resultant total lack of hands to the victim's lacking only one hand—likewise upsets the equality constraint). Additionally, if the hand that he severed was, before the mutilation, somehow paralyzed or unusable, it is not allowed for the culprit to lose a healthy, utilizable hand in retribution—again, because this upsets the equality constraint.

There exist still other constraints upon the application of *qisas*. In all cases, the victim must be an upright, practicing Muslim: specifically, adulterers and apostates do not possess the right to *qisas*. The victim must also not be the one who provoked or initiated the altercation leading to his death. In carrying out the *qisas*, one must be sure that only the culprit is harmed. Thus, one cannot put to death a pregnant woman. Rather, she will receive a stay of execution until, first, the baby has been delivered; and second, until she has suckled her baby, just once. Finally, the *qisas* is inapplicable if both the victim and perpetrator come from the same family.

In the case of mutilations, the decision on *qisas, diya* or *afw* is entirely the victim's. The one parameter that governs the character of the *qisas* is the equality constraint, which even extends to punishments: for example, the wounds done to the culprit will strive to match in extent, appearance and severity those done to the victim. The key difference is that, in the case of the culprit, *qisas* will be administered under anesthesia.

Diya

The principal *diya* is, as we mentioned earlier, that paid in compensation for premeditated murder. Those for semi-premeditated murder and manslaughter are less, as are those for the various forms of mutilations. Still, all *diya* are measured in proportion to that for premeditated murder. The currency of *diya*, as we also mentioned, is the camel. This is not an arbitrary choice: of great and lasting utility within the Arab world, the value of the camel serves as a means of standardizing the *diya* across time, insulating it from the effects of inflation as well as fluctuations within the marketplace. Specifically, we speak here of a camel's value *within* Saudi Arabia, the standard by which the Muslim world still measures the *diya*.

In the case of premeditated murder, the culprit must cull the *diya* from his own fortune, and must do so immediately. In this case of manslaughter, however, the *diya* will be provided by the clan to which the culprit belongs. In Arabic, the clan, in this capacity as wergild provider, is called *āqila* and is allotted three years to accumulate the relevant funds. In all cases, three categories of people are prohibited from paying the *diya*: the husband, the brothers of the culprit's mother, and the women of the family. Like the *qisas*, the *diya* attempts to evaluate, with the utmost precision, the harm done to the victim in question. What follows is a list of possible various *diyas* within Saudi Arabia, which has been included in the hope that it will engender in the reader an appreciation for the elaborate, painstaking precision of the *diya* system.

Incidence of appendage on human body	% of Diya	2010 U.S.D Equivalent	Example
1	100% — treated same as human life.	$26,881.72	Tongue
2	Each member worth 50% of full *diya*	$13,440.86	Eyes, arms
3	Each one worth 33% of full *diya*	$8,960.57	The nose (i.e. the two nostrils and the bridge)
4	Each one worth 25% of full *diya*	$6,720.43	Eyelid
10	Each one worth 10% of full *diya*	$2,688.17	Fingers, toes

Who will pay the Diya?

1) The perpetrator, in the case of premeditated murder
2) The clan of the perpetrator (with the exception of the maternal uncles, the husband, and the females of the clan), in the case of manslaughter
3) The government, in the case that:
    (a) the perpetrator is insolvent;
    (b) the clan is insolvent;
    (c) the killing is unsolved/the killer unknown;
    (d) the government bears responsibility for the death.

Translation

Newspaper: Lowering the interest rate to zero percent.

Osama Bin Laden: America abolished the interest rate?

Iman Al-Zawahri: Because it is forbidden [in Islam], ha ha ha

Language

The name "Osama bin Laden" has a literal meaning.

"Osama" means "lion," and "Laden" translates as "soft." Therefore, the name literally reads "Lion, son of Soft."

In the 1950s and 60s, Arab revolutionaries introduced the figures of a number of key Latin American radicals. These included contemporaries like Fidel Castro and Che Guevara, as well as historical figures like Simon Bolivar. These Arab revolutionaries—many of whom later led their respective countries, such as Egypt's Nasser—wished to present their post-colonial struggles as akin to the socialist uprisings throughout Latin America, and also to create the impression that their fight partook of a current global trend. Pictures of these Latin American radicals became common, and many streets and squares were named after them. In the present cartoon, the famous picture of Che has been altered through the addition of a large beard. The beard is meant to "Islamicize" him, or depict him as an Arab figure. This odd alteration—an Islamicized beard on a Latin American radical—would strike the Arab reader as very humorous.

Culture

In the Islamic faith, it is unlawful to give or receive interest for a loan or on account of credit. This holds not only for monetary exchanges but for goods as well. Though these business transactions are severely condemned, they are not uncommon among modern Muslims, some of whom take extortionate interest.

On the forehead of Iman al-Zawahiri is a mark associated with pious Muslims called in Arabic a "prayer raisin." It is caused by pressing the forehead on the prayer mat during prostration, and devout Muslims consider the presence of a prayer raisin to be a sign of extreme religious dedication. The prayer raisin takes the form of discoloration of the skin cause by repeated chafing and can build up into a callus, which can then become so thick that it forms a bump, protruding from the forehead. They are common in certain Arab countries, most notably Egypt, and they are almost never present on women. Generally, prayer raisins are viewed as intentionally brought about in an effort to appear to be a devout Muslim.

Men in jail, especially those accused of capital crimes, may become so religious that they display the prayer bump to help convince the judge they are innocent or repentant. One such is the man in the picture below, who is on death row, having been convicted of killing two young women.

The Origin of the Name "Al-Qaeda"

Osama bin Laden's first spiritual leader was Abdullah Azzam. Azzam kept bin Laden abreast of the goings-on in the Muslim world, and also stressed the necessity of liberating Afghanistan from the Soviet occupation. With the aid of his acquaintances, he arranged for bin Laden to undertake a series of secret trips throughout Afghanistan and Pakistan, beginning with Bishour and Karachi, where he first met the Afghani mujahedeen leaders. On these trips, bin Laden brought with him construction equipment (which he took from his father's successful construction company) in order to aid the mujahedeen in forging roads through mountainous terrain, as well as building combat training camps. In 1982, bin Laden settled in Afghanistan, where, two years later, he established the *Bait al-Ansar*, House of Supporters, an outpost committed to receiving those newly arrived in Afghanistan to fight in the jihad. Initially, bin Laden trained these men in the mujahedeen camps but, by 1986, he had already established a number of his own training camps throughout the country. In 1989, he opened an administrative office for the registration of mujahedeen, which was also responsible for contacting the family members of those who died in combat. Named "Al-Qaeda," or, "The Base," this office served as the namesake for bin Laden's current organization.

Translation

On Cassette: "New tape"
On Cannon: "Al-Qaeda"

Culture

Most Arabs do not see Al-Qaeda as an immediate threat. The immediate threat is Israel. Al-Qaeda and Hamas, the two most dangerous terrorist organizations to the West, were created by America and Israel respectively. Al-Qaeda was created to recruit Muslims to aid America in fighting against the Soviet Union in Afghanistan. Hamas was created in order to divert followers from the anti-Israel group FataH. These two groups have since become enemies to their creators. Arabs regard groups like Al-Qaeda and Hamas as having been created by foreign governments to pit Arabs against one another. However, they have turned against their creators, and this is a sign from God that it is dangerous to attempt to pit Muslim people against one another.

Al-Qaeda and Technology

In this cartoon, Al-Qaeda is depicted firing tapes from a cave. Tapes have been a very effective means of spreading Al-Qaeda's message, and have even helped Al-Qaeda to communicate hidden codes and messages to agents overseas. Tapes were not the first means used by Al-Qaeda to communicate to the outside world, however. Initially, Al-Qaeda sent faxes to news organizations, public officials, and even to random citizens whom they believed would be able to spread their message as quickly as possible. This was known as the Fax War. After the Fax War, Al-Qaeda began to rely on tapes, delivered to the News Channel Al-Jazeera exclusively, which would then broadcast the tapes. Once broadcast by Al-Jazeera, other news organizations would take these tapes and re-broadcast them, allowing them to reach a wider audience. Due to the pressure that Western governments placed on Al-Jazeera to cease broadcasting the tapes, Al-Qaeda began to make use of the Internet, and has found it to be a more successful means of communication. In 2003, there were only 12 websites for organizations such as Al-Qaeda. Today, there are about 17,800.

The Clouds Organization is the organization responsible for producing all the propaganda materials that Al-Qaeda uses online, setting up sites where visitors can download hundreds of tapes that contain messages from Al-Qaeda leaders and footage from its military operations. Al-Qaeda is always looking for recruits with an academic background in the field of information technology or for those with a natural ability to work in IT, in order to make use of the latest technology to suit their goals.

Translation

Title & Newspaper: American military bases in the Gulf.

Osama bin Laden: What a mess. Does that mean I have to blow up a World Trade Center in the Gulf too?

Tashmees

Expelling a person from a tribe or group was the harshest punishment someone could receive in old Arab culture. This is what happened to Osama Bin Laden when the royal family of Saudi Arabia expelled him

with the modern equivalent—stripping him of his citizenship. Those who are punished like this often become outlaws—violent criminals, who live in constant fear, since they feel that everyone is against them and that they are under constant threat of death. There is no authority to protect them anymore. This punishment is still practiced in many areas of the Arab world and goes under many names, but *tashmees*, is a form of ostracism with elements of the British "sending to Coventry." English has the phrase "to leave someone out in the cold," since the cold is the hostile environment, but originating in the desert, *tashmees* means "to leave out in the sun," from *shams* for "sun." The ostracized person no longer enjoys the tribe's protection, which was in the past essential for survival. Usually a tribe would issue such a punishment to someone for repeated misdeeds since the tribe is generally responsible for its members' actions. If a member acts irresponsibly or commits a crime, the whole tribe must make amends to those affected. When someone has repeated offenses, the tribe will no longer be willing to keep atoning for the person and will realize that it is in the best interest of the group to expel the irresponsible member. This punishment is not issued lightly, as signatures of five senior members of the tribe and three tribunal councils must consider the punishment. Most often the punished will be given a chance to make a case against the punishment.

Members of tribes, who have committed no crimes but are under surveillance by law enforcement, may be rejected because of the trouble they bring. People expelled for this reason will often go to the whole way and fully join the criminal world, through trafficking or terrorism, since they don't see any other means of survival after losing their place in the tribe. This is not difficult, since the inaccessible areas of the Arabian desert inhabited by these tribes have provided refuge to smugglers, drug-traffickers and terrorists.

Those subject to *tashmees* who don't become fully-fledged outlaws, will feel hopeless and marked out, unable to move to a metropolitan area of the country since they know no one there: the sentence is generally seen simply as a delayed execution. Those who have skills or a shop when punished will lose all their customers. They are treated as an outcast by other members, who know that if the punished makes a mistake there is no way of receiving compensation. If you are abused by someone subject to *tashmees*, there is no venue for retribution since they are not part of the society any longer.

Language

The name Zarqawi means that he is from Zarqa, which is a small village in Jordan.

Culture

Zarqawi was a Jordanian militant Islamist who ran a militant training camp in Afghanistan. He became known after going to Iraq and being responsible for a series of bombings, beheadings and attacks during the Iraq War. His capture proved so difficult that, this comic suggests, even the great American superheroes would fall into despair at the task of finding him. On June 7, 2006, however, two United States Air Force F-16C jets killed Zarqawi as he attended a meeting in an isolated safe house approximately 8 km (5 mi) north of Baqubah.

These American superheroes are well known in the Arab world since most Arab children read these cartoons in addition to Arab superhero cartoons. Like children in America are familiar with the stories of Aladdin, Ali Baba, and the Arabian Nights, Arab children read American-style children's books. These books are very popular and have been translated into Arabic since the late 50s. Many generations have grown up on these magazines in this part of the world. Here are some of these magazine covers in Arabic:

Superheroes aside, many Arabs view the inability of the U.S. government to "capture or kill" some "terrorists" as stemming from divine intervention. Despite the high price placed by America on these "terrorists" heads and the vast capabilities of the American military, the government has failed to catch

Osama bin Laden. Many Arabs perceive this failure as stemming from God's protection of bin Laden, which leads the population at large to protect bin Laden in turn.

One of the Reasons the United States Government Has Been Unable to Capture Bin Laden

Arabs are some of the most hospitable people on Earth. To understand the hospitality of the Arab people, one has to understand the environment within which they live. Generally speaking, the environment and terrain of a people shape their culture, and for Arabs, the harsh desert environment makes it a matter of life or death when choosing to provide shelter and nourishment to a fellow human being. The most deserving person of hospitality is the "mussafir," one who is on a journey. For example, very few Arabs will think about sitting down to a meal without inviting another to share in the meal, even if the person sharing the meal is a servant or a laborer. Some shop owners will eat their food outside their shop, to keep themselves visible, and will even offer to share their meal with any passers-by. Arab hospitality is illustrated in the Qur'an with the story of Prophet Ibrahim (Abraham) who invites angels to partake in a meal with him. God sent angels to warn Ibrahim that the following morning, destruction would befall the followers of Lut, known in the Bible as the inhabitants of Sodom and Gomorrah. Prior to visiting Ibrahim, these angels, taking up the appearance of handsome men, had visited Prophet Lut, known as Lot in the Old Testament. These handsome angels attracted the attention of the Lut's people who came knocking on Lut's door and tried to gain access to the angels. Lut stood at the door to protect his guests from the mob, saying, "Do you people have no reasonable men among you? Fear God and don't dishonor me by harming my guests. Here are my two daughters; they are better for you." (The English word "sodomy" refers to homosexual activity, derived from the name of the town of Sodom. In Arabic, the word "luat" refers to homosexuality, derived from the name of the Prophet Lut —known as Lot in the Bible—who lived among those people. He was their prophet. This was the first time anyone experienced homosexuality in history of the world.) The account of Abraham and Lut speaks to the extent to which Arabs are hospitable to their guests. Traditionally, Arabs should be willing to suffer almost any injury to themselves or their family in order to avoid their guest being mistreated while in their company. Arabs will go to extent of sacrificing the chastity of their wives or daughters for fear of offending their guests. Lut offered his daughters for the satisfaction of the mob in order to protect his guests. The same is the case with Osama bin laden. Despite a bounty worth $52 million, the people who have helped Osama bin Laden do so because the virtue of being hospitable to one's guest is worth infinitely more than a reward of $52 million. To this day, not only an Arab host himself but also the host's personal friends will work to extend hospitality to the host's guests; part of the friends' hospitality will be to restrain their familiar displays of friendship with the host and to replace them with more formal demonstrations, so that the guest may be honored by the respect shown his host. This hospitality should be extended to the guests of friends, and if an Arab encounters a friend with someone else he doesn't know on the street, he feels an obligation to invite both for a drink, or if that's not possible, at least to be very respectful towards them both, and more formal than usual with his friend. If an Arab encounters a friend walking with the friend's father or mother or sister, he must show the same respect that he extends to the guest of his friend.

Arabs take care to show due respect to the members of their friends' families when they meet them in public. This may be as simple as adopting a formal, reserved attitude or one may offer respectful greeting. Though it is appropriate to greet the matrons of a friend's family, one must not address or even make eye contact with his young, female relatives; the only polite acknowledgement is quietly to look down as she passes.

☪ Lut's act of offering his daughters to the rabid crowd reflects a long-standing Arab tradition: although no longer practiced today, male hosts used to grant their weary, homesick guests access to all of their possessions—including the sexual services of their wives or daughters.

☪ There are a number of dissimilarities between the Hebrew story of the Lot and the Qur'anic Lut that bear mentioning. While it records the death of his wife, The Qur'an says nothing of her metamorphosis into a pillar of salt, and also does not name the cities to which Lut prophesies. Most importantly, however, the Qur'an excludes the entire, incest-laden story of Lot's copulation with his daughters, which is present in the Book of Genesis.

Translation

Title: Al-Qaeda Condemns the Offensive Drawings

Al-Zawahiri: (crying) "Ahi ahi ahi, the offensive drawings hurt my feelings."

Language

"Ahi ahi ahi" is Arabic for the English sound of crying, such as "boohoo" or "wah wah."

Culture

The cartoon satirizes the hypocrisy of claiming to be offended by drawings, while flaunting murder. A lot of the cartoons in this section make fun of Osama bin Laden and Al-Qaeda, mocking their ideology and modus operandi.

Translation

Title: The evolution of Al-Qaeda bomb-rigging.

(*from right to left*)

Rigged airplane

Rigged car

Rigged bodies

Rigged shoe

Rigged packages

Rigged mosquito!!

[N.B. that since the Arabic reader starts from the right, this sequence represents a downward trend, both in scale and thinking.]

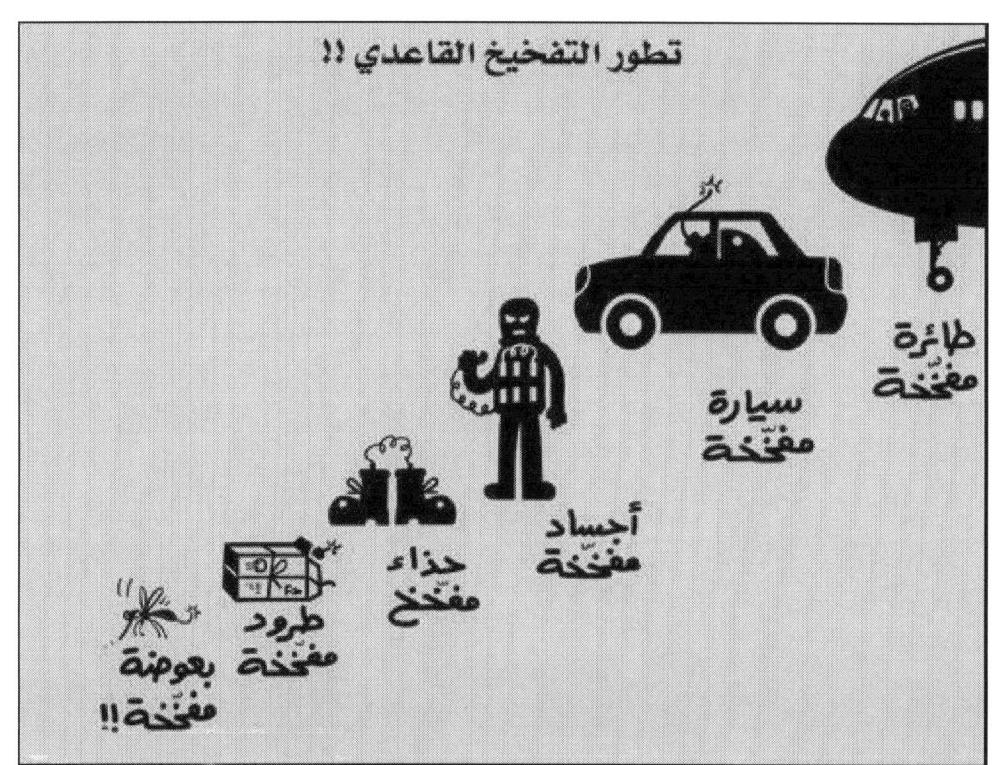

Translation

"No to violence"

Culture

Al Mounasa'ha — the Saudi Counseling Program

Around the 1970s, a profound and worrying turn towards violence spread through extremist fringes throughout the Arab world, and the influence of these groups expanded into the dangerous Islamist terrorist groups that pose such a danger to stability and peace today. Governments that follow in the secular tradition of the west have, in large part, responded to the intensification of terrorism through secular means such as military action and police investigation. Though many Arab governments, of course, employ very harsh means to control terrorist activities, such an approach is inadequate both because is only perpetuates the cycle of violence, but also because it cannot meet ideological needs of those governments of the Arab world that seek seriously to base their legitimacy upon their fidelity to Islam. Beyond the obvious threat to civic order that Islamist terrorists commonly pose to all governments, these states face an insidious challenge against their very foundations and cannot afford to cede the religious argument to the violent extremists.

One particularly insightful and effective strategy in this battle of religious philosophy has been Saudi Arabia's program to offer intensive counseling to those who have come under the influence of radical ideologies. The state's inescapable need to assume the truth of many of the basic premises that inspire the terrorists—e.g. the validity of Islam and the holiness of the Qur'an —forces them to engage intelligently and dynamically over points of difference. The program, run by the Ministry of the Interior as a voluntary adjunct to the criminal justice system, aims first to identify the specific points of error in offenders' thinking that led them to their violently heterodox opinions and then to disabuse them through rational argument. This reëducation program implies that people who commit crimes from the genuine wish to further the cause of Islam are not to be construed as evil—the impulse to serve Islam is inarguably virtuous—, rather they are simply suffering from poor information or at worst are the victims of malicious malinformers who took advantage of their naïveté.

As any who were genuinely convinced of the religious rightness of the actions for which the state has condemned them would be eager to justify themselves before learned and open-minded coreligionists, participation in the program is entirely voluntary for offenders, a fact which further distances the this counseling from any taint or savor of the punishing or retributive functions of the Saudi criminal justice system. If an offender should be convinced of his former waywardness, though, this is allowed to serve as a factor in commuting the sentences of those who have not actually been guilty of bloodshed. These repudiations of violence are great triumphs for the program and for the ideology of the state that the program promotes. Of course, the process is not without its dangers; in Sept. 2009, Deputy Interior Minister Prince Muhammad bin Nayef was wounded when a prisoner who had claimed to be willing to repent blew himself up with a surgically implanted bomb during a recantation ceremony at which the Prince was present.

In practice, the counseling program is administered by a subsidiary of the Interior Ministry known as the Advisory Committee, centered in Riyadh but with branches throughout the country. The work is thence divided four-fold into sub-committees that oversee the various aspects of the project. The central task of theological argument and dissuasion from violence is the responsibility of the Religious Subcommittee. Some 150 learned Muslims comprise this largest and most prestigious of the subcommittees, and membership is carefully shepherded. The central requirement is that members argue with care and genuine good-will "as if to their own brother." Selection for this position takes involves a range of considerations, from learning and soundness, to willingness to take such a firm and potentially dangerous stand against terrorists, to persuasive as opposed to hectoring style of argument, to an altruistic rather than place-seeking motivation.

Some fifty members comprise the Psychological and Social Subcommittee. They assess detainees' progress, assess the genuine nature of any supposed reformation, and works with the family and community around those in treatment to better the chances for a sustained recovery upon release. The Security Subcommittee is somewhat shrouded in secrecy, but its public roles, at least, include counseling offenders on how to avoid extremist influences in future, using lessons learned from those apprehended to predict future risks, and, prominently, monitoring released offenders to catch out recidivists. Finally, the Media Subcommittee promulgates the message and philosophy of the program to the wider public. For example, they are responsible for recent storylines on popular television shows that have depicted characters taken in by the bogus and dangerous claims of extremists who, after having been used as instruments towards terrorists' devilish ends, end up as tragic victims, ruined by their gullibility. The lessons of the un-Islamic wickedness of terrorist violence and the distorted nature of extremists' claims that the individual counseling attempts to impart to those who have already been fooled and then apprehended, the Media Subcommittee strives to make general to the entire Saudi nation, reaching both those who have been duped but not caught by the authorities and those who might, but for these warnings, have been duped in the future. This Saudi policy seems, in the end, remarkably potent and sophisticated. How wonderful if the way to curb violence were not to treat humankind like mules — that obey for fear of the whip — nor like forward curs — that are peaceable so long as their bellies are full —, but rather to address the noble glory of the rational human mind that longs to do good in the best way it knows.

Translation

On turban: "Al-Qaeda" The palm tree is the symbol of Saudi Arabi. Aside from being very common throughout the country, the palm tree resembles a classic oil gusher: the trunk is the tower itself, while the frond is the rich explosion of discovered oil.

Culture

Although criticized in the immediate wake of September 11th for failing to respond adequately to the terroristic threat, today Saudis pride themselves on their formidable counter-terrorism capacities. In the cartoon, Al-Qaeda attempts to devour the kingdom, finishing it off once and for all; but Saudi Arabia, the perpetual thorn in the side of the terrorist, resists defeat — and, in fact, poses an impediment to any other action. As mentioned above, the Saudis fight terrorism with both brute, outright force and subtler, less physically confrontational means. In 2006, leading counter-terrorist organizer (and victim of an assassination attempt) Prince Muhammad bin Nayef established the Center for Care and Counseling, an institute for the rehabilitation of convicted terrorist plotters. The center — staffed by social scientists and psychologists, as well as Sharia and religious scholars — offers two forms of treatment. The first is a program of one-on-one counseling, each session running to no more than two hours long. Often, this is not enough for the terrorist to disavow his former ideas and allegiances. Thus, in the second, longer program, social scientists and religious scholars lead twenty extremists in a six-week lecture series. The lectures cover the following topics: the merits of terrorism; Islamic jurisprudence regarding jihad; the pledge of loyalty (terrorists give the "pledge of loyalty," to their organization's leader; the class teaches the proper Islamic object of the pledge — the official head of state); self-esteem;

friendship to and distance from, teaching proper friendship to fellow Muslims; and the excommunication of the society. "Excommunication," in this case, refers to the determination of a society as an infidel society; through such a determination, collateral damage to the society from terroristic violence—even a nominally Muslim society—becomes *halal*, i.e. permissible.

There exist four traveling committees of terrorist counselors. They consist in:

The Religious Committee: a group of 150 scholars and university professors; through debate and discussion, they interact directly with the criminals.

The Psychology and Social Scientist Committee: contains 52 members (26 researchers and their 26 assistants); evaluates the psychological conditions and needs of the prisoners; evaluates aptitude for reintegration with society.

The Media Committee: focuses on education and the production of materials pertaining to the extremist-rehabilitation process.

The Security Committee: responsible for evaluating and monitoring the progress of the Religious and Psychological/Social Scientists Committees; posses the final say as to whether the prisoner is released or not; monitors the prisoner upon re-introduction into society; re-apprehending, if necessary, the extremist in question.

In addition to the preceding, the Center offers significant financial incentives as well: upon successful completion of the program, the reformed extremist will be provided with a house and a wife, as well as a means of supporting his children—the idea being to preoccupy him with family, such that he shies away from politics. To this end, the Center presents itself as the polar opposite of the severity of Guantanamo. In the latter, prisoners were rewarded with food and entertainment upon cooperation; in the former, such material goods are available to all subjects from the start.

In some Arab countries, terrorists are referred to as those of the "stray group" and the "martyrs of illusion." The presence of a terrorist within a family will shame the family in question, and prevent others from marrying into the family—a fact that is frequently underscored by the Center's employees.

☪ In his June 5th, 2009 visit to Saudi Arabia, U.S. Defense Secretary Robert Gates declared himself much impressed with the Center's progress, and commented that he would entertain the possibility of enrolling some Yemeni Guantanamo detainees in the Center's program.

Translation

"Enough both of you. You're going to lose your future and make me lose my reputation."

Language

In the Arabic language, all nouns have gender, and there is no neuter. Most Arab nations are feminine nouns, so it is standard for them to be represented as women, just as

the United States might be represented by Uncle Sam or, formerly, Columbia. In the cartoon, she is like a mother admonishing her fractious children, urging the terrorists to put aside their violent ideologies and the security forces to relax their harsh tactics. Both, she hopes, will put the country's well-being before their own selfish interests.

A woman's reputation, whether mother or sister, could be compromised if any members of the family were repeatedly involved in brawls or violence. No-one would want to marry into the family.

Culture

The war between law enforcements and terrorist groups in some Arab countries is intensifying so much that it is threatening the fabric of society and the state's international standing. In countries such as Lebanon, Algeria, Saudi Arabia, Egypt and Jordan, law enforcement officers have dramatically tried to quell thriving terrorist movements. Because of the intensity of these crackdowns and terrorist counterattacks, the names and reputations of the Arab countries are becoming tarnished in the media and internationally. The countries then become associated primarily with terrorism and counter-terrorism, ultimately scaring away tourists and foreign investors.

☪ on a domestic level: when the woman refers to tarnishing my reputation it refers to a fact that a household who is in constant loud fight that can be heard outside the house can actually ruin the reputation of this household especially the women who are of marriage age

☪ In this picture, it is very obvious that the man with the beard is a terrorist. Not long ago, growing a beard was a sign of fundamental Islamists and just having a beard was enough for someone to get arrested. When the government started cracking down on the Islamic fundamentalists, they shaved their beards as a first line of defense. Around the 80s, when a young man would first grow his beard, Islamic fundamentalists would congratulate him and assume that he was ready to join their ranks or was becoming serious about religion without asking if he was growing the beard because of fashion. The same phenomenon was very noticeable amongst women. A woman who forsook Western fashions for more traditional clothing would likewise be congratulated by her peers. Even those who, themselves, did not follow strict Islamic dress codes would often encourage friends to dress more conservatively.

Translation

Between '11': The Arab world
Under title: September

Culture

Arabs feel that they have become prisoners of the War on Terror in their countries and abroad. Hopefully, things will change for them after Obama's overtures to the Arab and Islamic world.

Translation

[In the top of this cartoon, we see three different views of the date, September 11th. First, at right, we see just the simple date as it has existed in every year. Then, in the middle, the day is redefined in 2001 by the attack on the World Trade Center. Finally, at left, the meaning of the day had been transformed by 2007 – the year of the cartoon's publication – into a symbol of the suspicion with which the Arab traveler is confronted as he moves through Western airports and interacts with security and customs officials.]

Suspect: Today, we celebrate the 6th anniversary of our friendship with the airport customs of the civilized world.

Culture

Arabs complain bitterly about racism and racial profiling that they encounter in airports all over the world, especially after Sept. 11th, 2001. It has become very hard for them to obtain visas and to navigate the security procedures around international travel, even for those people whose notable and dignified positions, one might think, would render them above suspicion.

The news of this unequal treatment and the harassment of distinguished personages have caused outrage in the Arab world. Calls are growing for foreigners to be given treatment in kind in Arab airports as a form of retaliation.

The Impact of 9/11 within the Arab world

In America, a popular, widespread assertion in the days following 9/11 held that life would never be the same again. Indeed, the scars of 9/11 are yet fresh in the flesh of the body politic. Too, amongst American politicians and pundits, the broad-stroke taxonomy of "pre" and "post" 9/11 is still all-too-commonly employed.

However, the American reader may be surprised to discover that this notion of 9/11's epochal, era-altering character was not confined to Western societies, and instead permeated the Arab world as well.

From the leaders of nations to the most vastly disconnected, modernity-shunning, nomadic citizen, 9/11's repercussions left no Arab untouched.

Much of the domestic Arab response to the World Trade Center attacks was carried out under the auspices of the Bush administration. Bush and his advisors regarded terrorism as a temperamental and violent potentiality, one which is born within, and travels between, the various unmonitored interstices of modern societies. Thus, the successful defeat of terroristic activities was thought to require a dual strategy of information centralization and hole-plugging, that is, the filling-in of the numerous cracks and crevices within a modern society's digital infrastructure. Accordingly, all citizens, structures and entities theretofore unplumbed by bureaucratic perspicacity needed to submit themselves to a quick and thorough assimilation.

The first radical change to the Arab world, then, was the introduction of various biometric methods for population monitoring. Entire communities of legally undocumented, wholly self-sufficient nomads were brought into jarring contact with the forefront of modern population technologies. In order to counteract the preponderance of lost or absent birth certificates, as well as the bureaucratic nightmare of Arab naming practices (to wit: it was not uncommon for one to have essentially *forgotten* one's legal name, and to be known only, to family and friends, by one's nickname), some Arab countries instituted a *national number* policy. Similar to the social security code — except more widely and casually used — the national number was intended to differentiate, in government records, Arab citizens from one another, as well as to serve as a convenient means of tracking their various activities. Such innovations incurred the ire of fundamentalists, as the biometric policing methods often required that men shave their beards and women unveil their faces; thus, these methods were considered to transgress both Islam (which mandates both the wearing of beards and veiling of women) and domestic law — which, according to Islam, must have the support and ratification of the populace.

The second substantial change involved the physical character of many Arab communities. More often than not, Arab towns and cities were the product of sporadic, piecemeal construction, rather than comprehensive pre-planning and focused development. Due to their haphazard construction, many roads and public areas rebuffed easy police access, as well as posed a clear potential danger in the case of emergency. Thus, numerous Arab governments undertook to re-structure urban areas, paving new roads and closing off particularly compromised locations.

On a similar note, Arab governments were also forced to address *random housing*. "Random housing," a translation of the Arabic term, refers to cheaply constructed apartment buildings that, due to their fairly comprehensive failure to comply to *any* building regulations, were denied access to publicly controlled amenities, such as electricity and running water. Whole scores of undocumented unknowns resided within these structures — and, because of the general anonymity they afforded, they were a favorite haunt of terrorists. Accordingly, Arab countries undertook the demolition of all random housing, followed by the raising of regulated, monitored apartment complexes.

Under further pressure from the Bush administration, some Arab countries were forced to confront numerous products of the influence of radical, fundamentalist Islam. For one, they were encouraged to crack down on the financial practices of firebrand imams, who often played a crucial rule in money-laundering and the funding of terrorist organizations. In addition, the Bush Whitehouse demanded they roll back some of the more conservative, traditional prohibitions limiting the population's civil liberties — indeed, Washington viewed the ostensibly restrictive, Islamist-inspired civil law codes as generative of terroristic violence. In this vein, Bush pushed for the democratization of Arab political practices. As a consequence, Egyptian president Hosni Mubarak was forced to hold a proper election to determine his re-assumption of his office. While Mubarak won by a generous margin, he nonetheless viewed the election's attendant necessities — debating, stumping, handshaking, etc. — as vastly humiliating, things unfit for a great nation's sitting leader.

Translation

On hand with axe: "The Ideology of moderation."
On hand with lighter: "The Ideology of extremism."
On bomb: "Terrorism."

Culture

The events of 9/11 resulted in the construction of new prisons, as well as new prison-rehabilitation program. In an attempt to *combat Ideology with ideology* (again, a translation from Arabic), terrorists imprisoned in Arab countries were submitted to a variety of Islamic re-education programs. The underlying assumption was that, at his the core, the terrorist was merely a *mis*reader of the *Qur'an*, a devoted man whose mistaken interpretation had led him to unconscionable acts of violence. Thus, prisoners were regularly exposed to moderate imams, who taught Islam's opposition to terroristic violence. Too, the prisoners' families were involved in the re-education process, and also used as a means of turning the prisoner's sympathy away from the pursuit of terrorism. (For example: the inmate's wife –along with the wife's entire family — would come visit the inmate in jail, and explain to him how, since his terroristic activity had put him in jeopardy with the law, and precluded him from maintaining a steady job, his beloved wife was suffering financial ruin.)

Not surprisingly, 9/11 led to increased religious strife between Christian and Muslim Arabs. Muslims perceived the much-touted War on Terror as a new Crusade — perhaps because Bush, in fact, publicly referred to the War on Terror as "this new crusade" (a statement which he later retracted). Christians abroad mobilized this changing global mentality as an opportunity to push their (admittedly benign) agenda in the Middle East, lobbying for the related causes of increased religious freedom and the construction of new churches throughout the region.

Many countries received financial aid in order to fight terrorism. Too, American used the War on Terror as an opportunity to insinuate itself into regional politics, using anti-terror funding in the construction of their two biggest embassies — those in Iraq and the Sudan. Finally, the events of 9/11 underscored the fact that, more than ever, the world needed a speedy resolution to that chronic problem of the Middle East: the Palestinian issue.

☪ Many Arab politicians, borrowing the common American practice, now wear flag pins on their lapels. Moreover, the persistence of America's PATRIOT Act has served as an excuse for the continued existence of laws inhibiting civil rights in Arab countries, a much less benign example of political mimickry.

Translation

On shirt: "Arab People"
On left nozzle: "War on terror"
On right nozzle: "Terrorism"

Culture

Arab people consider themselves to be in a bad position. They are caught between the rock of terrorism and the hard place of the war on terror. They are both the victims of terrorism themselves and considered to be terrorists.

Translation

Judging from the sleeves, we can roughly guess the nationalities at loggerheads in this cartoon: on the left in the suit: a westerner, on the right in traditional Arab clothes: an Arab.
TERRORIST!!!

Culture

The issue of mutual accusations of terrorism raised by the cartoon was starkly illustrated during U.S. Secretary of State Clinton's visit to

Pakistan in late 2009. During her visit, which was marred by ghastly terrorist attacks in protest, Clinton participated in a live television interview with prominent female news-anchors and a large, mostly female audience. Someone in the audience challenged Clinton over the American use of Predator drones—unmanned aircraft armed with guided missiles that the U.S. has used to great effect to eliminate terrorist leaders beyond the reach of ground forces in Afghanistan—calling such bombings "executions without trial." Another audience member went further, demanding the Secretary define terrorism and wondering whether Clinton believed both that drone attacks and that week's devastating market bombing could both be classified as terrorism. Maintaining her government's distinction, Clinton answered, "No, I do not."

Translation

Police: "Confess, where did you get the weapons?"

Man: "From you sir. You armed us so that we could rid the region of terrorist groups."

Arrow: "Drug dealer from Nakhila"

Culture

In some Arab countries, law enforcement agencies have armed drug dealers, enlisting their aid in the fight against terrorism. The reason for this is that most drug dealers are also smugglers, and thus, in their many trips across borders, traverse the same vast, uninhabited desert terrain that serves as campsites and training grounds for terrorist organizations. Police forces find such areas difficult to both navigate and travel with the equipment they possess. Of course, drug-trafficking is a criminal enterprise, and these drug-smuggling militia bands often use their government-granted weapons to illicit ends. Given both the American origin of the weaponry and the nature of the government arrangement, the guns in questioned are not properly licensed for use. Accordingly, the drug dealer in the cartoon has been arrested for carrying unlicensed arms—only to reveal that he did, in fact, receive these guns from the very government that now holds him in custody for their possession.

☪ In the Arab world, gun-ownership is considered one of the citizenry's fundamental rights. In this, the reader might note the analogy to America's National Rifle Association (NRA), which holds that the populace possesses both a responsibility for self-protection and the inalienable right to ensure it. Similarly, Arab communities view weaponry primarily as a means of self-defense. Guns are most abundant in rural areas, which endure perpetual tribal warfare, as well as the very real specter of revenge killings. Here, a man will brandish his weapon openly, often employing it as a walking stick. Many Arab countries lack acutely a well-funded and reliable police force—especially these more rural areas, where the police will often take hours to respond to a distress call. Accordingly, the local population must take up the burden of policing its streets, and a household gun is essential for guarding against thieves, wild animals, and revenge killings. Most guns in the Arab world are found in substantially lawless countries, such as Somalia, or countries where the government lacks a firm grip on security, such as Yemen. The Arab gun of choice is the Kalashnikov, a Russian automatic weapon. Arab gun-owners prefer Russian-manufactured weapons to all others, as they require very little maintenance and function well in harsh climates. The Kalashnikov's unique popularity resulted from a number of historical contingencies. First, due to long-standing trade embargos maintained by Western powers, the Arab world's main source of weaponry for many years was Russia. More importantly, the Kalashnikov was the staple weapon of the Russian infantry during the invasion of Afghanistan and, in the course of their successful resistance against Russian power, the mujahedeen appropriated the weapon as a symbol of Islamic strength and fortitude. In this vein, patriotic folk songs have been composed to the gun, and Osama bin Laden is often depicted cradling the Kalashnikov he stripped from the corpse of a slain Russian general. The least common weapons in the Arab world are American, which are more high-maintenance than most. (In fact, due to their expensive upkeep and general aesthetic quality, American weapons have become something of a status symbol among wealthy Arab gun-owners.) After the Kalashnikov, many Arab gun-owners prefer shoulder-mounted rockets and RPGs, which can be purchased for as little as $100. These guns are typically acquired by corrupt government or military officials, who place bulk gun orders with Russia or China and sell the wares to the general public.

The wide availability of guns throughout the Arab world is one of the international community's top concerns in combating terrorism. Recently, Western powers have sought to instate a weapon "buy back" policy similar to that which they had successfully adopted in their own countries. Such a plan would provide cash for guns that were turned in off the street.

Translation

"Olympics of the war on terror"

Culture

It seems as if the whole world is in competition to crack down on terrorism as if it were an event at the Olympic Games, transforming the Olympic rings into the muzzles of smoking guns.

Translation

On the book cover:
How to Defame Islam with a Press of a Button.
On the man: The Taliban movement.

Culture

This cartoon refers to the dynamiting of the Buddhas of Bamyan in 2001. Taliban leaders considered the statues—two majestic, towering Buddhas carved into the Afghani mountainside—to violate prohibitions of idol worship put forth by Sharia Law. The destruction of the statues was met with international outcry, viewed as evidence of the intolerance of the Taliban and Islamists.

The cited motive for the detonation—perverse, ungodly idol worship—is, at the very least, familiar to Westerners reared in the Judeo-Christian tradition. What may strike the reader as peculiar, however, is that, in Somalia, Islamic extremist groups are currently defaced, vandalizing and, when possible, razing the tombs of Muslim piousmen. While they are spurred into action by what is, loosely speaking, a form of idol worship, the matter at hand is of an altogether more abstract, nuanced and theological nature.

Intercession in Islam

Intercessionism in the Abrahamic faiths denotes the capacity of holy men—prophets, clerics, etc.—to "intercede" with God on behalf of believers. The most obvious example of this is, of course, the way in which Christians regard Jesus Christ as the necessary intercessor—as, in a way, intercession itself. Similar paradigms are at play when Christians pray to saints, or the Virgin Mary.

In Islam, issues of intercessions are far more fraught and contentious. Muslim laypersons believe that, through the appropriate mixture of devotion, submission and favoritism, Muslim piousmen of yesteryear can be persuaded to intercede on their behalf upon Judgment Day. But fundamentalists—and, to a less extreme extent, more conservative Muslims—are disdainful of widely held intercessionary hopes. The sole agent in matters spiritual and cosmic is God: before His ubiquitous gaze, it is every man for himself. Thereby, people are required to take a more comprehensive responsibility for themselves and their behavior, instilled with the certain, profound awareness that the sole provider, advocate and judge is God—and no fond murmurings from pious men can do anything to change this. The flip side of this is that, in addition to personal requests for intercession, personal intercessions on behalf of loved ones are also deemed inefficacious. To this end, the Qur'an believers not to overly concernn themselves with the ways of loved ones. God, it reminds the reader, will call those whom he sees fit.

Translation

The TV interviewer's microphone identifies him as a reporter from the: Free One

Reporter: What is your understanding of terrorism?

The westerner immediately thinks of a mosque with the words: God is most great, God is the most great.

The news ticker at the bottom reads: The Israeli forces leveled three houses in the Gaza Strip / Iraqis are being killed as a result of American bombardment

Culture

Arabs realize that many westerners associate terrorism with Islam. Debate and public discussion on the matter has covered the Arab world, and great efforts have been made to break this association in the minds of westerners, thereby dispelling dangerous thoughts of a "clash of civilizations." Many westerns leaders—Bush, Blair, Merkel, and so on—, have stressed that their military actions in the Middle East are intended strictly against terrorism and emphatically not against Islam; the reality of the conflicts on the ground, however, make many Muslims doubt the veracity of these claims.

The sheer violence that western armies have visited upon the Arab world gives reason enough for Arabs to be suspicious, but these doubts are vastly deepened by news of western soldiers' sacrilegious outrages, such as the flushing of the Qur'an down the toilet. Islamophobic propaganda in the west, too, naturally heightens the sense of alienation and discord.

For example, Switzerland recently banned the building of any further minarets, after a campaign illustrated by the poster at right, depicting a host of threatening-missile shaped minarets rearing up over a Swiss flag with an ominous and shifty-looking Muslim woman in the foreground.

Cultural differences can make communication confused and difficult; when, for example, Arab media monitor as a matter of course as the western media, they are bound to hear people like conservative talk-show hosts such as Rush Limbaugh and Michael Savage. More inflammatory even than their opinions about Muslims and Islam are those of their callers-in, some of whom bay for bombings of the holiest Muslim site, the Kaabah. Familiar with a media culture in which the government exercises strict control over opinions broadcast, Arabs listening to these belligerent opinions can easily confuse them with the official positions of the American government. In spite of all these difficulties, the effort continues to end the habitual miscommunication between the west and the Arab world, to listen and to understand what is said.

Translation

Title: Switzerland Bans the Building of Minarets

Culture

With the proliferation of immigration to Western Europe from the Arab world, many Europeans have become anxious about a perceived Islamization of their countries and some governments have taken strong measures to maintain the Christian, or at least un-Islamic, character of their countries. France, for example, restricts the wearing of headscarves and veils in its

public schools and has discussed banning the burka; the United Kingdom elected two members of the fascistic, anti-Islamic British National Party to the European Parliament in the spring of 2009; the Italian legislature is debating a bill to limit mosque construction and the sounding of the call to prayer; and, as this cartoon records, Switzerland made international headlines by banning the construction of new minarets. Though some of these measures rankle as heavy-handed and intrusive, opinion in the Arab world has tended to fall on the side of accepting these restrictions as the prerogative of the native populations. Faithful Muslims believe that Islam will inexorably rise to become the world's dominant religion as foretold in the Qur'an, so measures to halt its spread are doomed to be ineffective.

Translation

"[Islamic fundamentalist] conservatives don't see the difference between 'Star Academy' and terrorism."
On the bomb: "Tick, tick, tick"

Culture

Star Academy is a highly successful television show format that has been broadcasted in many Arab countries and internationally. It is a pop-music talent contest with viewer voting and reality show elements. Some Arab commentators condemn such programs

as having a bad moral effect on Arab youth as much as they condemn terrorism; hence the cartoon depicts conservatives as unable to distinguish the two.

Translation

Title between diamonds: [Islamic fundamentalist] Conservatives Abroad

Man being interviewed: Why are the Swiss afraid of us? What have we done?

Starting with top arrow pointing to tall woman, then proceeding counter-clockwise: Education is unlawful [in Islam] / Only one eye because two are unlawful / Voice [of women] is unlawful / Perfume is unlawful / Circumcision is mandatory

Arrow pointing to the small girl: Because of [to prevent] temptation

Culture

In the mid-1980s, liberal Western countries generally opened their doors to fundamentalist Muslims who, it was believed, were being persecuted in their home countries for their religious beliefs. Though a laudable effort, many of those who were allowed to immigrate wanted not merely to live quietly according to their faith but rather violently to overthrow societies that they viewed as heathenish or impious, including not only their countries of origin but also the Western countries that had given them sanctuary. The most extreme Islamic fundamentalists subscribe to all the beliefs listed here about what is lawful, and this cartoon argues that Muslims should not be surprised at Western wariness when so much of what the West sees of Muslims is dominated by this vocal but tiny minority.

☪ A male Islamists who follows sunnah is required to simultaneously grow his beard and trim his moustache. This practice is illustrated by the two men in the cartoon above.

☪ Many Arab perfumes are alcohol-free.

Fitna, or Temptation

In Islam, the temptation that tests the strength of a person's morality, faith, and character is known as *fitna*, a deeply challenging lure from the path of righteousness. *Fitna* is a crucial aspect of every Muslim's experience of his or her spiritual life, and facing and overcoming *fitna* is a hallmark of a strong faith.

Fitna, though, has also been open to a range of reinterpretation in fundamentalist community, and their understanding of the concept can be very much at variance with the mainstream view. Much of the restrictions and strictures that characterize fundamentalist Islam are measures to reduce the temptation to act or think impurely. In their eagerness to avoid the allurements of *fitna*, these extreme conservatives place ever-increasing restrictions women to prevent possible seduction. In this cartoon, the man only allows the women in his family to uncover one eye, and they must maintain strict silence. Most disturbingly of all, he apparently views his tiny daughter as a potential source of sexual temptation.

Translation

Right panel: Thinking
Left panel: Declaring someone an infidel (Excommunication)

[N.B. Placing the index finger to the temple is a way of saying "use your head," much like the tapping version used in the U.S.]

Language

The two words *takfir* and *tafkir* are sound similar because they have the same letters but with the central letters interchanged.

The word *takfir* means to judge somebody to be a *kafir* or infidel, because they have shown themselves to be an infidel by their behavior.

Culture

The implication of the cartoon is that if you use your head and think about matters, you will end up being labeled a *kafir* by fundamentalists, which could lead to execution.

Fundamentalists and a large group of Muslims believe that there are areas of religion that should not be discussed, and that opinions published a hundreds of years ago should be accepted without question—disagreement is a sign of heresy, apostasy or lapsing. There are six conditions for a Muslim to be declared apostate: declaring an open hostility toward the Qur'an and sunnah, and inviting others to refuse its commandments; attacking the companions of the Prophet and accusing them falsely; attacking the Qur'an and its origins; denying the Oneness of God, His secrets and the world beyond; accepting in any secular doctrine that excludes God, such as Marxism or secularism; accepting or defending writings and opinions that put forward any of the foregoing points, such as *The Satanic Verses*.

The accusation of *takfir* is serious, and can genuinely lead to a death sentence such as the fatwah against Salman Rushdie, or, in any country where Sharia law is followed, may escalate so that a person is made into a non-person, losing many rights, and a man may be forcibly separated from his wife (since a Muslim woman is not permitted to be married to a non-Muslim). A teacher of Sharia law in a university could lose his job on the grounds of having written or defended an opinion that is judged as heresy in Islam.

This can be taken a step farther, so that a whole society may be declared infidel by *takfir*, meaning that it has deviated from the teachings of Islam and is a *kafir* or infidel society. In this case, it is, of course, legitimate to use terrorism against it.

Translation

[*Obama's newspaper carries the headline:* Incident of Ft. Hood Base]

The Man in the middle with bloody hands (identified as Benjamin Netanyahu): Didn't I tell you those Muslims were terrorists?

[*The hoodie is identified as:* The Killer of Marwa al-Sherbini]

Hoodie: That's true!

Culture

This cartoon commemorates the death of Marwa al-Sherbini, known as "the headscarf martyr." A German Arab living in Dresden, accompanying her child to the playground, she fell into a dispute with one Alex Wiens (shown in the cartoon as the hoodie with a bloody knife) over access to the swings. Wiens flew into a racist rage and insulted her headscarf, growing so belligerent that police were called and al-Sherbini successfully sued him. Wiens appealed, and when the case was heard, he attacked the pregnant Marwa and her husband with a knife, fatally wounding her.

The incident grabbed international attention, with many protesting the grotesque level of racism Wiens exhibited. Since her death in July of 2009, Arab popular opinion has embraced the memory of Marwa and considers it evidence of malignant racism endemic in Western society. German officials, for their part, quickly argued that such attitudes are horrifying but thankfully rare in modern Germany, and Wiens was sentenced to life imprisonment.

12 — How Arabs View America

Translation

Wife: You know father of Saba, our relationship with America is like our relationship with onions: they make us cry and still we can't dispense with them.

Husband: O peace.

Language

The husband's words *ya salaam*, "O peace," have many meanings in different contexts, which are discussed as they occur. Here they probably mean "How true."[22]

"Father of so and so" is the title that a father will be called, usualy the name used is that of the oldest son, mothers will also be called this way, mother of so and so; it could be her son's or daughte'rs name.

Culture

The wife's characterization of the Arab world's relationship with the U.S. being like an onion is true. The whole region has a paradoxical relationship with the United States.

America's presence is indispensable to the region. It helps to improve the life of Gulf citizens in return for alliances. The U.S. offers protection to the oil rich countries of the region and economic stimulus through trade, as well as encouraging democracy. The Arab world benefits from America's modern technology, and advanced science, and there is hardly a single Arab house that doesn't have an American product such as a car or an electrical appliance, and many people proudly wear American-style clothes, eat American-style food and drink American-style drinks. Arab and Muslim citizens gladly buy these products despite the availability of others from countries such as Japan, China and Europe, and some of them will prefer these goods over local products. In some countries the whole population depends on American wheat and corn.

America has almost total control over the Arab oil supply, with most of this oil being extracted by American companies, and Arabs perceive that America benefits from this oil more than the producer countries. Many notice that oil by-products are sold to the American consumer at prices that are lower than those available to the Arab consumer, despite the fact that the average American's income is many times greater than the average Arab's. American interests in the Islamic and Arab world are totally guaranteed by bilateral agreements between each country and the United States, and there is an

---

[22] See "10 — Arab Leaders," p.235.

American military presence in almost all Arab and Muslim countries. The largest American military base outside of the U.S. is located in Qatar, which is the smallest Arab and Muslim country in area and population. It is also known that the American territory has never been attacked by an Arab or Muslim state, while America has occupied, bombed, and devastated Iraq and Afghanistan. The U.S. also attacked Lebanon in 1982, later bombed Libya and Somalia, and then used long-range missiles to destroy a medical factory in Sudan. America gives financial aid to Israel, as well as guaranteeing its military superiority, which has enabled Israel's occupation of Palestinian and Syrian territory. America also uses its power of veto as a Permanent Member of the UN Security Council to prevent condemnation of Israel, and turns a blind eye to Israel's covert operations against the Palestinians, which are seen as state terrorism in the Arab world.

The wife relates the U.S. to an onion because of this dichotomy. No Arab meal can be cooked without one. Arabs rely heavily on onions, putting them in everything, even breakfast foods such as fava beans and split-pea soups. It is the common denominator of Arab cuisine, being found in all types of food for both rich and poor. It can be eaten raw or cooked, with stew or sauce, with soups or fish. It is bought in bulk in sacks and stored on balconies with the garlic to keep dry. Even though it is so helpful, it still stings your eyes when you prepare it. The U.S. is vital to the Arab world, it is found in every part, but it still hurts to work with it.

Arabs believe that the health benefits of eating raw onion are numerous; eating it daily is thought to be an aphrodisiac. Devout Muslims refrain from eating onion and garlic before praying and before reading the Quran because of the smell. A lot of people believe that eating onions will sterilize the mouth and that the smell is a small price to pay for the overall health benefits.

Because of the importance of onions in Arab life, proverbs about them are commonplace. "The onion of the beloved is a lamb," means that when somebody loves you but has limited resources he may give you something very cheap, like an onion, but that this expresses his love as much as preparing lamb, which typically signifies total hospitality. An equivalent phrase in English would be, "It's the thought that counts."

One day onion and one day honey,' refers to the ups and downs of life similar to the English phrase, "peaks and troughs" or "the rough with the smooth."

"The first period of married life is honey, the middle is laziness and the last is onion." This phrase is tongue in cheek: it refers to the expected decline in a marriage once a couple has been together for too long.

"Fast and fast and break his fast on an onion" is a proverb that indicates that someone is self-disciplined and restrained but then does not choose to enjoy the reward that seemed to be his goal. It would be expected that after a long period of fasting an individual would reward himself by having a really delicious meal, so to break his fast with an onion would be seen as selling himself short. Keep in mind that the individual featured in the proverb is making the choice to eat the onion, to deny himself the reward at the end of his disciplined pursuit, so it expresses the observer's surprise.

"For if your father is an onion, and your mother is garlic, how could you get a good smell." This means you have little chance of turning out well if you come from a bad family.

"Garlic is making fun of onion," is the equivalent Arabic phrase of the western phrase "The pot calling the kettle black."

"Eat onion for a year and then honey," suggests that things can only get better; you have to endure hardship for a period after which comes the reward.

"This person is like an onion, he sticks his nose in everybody's business." As in the cartoon above, this proverb refers to the dependence of Arab cuisine on onions.

☪ The long time involved in meal preparation provides an opportunity for husbands and wives to talk. The woman will do all the preparation, doing things such as cleaning vegetables or any simple menial activity, while the husband will drink tea and read the newspaper, discussing its topics with his wife. The implied situation is that the subject of America has come up from his reading and she is bringing a homely analogy to the conversation.

☪ Note the size of the wife and her husband. As is seen elsewhere in the book, husbands, after years of marriage, get skinnier while the opposite is true of the wives. If you ask a married Arab man why he lost weight, he would most likely reply, 'because of the stress of life.' Note also that the wife's hair is covered by a scarf, which is worn primarily to protect her hair from the dust while cleaning the house and carrying out other daily tasks.

Although eating raw onions in the morning is delicious for Arabs, if you are brave enough take a bus ride with morning commuters in any Arab city, you risk passing out from the smell of onion flatulence.

Translation

Title: A dialogue with America
Uncle Sam: Why you hate us?

Culture

When Arabs hear this question—"Why do you hate us?"—which surfaced soon after Sept. 11, 2001, their first reaction is to ask: "Why do you kill us?" Muslims in other parts of the world may express their frustration with America by burning flags and effigies, demonstrating in the streets and kidnapping tourists. Arabs' displays of contempt are much less dramatic: they pray for the destruction of America and when something negative happens to Americans, such as a financial crisis and a recession, Arabs experience a certain *Schadenfreude*.

These expressions of ill-will can take the form of personal writings, graffiti in public spaces, or appear in newspaper articles, and an imam might end Friday service by calling for the destruction of America. Americans who read Arabic fluently may be shocked by the intensity of hatred that people articulate toward America in comments on the websites of major newspapers. This is not without exception, but just as in America, angry people are more likely to express their opinions, and voices of reason are the minority. The most vocal commenters are typically not very sophisticated or knowledgable about America—they only hear the negative aspects of American culture and base their opinions accordingly. The American Department of State is also proactive in countering extreme sentiments. A team of media experts monitors these comments and responds, sometimes overtly and sometimes covertly, in order to counteract incorrect information.

Translation

Title: The Third Anniversary of September 11th.

Culture

Initially, Arabs were highly sympathetic to the United States for the terrorist attacks of 9/11. However, the United States' actions since then have caused much suffering for Arabs, so their sympathy has diminished with each passing anniversary. On the third anniversary, this cartoon showed Uncle Sam using an airplane to wreak misplaced vengeance on the world. Some Arabs find that the American commemoration of the anniversaries of the 9/11 grate, resuscitating resentments, and note that many more people have died in attacks on Gaza than died at the World Trade Center, but that Americans value some lives more than others. The cartoons that appear on the anniversaries of the attacks act as a kind of barometer of opinion in the Arab world toward the fallout from American action in that year.

Reflecting a collectively poor self-esteem, many Arabs believe that the terrorist attacks could not possibly have been committed by nineteen Arabs, because of the high level of sophistication involved in pulling off such a logistically challenging operation. Some of these think that America's own agencies were behind the attacks, and staged them because they feared the rise of Islam and sought to manufacture an excuse to attack the Muslim world and to seize control of their natural resources: oil and gas, water, cotton, gold. Others believe that Al-Qaeda is an American creation and Osama bin Laden an American agent, instructed to engineer the attack by his controllers. Another section of the people accepts the general explanation, but that God wanted people to see the act, as is shown by the exceptionally clear weather conditions that were in operation on the day in question.

Translation

Title: Terry Jones, the extremist pastor who is planning to burn copies of the Noble Qur'an on the anniversary of Sept. 11.

On his jacket: The culture of hate and terrorism.

Culture

Terry Jones, a Florida pastor, threatened to burn copies of the Qur'an on September 11, 2010, but changed his mind under pressure to consider the safety of U.S. citizens abroad. There is extensive media coverage any time there is a desecration of the Qur'an or an attack on Muslims in the West.

Terry Jones may be surprised to learn that in Islam, the burning of the Qur'an is actually *not* a sin. In fact, it's the most dignified way of disposing of the Qur'an or any paper that contains its verses. Arabs use old newspapers in a variety of ways; but first, they must scan it to make sure that it doesn't contain any references to God, or verses from the Qur'an or Hadith (sayings of the Prophet). It is very likely that even newspaper articles having nothing to do with religion would contain such language. This is because religion permeates every aspect of Arab society. Muslims are taught from a very young age to relate the Qur'an and Hadith to everyday activities.

At the same time, the act of burning the Qur'an by non-Muslims is still considered an insult because it is an act of intentional ill will and involves non-believers touching the Qur'an, which should only be touched by Muslims after purification.

When Their Religion Comes Under Assault, the Reactions of Arab Muslims Differ from Those of Other Muslims

Arab-speaking Muslims have the clearest understanding of the Qur'an, which was written in Arabic. (The Qur'an is only meant to be read in Arabic, even for non-Arabic-speaking Muslims. They learn from a very young age to recite and read the Qur'an in Arabic, even if they don't understand it.) This can help to explain why their reactions are calmer when the Qur'an is desecrated. The reason is that in the Qur'an, God says: "We truly revealed The Book and we indeed will protect it." So even though Arab Muslims may feel angry when the Qur'an is desecrated, they believe that God is more capable of protecting his work than they are. This is partly because of their sophisticated knowledge of Arabic, but also from a sense of religious fatalism. They also live in political environments that do not encourage open displays of protest or demonstration—for any reason.

The Terry Jones story was covered so extensively in the media that many cartoons appeared in Arab newspapers. In the cartoon on the right, the text next to the burning building says "The extremism of bin Laden"; the text next to the burning match says "The extremism of Terry Jones." Although this particular incident was quickly forgotten, deliberate insults to Islam are repeated with some frequency and provoke a similar reaction.

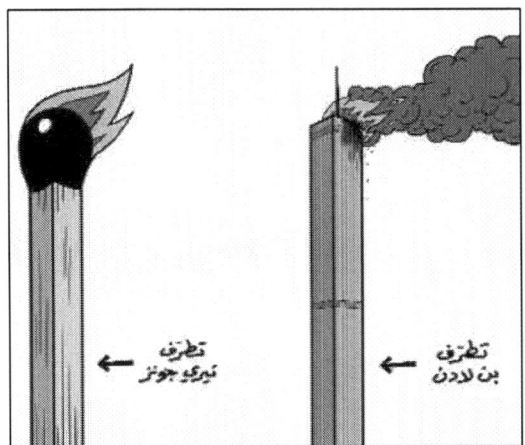

The Mosque near Ground Zero and similar aggravations.

According to the Qur'an, it is God's order that Muslims should not antagonize non-Muslims, so that non-Muslims will not disrespect God. Therefore, because Muslims know that building a mosque near the site of the World Trade Center angers non-Muslims, their persistence in going ahead with their plans is actually against scriptural teaching. "Don't curse those who pray to gods other than Allah; because if you do, they will curse Allah."[23]

Translation

Imam: Is that what they call "One hour for your heart and one hour for your God?" How wonderful!

On sign: Donate for the building of a mosque and...a swimming pool and a gym.

Language

"One hour for your heart and one hour for your God" is an Arabic proverb, urging individuals to split their time between worship and leisure so that they do not grow bored with either. An American equivalent might be "Variety is the spice of life" or "All work and no play makes Jack a dull boy." "One hour for your heart" specifically refers to humorous activities—there was an old radio comedy program called *One Hour For Your Heart*, which featured jokes and skits.

The imam in the cartoon, representing collective Muslim opinion (and *not* the imam behind the project), uses this proverb to describe the Ground Zero mosque, because he finds the idea of having a swimming pool and a gym in the same building as the mosque offensive.

Here the phrase *ya salaam*, "O peace," has the import of "How wonderful," though in an ironic way.

---

[23] Al-Qur'an, 006.108 (*Al-Anaam* [The Cattle, Livestock]).

Culture

When the news of the objections to the construction of a mosque in the vicinity of Ground Zero reached the Arab world, support for the project was unanimous. Many Muslims thought that the mosque would be a grand structure, the centerpiece of the proposed building, and when they discovered that it would, in fact, be in the basement, and would also house a swimming pool, restaurant, and gym, their support of the imam turned to mockery. The idea of a mosque being located in the same building as women in skimpy swimsuits, a Western restaurant that would likely serve pork and alcohol, and a gym with popular music seemed, for many Muslims, a sign of disrespect. Those who once had supported the imam lampooned the plan by asking why they weren't going the whole way and including a bar and nightclub in the center.

However, many mosques in the Arab world are located on the first floor (ground floor) of an apartment building, where all sorts of things could take place in the rooms above them.

Translation

Title: America's to blame for not getting involved in the Lebanon Crisis.

Bush: "Why do I have to get involved when *our group* is breaking down the world?"

Language

In Arabic, saying that someone is, "breaking down the world" means that he is doing a really good job.

When an Arab uses one of the phrases that means "our group," you know there is a strong association between him and the people of the group. "Our group" here means our people, Israel, though with the appropriate context and grammar, it commonly means "my wife."

Culture

The Lebanon Crisis that is mentioned in the title refers to the 2006 war between Hezbollah and Israel.

Constructive chaos and the new Middle East

America didn't object to the war Israel waged on Lebanon despite the devastating effect it had on the country. The reasoning for this was that Hezbollah is a terrorist organization that had to be taken out in order to create a new, peaceful Middle East. The rationale is what Condoleezza Rice referred to as "Constructive Chaos" — the theory that blood must be shed in order to bring about stability. She is quoted as saying, "I have no interest in diplomacy for the sake of returning Lebanon and Israel to the status quo.... I think it would be a mistake. What we're seeing here, in a sense, is the growing — the birth pangs of a new Middle East and whatever we do we have to be certain that we're pushing forward to the new Middle East not going back to the old one." Tellingly, the Constructive Chaos theory echoes the "War is Peace" slogan used by the government in George Orwell's *1984*. Arabs were far from pleased when the George W. Bush administration began inventing new geopolitical terms, such as the Greater Middle East and the New Middle East. Arabs have a highly specific understanding of what the Middle East means, its boundaries and its cultures. In every part of the world, redrawing boundaries has always been fraught with conflict. By attempting to rename it, the Bush Administration was attempting to impose a new identity on the region. This cartoon depicts Rice as a midwife delivering the

"New Middle East" out of the "Old Middle East." Little does Rice know that she's also delivering a brand new type of Lebanese and Palestinian resistance, as written on the babies' bandanas.

Translation

Title: The Banner of Constructive Chaos.

This banner represents numerous factions in the Middle East. On the top and bottom panels are written the words

Sunni, Shiaa, Christian, Muslim, Arab, Foreign, Salafi, Moderate, Religious, Secular, Fighter, Terrorist, Traitor.

The triangle on the right of the banner says "Hamas" while the one on the left says "FataH." The star in the middle says "March," as in the month. To the left of the star is written "God" and to the right it

says "is the most great." The cedar tree on the left has the number fourteen on it, while the tree on the right features the number eight, referring to the anti-Syrian Christian-Sunni March 14 Alliance, and the pro-Syrian Shiaa -Hezbollah March 8 Alliance.

Language

In Arabic, when somebody uses the word "banner" (*rayah*) as opposed to "flag" (*alem*) it most often has religious connotations because the word banner is associated with Islam.

Culture

Though this cartoon does not mention America explicitly, it is intentionally ambiguous. Some Arabs will see this banner and conclude that Constructive Chaos is simply the result of many conflicting interests and warring parties. Other people believe that these groups have been created since America became involved in the Arab world, especially since its involvement in Lebanon. These separate groups used to live peacefully together, but internal fighting has been encouraged by America. When people are distracted with fighting internal conflicts, they will be less focused on fighting a common enemy. Some Arabs believe that this fragmentation is a direct result of American Constructive Chaos.

Translation

In the first cartoon, the prisoner stands on the word: (The) Freedom
In the second cartoon, Obama stands on a box printed with: (The) Change

☪ In the first cartoon, note that the electrical wires attached to the prisoner's hands hang such that they form an outline of the map of the United States of America.

Language

Notice that the last letter in the word "the freedom" – "horaya(t)," called *taa marbouta* – is muzzled. It is a visual pun upon the Arabic letter. *Taa marbouta* can be translated as a "tied/bound taa," and the cartoon puns on this by " binding" the *taa marbouta* with a muzzle, meaning that freedom itself is restricted.

Culture

All three of these cartoons take as their subject the torture of prisoners at Iraq's Abu Ghraib prison by American soldiers and specifically the infamous photos that documented the abuse. The second references a photo showing a detainee's hands attached to wires. He was told that he if he stepped off the box he would be electrocuted. The photo came to represent torture at Abu Ghraib prison in Iraq at the hands of the American military. This image is still being used in the Arabic media to depict America's aggression towards Arabs.

Translation

"There is no torture in American prisons"

Culture

This cartoon appeared during the 2008 American presidential campaign. Its message is that regardless of who wins, the next president will be in the pocket of the Jewish/Israeli lobby. Traditionally, a major aspect of the presidential contest is trying to prove who is more loyal to the state of Israel and concerned with its security. Candidates have promised to move the American embassy to Jerusalem and place a

strong emphasis on Judeo-Christian ties, without ever paying attention to Arab countries or politicians in the same way. This worries Arabs, who are keenly aware of the profound influence Israeli lobbies have on American foreign policy and are thus convinced that any peace negotiations with Israel will be futile. Instead of anticipating peace, they are better off preparing for war. Nevertheless, they have attempted to influence American public opinion in the public arena on the suffering in Palestine and other Arab causes. The relationship between America and the Arab world reached its lowest levels during the Bush administration, highlighted by the mistreatment of Arab government officials in Washington, D.C. Since the 1970s, the visits of such officials were marred by organized demonstrations by oppositionists in exile or oppressed minorities alongside Israeli sympathizers in Washington. This influenced American policymakers and resulted in a high level of discomfort for Arab officials. Ultimately, these continued interruptions resulted in some of these leaders deciding to stop their traditional visits to the United States. Most notable was the president of Egypt who was resentful of dismissive and disrespectful treatment by the Bush administration, and broke the Egyptian tradition of making annual trips to the American president. The Obama administration has recognized the impracticability of a policy of "going it alone" diplomatically and economically, and it has aimed to approach Arab leaders with comradely respect. Increasingly, encouraging signals have emerged from the Obama administration that the American government will not follow the same path adopted by Bush; this policy change is particularly illustrated by the charismatic speech that Obama delivered in Cairo and his positive overtures toward the Islamic world in addressing the issue of Israeli settlements in the West Bank and throughout Israel.

☪Although the Westerner probably does not notice it, Western politicians engage in a minor form of smile-based warfare with regard to the Palestinian/Israel conflict. Yes, "smile-based": throughout the Arab world, it is a legitimate, widely held perception that, when meeting with Israeli leaders, Western politicians will implicitly broadcast their support for Israel with a wide, toothy, ear-to-ear grin. When meeting with Palestinian leaders, on the other hand, they will

invariably glower—or, at the very least, display a curt and somber countenance. Intended or not, it sends to the Palestinian supporters a message of stern disapproval. In this cartoon Ehud Olmert is given a banana by Condaleezza Rice, while she throws the peel to Mahmoud Abbas.

Apropos of perceived double standards: numerous Arabs believe that Western leaders treat the Jewish Holocaust with much more seriousness and reverence than they do the daily, ongoing tragedy of the Palestinians. Indeed, many Arabs feel that Western leaders regard this suffering—hideous in scope—as marginal and that they discount it.

Translation

Coming from Mickey's horn, from the top: Syria / Iran / Hezbollah / Jihad

In this cartoon, America (depicted as Mickey Mouse) is a noisy horn tooted by the Israeli lobby, mindlessly repeating slogans, trite excuses and justifications for its support of Israel against perceived and inflated threats.

Translation

Title: American Satellite Television: The Free One

The Free One

[N.B. *The letter Alif in the Arabic word for "The Free One" (Al-Hurra) is depicted as an American soldier in military uniform with his feet on a dead person.*]

Culture

The United States established several satellite TV and radio stations in its war to

win the hearts and minds of Muslims and Arabs, and deliver its point of view to Arab audiences. Two of these are Radio Sawa and Al-Hurra satellite television. Arabs are suspicious of these new channels and do not really watch them, as depicted in this cartoon. This cartoon refers to Al-Hurra, the U.S. taxpayer-funded news network launched in 2004 to, as President Bush put it, 'cut through the barriers of hateful propaganda' in the Arab world.

Arabs believe that Al-Hurra is biased. They give such evidence as its management preventing reporters from the station from talking to any member of the Hamas organization. It also prevents its reporters from speaking to anyone from Gaza. It limits the amount of coverage given to Iranian points of view. Al-

Hurra did not cover the killing of Marwa El-Sherbini who was killed in Germany because she was wearing the Islamic hijab, because it was a religious topic. In the meantime the management of Al-Hurra TV gave extensive coverage to Gilad Shaleet the Israeli soldier who was kidnapped by Hamas. They interviewed his relatives and re-broadcast the interview many times. Al-Hurra would not interview any relatives of Palestinian prisoners.

Arabs do not consider Al-Hurra, or *The Free One*, to be the only outlet of American propaganda. Others operated in the Arab world by Arab media professionals have content that makes some viewers suspicious that, "despite their Arabic tongue, they have become infiltrated by Zionist propaganda, Western culture, and American ideology," all of which have detrimental effects on conservative Arab culture and youth. Certain topics discussed by the stations are not approved of by conservative elements in the Arab world, and are topics that would never be discussed in the mainstream Arabic media. The Dubai-based television station Al-Arabiya, MBC, and the *Middle-East* newspaper (al-Sharq al-Awsat) are all accused of being like this.

Arabs notice that the topics covered by the al-Arabiya website are primarily sexual and deviant in nature, ranging from Spaniards' quick but satisfying sexual encounters to Bahraini women who go through female circumcision so as to visit Mecca, to a Syrian girl whose brother raped her and was then sold in a slave market, to topics on how "the Gays are Coming." Usually critics of these topics don't dispute their truth, but when a major television station devotes its coverage to such sensationalist, culturally insensitive topics, it raises a flag to them that the station disseminates propaganda and corrupts the morals of the society.

Reading comments in Arabic newspapers, it is not unusual to read Arabs of one nationality attacking those of another when one party is seen as having insulted the other's tradition or because of an incident involving both nationalities, but usually the written attack is tactful. On the Arabiya website the style of attack is often vitriolic and very insulting, which has led some Arabs to believe it is orchestrated by groups who want to spread division and deepen disagreement between Arabs, and not just the opinion of an exasperated citizen.

In this cartoon, the world is covering its face while feeding Palestine (written on the leg of meat) to Israel, depicted as a wild dog on the end of a leash held by the Americans. The Arab world blames America for Israel's aggression, and many cartoons depict America as condoning this aggression. This notion has a strong hold on the Arab mentality, especially when Arabs see that the weapons that the Israeli army uses to attack their brethren in Palestine and Lebanon are manufactured in America, and that international legislation condemning Israel has been vetoed by America. This perception has deepened. Unfortunately, it is only after leaving office that most

American presidents, such as Nixon, Ford, Carter, George H. W. Bush, and Clinton, have come to realize the plight of the Palestinians and tried to help them. Their help, however, is both too little and too late, because these men no longer wield the power they possessed while in office. These gestures from prominent American public figures do give Arabs hope that perhaps, one day, people in power might give the Palestinian problem the attention it deserves early in their tenure. Obama has realized some of these hopes by addressing the Palestinian conflict in the first year of his administration.

Translation

Grant Wood's painting *American Gothic* is seen as a symbol of American moral obligation, but there is a stark contrast between these obligations and the reality of America's recent actions during the war in Iraq.

Culture

After the 9/11 terrorist attacks, the outpouring of love and sympathy from the Arab world to America was very sincere. Even Iran, which was classified by Bush as part of the "Axis of Evil," was sympathetic. Unfortunately, the American response to the attacks succeeded in turning these positive feelings into hatred and disdain. The pictures of American combat in Iraq, including those of the torture of the prisoners at Abu Ghraib, were used by terrorists and their sympathizers as recruiting tools. American ignorance of Arab culture also contributed heavily to what went wrong, starting with the invasion of Iraq and the detention of prisoners in Guantanamo. Almost all Arab countries give a hero's welcome to any citizen returning home from Guantanamo. The Americans had a steep learning curve regarding Arab culture, but their understanding has steadily increased.

Translation

"Terrorists are behind this explosion."

Culture

After the terrorist attacks of 9/11, the immediate reaction to any disaster was to look for possible links to terrorism, even when it was clear from the outset that this was impossible. In a similar way, when the Space Shuttle Columbia exploded in 2003, the authorities decided to announce formally that it was not terrorism-related, as if to imply that it could somehow have been connected with terrorism. Some Arabs believe that the explosion of the shuttle was an act of God, since one of the crew-members was an ex-Israeli fighter pilot, and a large amount of debris fell onto a small city in Texas, called Palestine. This type of reaction is also found in the Arab world, and many Arabs will blame other countries, primarily Israel, for any incident that does not have an immediate culprit.

Translation

The fava beans are sour! ...This must be an European, American, Zionist, international conspiracy.
[N.B. Fava beans are considered a lowly food and are a staple breakfast of the poor, as indicated by the man's patched clothes.]

Culture

Just as some people in America and Europe will blame Arab terrorism for any misfortune, no matter how plainly unconnected, some Arab people will blame anything that does not have a clear culprit on American, European, and Israeli conspiracy.

Conspiracy Thinking

In the Arab world, there exists a general predisposition toward what some sociologists have termed "conspiracy thinking." "Conspiracy thinking" refers to the tendency of an individual person or society to explain the world in terms of conspiracies, or the hidden, coordinated machinations of various, often powerful persons or entities toward nefarious ends. Such thinking is remarkably prevalent throughout much of Arab society. For example, within the Arab world, the Iraqi invasion of Kuwait was largely considered either an Israeli venture to discredit the Palestinian cause, a Zionist-American attempt to undermine and disarm Iraq, or an American imperialist effort to weaken the power base of the Saudi royal family. Likewise, the later execution of Saddam Hussein was considered the result of a joint American-Israeli-Iranian conspiracy to destabilize power relations in the region, silence opposition, and seize lucrative oil wealth.

The preponderance of conspiracy thinking within the Arab world can be traced back to a few decisive influencing factors. First and foremost, conspiracy thinking presupposes the existence of an "actual" reality—reality as it *really* is, behind the merely "familiar" reality of perceptible, everyday life. This distinction has deep roots in Arab culture, and is exemplified in the core concepts of "*zahir*," or "outer," and "*batin*," or "inner." The "*zahir*" comprises everything that is available even to the most ignorant, unlearned and innocent of eyes, and can be taken to refer to anything from the small, simple things of quotidian life to phenomenal reality and appearance itself. The "*batin*," reality, meanwhile, refers to that which is beyond appearance—thus, to something like an esoteric, privileged realm of higher truths or fundamental *noumena*, visible only to the trained or enlightened. Religious? Philosophical?

This metaphysical or ontological distinction between *zahir* and *batin* sets the stage for the socio-political distinction between, on the one hand, the political "mere appearance" and, on the other, the secret and concealed political *actuality* that conspiracy thinking claims to uncover.

In addition to the duality of inner and outer realities, sociologists explain the high incidence of Arab conspiracy thinking by referencing Arab child-rearing practices, as well as cultural attitudes toward sexuality, both of which are thought to reinforce the inner/outer distinction. The typical Arab male child will pass through two vastly different stages: one dominated by his mother, the other dominated by his father. The necessary severance of the child's close connection to his mother, in order to facilitate his introduction into—and eventual assumption of—patriarchal mores and authority, is said to constitute a traumatic nucleus within Arab life. The fear of its repetition, as well as the sense of different realities that it engenders, is believed to cultivate and inflame conspiracy thinking among Arab males. The strict taboos and prohibitions on sexuality, meanwhile, are thought to function in a similar manner: the exclusion of sexuality from public discourse creates, in a sense, two "realities," while a fear of discovery and shame, as well as a certain felt "passivity" in the face of one's inability to curtail or fully neglect one's sexual desires, lays the foundation for further conspiracy thinking.

"Passivity," in this sense, is important to conspiracy thinking and arises from other circumstances besides the merely sexual ones. In fact, years of colonial occupation, followed by the unceasing threat of American, Israeli (or, at one point, Soviet) imperialist incursions into the region, have continuously engendered a sense of vulnerability, paranoia and passivity amongst many Arabs, and also resulted in the existence of numerous *genuine* foreign imperialist conspiracies. Of course, the existence of very real conspiracies—particularly pertaining to CIA involvement in the region—has only strengthened and increased conspiracy-thinking within the Arab world.

The Origin of Conspiracy Thinking

Does this tendency in thought have a concrete historical origin? The preceding paragraphs may give the impression that conspiracy thinking is, primarily, a cultural artifact, a practice that was formed and conditioned in the forge of specific socio-cultural arrangements and then, only derivatively, reinforced by historical contingencies. In point of fact, however, such clear discriminations—e.g. between socially conditioned and historically conditioned—are not altogether easy to fashion. To this end, a noxious cluster of events during the First World War are probably behind the *realization* of conspiracy thinking within the Arab world. In this paradigm, the various cultural practices outlined above served as untapped prerequisites, the *potential* for a proliferated conspiracy thinking that, until the catalyzing, imperialist machinations of the First World War, lay dormant.

Hussein-McMahon

In World War I, the ailing Ottoman Empire entered the fray on the side of Germany, and thus engaged British forces in the East. From the outset, the Western European powers regarded the Ottoman Empire as an ailing beast, and that, once it was slain in the course of the war, it could yield ample opportunity for European influence and growth (the Sick Man of Europe). Thus, in the course of the war, Britain strove to undermine the Ottoman Empire from within. While waging a fierce war over Egypt, British diplomats contacted Hussein, the *sharif* and *amir* of Mecca. In an extended correspondence between Hussein and British high commissioner Sir Henry McMahon, which both parties agonized over, the British attempted to goad and persuade Hussein into initiating a pan-Arab rebellion against the Ottoman overlords. In return, the British promised to collaborate with Hussein in establishing independent Arab governments in the Arabian Peninsula and most portions of the Fertile Crescent. Crucially, however, "portions of Syria lying to the west of the areas of Damascus, Homs, Harna and Aleppo" would be governed by European colonial authorities. Whether or not this area included Palestine remained notoriously unclear.

Finally, when the Ottoman Arabs did revolt, they did so in the belief that, if they proved victorious, Europe would grant them blanket self-rule throughout the region. Of course, this was not the case. (T. E. Lawrence, who pledged as much to his numerous Arab troops, never forgave the British for reneging on their initial promises.)

In a mere three-week-long span, British treacherousness was exposed, as their various duplicitous, under-the-table agreements, determining the fate of post-Ottoman Arabia, were made public.

The Sykes-Picot Agreement

Although modern scholars have concluded that the Sykes-Picot Agreement does not violate the promises of the Hussein-McMahon correspondence, this can only really be claimed by means of very literal and lawyerly hair-splitting of the semantics. Thus, the various promises of Arab self-determination, while ubiquitous during the Arab revolt, were revealed, in the final assessment, to have been promises only, and never officially committed to paper. And the Hussein-McMahon correspondence, while ensuring some form of Arab sovereignty, did not rule out the possibility that such sovereignty would exist under some form of European oversight. (A puppet government is, after all, still a "government.") Thus, in 1915, Britain, France and Italy, with the aid and input of Russia, convened to apportion the various sectors of the soon-to-be-felled Ottoman Empire. The Arabian Desert was the sole region assigned to unhampered Arab rule: the rest of the Arab world was divided between French, British and Italian direct rule, while minor enclaves around Jaffa and Jerusalem were placed under international rule.

The Balfour Declaration

Unfortunately, the public release of the Sykes-Picot Agreement (arranged by Lenin's new Communist regime in Russia, committed to the eradication of precisely the sort of imperialist violence and presumption exemplified by the agreement in question) was the second revelation of Western imperial conspiracy. Three weeks earlier, Britain had issued the Balfour Declaration. Still a source of enormous contention with regard to the Israeli-Palestinian conflict, the Balfour Declaration is one of the most zealously debated documents in 20th Century history. The document, in full, reads as follows:

> *His Majesty's Government views with favour the establishment in Palestine of a national home for the Jewish people, and will use their best endeavors to facilitate the achievement of this object, it being clearly understood that nothing shall be done which may prejudice the civil and religious rights of the existing non-Jewish communities in Palestine, or the rights and political status enjoyed by Jews in any other country.*

To begin with, the present declaration is a marvelous feat of lawyerly equivocation. The government *favors* the establishment of a Jewish homeland, but commits no resources to the goal, nor does it provide any concrete details as to how it might be realized; it refrains from "prejudicing the civil and religious rights of the existing non-Jewish communities" — but, by its exclusion, will it therefore prejudice their political rights?

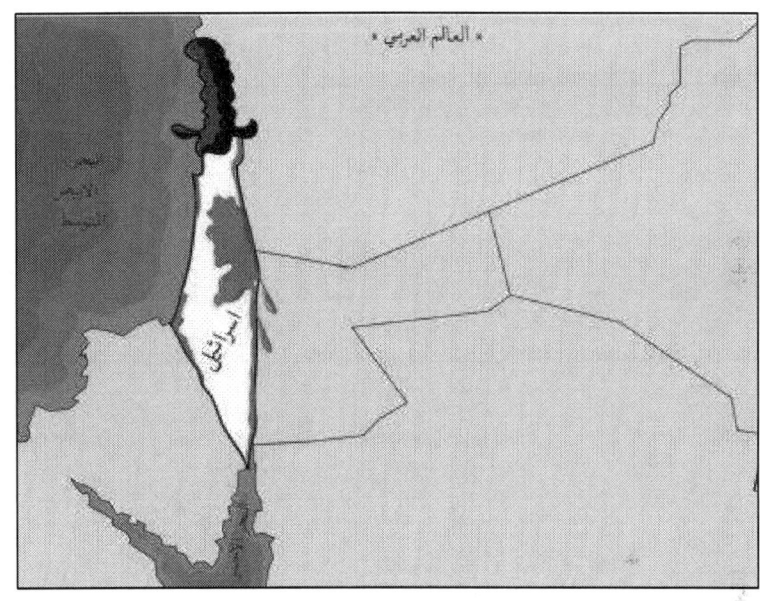

No one knows why, exactly, the British condoned the issuing of such a statement. Some believe the British severely overestimated Zionist power within post-Ottoman Palestine, and sought allies in their re-building and occupation efforts. (One scholar, in fact, explains the decision by Prime Minister Lloyd George's belief in certain anti-Semitic propaganda, which credited the international Jewish community with far more power than it actually wielded: fearing the inflated specter, he acquiesced to their supposed demands.) Finally, some think it the product of the tirelessly lobbying of British journalist and preeminent leader of European Zionism, Chaim Weizmann.

Taken together, the publication in rapid succession of the Balfour Declaration and the Sykes-Picot Agreement are probably at the root of Arab conspiracy thinking. They do not, however, mark the end of genuine conspiracy. There is however a far more contemporary instance of what is seen as furtive Western meddling in Arab affairs: NSSM 200.

National Security Study Memorandum 200

"National Security Study Memorandum 200: Implications of Worldwide Population Growth for U.S. Security and Overseas Interests" (NSSM 200) was a 1975 multi-departmental study completed under the auspices of United States National Security Council. The endeavor's mastermind and driving force was then-Secretary of State Henry Kissinger. Even before he ordered the study, Kissinger was convinced that continual population growth within a number of key nation-states would severely jeopardize U.S. interests. In his initial letter calling for the report, Kissinger outlined a number of his key concerns. Unmitigated population growth, he stated, would severely stress the over-populated country's agricultural system, resulting in a (perhaps prohibitive) dependence upon overseas food products. Coupled with similar stress being placed on public agencies (health care, law enforcement, etc.), scarcity could lead to civil unrest—which, in turn, might threaten foreign access to their natural resources. To that end, the availability of essential U.S. imports—for example, oil—would be dramatically restricted, as over-populated, oil-rich countries would be required to first share these resources with the numerous native inhabitants. Finally, population growth among certain demographics had the potential to upset the already precarious ethnic balances within a variety of regions.

To put it another way, the ostensibly self-evident threat of population growth was, at the study's outset, a foregone conclusion. Thus, the study focused far more on means of strategically combating and curtailing population growth within twelve key, developing countries. Of this list, Egypt is the only Arab country mentioned. With regard to Egypt, ethnic balance within the Middle East was a crucial concern: already reeling in the wake of the 1973 war, Israel's Jewish core could suffer a decisive blow if regional demographics shifted so significantly in favor of the Arabs. And Egypt's projected "shift" was nothing if not significant: 33 million large in 1973, Egypt was projected to grow to 66 million by the end of the century (in fact, the estimations were too modest: as of 2000, Egypt's population was roughly 80 million people).

When NSSM 200 was made public in 1990, by means of the Freedom of Information Act, the Arab public was appalled to discover the duplicity involved in U.S. population policy. Essentially, NSSM 200 (which was strictly adhered to by the Ford administration) recommended an aggressive campaign of misinformation and family planning. The U.S. was to insinuate itself into the population divisions of the UN, so as to hide its leading role in the global family-planning movement. Then, under the guise of the international community, U.S. officials would doggedly lobby the leaders of the twelve states mentioned in the report, flooding them with information as to the supposed benefits of population control (e.g. how economic growth was impossible without it), as well as an unending supply of contraceptives (and, in some cases, funding for abortions). Without trying to appear "coercive," U.S. agents would strategically withhold valuable agricultural and economic aid (e.g. food, medicine, technology) from countries that did not eagerly comply with U.S. recommendations as to family planning.

In mid-70s Egypt, the pro-contraception, family-planning campaign was everywhere: posters proclaimed the untold benefits of keeping the family small, and condoms were even distributed in mosque clinics. But the campaign was ultimately unsuccessful: despite the abundance of advertising, the majority of the population still considered "family planning" to be in irresolvable opposition to Islamic tradition.

Nowhere in the *Qur'an* are family-planning practices (contraception, etc.) explicitly prohibited. But Muslims—like all people, everywhere, at all times—will often over-emphasize one portion of a directive (in this case, an *ayah*) to the exclusion of the rest. Thus, in the *Qur'an*, God does bar the killing of children for reasons of poverty. At the time of its revelation, indigent Arabs commonly put to death young children if they felt they could not adequately provide for them. God outlaws this practice and promises that, if the children are left alive, both the family and the children will be provided for. Unlike the Bible, however, nowhere does the *Qur'an* say, "be fruitful and multiply," and though the connection between the child-murder verse and modern-day contraception is, perhaps, a bit tenuous, it is nonetheless considered by the majority of Muslims to be the authoritative ruling on matters of family planning.

When NSSM 200 was made public, Arabs were horrified at the extent to which the U.S. had intruded in something so personal—and seemingly secure—as foreign reproduction. It led some to wonder if such meddling constitutes a crime against humanity, and also to speculate that the U.S. might be responsible for other population control mechanisms, such as the calamitous spread of AIDS.

Translation

Tony Blair: "What's the big deal? When I kill a person and walk in his funeral, I'm going to have fun until they oust me."

Chicken: "Patience, God."

☪ Cartoonists may include a small animal as a tool to voice the author's own opinions. The chicken's words here also show that the offense is so great that even the simplest creatures have an opinion about the situation.

Language

The phrase "killing a man and taking part in his funeral" is an Arabic proverb to descibe a brazenly callous person. It originated when a murderer attended the funeral of his victim in order to keep up appearances and avoid suspicion or because he was sadistic and vengeful. By asking God for patience, the chicken indicates that she is reaching the end of her tether. According to the Qur'an, the patience to endure afflictions can only come from God. Arabs value this quality, so they use this phrase when they feel that they are being tested.

Culture

Shortly after leaving office as Prime Minister of Great Britain, the United Nations appointed Tony Blair as the special peace envoy to the Middle East. People in the Middle East found this ridiculous and insulting. Arabs wondered how someone who had played such a large role in the killing of so many Iraqis could help to foster peace in the region. For Arabs, the appointment was clearly compensation for Blair's support of the war.

☪ It is typical that people physically carry their deceased from the house to the mosque, where they pray over the body, and then on to the cemetery, rather than in a car (though on their shoulders, rather than overhead as depicted in the cartoon). Every step that a person carries the deceased is considered an act of piety, that will be rewarded by God. Numerous pallbearers take turns carrying the deceased in order that as many people as possible have a chance to earn their reward. Walking also gives by-standers the opportunity to pray for the dead person en route. Pallbearers are most likely not the closest relatives, who are usually overcome with grief and walk hand in hand just behind the casket with those closest to them. Women are encouraged not to participate in funeral processions because their wailing is considered an objection to the will of God and therefore a sin. If women insist on joining the procession, they walk behind the men. If a car is used to carry a dead person, it is black and understated.

The body is not buried in the coffin, which is returned to the mosque or funeral house, where the caskets are often kept in a back yard for use again.

☪ Blair's handkerchief is an emasculating symbol, which is a common way for Arabs to demean their adversaries. Handkerchiefs are used at funerals only by women, who express grief by holding a large handkerchief at two corners, one in either hand, then tugging repeatedly at these corners, pulling them back and forwards, while calling out lamentations and praises to the deceased. Short phrases of lamentation culminate in their highest pitch and coincide with the full extension of the handkerchief. Then the mourner will close her handkerchief and repeat the sequence with a different phrase of lamentation. This can go on for hours. This stretching-and-wailing is a highly traditional form of mourning that has existed in the Middle East for thousands of years, as seen by references in the Old Testament. Traditionally, women have felt the loss of their husbands more, because they depend on them to support the family financially and for their standing in society. Nowdays, especially in cities and among more educated people, women express their grief less dramatically.

Translation

Cage: Iraq
Sign: We are working for your freedom...

Culture

After the invasion of Iraq by the United States, Iraq became a quagmire from which the U.S. was unable extricate itself. Many Arab leaders and entities whom the United States consulted prior to the invasion advised against the move. The strongest advice against invasion came from President Mubarak of Egypt, while Jordan tacitly approved the invasion. The Gulf countries such as Kuwait and Saudi Arabia favored the invasion because their countries had suffered at the hands of Saddam's SCUD missiles during the first Gulf War. Since the invasion, most of the fears of those who opposed the American invasion of Iraq have come true.

The United States has consistently been reluctant to listen to countries whose advice seems to run counter to the American agenda, even if that advice comes from friends who have the United States' best interests in mind. The United States mistakenly regards any advice against particular moves in the Middle East as opposition to all its policies, and in turn retaliates in different ways. The most recent victim of this sort of retaliation was Egypt, which had advised against certain American policies. Historically, the United States has not had smooth relations with Egyptian heads of international organizations or diplomats who deal with the United States on a regular basis. This began when Secretary of State Madeleine Albright had difficulty working with Egyptian Foreign Minister Amr Mousa, and convinced Egyptian President Mubarak to assign Mousa to be head of the Arab League because he was deemed too rigid in his pro-Arab stance. Boutros Boutros-Ghali, Secretary General of the United Nations from 1992-1997 presented some difficulty for the American Administration during his tenure. Muhammad El-Baradei, the head of the International Atomic Energy Agency, opposed the invasion of Iraq as there was no proof that Iraq possessed weapons of mass destruction. Nor was he in favor of military action against Iran. In keeping with this trend, the United States launched a fierce and successful campaign to dissuade the members of the UN organization UNESCO from electing Egyptian Farouq Housni as its head in the autumn of 2009.

The American opposition to this appointment was so strong, that the American representative threatened to quit the organization and to cut American aid if Housni were elected.

Translation

"Baghdad"

Language

What does Baghdad mean?

There are many possible meanings of the name of the city of Baghdad. In Aramaic, the "b" in "Baghdad" may have been a truncation of the word "*bait,*" which means "house." The "*ghdad*" means thread, yarn, spider web or sheep, which indicates that the meaning of the "Baghdad"

could be "the house of sheep" or "the house of yarn," etc. Also in Aramaic, the word "*bagh*" may refer to a lover or either the maternal or the paternal uncle and the word "*dad*" means garden, indicating that the word Baghdad is "the garden of one's lover" or "the garden of one's uncle." In old Arabic, depending on the vocalization of the word, "*bagh*" may mean "erupted" or may refer to the width of a woman's eye. The word "*dad*" may mean "entertainment" or "play," or it could be the proper name of a woman, indicating that "Baghdad" may refer to the width of the eye of a woman called Dad, or it may mean that the entertainment has started.

Culture

The word *Baghdad* is carrying the torch of liberty. All Iraqis hope that Baghdad will be free after occupation. And terrorism.

Translation

First tissue box: "Iraq"
Tissue box being used: "Palestine"
Band on arm: map of the Arab world

Culture

The weeping Arab has been going through an old box of tissues representing Palestine; in other words, the lengthy history of violence and chaos there has been causing him anguish for a long time. Far from reaching the end of his tears, though, a fresh new box of grief has appeared: Iraq.

Translation

Title: Wave of Resistance
Wave: Fallujah

Culture

As part of the occupation of Iraq, the First Battle of Fallujah in April 2004, code-named Operation Vigilant Resolve, was an initially unsuccessful attempt by the U.S. military to capture the city of Fallujah. The chief catalyst for the operation was the highly publicized killing and mutilation of four Blackwater private military contractors, and the killing of five U.S. soldiers in Habbaniya several days earlier.

This cartoon appeared when Iraqi resistance to the American army was particularly fierce and strong.

Translation

Title: The dream of one of the mujahideen

Arrow pointing to city: Fallujah

"The turban of the prophet Muhammad. God, peace and prayer be upon him."

[N.B. The mujahid's dream attributes Fallujah's preservation to divine protection.]

Culture

The siege of Fallujah proved the endurance of the mujahedeen under siege. This cartoon depicts the help of divine intervention. In Arab culture, people have such high respect and admiration for the Prophet Muhammad, that even a piece of his clothing will bring blessings. As with the relics of Jesus or a saint in the Catholic Church, these are thought to confer special protection or blessing to the mosque or place that holds them. Despite its many mosques, Fallujah does not have any actual relics of the Prophet, but the cartoon suggests that the city's endurance through the siege was as if it had the cloth of the Prophet's turban surrounding it to protect and bless it.

Mukhallafat en-nebee, "What the Prophet Muhammad left behind," relics of the Prophet.

Many mosques throughout the Muslim world have the personal effects of pious people such as a copy of the Quran from which they read, their walking stick, cloak, or other pieces of their clothes. A mosque is considered to be more religiously significant among worshipers when it has these types of artifacts.

Just as relics associated with Jesus—for instance the crown of thorns, the cross or the shroud—are the most valued in the Catholic church, the most highly prized items in Islam are relics of the Prophet Muhammad. Muhammad's body and the majority of his relics are in Medina, but in al-Hussein mosque in Cairo, for instance, there are few of his personal effects, called *mukhallafat en-nebee*, which means "what the Prophet (Muhammad) left behind." The items are: two *sebHahs* (rosaries), his *mus-Haf* (copy of the Quran -in unarranged fragments), his *muk-Hul'ah* (the vessel in which he kept the black powder with which he painted the edges of his eyelids), two *seggadehs* (prayer carpets), a hand-mill, a staff, and a tooth-pick, among other items.

Translation

[*This cartoon is a conversation between Rice and Bush about how they will handle the last Palestinian-Israeli clash.*]

Bush: Do you like [What do you think of] these Palestinians beating up the poor Jews?

Rice: I wouldn't be myself, Rice Khanoom, and you wouldn't be my uncle, leader Bush, if I didn't make their women widows.

[*Bush is pointing out to Condoleezza Rice that the Palestinians are very violent towards the Jews. She is replying that she wouldn't be able to look herself in the mirror until she has avenged the poor and mistreated Jews. In her loyalty to President Bush she must prove herself by destroying the Palestinians and making their women widows.*]

☪ Bush and Condoleezza are dressed as two characters from *Bab al-Hara*, "The Alley Gate," one of the most popular television series in the Arab world in 2008.

Language

In Arabic, when you say "I wouldn't be [your own name]," it is like saying "I wouldn't be true to myself" or "I wouldn't maintain your integrity" if you didn't rectify the situation. In the case of Condoleezza Rice, she will rectify the situation by responding with overwhelming force to the injustice that has befallen the Jews.

In Arabic, when you say "Do you like what's happening…?" to introduce a bad situation, it can be translated in English as the somewhat accusatory "Are you happy now…?" or "Are you satisfied…?" implying, "…with what you've done/caused." But unlike in English, the implied accusation is not necessarily targeting the person to whom you're talking; instead of squarely laying the blame on that person, it can imply that they have an indirect responsibility for whatever is happening. This subtlety of the language is significant here.

☪ The choice of "Khanoom" as Rice's last name and the clothes she wears indicate that she is totally Arab; she talks like them, dresses like them and has a last name like them. The name Khanoom is of Mongolian origin and is often added to a woman's name as a token of respect.

Culture

Bush's election to his first term was celebrated in the Arab world, particularly in the oil-rich Arab countries, due to Bush Sr.'s legacy in these countries. He had liberated Kuwait from the Iraqis, and there were strong ties between the Bush and Cheney families and the Saudi royal family, illustrated by the fact that the Saudi ambassador to the United States, Bandar Bin Sultan, was nicknamed Bandar Bush. Even after his ambassadorship ended, he kept in contact with the Bush administration, and conducted business on behalf of the Saudi royal family, without the knowledge of the Saudi embassy. Furthermore, Bush Sr.'s attitude towards the Israelis had been, though not harsh, not particularly generous, so in Arab eyes he was impartial and fair.

Arab perception of Bush changed during his first term, and of course was greatly affected by the course of action Bush took after 9/11. Some Arabs now perceive the Bush era United States as a staunch ally of an aggressive Israel, despite the fact that Israel was the one doing the beating up. The writer is being sarcastic; everyone in the Middle East knows that the truth is exactly opposite of what's presented in the cartoon.

Translation

Title: Rice visits the region.

Culture

Because of the pressure that Condoleezza Rice exerted on many Arab governments in the Middle East, she has not been depicted in a positive light by the state-run media. During Rice's visit to Libya, Gaddafi admired her so much that his behavior bordered on flirtation. His admiration of her stemmed from her humiliation of other leaders of large Arab countries, whom he has historically hated. Despite the negative perception of Rice by Arab leaders, both she and Bush were showered with gifts by these same leaders during their tenure.

Historically American presidents have used their Secretaries of State as tough negotiators, the bearers of bad news and the people to deal with difficult details, so that the Secretaries of State seldom enjoy a good reputation in the Arab world.

☪ U.S. presidents are very aware that women in positions of power can cause discomfort to traditional Arab leaders, and it is perceived that female Secretaries of State have been used to underline the inferior position of the Arab officials. This perception can be reinforced by an overtly bossy manner or by behavior that is known to be inappropriate in Middle Eastern contexts—since the people involved must be aware of how this behavior will be received, any insult must be calculated, and at a high level.

Translation

Sign: "The Middle East"

Culture

This cartoon mocks America's "cowboy" attitude, involving itself in the Middle East without proper knowledge of its culture

☪ In Arab cartoons, there is no concept of political correctness. Cartoons depict blind, disabled, overweight and older people in order to be humorous and to convey their message. The most common butts of jokes are those who are under the influence of drugs in both cartoons and with stand-up comedians, who will jokingly label whole groups of people drug users.

☪ Stand-up comedy is an extremely popular form of entertainment. The act is based on jokes, though it is beginning to follow the shift toward observational humor that has become more dominant in English. There are some other minor differences between stand-up comedy in America and in the Arab world. In America, when a comedian has delivered his joke, a rim shot is sometimes played on the drums. In the Arab world, however, the rim shot is played on several instruments. The delivery of jokes in Arabic is often very fast, and in fact, an Egyptian comedian named Hamada Sultan once held the Guinness record for speediest joke delivery.

Translation

Title: After Bush's tour of the region...
Woman: "I hope President Bush won't be like 'a witness who saw nothing.'"
Bottom: "My apology to the artist Adel Imam."

☪ The dove of peace can be portrayed as a woman with wings and an olive branch.

Language

Shahed Mashafsh Haga (*The Witness Who Saw Nothing*) is the name of a play written for Adel Imam, a popular Egyptian movie actor and stage comedian. The play is about Sarhan Abdel Basir, a simple actor who plays a bunny in a children's program and lives below a well-known belly dancer, called Enayat. He is the last person who saw her alive but can't remember any details.

In Arabic printed media, when the name of a person or his work is mentioned in an unrelated context, he deserves an apology. (In Europe cartoons that borrow from other media, especially those that copy an artist or famous artwork, will usually include "with apologies to [the artist]," and the Arab custom may be taken from this practice.) The apology is usually written at the bottom of the picture or satire, and indicates respect. On the other hand when the line is written as "Without apology," or "Without my apology," it means the person who is quoted from is not worth an apology, and this could be for several reasons, one of which is his views don't conform to the culture of the audience's country.

Culture

The worry in this cartoon is that despite President Bush's visit and subsequent witnessing of the conditions on the ground, the suffering of the Palestinian people will not change.

Catchphrases and the titles of songs, movies, and plays are often use in Arab cartoons and in coversations as comic lines to elicit laughter and emphasize the point. Even though the line may be serious, the shift of context makes it amusing. *The Witness Who Saw Nothing* is one of the few plays which has many quotable lines that have taken on a life of their own separate from the play.

Translation

The Arab ruler: "Would you please allow me just to condemn what's going on?"

Man being stabbed: Iraq

Culture

This picture illustrates the fear that most Arab leaders have felt towards the United States during its invasion of and subsequent war with Iraq. Most of these leaders knew of the invasion beforehand, but none attempted to stop it, making the excuse that it was too late to change the course of events. This attitude resulted in demonstrations by most Arab people and a deteriorating relationship between leaders and citizens, as illustrated by cartoons such as the one above.

There is a dark humor to the ruler's use of the word "condemn" within the cartoon. Acts of American or Israeli aggression are usually met with swift "condemnations" or "denouncements" from all sectors of Arab politics. Such politicians act as though the issuing of an official condemnation is a sobering, serious act, one whose ramifications throughout the international community are widespread and immediately felt. In conducting the matter with pomp and circumstance, politicians hope that the verbal condemnation will be perceived as a wholly sufficient reaction to acts of ostensibly imperialist violence.

Of course, this is far from the case. Like here in America, Arab populations often take their politicians to task for being, as the saying goes, all talk and no action. Inevitably, the increasingly frequent need for official condemnations has revealed to the public the ineffectualness of just this sort of action: for if such "condemnations" worked, the need for them would surely cease. Consequently, Arab laypersons have begun to regard these varied and all too common expressions of official displeasure as politically motivated acts of self-preservation—attempts on the part of politicians to obviate the pressing need for direct and concrete action, all the while creating the illusion that precisely this sort action is being done.

Thus, the cartoon strives to reveal the official condemnation for the hollow gesture that many believe it to be. A means of placating the conflicting interests of, on the one hand, American and Israeli imperial powers, and, on the other hand, the suffering and afflicted Arab peoples, condemnations seek to create the illusion of effective action without bringing about the attendant difficulties that true action entails.

Translation

On cylinder: The concept of American democracy
On the hole in ground: The Arab world

Culture

Looking back on the American-style democracy that the Bush administration attempted to impose upon Arab countries, it is now obvious that the strategy was a failure, as illustrated in the cartoon above. Most Arab leaders are reluctant to implement democratic measures on the grounds that their people are not ready for this type of government, because their citizens do not have adequate education or levels of literacy. The American government has refused to accept this excuse, though the Obama administration has modified its stance on the democratization process.

☪The Bush administration succeeded in persuading Arab leaders not to fear freedom of expression. Now in many Arabic newspapers citizens can voice their opinions in on-line editions without being censored by the newspapers' staff. This is an unpredictable gain and the pendulum could easily swing back. Libyan newspapers contain the icon to the right, where the symbol indicates no cuts and the comment below reads "The country without the scissors of the censor except for national constants: Muamar al-Qazafi, Islam and National Unity." Westerners might criticize the exceptions, Arabs would criticize al-Qazafi's name appearing before Islam.

Translation

"Listen to me carefully, if you don't straighten up, we'll bring you **democracy** the way we did in Iraq. Understood?"

Culture

When the United States invaded Iraq and deposed Saddam Hussein during the presidency of George W. Bush, other Arab leaders in the region took notice. They began to allow their own citizens more freedom out of fear of being targeted by America. This cartoon depicts how intimidated the Arab leaders are by the threat of American force.

This fear of American intervention prompted a wave of democratic changes: Egypt held a presidential election, Libya declared its nuclear program, Saudi Arabia started debating co-education and allowing women to drive. In other parts female circumcision was outlawed, underage-marriage laws were enacted, and the opposition was given more room to voice their opinion. Freedom of the press was granted in many Arab countries, while many other legal changes that made life easier for women and minority groups came into place, and changes are still being made.

☪ Arab intellectuals believe that lack of democracy is not the reason that terrorism came about, it is the torture in their countries' jails that the fundamentalists went through that changed their methods to more violent ones.

Translation

Title: A Commemorative Picture of Arab Dignity.

Culture

Hitting someone on the back of the neck is considered a major insult in Arab culture. This gesture is almost as insulting as throwing a shoe at someone, as happened to former President Bush a few years ago — and is easier to perform! This is a culturally sensitive issue, because in the Western world, hitting or squeezing someone on the back of the neck or the shoulders is often considered a friendly gesture or a greeting. Also, tapping someone on the bottom — as sports players often do — is insulting in

Arab cultures. A word of advice to travelers in Arab countries: unless you're sure how a gesture will be received, don't use it!

This picture illustrates the Arab sense that they are disrespected by the international community. In the picture, the leaders of five major Arab countries have received this highly insulting blow to their—and to Arab—dignity.

This picture also illustrates the type of clothes worn by Arabs from different countries. The man on the far right is probably from a Gulf country, the next (to the left) is probably a Palestinian, the next from Sudan, the next, wearing Western-style clothes is probably Egyptian or Lebanese, and the leftmost could be Libyan.

The weight carried by the gesture of slapping the back of someone's neck is reflected in the proverb, "The tongue is the enemy of the neck." This means that a person should mind what he says, lest those who hear get angry and give him such a slap.

Translation

Arab government official: We are not under any pressure from abroad—yes, by God!

Language

"Yes, by God!" is a type of oath, similar to "I swear to God that..." in English. It is the only oath in Arabic that occurs at the endof the phrase rather than the beginning. Its placing reflects the fact that this particular oath is associated primarily with the disingenuous and the simple-minded. Others do use "Yes, by God," but they do so in order to be humorous or facetious. Accordingly, placing this particular oath in the official's mouth both heightens the humor (i.e. a high-minded official using a simple-minded person's oath) and underscores his dishonesty.

The oath "Ai walahai" is funny because it is an overly casual, unserious way of swearing, and it also comes from a song.

Culture

The Bush administration put a lot of pressure on Arab governments following the 9/11 attacks to spread democracy and redraw the map of the Middle East in the belief that giving Arab people freedom was the way to fight extremism. This effort was not a total failure and resulted in the relaxation of censorship, the establishment of human rights groups, and the increased recognition of minority rights. Most Arab rulers, fearing the same fate as Saddam Hussein, have grudgingly yielded to American pressure. Despite the denial of Arab leaders of influence from the United States, Arab people know that the new democratic measures are a direct result of the American government's pressure on their governments

Translation

[N.B. The crescent is the symbol of Islam.]

Culture

In this cartoon, President Bush suffers from an acute case of Islamophobia. When the crescent appears above the Capitol building, the dome also bears similarities to the dome of a mosque. Arabs are aware of the phenomenon of Islamophobia and either use the same term to describe it or the phrase "fear of Islam." As a result of this awareness, private citizens, organizations, and politicians have taken steps to overcome Islamophobia. Arabs send religious delegations to major Western cities to provide Westerners with a better understanding and conception of Islam. However, much damage has already been done, and this kind of paranoia is likely to persist for a long time.

Translation

Sign: War on Poverty
Man [labeled Africa]: "God willing, it won't be like the war on terror!"

Culture

This cartoon depicts President Bush as a representative of the G8 talking to a poor man from Africa and declaring a war on poverty.[24] Arab people criticize the violent rhetoric of the United States displayed by its reliance on the phrase "war on…" The word *war* has very negative connotations in the Arab world, which Americans realized too late. The Obama administration has tried to move away from the phrase "global war on terror" and move towards "overseas contingency operation."

Despite the fact that African countries have all of the necessary resources for prosperity, they share many problems with Arab countries that prevent them from achieving their goals. These problems include poor management, corruption, and tyrannical leadership. The Libyan leader Muammar al-Gaddafi has proposed the creation of a United States of Africa, which would be modeled after the United States of America, in order to consolidate the continent's resources and advance the African cause. In return, Africans named him "the king of kings."

The African's reaction plays into whatever negative impression the reader may have about the "war on terror," whether it is its conception, its cost, the fact that it seems impossible to see an end, or anything else.

Africans in Arab cartoons tend to be portrayed as simple tribal people.

---

[24] See "2 — Social Life" for this depiction of Africans in cartoons, p.33.

In sha' Allah or "If God wills"

The belief in predestination renders the true Muslim utterly devoid of presumption with regard to his future actions or to any future events. He never speaks of anything that he intends to do, or of any circumstance that he expects and hopes may come to pass, without adding, "If it be the will of God," "if God wills," or "God willing." These words can be used to indicate hope for an event in the future and it can also be used to provide wiggle room for someone who may feel obligated to agree to do something, but reluctant to do it.

Language

Arabic grammarians criticize the writing of *in sha' Allah* as two words (*insha Allah* as in the cartoon) as wrong and blasphemous, since the second correctly means "the building of God." However, the mistake is widespread.

Culture

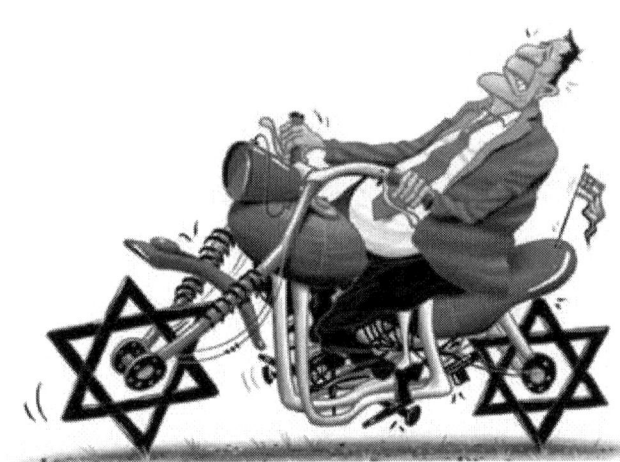

The Arab world's main grievance with the United States is its support of Israel. The Arab world does not comprehend how the United States could forego good relations with the Arab world and its vast resources in exchange for supporting a country with only a few million people that is in a constant state of aggression.

The tires of the motorcycle being ridden by the American in the picture are in the shape of the Jewish symbol of the Star of David, a tire shape which is not conducive to movement of the motorcycle. This is a metaphor for the United States' campaign to win over the Arab people. So long as the United States supports Israel, it will gain no ground in the way of winning over the hearts and minds of the Arabs.

In 1777, Morocco was the very first nation to recognize the sovereignty of a newly independent United States. The Treaty of Peace and Friendship between the U.S. and Morocco, negotiated in 1787, is the longest unbroken treaty relationship in U.S. history.

☪ The motorcycle is an important and significant mode of transportation, mainly for those who cannot afford a car. Legally, they are often regarded as being closer to a bicycle than a car, and may not need license plates or insurance. Vendors who in the past used bicycles, such as milk-sellers, will move up to a motorcycle once they have made enough money, while those who wish to get into the business of taxiing can start on a motorcycle with passengers riding pillion.

Few riders wear helmets or protective clothing, and motorcycles cause many deaths, so that governments are beginning to mount major safety campaigns and crack down on motorcyclists. Another cause of their concern is the increasing use of motorcycles by Al-Qaeda affiliates in drive-by shootings and suicide missions. There are now curfew hours for riding motorcycles and compulsory registration, which does not sit well with motorcyclists, who point that the use of cars in bombings and has not provoked any similar measures against cars. However, in Arab countries most terrorist crimes rely on motorcycles, mainly because of their maneuvrability in congested traffic.

Culture

This cartoon depicts how proud Arabs are of the Iraqi journalist who threw his shoes at President Bush during Bush's final visit to Iraq.

☪ Muntadar al-Zeidi was the Iraqi reporter who threw his shoes at President George W. Bush in the middle of a press conference regarding the signing of a security agreement. In Arabic, he yelled: "This is a farewell kiss, you dog. This is from the widows, the orphans and those who were killed in Iraq."

Translation

Title: Eternal events of the 14th of December

On right shoe: Nuclear shoe

On left shoe: Mother of all shoes

On podium: Shoe and awe (as in shock and awe)

The shoe theme is further emphasized by the symbol with the number 43 printed on the podium (the President was the 43rd president of the U.S.), framed within the symbol that is stamped on products to indicate genuine leather.

☪ Size 43 is an actual size for shoes in the Arab world—which follows the British measurement—a measurement equivalent to the American size 10.5, the actual President Bush's shoe size.

Culture

In Arab culture the act of throwing is insulting in and of itself, even if the object being thrown seems benign in Western culture. For example, throwing water, a playful act in the West, is tantamount to throwing blood at an Arab. In the U.S., the thrown shoe was viewed simply as an aggressive gesture, but the streets of most Arab countries are very dirty and shoes represent something that others should not have to be exposed to. Culturally, the shoe is viewed as so unpleasant, it is insulting just to see its bottom. Shoes are always placed sole to sole when being carried or placed on the ground, in order to avoid dirtying the floor or exposing the soles to others. In an Arab house, a person will overturn an upside-down shoe, so the bottom is no longer visible, since some people believe that the soles of shoes should be turned away from God. When praying or at a mosque, shoes are placed next to columns or on shoe racks. Placing shoes on their sides also takes up less floor space, so there is more room for more shoes in one area. Arabs also avoid exposing the soles of their shoes to others by not crossing their legs and picking up someone else's shoes is considered an extremely big favor and requires profuse thanks. Calling somebody a shoe is a harsh insult and means that the person is debased and immoral. One may also express his extreme anger and disrespect by beating another with a shoe. It is not unusual for a poorer Arab mother to become so angry with her children that she beats them with her slippers. The phrase some Arabs utter to express complete disregard and disrespect for an issue or person comes from these ideas: "[*this person or thing*] is on my shoe." The Qur'an mentions in several places that shoes must be removed in holy places, such as when God spoke to Moses in the desert, He commanded Moses to remove his shoes, as he was on holy ground. 25

Translation

On Podium: White House

Under the White House: All sizes

"America will *shine* and it will remain the *Coach*. It is true that the creative chaos turned out *outsize*. And the world *split into two* and became a *right one* and a *left one* but the solution is that democracy should be a *last* that fits the *size* of every country."

The language used in this cartoon uses vocabulary that is related to shoes: "Coach" is a brand and "last" is the cobbler's mold.

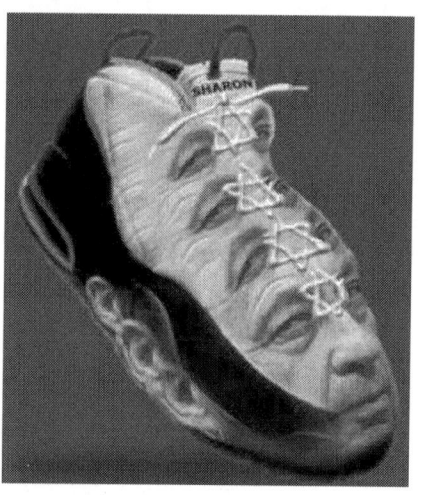

Translation

In the cartoon, the face of the most hated man in the Arab world—Israeli Prime Minister Ariel Sharon—is shown superimposed on a shoe. Any identification of a person with a shoe is considered immensely insulting, so plastering this shoe with Sharon's face is a tremendous insult.

The symbolic weight of shoes as insulting objects does not, however, infect shoes as consumer products. Before they are purchased and used, there is no stigma attached to shoes, and shoe stores and salesmen are at the pinnacle of retail luxury, selling to passionately eager shoppers. However, the high-status of new shoe stores does not communicate to those who repair shoes, as these tradesmen are relegated to extremely low status.

---

25 "Verily I am thy Lord! Therefore (in My presence) put off thy shoes: thou art in the sacred valley *Tuwa*. Qur'an, 20.012 (Ta-Ha [Mystic letters Ta-Ha])

Translation

President Bush: "If I knew my end, I wouldn't have started."

Culture

In this cartoon, the phrase that President George W. Bush is saying is the title of a song by the famous Egyptian singer, Abdel Haleem Hafez. Sometimes, Arab people will use the titles of famous songs or movies in order to make their point stronger and more relatable.

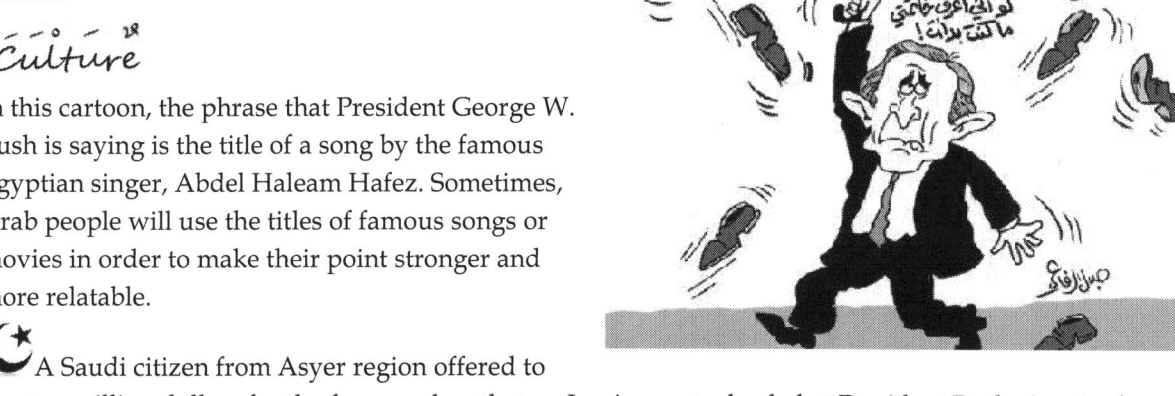

☪ A Saudi citizen from Asyer region offered to pay ten million dollars for the famous shoe that an Iraqi reporter hurled at President Bush. A retired primary school teacher, sixty-year-old Hassam Muhammad Makhfa owns a number of lucrative properties in southwestern Saudi Arabia. The shoe, declared Makhfa, is more valuable than all of his land put together. Calling it "a medal of freedom," he intends to pass down the shoe to his children. He hopes that his purchase will help restore pride and dignity to the Arab world, which suffered ignominy through the American occupation of Iraq and Afghanistan.

Translation

"The road to solving the Middle East problems."

Culture

Several years before the war of October 1973, many Arab leaders began to realize that the solution to the Israeli-Palestine conflict lay in the hands of the United States. In the years following the war, Egyptian President Anwar al-Sadat correctly stated that America held "99% of the cards in its hands." This is the case

because most Arab countries, up until the war of 1973, were aligned with the Soviet Union, depending on the Soviets to supply their weapons and to stand by them as an ally in international organizations. Because the Soviet Union was such a large bureaucracy, the help needed by the Arab countries did not come as fast or efficiently as Israeli aid came from the United States did. Once, Egypt requested spare tires from the Soviet Union for its fighter jets. Instead, Egypt received sneakers instead, all of which were left feet.

The Arab people still believe that the United States can help them in resolving the Israel-Palestine conflict better than any other country can. The Arabs, however, have yet to master the intricacies of American politics, and have not figured out how to use American influence to their advantage.

Translation

Dove of Peace: I have a feeling that some people want to kill me, doctor.

Culture

Like the distressed dove in the cartoon, people in the Arab world feel threatened from many sides. Sneaking up on the bird as it expresses its anxiety are an Israeli soldier, a member of an Arab secret police, and a terrorist. As Arabs look for protection from America, so the dove hopes that Uncle Sam will be able to help her. Little does the dove know, though, that Uncle Sam

is yet another murderous attacker. A common view among Arab citizens is that, despite the fact that each of these people pictured are warring with one another, the violence of their incessant squabble mean that the ultimate victim is the peace and stability of the Arab world.

☪ In the Arab world, a heavy stigma is attached to psychoanalysis. Unlike in America, analysts and psychologists do not usually run independent practices, set up to serve the layperson in his or her day-to-day struggles. Rather, psychological counseling is reserved for those with genuinely severe mental health issues, as well as a handful of elites.

Translation

"Uncle Sam is ready for Iran or anyone else."

Culture

Arabs' perception of President Bush is clear from this Egyptian cartoon depiction of him as a rattlesnake. Arabs felt great pride when the Iraqi journalist threw his shoes at Bush, because they felt that he expressed what many Arab people felt.

Nixon and Johnson were also disliked during their time mostly for their support for Israel. The most liked is Obama, and before him Clinton.

Translation

[*An Arabic reader, approaching this from right to left, would find the word Iran; an English reader, approaching it from left to right, would see the abbreviation U.S.A. The artist has managed, through his mastery of calligraphy, to present two distinct messages – in two languages! – in a single, fascinating image.*]

Language

Whenever a word is written as another word, through skillful calligraphy, or is transformed into another word (whether within Arabic or between Arabic and another alphabet), it is considered to show an underlying truth: above, the U.S.A is no different from Iran – presumably in its sabotage of the Arab world. Below, that Iran is as much an enemy as Israel.

Translation

Israel is the enemy
[*intermediate form*]
Iran is the enemy
[*N.B. The word Israel on the right is gradually changing into Iran.*]

Culture

Many Americans were first aware of anti-American Islamic rhetoric from the Ayatollah Khomeini in the wake of the Iranian Revolution, and they are therefore sometimes bemused by the hostility with which Iran is regarded by the Arab world. The main reason is the religious divide between Shiaa and Sunni Islam, although during the war between Iran and Iraq, the Sunni countries of the region were not particularly partisan in favor of Iraq and their message was one praying for peace between these two Muslim countries. Iran has been regarded as an expansionist regime, seeking to spread its ideology, and then increase its influence. A bone of contention has been the annexation of three islands from UAE and their sponsorship of Hezbullah in Lebanon.

Translation

In right-hand cartoon, an arrow points to the tiny nuclear warhead on the left: "Iranian nuclear"

Translation

Under large picture: "The Dream"
Under small picture: "The Reality"

Culture

This cartoon depicts an Arab man standing in front of two representations of the United States. The man is very much enamored of the larger image of a beautiful woman, entitled "The Dream." He does not seem interested in seeing the smaller image of an extremely unattractive woman, entitled "The Reality."

☪ Symbolically, this cartoon represents the experience of many an Arab who spent his life with the radiant dream of an impossibly prosperous and happy land called America: the dream

manufactured by Hollywood and the media, spread by rumor and rhetoric, and fired by imagination and hope. Living with bleak prospects in decrepit countries, he could be sustained by the knowledge and trust that such a paradisiacal paragon existed and lit the world, even if from a distance. Can we wonder that such a one would gaze longingly at such a picture?

But the world is not Paradise, and the perfect cannot exist here. When America made itself known as it is — not only a disappointingly flawed land but a land that has made war on Arabs, has insulted Arabs, has tortured Arabs — then that picture that had been clung to for so long and against both reason and evidence, that picture burned before the passionate on-lookers eyes. The once-treasured image is now shown up as lies and betrayal, and the flawed reality inflates in monstrosity as the dream's destroyer. America's smallest flaws seem enough vile deformities, and America's many, grievous faults swell to a blackness that inks over the firmament and the soul.

Translation

Title: Happy Summer

America as a prostitute: Let 'em say what they say. I don't care what anyone says.

Culture

Some Arabs perceive America as pursuing her own interests. They believe that the United States would support tyrannical dictators if they were in the country's best interest, and that it is not genuinely interested in democracy or human rights.

Street Walkers

In this cartoon you can see a stereotypical cartoon of a prostitute. In actuality prostitutes in Arab countries do not dress in a tarty way, some even wear Islamic clothes so as not to attract attention to themselves and their illegal profession. For many prostitutes the business is brisk: the encounter would take place in the customer's car most of the time, and it is not unusual to see a line of cars waiting for a prostitute. If the police see a lot of cars parked they will assume that it is because of prostitutes working; however all they are able to do is ask the cars to move away. Prostitutes have a lot of business because sex outside of marriage is not as readily available as in the western world. The majority of people running the prostitution rings are female. If her women walk the street she will sit in a car at the same location to negotiate the price and resolve any disputes with customers. Because it is not always obvious from her dress, any woman standing by herself late at night in disreputable areas can be mistaken for a prostitute. This obviously is a source of irritation for women who are not prostituting themselves.

Translation

Title: Victory of Barak Obama

Praying man: O Lord, make him as was Nagashi to us! Make him as Abraha was to our enemies! Make him as Ahntara on injustice and as Kafur on the unjust! Make him like Bilal in saying the truth.

 The cartoon makes a pun on Obama's name: *Robama* is an Arabic word meaning, "Maybe."

Culture

Arabs have many ways of praying to God, and one of these is to pray that someone will meet their expectations by likening him to the national and religious heroes they cherish. In this cartoon, the man hopes that Obama will express the characteristics of the following five personages:

Nagashi (Negus): a title in Ge'ez, Tigrinya, Tigre, and Amharic used for a king and at times also a vassal ruler in pre-1974 Ethiopia and pre-1890 Eritrea. It was subsequently used to translate the word "king" in Biblical and other literature. It is a noun derived from the ancient Semitic verbal root N - G - Ś meaning "to reign." Much as classical Greek tradition uses the presumed Cretan title *Minos* as the proper name of particular kings of Knossos, the term *Nagashi* is understood here to refer to a particular, historical ruler of Ethiopia and Eritrea. In the early days of Islam, the faithful fled the baleful onslaught of the Quraysh and sought refuge in the lands of the *Nagashi*. Though he was initially a devout Christian, over time his Muslim wards converted him to Islam.

Abraha: a fiercely Christian king of Yemen who undertook to destroy the Kaabah with a vast army that included war elephants, which were an unheard-of innovation at the time. According to tradition, his attack was foiled when God sent a vast flock of birds to pelt his forces with stones that made them like an empty field of stalks (of which the corn has been eaten up by cattle).

Ahntara Ibn Shaddād al-'Absī: a revered poet and fearless warrior who is renowned for the victories he achieved for his tribe.

Abu al-Misk **Kafur**: a ruler of the Ikhshidid who is revered for protecting his people from the attacks of the Hamdaníds, Fatimíds, and the Nubians.

Bilal ibn Rabah: first *muezzin*, amongst the slaves freed by Abu Bakr, who was the closest companion of the Prophet Muhammad. Bilal was noted for his beautiful voice, with which he called the people to prayer.

Translation

Before Obama's revision, the sign reads: Uncle Sam
After the revision, the sign reads: Uncle Salaam

Language

With the addition of the letter "L," the Arabic word for Sam can be transformed into "Salaam," or peace.

☪ Barack Obama's nickname in the Arab world is "Abu Samra," which means "father of olive skin." As the concept "black" has generally negative connotations, Arab men and women use "Abu Samra" as a title of endearment for those with darker skin. The term "Abu Samra" derives from a popular song from the 1950s.

On the other hand, for those with lighter skin, like Caucasians, Arabs reserve the term "Abu Shaqra," which means "father of blonde hair." "Abu Shaqra" is also the name of a famous restaurant in Egypt.

Translation

The arrow identifies the medal as: The Nobel Pre-Peace Prize

Culture

Many Arabs share the opinion with much of the world that the awarding of the Nobel Peace Prize to President Obama was premature, as no real peace had been achieved in the Middle East because of him. Some Arabs believe that the real recipient of the award is the American people for electing Obama.

Translation

Title: The feeble dollar

Language

The title of the cartoon is a pun on the popular phrase "The Mighty Dollar."

Culture

The economies of a number of Arab countries are linked to the United States' economy, and their foreign currency reserves consist mainly of the U.S. Dollar because of its strength. Some Arab citizens who do not have faith in their country's currency have converted their money to dollars, and have saved it in banks where these are accepted, although dollar accounts accrue interest at lower rates than if they were in their own currency. Thus, the alarming weakness of the American financial system that affected the value of the dollar prompted concerned government officials and citizens to call for diversification of currencies in the foreign reserves. Many terrorists are betting against the continuing strength of the American economy, and have advised their compatriots to do away with their savings in dollars in anticipation of America's downfall, while their move to encourage selling of the dollar also seeks to destabilize it further. This kind of effort to undermine is part of the same strategy as the small, cheap initiatives from the terrorists (a letter bomb or a single passenger) that are met with huge, expensive security responses from the West, which they refer to as "bleeding" their economies.

The Black Market for Dollars and other Western Currencies

In most Arab countries there is a dual market for buying and selling foreign currencies: there is the banking system and there is the black market. The banking system is the legitimate way to buy and sell foreign currencies but banks often pay less than the prices people can get for western currencies on the black market. People who buy and sell on the black market are usually individuals and shop owners generally operating in tourist areas. A lot of money can be made from tourists, who know that in Arab countries they can get more for their dollar than they can at home. An individual or shop owner can make good money by selling western currencies to natives. Arab natives buy on the black market because they cannot buy western currencies from banks—no one is allowed to take foreign currency out of the country unless they can prove that they got the money legitimately.

Central banks in Arab countries are trying to eliminate the black market on the grounds that foreign currencies are needed for the development of the country; if there are no dollars available then it will have a damaging effect on the economy. The banks try to bridge the gap between prices people can get for western currencies on the black market and prices they can get at the banks, they also try to get laws against the black market enforced on the grounds that the black market is damaging for the economy.

Arabs usually benefit most from the exchange rate during the summer, especially August. In addition to tourists, expatriates return to their native Arab countries and invest the money they've made abroad. Expatriates and anyone else entering the country have to declare what foreign money they are bringing in to the country. If they do not declare the foreign money they are bringing in, they will neither be able to legally exchange it nor bring it back home with them.

Organizations will sometimes try to manipulate the market in buying and selling foreign currencies in order to create political or economic instability. When Lebanon's relations with Syria were strained due to the suspected Syrian involvement in the killing of Rafiq Al-Hariri, Lebanon bought all the dollars they were able to. Syrians found there were no dollars available in their country, and this created instability in the country. Iran supplied Syria with dollars in order to stabilize the market. Business men can also artificially inflate the market by buying up as many dollars or western currencies they can and selling them back at a premium.

13 — Sand Clock

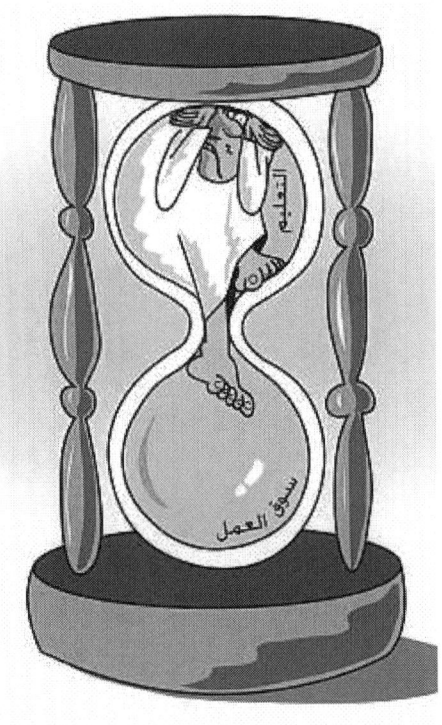

The Arabic term for hourglass is literally translated as "sand clock." The hourglass is a common motif in Arab cartoons, no doubt because sand is ubiquitous in the region.

The hourglass in Arab cartoons conveys messages regarding the device's primary function—keeping time. The image in the upper-right bears the title "Timetable for starting [Israeli-Palestinian] peace talks." This cartoon implies that there has been no set time frame imposed on parties involved in the peace talks, leading to a permanent impasse.

The cartoon on the lower right portrays a bleak view of the future of the Arab world. The challenges are numerous: increasing unemployment, terrorism, dwindling oil revenues, overpopulation, abuse of human rights, the chasm between rich and poor, gender inequality, inadequate education, the nuclear threats posed by Israel and Iran… the sands run quickly.

The cartoon in the upper left also plays off the shape of the glass—a typical Arab finds it hard to squeeze between the upper bulb's "education system" and the lower one's "labor market."

14 – Mazayen al-Ebel, the Camel Beauty Show

Language

Ebel or *ibl* is a collective noun referring to female and male camels, while *jamal* is the male and *naqa* is the female. It is a sign of the Arabs great affection for the camel, that it has a wide variety of names, and there are more than forty different terms to describe camel breeds, ages and races.

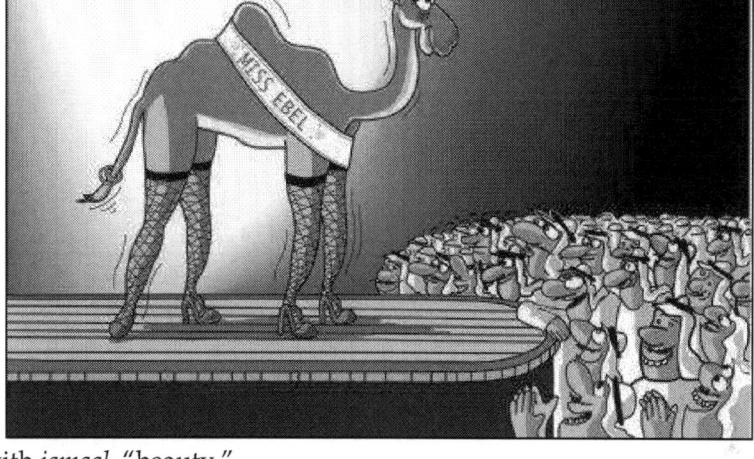

Beauty contests are actually slightly pointless, because all camels are regarded as beautiful, indeed the word for camel in Arabic shares a root with *jamaal*, "beauty."

Culture

The camel has been a very close companion to the Arabs for centuries. The camel was friend, food, a piece of war equipment, and because of it early Muslims were able to spread Islam in the Middle East and Africa. The value of a camel lies in its milk, meat, racing-prowess and potentially also in camel shows.

Camel shows

Mazayin al-ebel (camel shows) center on the display and appreciation of camels in all aspects. They include lectures delivered by experts and professors on topics related to camels. They discuss different breeds of camels, their potential diseases, and the natural miracle that is the camel is, able to withstand a brutal environment and thrive. They also talk about cross-breeding, and what breeds are suitable for which environment. Lectures also discuss camel meat and milk for food production, and then how to market the product. Others talk of how humans, as instructed in the Qur'an[26], must contemplate how camels were created; or, how to raise camels, their behavior, intelligence, interaction with environment, and their choice of foods. Because of all the stray camels in the desert, lectures will discuss the dangers of these wild camels on roads. Lectures will also deal with the health of camels, their diseases, how these may be communicated to humans, as well as prevention and treatment. Representatives from the government also are on hand to advise what the state offers and discuss veterinary facilities for camels.

There are also camel races at these events, cultural exchanges, and poetry evenings, with discussions on the importance of camels in the lives of people of the Sahara, camels' traits and their relations with those who care for them, or their place in Arabic literature, poems and proverbs. People believe that camels are strongly tied to traditional culture and history, having provided them with food and transportation for

---

[26] "Do they not look at the Camels, how they are made?" Al-Qur'an 088.017 (*Al-Ghashiya* [The Overwhelming, The Pall]).

thousands of years, and they should be celebrated, not neglected, even though they don't have the same use of them anymore. Arabs still use camel meat and milk, and believe that their urine can cure cancer. An Arab proverb states: "He who doesn't know a hawk will grill it," meaning that someone who doesn't know the utility and inherent value and beauty of an animal will simply take it for granted and eat it. They apply this sentiment to camels, seeing their beauty and helpfulness, rather than regarding them simply as livestock. They are viewed the same way Westerners view dogs, and disregard for camels is seen the same way we do disregard or abuse of dogs.

Gulf people are sensitive about their camel celebrations. There is strong opposition to having camel shows that cost 3 million dollars in countries where poverty is ubiquitous. Further objections relate to the way that certain camel shows are based on tribal divisions and open only to one group, involving strong appeals to clannish instinct and feelings of superiority. This emphasizes differences and reignites ancient tensions, undermining social harmony and hindering progress in the region. These critics advocate abolishing this type of show and holding only shows that are completely open to everybody and all tribes. Furthermore, many sarcastic Arabs, frustrated with their own countries' failures to advance as rapidly in fields of technology and industry as rival countries—or worse, countries the Arabs regards as inferior—, respond to news of any new, foreign triumph with a sigh of, "Yes? And how is our camel show doing?"

☪ Camel shows can involve enormous transactions of money and the business is unregulated. It is, therefore, a popular means of money laundering.

Camel milk

The UAE is planning to export camel milk to the U.S., Hong Kong, and China. It is looks like cow's milk, but is healthier and has greater nutritional value, and some scientists claim that camel milk is second only to a mother's milk, with a similar constitution. Bedouins enjoy general good health, despite a lack of vegetables and fruit, and this may be attributed to the milk. It is good for those who are lactose intolerant and contains high levels of insulin.

☪ This sheet displays vital information on the ownership details of family-owned camels. On the far right appears the name of the family (the fourth family from the bottom, for example, is Mahfouz); the next column over shows the mark that each family uses to brand their camels with (the aforementioned family insignia, for example, is a mallet and a crescent); the column second to the left is the name of the insignia; and the column to the far left is where the brand is placed on the camel (the location on this family's camel, for example, is on the left side of the animal's neck). This is crucial for keeping track of a family's herd, as various families' animals often graze together, and the brands differentiate the herds, which also prevents theft.

14 — Mazayen al-Ebel, the Camel Beauty Show

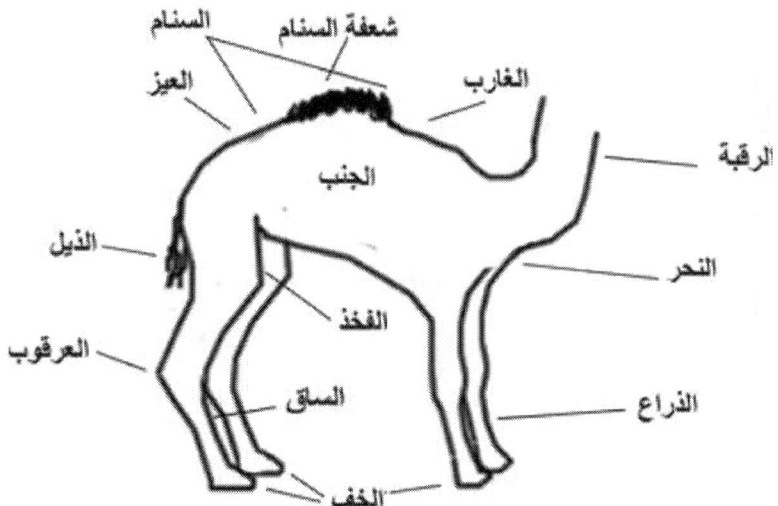

Translation

From the tail, clockwise: Tail, Croup, Hump, Cusp of the Hump, Withers, Neck, Throat (called "to slaughter" in Arabic because this is the area that is cut when killing a camel), Forearm, Hoof, Leg, Hock. On the side of the camel it is written, "The side."

Culture

This picture shows body parts that will be discussed to show the standards of camel beauty, and how each body part should contribute to how a beautiful camel should look. There are a number of key features of a camel that can contribute to how it is perceived, but the main ones are as follows:

1) The side: a camel with a long side (right), is better than one with a short side.

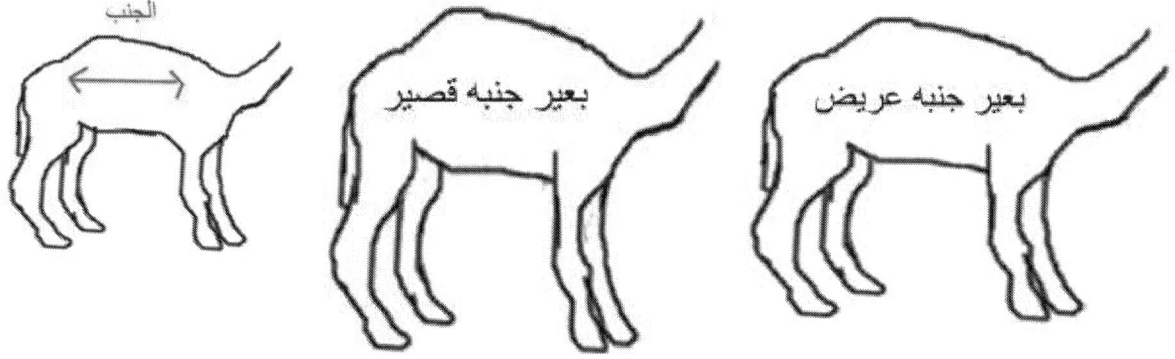

2) A camel with equally tall front and hind legs (left) is more attractive. Notice the camel on the right has longer hind legs, but this can be compensated for by other attributes.

3) A tall camel (left) is better than a short one (right).

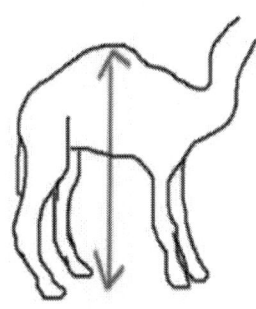

4) A camel with a pronounced hock (left) is better than one with a less defined one (right).

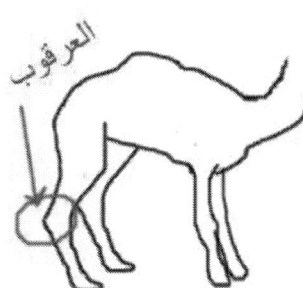

5) A hump that is tall and closer to the rear (left) is better than a short one close to the front (right).

6) The croup must be short and steep (left) rather than long and high (right).

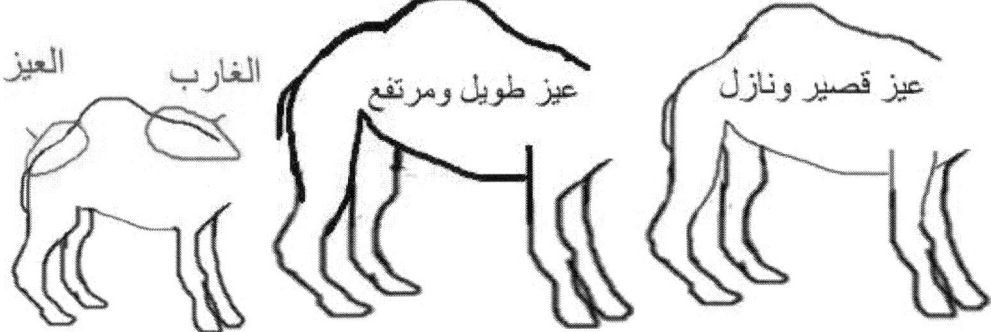

7) The neck must be slim and erect (left), as opposed to thick and slumped (right).

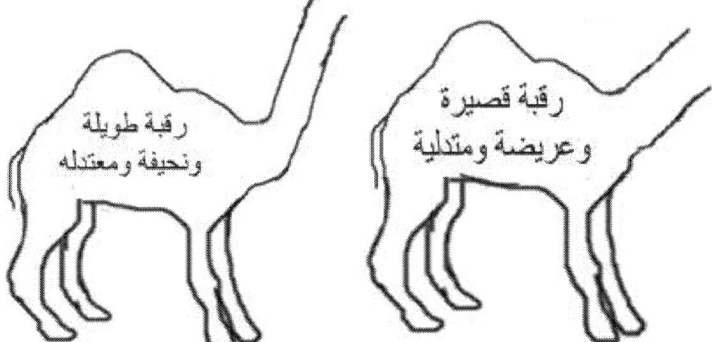

8) Brown camels should have a short and wide tail (right), while black ones should have a long and wide one (left).

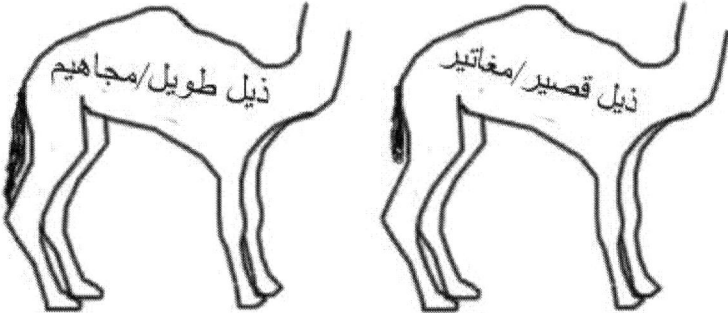

9) A camel with a wide stance is better than one with legs close together.

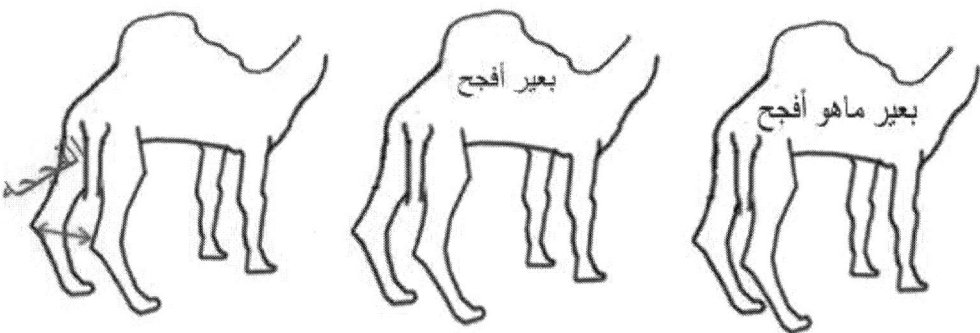

Camels Under Siege

There are no wild camels in the Middle East—they are all owned by families, which can comprise hundreds of people. The family groups brand their camels and send them out to the desert to graze with other camels, similar to the system of grazing cattle on public lands in the American West. But the desert is no longer deserted. Roads and other developments encroach further into wild lands every year. Now, camels are a frequent victim of trucks and buses. So frequent, in fact, that a single herd can lose up to 30 members in a month. This is an enormous financial burden for the families that own them because camels represent an important source of livelihood and are very expensive to replace—each one can be worth thousands of dollars. Some truck drivers become so aggravated by the frequent need to stop for camel crossings that they kill them intentionally with their massive trailers. Some camel owners have begun to equip their animals with large reflective triangles, so they are less likely to be hit by traffic at night. It has been proposed that all camels should be required by law to have reflectors, but the enforcement of this would be extremely difficult.

Oil companies pose another threat. When they survey the desert for new drilling spots, they frequently leave open wells or slicks of oil across the sand. This is fatal for camels, which can mistake the oil for water. Also fatal is radiation from certain equipment that oil companies use.

Camels' continuing role in Arab countries

The camel is naturally the most dominant animal in Arabian Peninsula, and is particularly well adapted to the desert climate that affects the whole Arab region. Both single and two-humped camels are common throughout the region, but the two-humped camel is stronger and more prevalent in the Levant. During the desert winter they can survive without water for a week, and can do without water entirely if they are fed grass; in summer need water once every four days, being able to store it in a second stomach. They are able to scent water and, sensing how far away it is, they are said to be able to ration their use accordingly. If necessary they can survive for a month without food, and females have more endurance in summer, the males in winter.

The original strains of camel are the white, black, red, and blue: black and red are used for transport, while the white are only really used to lead a herd or camel train. The blue are the least desirable, being renowned for their bad temper. Camels are naturally herd-animals and will be trained to respond to the call of the herder in charge of them—and a single trainer can control up to a thousand camels. They need to be trained to travel or act independently, since this is not natural behavior, but a runaway camel in any context is impossible to control.

Unlike a horse a camel moves silently, whether it is running or walking. At a trot it makes on average 67 steps a minute, each step covering a 1 meter or yard, so an average camel covers 4 km or 2.5 miles an hour, though at a gallop its speed can reach 12-15 km or over 9 miles per hour. A camel can carry two people.

War Camels

The *Hajana* or Camel Corps retains its place in the armies of Arab countries, where the camels' special qualities continue to be extremely useful. It has a particular role in law enforcement in otherwise inaccessible places and is also used in border patrol. It can effectively be fed in advance, and will be able to operate for a month without food, which considerably lightens the burden of what needs to be taken along. The noiselessness of its movement is very useful, but it needs muzzling to make it truly silent. A group of camels at rest is very compact, since they naturally pack together, either standing or sitting, which means that they can be hidden far more readily than horses or vehicles.

15 — Soccer

Translation

Title: Alley Tournaments

Man on the roof in beanie (right): You broke the TV and you decided to boycott the Asian cup finals so you can watch alley tournaments?

Man throwing shoe: Of course because here if I don't like the game I can hit the players in the stomach… may God break your legs, Mahjuob… take that!

The two barrels filled with stones that have two-by-four sticking out of them are being used as goal posts. Despite the fact that there is no cross bar on the goal a player can visually judge whether a goal should be allowed or not.

These soccer games take place during the afternoon, once school has finished, but while tired people want to nap because of the heat. Fights and yelling will break out between players and the surrounding neighborhood because they are disturbing people. If the players don't go away, the yelling can escalate until the mothers come to take the offending players inside.

The sure fire way for making the area near ones house undesirable to would be players is to spray it with water from a garden hose. The area turns muddy and it is far from ideal to play on.

Breaking a neighbor's window with a misplaced kick of the ball is always a possibility. Luckily windows in Arab houses are often protected by shutters made from wood.

The main concern when playing in the street is that the ball will hit a passing person; the worst case scenario would be to hit a pregnant woman.

Even important alley tournament games have to stop for every passing car.

These after school matches most commonly end when a mother tells her son to come home.

The man who is standing next to the woman holding the seven, is being restrained. He is angry, holding a rock, and his hand gesture, which looks like the western "O.K." gesture, is actually a threat in Arab culture.

What's more the western gesture for aggression, that is using two fingers to indicate eye contact, would be interpreted by an Arab as a sign of attraction meaning, "I've got my eye on you," but in a flirtatious way.

When a virtuoso player manages to pass a soccer ball between the legs of an opponent standing in front of him — a move called the "bridge" —, it demonstrates his consummate ability; humiliates the other player who can't even manage to close his legs in time to stop the pass; and absolutely delights any Arab soccer fans who are watching.

Culture

On almost every street and alley there is a football match taking place, the young people don't need much space or equipment to turn any alley or street into their own stadium. When the school day is over students will often start a soccer match near their school or by their homes.

Usually no one will watch these kids playing soccer. But when the kids that play soccer in the street grow up their love for the games does not diminish. Their talent becomes obvious and they start forming teams. They play against each other and against teams from different neighborhoods. From starting out in these neighborhood teams it is possible to move up the professional ladder. These mature games are more organized and resemble a real match with a referee and soccer kits. These games take place on wide streets with complete, eleven players, teams.

Many talented players were discovered by scouts when they were playing in the streets.

To play football you don't need a playground a partner or even a real football, footballs can be made out of balls of socks or old discarded bits of fabric. Arabs who really want to play can play what is known in England as "Walley," that is playing alone kicking the ball against a wall. It is common to see Arab schoolboys walking home and at the same time kicking a ball or any other piece of rubbish between themselves.

A typical piece of vandalism is slashing open any stuffed seat, for example on a bus, subway or even in the movie theatre and taking the sponge stuffing. This filling makes the perfect football when rolled into the shape of a ball it has more bounce than a ball made of a sock filled with rags. The filling from movie-theater seats is the best sponge and, what's more, the movie-theater provides cover of darkness. It is typically difficult to find an unslashed seat in an Arab movie-theater.

Translation

Title: On to the next thing

On Bus: "Leader Transportation"

Language

The title of this cartoon is asking for the next challenge with bravado. The winning team will again be victorious and get another trophy like the one on the top of the bus.

Culture

In the Arab world, soccer (called "football") is a very serious business. Millions of dollars are spent on hiring foreign players and coaches. Some native players achieve international status and sometimes are hired by big European and American clubs. Soccer's prominence overshadows other sports in spite of both the repeated disappointments that native soccer teams give to their fans and the many success stories of other sports. Even players with tremendous accomplishments who gain international acclaim and success in other sports don't get a small percentage of the attention paid to a mediocre soccer player.

Translation

On newspaper: "Egypt national team beats Cameroon and The Sudan"

"What Book Exhibition are you talking about? These two days, I'm not interested at all in books.

You see a lot of cartoons in the Arab world in which the characters depicted have been drawn with soccer balls for heads. This clearly indicates the individual's blind obsession with the game.

Language

The English expression, *these days* is equivalent to the Arabic expression *these two days*.

Culture

This cartoon represents the Arab obsession with soccer and shows it to be an all consuming addiction. Usually a Book Exhibition would be a very important event in Arab culture. Book Exhibitions generally happen annually, attended by thousands of people, they are an opportunity for individuals to access books from all around the world. Books that are not so readily available in their heavily censored communities. In this cartoon the Book Exhibition is happening at the same time as an important soccer match and so even though a Book Exhibition may be the more ' high brow' worthy event, the soccer match is the thing that will really get people's attention.

Translation

Title: A high school exam coincides with Euro 2008

Literal translation: I am sitting in a higher floor. I am making the last milled batch, and I am making a head. Depart away from me.

Translation for people who aren't Arab teenagers: I am feeling good, please go away.

Language

Like all youth around the world, young Arabs use a slang that no one understands but them. The slang used by the youth is usually an amalgamation of foreign words—mostly English—sports metaphors and terms commonly used by drug users. The form used in texting and messaging is called *Franco*. In this cartoon, the student's mind is on soccer, and he has no interest in interacting with the proctor.

☪ In the cartoon, the students are shown seated at special, collapsible desks. These are stored during the majority of the year and brought out for use in semester-end test taking, which typically occurs outdoors, in large tents. The professor, meanwhile, is seen wearing a "summer suit." Made of lighter, breezier fabric than typical formal attire, the summer suit is a mainstay in those months of formidable heat, and will even be worn by Arab heads of state.

Translation

"This is not soccer. This is music. Make me dance."

Language

When you describe the seamless and perfect performance of soccer players as *music you can dance to*, you mean that they are doing an outstanding job; they are playing extremely well. The guy in this cartoon uses this expression to describe the performance as music to his ears. Although this expression is not widespread in America, most Americans would understand its meaning because they often describe their satisfaction with what they hear or see as "music to their ears." In Arabic, the phrase said to musicians, "make me dance" is equivalent to "start playing music so that I can dance."

Culture

The staff in the soccer fan's hand shows that he is eager to do one of the traditional dances of Egypt, the *taH-teeb*. Performers of this folk dance wave the staff in complicated patterns, swinging it around and over themselves in a display deriving from ancient techniques of swordplay. The intricate motions of this staff dance are highly evolved, and skilled dancers can achieve remarkable feats.

Translation

Title: A Greeting to the Knights of Code-Breaking, who made watching the World Cup possible for all.

[N.B. the four-pointed frame on the far right is from the internal metal rods used in reinforced concrete columns, left exposed on a roof so that the building can be continued if the owner wants.]

Language

Much as in English one might refer to someone who has distinguished himself in a particular event or field as a "Hero of X," so Arab speakers refer to "Knights of X." The Arabic word *tashfir* relates to "liberating" or bypassing the black boxes or set-top boxes that cable and satellite companies use to decode their signal.

Culture

Cable companies take advantage of the general Arab love for soccer and charge extra for coverage of major matches like the World Cup. The tech-savvy can become heroes to those soccer fans who are unable to pay these exhorbitant fees by pirating the signals and helping people to circumvent the cable companies.

Also, governments recognize their citizens intense interest in soccer, and many choose to negotiate with cable companies for free broadcasts of matches in which the national team is participating, and other governments distribute "decoding cards," which allow people temporary access to cable channels.

Those who are too poor to afford a TV but still want to watch important matches go to cafés with televisions, though even here they are generally charged cover fees.

15 — Soccer 341

Translation

[*The words above the Algerian flag (on the right) identify the man as:* An Algerian Citizen.
The words above the flag with the skull-and-crossbones (on the left) identify the devil as: An Algerian Fan.]

Culture

In November 2009, a spate of soccer violence errupted around a series of World Cup qualifying matches between Egypt and Algeria. Both nations have numerous keen soccer fans, proud of sporting histories, and have suffered through long fallow periods without appearances at the World Cup finals. Excitement over the prospect of finally making it through grew precipitously in both countries, and each nation's enthusiasm fed its rival's passion. Reports of rowdy crowds in one country harassing the other's supporters or teams were breathlessly reported in the other country's press, so larger, vengeful demonstrations would pour onto the streets; naturally, these inspired their own reprisals. As the series of matches wore on, crowds in their thousands ran riot in the streets—Egyptian mobs targeting Algerian citizens, businesses, and embassy buildings in Egypt, and Algerians targeting Egyptians in Algeria. The chaos grew into a major diplomatic crisis, with embassies attacked and ambassadors withdrawn.

Translation

[The patches on this soccer ball have been arranged to resemble a map of Arab world. The ball is quickly leaking air and becoming deflated.]

☪ In a way, many Arab societies blamed soccer for Israel's victory in the 1967 war. They refer to this war as "*al-naksa*" ("the set back"), a term traditionally used to denote the relapse of a disease or illness. The 1967 war wasn't labeled *al-naksa* until a few months after the Israeli triumph, when Arab countries wished to express that it was a temporary, and not permanent, loss—and that a full recovery was well on its way. It was thought that the defeat resulted from the Arab preoccupation with numerous forms of entertainment, chief among which was soccer. This preoccupation was said to have harmed the vigilance and military preparedness of the Arab powers before the war's outbreak. In order to ensure that no such set back recurred, the Egyptian government suspended indefinitely the country's two major, transnational soccer tournaments. Additionally, cultural industries underwent a major reorientation, with many artists and performers shifting their focus from local profit-making to international fund-raising for the war effort. The prohibition on soccer tournaments remained in place for a number of years. Today, however, the Arab obsession with soccer has again reached a fever pitch, as violent fighting recently broke out between Egyptians and Algerians over a soccer-related dispute. The cartoon draws a parallel between soccer's current popularity and the situation in the mid 1960s, thus issuing an implicit reminder of the dangers of such a preoccupation.

Translation

Title: Without apology to Karl Marx.

"Soccer is the opiate of the people."

The ball in the picture has been turned into a kind of bong (in Arabic *goza*, from its origin as an empty coconut shell). There is a burning coal on the top and a bamboo pipe coming out of the side of the ball.

Language

In this cartoon a famous Karl Marx quote has been adapted. The meaning here is clearly that soccer is something that distracts the populace from everything else that is going on.

When someone is quoted in a cartoon the cartoonist will usually say "with apology to the author," here they say "without apology," because Karl Marx's original statement is "religion is the opiate of the people," which is counter to what the majority of the Arabs believe.

Translation

Man with moustache: What do you want before the execution?

Other man: Change this red suit for me.

An arrow pointing to the man on the left indicates that he is a fanatical Zamalek supporter.

Culture

Soccer has a large an extremely passionate following in the Arab world. Fans avidly follow their favorite teams and can come into violent conflict with fans of rivals. In this cartoon,

the large mustachioed man is the executioner, about to do away with the smaller man, who is dressed, as is the custom for one who is about to be executed, in a red suit. Adding to the not inconsiderable misfortune of being about to be executed, the prisoner suffers because his favorite team, *Zamalek*, has a jersey of white with two red stripes, and their hated rival, *Ahly*, has a solid red jersey not unlike the Death Row uniform he wears. In other words, he is being forced to go to his death dressed as a traitor to his soccer team. The depth of his passion for the game, then, is clearly shown when he makes this outrage the subject of his final wish.

☪ In every Arab country there are two major teams that dominate the game, and usually most of the country are fans of one or the other, inheriting their allegiance from their family — indeed supporting the wrong team can be a deal-breaker when it comes to marriage, since it indicates a lot more than just sports.[27] The fans of other teams are seldom as significant a force, and depend on where they live or the industry that they are associated these teams belong or if the team represent industry (e.g. iron and steel). Most of the top players play for the "summit clubs," the premier or major league, and sometimes talented palyers from the less successful teams are recruited into the big two.

Translation

Title: Pre-game interviews

Next to clown: "Administrator"

Culture

Fans often consider pre-game interviews to be idiotic or silly. In the past soccer matches were broadcast on TV and radio without interviews from the team's officials, such as the trainer and manager. With the introduction of a Western style of production, interviews have become common, but because most of those "officials" are not adequately educated their comments are silly.

Translation

"Now let's go over to Zaid Sports City in Abu Dhabi to watch the finals of Gulf 18 between two teams who made fun of us, disgraced us, and wiped the floor with us!"

Language

The phrase "to wipe/mop the floor with someone" is exactly the same as in English, meaning to humiliate or beat someone totally.

Culture

Most Arab soccer teams do not perform on a level that corresponds with the amount of compensation that they receive. Arab society is very critical of the attention and lavish gifts that are bestowed on soccer players, instead of on people who have a genuine positive effect on

---

[27] The division of society by sports allegiance is seen elsewhere, of course, and can be as important as political parties. In some ways the archetype for both is in division of the Byzantine populace between the Blue and Green teams of chariot-racing teams that were tantamount to political affiliations.

society. Despite this praise, the teams continue to underperform, especially against foreign teams.

Translation

Man with whistle: "Foreign referee"

Two soccer players: "It is clear that we should start learning soccer all over again."

Other arrow: "Our Players"

Culture

When there is an important soccer game in Arab countries between two top teams, the teams hire a foreign referee to ensure impartiality. Because foreign referees are accustomed to high standards, they are more critical of

the players and fault them more often than local referees. In soccer, a red card is more serious than a yellow card and can result in a player being sent off for the rest of the match.

☪ Players' numbers may change between games and their names do not normally appear on their shirt.

Translation

Title: Regulations that apply to professional athletes?!

Book: 1000 explanations and explanations

Writing: Regulations for Professional Athletes…

Culture

Before the 1990s, most sports players were amateurs and did not receive the copious amounts of money they now receive. After the introduction of professionalism, however, these players began to be paid far more than their earlier counterparts in the 1960s and '70s. In the past, it was not unusual for famous players to work menial jobs to make ends meet in the absence of the high salaries that are now common for athletes.

This cartoon depicts the complexity now involved in becoming a professional athlete. The humor arises from the fact that (what should be) the

simple act of joining a team as a professional—represented by the mere two page "Regulations..."—is mired by excessive amount of legal maneuvering, interpretation and negotiation, which is represented by the tome "1000 explanations..."This complexity arises from the fact that, in signing a player from a different team, his new team must pay not only the player, but also the player's original team. These elaborate legal entanglements, then, come from the fact that the original team wants to ensure that it will be paid amply.

Many Arab players receive offers to play professionally for Western teams, through which they can earn a lot more money. Teams such as Chelsea (in Great Britain) and Real Madrid (in Spain) can afford to pay high sums to acquire these Arab players. Their transfer, however, can be hampered by a number of other factors besides their original contract. A player that accepts an offer from a foreign team in a critical season may be criticized as a traitor by fans in his country, and both the player and his family may be treated as pariahs.

Translation

Son: "O God, O God! Yes, yes! Shoot, shoot! Yes, yes! Goal!

Father: "I wish I knew what subject he's studying."

On the back of the son's shirt: "High School (Exam)" crossed out in a red circle.

Culture

Many teenagers will not focus on their studies if their favorite sports team is playing on TV.

In Arab homes, parents will always watch their children to ensure that they are studying

and not doing other activities. For example, children may only be allowed to watch television on the weekends, as not to interfere with their studying. In this cartoon, the young man is hiding the TV under his book so that his father will not see, because he is not allowed to watch it when he has studying to do. It is easy to tell when an Arab student is studying hard, because he will be reading the material in an audible voice. The Arab education system mostly relies on memorization and, in order for a student to memorize the material, they will often repeat it aloud. In this cartoon, the father thinks that his son is studying, because he can hear him reciting something, though he does not know what subject is.

 In the next cartoon, the father seems to have changed his mind about his son's studying.

Translation

Title: Astronomical salaries for professional soccer players

Father:

Boy, enough studying, reading and all that nonsense. Go outside and play soccer — that's something that'll really pay off in the future.

The father is using exactly the opposite advice Arab parents would usually give their child if they saw them playing football or engaging in other non-curricular activities.

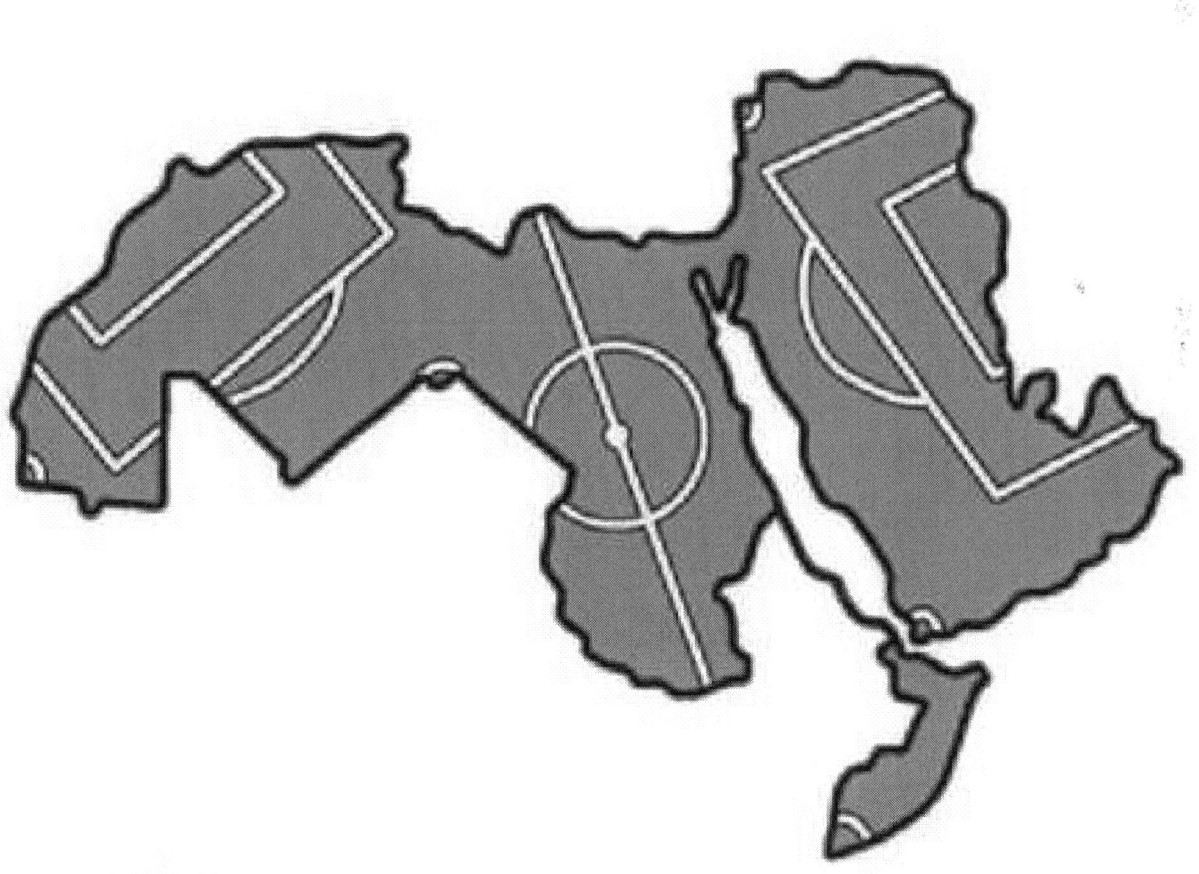

16 – Education

Translation

The sign in front of the dilapidated building reads, "Government school."
The other buildings sign says, "Foreign school."

Government school: Sweet swine flu! It's an opportunity to get a shower!

Man in window: Recite, boy! What are the symptoms of swine flu?!

Boy (out of picture): AIYEEE!

Language

As in colloquial English, many Arabic dialects use the word "sweet" to express that a thing is good, welcome, or desirable. Furthermore, it can be used in exclamations, where it expresses that the object so described—in this cartoon, swine flu—has come at the perfect time.

Culture

In Arab countries, there are several types of educational establishment: government schools, private schools, and schools that teach in a foreign language. Generally speaking, the free government schools have the lowest quality of education; private schools have fees and the quality of education is better; and best of all are the language schools, which are either supported by foreign governments to promote their language and culture or by the local government and private foundations to provide intensive language instruction. These language schools have recently grown in international prominence as the governments of the world have determined to curb religious extremism and prejudice against minorities through education. The lines sometimes blur between these categories since some Arab governments try harder to give quality education and offer subjects typically offered only in private and language schools.

The gulf between foreign schools and government-run schools is like that between heaven and earth. The government school in the cartoon is ringed with a forbidding spiked fence like a prison, designed to pen in the unfortunate children who have to attend and risk a beating. The grounds are filled with dying trees, the roof used for storing discarded materials, and the structure is crumbling. Foreign schools, in comparison, are well-funded and well-maintained. The foreign schools, understandably, produce students of a relatively high average competence. Paradoxically, though, the very best students tend to come from the government schools. Those students' poverty-stricken lives of deprivation and hardship seem to motivate them to work harder to claw themselves up to higher acheivment. These high scores are vital if these students are to compete successfully after graduation with those who attended foreign schools, whose family connections, westernized looks, foreign language experience, and refined deportment can make up for more mediocre scores as they seek out coveted high-paying positions with prestigious foreign companies. Foreign schools and foreign companies both have a great deal of cachet in the Arab world, and the exposure to western ways that one learns in the former leads one naturally to the latter. Of course, this can give rise to cultural clashes when Arab parents realize what their children are being taught in these foreign schools, which are often accused of sneaking in proselytyzation for Christianity, of putting a negative spin on revered Arab historical figures, and of presenting an account of current events that favors Israel and others whom the government would rather not promote.

☪ Whenever a school in an Arab world shuts down for an extended period time — say, because of the outbreak of epidemic, like Swine Flu — private teachers become highly in demand, and reap great profits from such inconveniences and misfortunes.

Translation

Title: Fashkool's style of studying.

Guy on right: "Aboud, wait a while, we're going to drink the lesson together.

Guy on left: "No, I'd like to eat it dry today. I want to perform well on my exam this time."

[N.B. Arab kettles are often very large, to keep a good supply of boiling water for tea.]

Culture

People who are sick may boil a slip of paper with a prayer written on it in water and drink the liquid. They do this to fuse that blessing with their body in hope of a cure. In this cartoon, these two students apply this concept to studying.

☪ In Arab countries, when you travel, it is customary for the person who is leaving to receive a blessing on a piece of paper. It is also customary for Arab Muslims to say to one another when taking leave for an extended period, "There is no deity but Allah, Muhammad is God's Apostle." The first person will say the first half of the sentence, while the second person will speak the latter. Sometimes the two people will write the whole phrase down on a sheet of paper and cut that paper in half, giving the first part to one person and the second part to the other. By doing this, they are ensuring that the person who says or holds onto the second half of the phrase will meet with them again. The whole statement is a Muslim's profession of faith, and both halves are necessary to be a true believer. Since the phrase cannot be incomplete, splitting the phrase among two people promises to keep bringing them back together. The same effect can be achieved in conversation, with one person giving the first half of the phrase as a pledge that they will meet again to finish the second.

☪ In the strongest possible contrast to this practice of drinking in the power and wisdom of text by physically ingesting it, Arabs also speak of a wholly worthless paper as something to be dampened and drunk. In this case, the implication is that the importance of what is written is so slight that it can dissolve into mere liquid. The two quite contradictory takes on the concept of drinking a piece of paper, puzzling though they are to foreigners encountering them for the first time, coexist happily in the Arab imagination and can be differentiated by context and intonation.

The humor here is that Aboud, the boy on the left, thinks that the dry form is more concentrated and will be more effective than the "diluted" form with water.

Translation

Title: Abu Hameed and Hamoud keep studying.

"And the air hostess approached us and said that the driver of the airplane has epilepsy and they need somebody to make the airplane *fall down*. I drove the tractor in my father's farm and I don't see a difference between driving a Jumbo and dad's tractor so I told the hostess that I was ready to make it fall down. And *on the day* I arrived at the runway, I found that there were a lot of ambulances and fire trucks and I said, "What is that? You don't trust me?" So I started going back and right after that the airport operations manager, George *bin* David, kept calling and begging, 'It's OK, it's ok, Abu Humaid, there is trust, and I will remove the fire trucks and ambulances.' After that, they gave me vouchers to fly free the rest of my life and four hostesses that I transferred their sponsorship to the name of my father and we employ them as maids in my mother's house."

This is a Saudi cartoon and Saudis are not renowned for their sense of humor, however there is here a kind of absurd comedy. There is the additional detail of translating a Western name into Arab style—George Davidson, or maybe he knows the man's father.

Culture

As in America, Arab teenagers have a tendency to spin tall tales to their friends to gain respect. In this cartoon, one boy is telling his friend that when he was flying somewhere, the pilot lost control. Because he drove a tractor at his father's house, the boy said he was qualified and took over. He landed the plane successfully and was given tickets for the rest of his life as well as the services of four female airhostesses. He transferred their sponsorship and employed them as housekeepers in his mother's house.

☪ These boys are sitting on the floor. Most Arabs enjoy sitting on the floor to eat, to do work, etc. Though it may seem precarious, it is common for people to perch teacups on their knees, as the boy in the cartoon has.

☪ Work visas can be sold or transferred between employers if their initial holder doesn't need them. This is what is meant by the airhostesses' "sponsorships."

Translation

Title: Studying with Friends

Boy with book: It didn't work... send it again.

Boy on floor: I told you your cell phone doesn't support Java games.

Culture

Arab kids like to study with each other for mutual motivation. The theory goes that,

because they are all studying the same material, the students could quiz each other on their subjects, and since Arab education relies on rote memorization, students need partners to read along as they recite their newly conned texts. The friends meet at one of their houses, where their host's parents can supervise them—as well as hospitably ply them with food and drinks. As society's pace increases and families become busier, though, parents cannot keep so careful a watch as they once did, and these study sessions can degenerate into scenes such as that depicted in the cartoon, in which the students are wasting time and playing games.

It can be inferred from their attitude that the exams are still distantly in the future. Students must endure a variety of exams throughout the year: monthly exams, mid-terms, and final exams to cover the entire year's subject matter. As they near, Arab students will take their studies far more seriously, and the study partnerships will be much more likely to be resolved and diligent.

Group study is an important part of education at all levels in the Arab world. Large class sizes make it difficult for students to get adequate individual attention from their teachers and professors, so it is vital for students to team up with smart friends who will be able to work through difficult topics and share ideas.

☪Despite the prominent role that study with friends plays in the career of an Arab student, it is a notable fact that group projects are almost unknown in Arab educational systems. Their emphasis is solidly on individual work and achievement, with very little effort made to instill cooperative and collaborative skills. Arab adults, as a consequence of this training, tend by and large to prefer to work alone rather than as part of a team.

☪In this, as in the previous two cartoons, judging from their titles, reflect adults' opinion that friends studying together are more likely to distract each other than to be productive.

Cramming in the mosque

The favored place to study for many Arab students cramming for exams is the mosque. It is not unusual to see Arab students walking back and forth in mosques trying to memorize their material. They choose mosques because, between the prayer times, they are largely deserted, and are peaceful and cool, this last being a great benefit during the hot summer months in which students normally sit their exams. By studying in the house of God, they also hope to receive blessing to help them in their exams, taking part in prayers at the appointed times—a level of devotion that will last until the exams are over but seldom longer. Partly because of this, some people frown on the habit, thinking that the mosque should be reserved for prayer and that the students are insincere in their renewed piety.

☪Memorization is habitually associated with walking a few steps back and forward, and outside exams they will be seen doing their last-minute cramming each pacing his own short line.[28]

Translation

Chess piece: "Teacher"
Man with back to us: "Ministry of Knowledge"
Man facing us: "Department of Education"

Culture

Most Arab countries are chronically changing their educational systems. The changes can be drastic, with certifications being canceled, degrees being combined or separated, and even entire school grades being eliminated. The resulting confusion makes a terrible muddle for students and parents.

The equivalent of the U.S.'s Dept. of Education has a variety of names in Arab countries, and these names are not stable. For example, Egypt's has traditionally been called the Ministry of Upbringing & Education. The emphasis is decidedly on the Upbringing, concentrating on good morals and sound values. The Ministry's name, though, has gone through a number of changes, with the "Upbringing" being

---

[28] Aristotle's habit of walking as he taught led to his school of philosophy being called the Peripatetic School, and it is possible that this tradition lies behind the custom.

alternately added and dropped—yet another symptom of the ceaseless turmoil in the educational system. Whatever their name, they oversee the educational system from high schools down.

Ministries of Knowledge typically have the responsibility to spread knowledge to the general public. They oversee the publishing of all books (non-fiction and high literature) and other media that might serve to educate the citizens. In addition, they create special projects to further knowledge, such as commissioning translations, publishing classic titles affordably, or building libraries.

In addition, there are Ministries (or Departments) of Higher Education to oversee the universities.

In this cartoon, the Department of Education and the Ministry of Knowledge are fighting a turf war over their conflicting powers and responsibilities. The poor teacher (and, of course, the students) are helplessly caught in the middle of their power struggle.

Translation

Left to right

"A teacher"

Next to the list: "Superintendent"

On list: "Educational goals"

Culture

In this cartoon, the dreams of an ineffective teacher are haunted by his superintendent, who chastises him for failing to do his job and not teaching his pupils what he should. The composed, authoritative image of the superintendent is in stark contrast to the fretful, writhing teacher, quite undignified and ridiculous. Teachers are generally figures to be mocked and scorned in Arab cartoons, paragons of inefficiency, incapability, and ineffectiveness. The well-thought out goals for teaching are foiled on the ground by the bumbling of the schoolroom teacher.

This broad brush of mockery is an unfair slur against many diligent teachers in the Arab world, but their efforts are frequently undermined by insufficient funding, inadequate pay, and overcrowded classrooms. However, the sleek clothing of the superintendent suggests that this is an oil rich country and therefore would probably able to afford to fund a proper education, if the teacher could only manage to deliver it to his pupils.

☪ The Saudi Arabian Ministry of Education, like many other national education ministries, maintains a national "question bank," an extensive stock of appropriate exam questions. Doubtless, its purpose is to avoid incidents like the following.

A teacher in *al-Medina al-Munawara* (literally "the lighted city") evoked a small storm of public turmoil and political scrutiny when he included a number of "controversial questions" in an exam he prepared for his 10th grade class. One characteristic question read: "An English-language teacher, a Muslim singer, a Christian [sports] fan and an infidel [sports] coach: which ones should you love, and which ones should you hate, for the sake of Allah?" Another: "Turkey is wearing *forgive me father* pants; Muhammad Nour is wearing sunnah pants; and Yasser al-Qhatami is wearing *halves*. Who has more shame: Turkey, Muhammad, Yasser or none of the above?" (Note: "forgive me father" is the Arabic name for the common American-style of pant that is oversized and loose, so baggy as to be falling down well below the waste; "halves," meanwhile, are the Arabic name for clamdigger pants, while sunnah-style pants are those recommended by the Prophet Muhammad.)

The Western reader will surely be surprised by the fact that, on the surface, there appears nothing self-evidently "controversial" about the questions under consideration. Or, to put it another way, while Westerners would suspect a lack of controversial content from the (strictly Islamic) Saudi point of view, they themselves might take offense at the implicit disparagement of Western cultural and religious traditions — a disparagement, presumably, that is rigidly in line with Saudi educational dogma. And, in fact, one will find numerous references to the "infidel West" peppered throughout Saudi textbooks. Nonetheless, the Saudi did find these mentions of the West and Christianity to be enormously controversial — but not for the reason one expects.

That is, the question's "controversy" — its subversive core — lies not in the question itself, but in the potential (and potentially dangerous) avenues of response that the questions open up. In handling banned, taboo topics like Western culture and Christianity, Saudi educators prefer to instill students with information — and not induce them to reflect upon the matters at hand. The danger of the question, then, is that the students could re-interrogate the obvious "right" answer and, to everyone's horror, pay a second glance to the other options.

Love and Hate for the Sake of Allah

Notice that, in the first quoted question, the test-taker is enjoined to determine love and hate "for the sake of Allah." This is different from love and hate as we typically conceive of them. Rather, to love or hate someone "in the sake of Allah" is to allow your disposition toward, and feelings for, another person (or group) to be determined solely by that person's (or group's) relationship with Allah. The "true Muslim" is enjoined to love *only* for the sake of Allah, and hate *only* for the sake of Allah. The degree to which one has accomplished this feat is directly (positively) correlated with the extent of one's piousness. In other words, this dispositional triangulation is considered a necessary component of the Muslim faith. It should not be confused with al-*wala' wal bara'*, which pertains more to individual friendships than the broad-strokes of emotional alignment.

Translation

[*The cartoon reads from right to left. Notice the man's clothes are heavily patched, indicating his poverty.*]

"The teacher before annual adjustment"

"The teacher after annual adjustment of 10 Riyals."

Culture

As discussed earlier, teachers don't make enough money. When they do get raises or adjustments to their salary, it is still not enough.

Translation

First Title: **Stages of an employee's life**

(From right to left)

First year–employee

After 15 years–division head

After 35 years–general manager

Second title: **Stages of a teacher's life**

(From right to left)

First year–a teacher

After 15 years–still a teacher

After 35 years–a teacher and 6 honey-bee hives

Culture

Arabs respect their teachers but some think that teaching is the profession of someone who can't do any other. As you might expect, teachers in government schools are the lowest paid and least qualified teachers in the whole system. It is, to be sure, a poorly paid profession.

The governments of Arab countries have established programs for people of limited incomes to engage in a variety of entrepreneurial enterprises. For example, if one agrees to start a chicken farm as a sideline, the government will make quality chickens and coops available. Underpaid teachers would be prime candidates for such aid. Such a program, then, is understood to be the source of the beehives for the teacher who has been in his job for 35 years.

☪ Honey is mentioned in the Qur'an as a curative substance and is widely used throughout the Arab world — just the sort of produce encouraged by this type of government scheme.

Translation

Title: The Brother is supposed to be a School Student

(From top right and going counterclockwise)

He is scowling because he doesn't like what's going on.

Third generation telephone

Expensive sneakers

¾ pants (crab-catchers)

Backpack content: messed-up notebook, knife, broken ink pen

Latest fashion

Bottom title: On top of that, he's coming to class ten minutes late!!

Why?

Because he overslept!!

Culture

The Arab student is in a tacit contract with his parents: they will give him everything he needs, and in return he is expected to behave as a good student. This student has a panoply of luxuries at his disposal, including the latest fashion in pants, shoes and hairstyle, but he is not taking care of his school supplies and on top of everything he is late because of oversleeping. Adults will look at him in bafflement: he has everything he needs to excel, but is failing to give the only thing that's asked on his side.

☪ Arabs constantly criticize their youth for imitating Western habits: smoking, hanging out too much, and going on the Internet for extended periods of time. The constant criticism that teenagers receive from their parents and the media can be unhealthy for their self-esteem. Rather than conforming to the traditional demands, many young Arabs adopt yet another storied Western tradition: teenage rebellion. Actually achieving independence is very difficult, given troubled economies and the social expectation that people will be a part of a large and integrated family network, but the dream of freedom — and even of leaving their country — is cherished by many young Arabs.

Translation

المدارس تطلب تبرعات عينية تحايلا على قرار الوزير

والمدرسة محتاجة لمراوح للفصول.. وتايرين.. تاير كحلى وتاير رمادى مقاس ٤٨

Title: Schools are now asking for contributions in kind as a way to work around the Minister of Education's decision (that schools not be allowed to ask for monetary contributions).

Headmistress: "And the school needs fans for the classrooms and two woman's suits– one red and one gray in size 48."

The suits are evidently for the headmistress herself.

Culture

In many Arab countries, it used to be that school teachers constantly asked their pupils for monetary donations: for maintenance work, for extra furniture, for field trips, for classroom decorations— even money for the custodian, who often can't survive on his or her salary alone. While education is largely free in the Arab world, these classroom requests constituted a hefty sum of hidden fees, and varied according to the average wealth of the student body. Education ministries thought that the practice was getting out of hand, and banned teachers from soliciting funding from their students. In response, schools began asking for the actual objects they needed, rather than the funds necessary to purchase them. Now requests for objects such as, say, fans have become quite common, while teachers will often inquire as to whether students' parents work in relevant fields—carpentry, for example. Of course, the teacher's request for two new suits is intended to be humorous.

☪ Beyond maintenance and cleaning duties, custodians in Arab schools also work as waiters and waitresses, preparing tea and coffee and running errands for the teachers—an act that will usually earn them a tip.

☪ As happens probably everywhere, good kindergartens have long waiting lists and are difficult to enroll in.

☪ Arab countries use SI (metric or "European") rather than Imperial or United States customary units. For example, distances are measured in kilometers, weight in kilograms, temperature in Celsius, etc.

Translation

On blackboard: "Test."

Culture

These students are looking around during the absence of their teacher, exam proctor or invigilator. All of them have twisted necks from looking at other students' tests, or looking at the door.

Exam procedure is very similar to most of the rest of the world, as are attempts at cheating. Usually the proctor will

order the examinees to look at their own answer sheet and nowhere else. Sometimes a compassionate proctor, if he feels the exam is very hard, or that it is very easy and most have left except a few stragglers, will not explicitly allow cheating, but leave the room and give the students the opportunity to help each other. Students usually come to the hall with their books and notes, but these will be piled in the corner of the exam hall. If somebody does get caught cheating it must be with physical evidence. It all depends on the personality of those involved, but generally you must be caught red-handed with a cheat sheet. When this happens, the proctor will call the exam hall president, who has a red pen to write on the perpetrator's exam sheet that he has been caught cheating and the exam has been canceled. Other incriminating evidence can be any writing related to the exam that is on his body or clothes. Before the exam starts, proctors and the exam hall president will remind the test takers to get rid of everything that could be used in cheating, such as cheat sheets, calculators, cell phones, head phones, and recorders. Those in charge have the right to body search the students if they feel something is being hidden. This warning before the exam can be so sobering that students who have materials on them will voluntarily give them to the proctor.

Going to the bathroom, and returning, can also subject you to search. Arab students, now, use high tech equipment to help them cheat, and eighty percent of cheating now involves cell phones. Those wearing *niqab* are not allowed to keep it in place in exam halls due to the way it completely covers the body. Cheating is most prevalent among male students. In a large country like Egypt, where there around 1.6 million university students take an exam, there are between seven and ten thousand students caught cheating. Cheating in university is prevalent in what, in Arabic, are called "theory colleges," or those teaching the social sciences and humanities, such as law school, accounting, and languages, while there are hardly any cases of cheating at science and engineering schools.

☪ The exam format in Arab schools and universities is "long form," with large amounts of written work and essays required.

There are many Arabic proverbs associated with exams. The most famous is: "on the day of exam the person will be honored or humiliated" (*youm al-imtihan youkrem al-mraa ow youhan*). Arabs students usually, before they start the test, must recite a lot of prayers and sublication, to ask for God's help. There are religious television programs that tell the students about certain verses of the Qur'an and certain words that must be used to pass the exam.

Translation

Title: After the test
Top of door: "Examination hall"
On Student: "Student"
On paper: "Questions"
On guy running: "Teacher"

Culture

There is a famous Arabic proverb that says, "Our country is a country of certificates." Having a formal education or formal training is the key to success. Without such certification, life is extremely hard. This is why education is very important to Arab people. Arab education relies heavily upon memorization, and there exists a major industry that thrives by selling practice exams to students. But when an exam is "out of curriculum," that is, tests students on their critical thinking or on information that requires reading outside of the textbooks, students become angry. This cartoon depicts one such situation, wherein the students are upset because the test is harder than they expect. When students cannot answer questions on the exams, their reactions to this can be very violent as certification is a matter of life or death for them. Female students may scream while taking the exam or sob until they faint. Male students may be seen destroying chairs or desks or they rip up their answer sheets, on the belief that if there is no answer sheet, the teacher will give them a chance to make up the exam. Certification exams are not created by one teacher in particular, but rather by a committee of teachers whose intention is impartiality and coverage of all the required material. When a certification exam is extremely difficult, there may be a public outcry against the Department of Education, which may in response redistribute the grades.

If an upcoming exam is not a required certification exam, the teacher will often give hints or provide examples of what sorts of questions will be on the exam. These class periods are usually the most attended.

Translation

Father: May God grant you success Ashraf, my son. Do the best you can, you see with your own eyes what your private lessons did to us.

Culture

Arab families will spend a lot of money to prepare their children for their high school exams. This family has spent everything they had for their son's education; they even sold their own clothes. In an Egyptian survey in 2010, 39% of families said that half of their income went on school expenses, 22.6% spent over a third, and 18.1% spent over a quarter. The same study found that 66% of students relied on private tutoring.

☪ This boy is carrying everything that he will need to take his exam in his hands because, just as when U.S. teenagers take the SATs, he is not allowed to carry a calculator, a bag or anything extra into the exam room.

During normal school, students carry bags to school—these are usually large for the younger pupils and get smaller as they progress further in the school system. Those who not engaged in their education or regard school as a waste of time will signal their disaffection by carrying only the most necessary items to class. Such an attitude has a certain rebel cool that earns peer-group admiration, but can be a calculated pose to mislead others into neglecting their studies so that the apparent rebel can shine all the more in final exams.

☪ Arab governments are proud to say that they provide free education from elementary through high school. But in reality, the associated costs of giving their children a quality education can all but ruin a family. In Egypt for example, education is free, but there are a variety of costs that can make high school a financial burden to all but the wealthiest families. Private lessons, comprising one or two students and a teacher, guarantee an excellent education, but are extremely expensive. For students who can't afford the high cost of private lessons, most schools and some mosques offer evening study groups for eight to ten students to receive extra instruction. These study groups—"strengthening groups" is the literal translation—also cost money, but rather than paying the teachers directly, families pay the school, which then compensates the teacher. Textbooks provided by the government tend to be written in a dry and pedantic style, so many students spend the money to buy "external books"—books written by well known teachers or college professors—that address the same subjects in a more appealing and interesting way. Some students also buy "summaries," which are similar to Cliffs Notes in the U.S., in order to learn the main points that they will be tested on in a given subject.

Translation

"Private teacher"

[N. B. Having big pockets and a bar code is a sign of being expensive in a cartoon — bar codes are only used on imported or luxury goods.]

☪ Teachers' appearance is usually not as disheveled as shown in this cartoon, and most are smartly dressed — something they can afford because of private tutoring.

 Private tutors who are extremely good and have high reputations often give themselves special names: "The Emperor of Chemistry," "The King of Physics," and "The Prince of Mathematics," for example.

Culture

Private teachers are a widespread phenomenon in Arab education, especially in countries with large populations and limited economic means. This is due to the lack of personal attention students receive from teachers in school because of class size.

School teachers are not adequately paid, and so they give private lessons to their own students to supplement their income, and no-one works solely as a private teacher. Students can indirectly bribe a teacher by asking them for private lessons, even though they may not need tutoring, to guarantee that they receive good grades (and, to recruit students, the teacher will assure them that studying with him will enable them to pass the exam). Teachers then give their tutees strong hints and, in some instances, actual exams with correct answers in advance to ensure good grades. Because the bulk of a teacher's income derives from giving private lessons, teachers neglect their classes and focus on their private lessons, while students neglect their studies because they know they will receive good grades. These trends ultimately lead to the deterioration of the education system.

This method of obtaining good grades works at all educational levels except the sixth, ninth, and the twelfth grades, when teachers who are unfamiliar with the students or the school are responsible for grading their papers. Private teachers are still needed in these grades but students seek good tutors and not necessarily their own teacher, because their particular teacher does not have control over the grades. The prices of these private lessons range from inexpensive fees to astronomical amounts for star teachers.

☪ The peak season for private tutors falls in the last month before exams, when the highest earners can make as much as half a million Egyptian pounds. In Arab cartoons, perhaps understandably therefore, private teachers are often depicted as greedy people who have forgotten the true mission of a teacher. There is something of a running battle between the Education Minister and the teachers who earn large sums through private teaching, where the Minister can threaten to move a teacher to a new area where his reputation and earning potential will be greatly reduced—this is motivated by a desire to make them focus on their work in school, and also by jealousy.

Translation

Lecturing teacher: All of us are one nation. . . .
All of us are going to meet one destiny. . . .
All of us are going to take [private] lessons with one teacher.

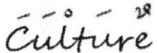 Pan-Arabism used the slogans: "One nation, one destiny, and one language," which the teacher subverts for his own ends.

Culture

In this cartoon, a teacher is inviting his student to take private classes. A teacher will not usually invite his students to take private classes that he is offering, and instead the students will inquire into his ability to tutor them privately. Students are usually good judges of character about which teachers are amenable to improving their grades in return for the income from private lessons, generally choosing the less strict, less distant, and less respected teachers.

☪ The student in the present cartoon is seated at a typical Arab school desk. The desk and chair constitute one conjoined unit. The desk itself, meanwhile, is divided into two parts, the large slanted surface and the flat, smaller surface above it. On the latter area, the student will keep his pencils and various tools; on the former, he will do his writing and note-taking. Too, the slanted surface lifts to reveal a large storage space within the desk itself. Therein, the student will keep his notes, textbooks and whatever else he may need for class.

Translation "How am I going to pay **the rent**? How am I going to renew **my ID**? How am I going to eat boiled **eggs**?"

On sign: Farghly for private lesson.

New fees because of exams.

(From top to bottom)

Teaching the subject (without beating) 3700 Riyals

Teaching the subject (with beating) 3700 Riyals

Solving exam questions 450 Riyals

Recitation 300 Riyals

Covering a book with paper 600 Riyals

Writing cheat sheets 1500 Riyals

The parentheses are used in the Arabic to indicate emphasis (and appear in the translation in bold), and all of these things are becoming increasingly expensive.

Giving the teacher the name Farghly and making him bald with thick glasses is funny for Arabs since it alludes to a character in a very funny play, *School of the Trouble Makers*.[29]

One of the items listed is covering books with paper, something that students usually do for themselves or that is done by their mother, using brown wrapping paper to protect the covers of textbooks and notebooks.

Culture

Arab private teachers' fees will vary according to both the subject and the grade. The highest fees are charged for the three major certification exams, the 6th, 9th and 12th, since each of these exams requires high scores in order for a child to move on to the next level of education. As for subjects, foreign languages, especially English, usually command the highest fee. The subjects that most students do not need private lessons for are usually history and geography.

As in this cartoon, private teachers will not only explain a topic that is not clearly explained in the government-issued textbooks, he will also write easy-to-digest notes on the subject, which will be easier for the student to memorize. A private teacher will also help students with practice tests, helping them to prepare for the actual exam. A dishonest tutor may also help the student in writing a cheat-sheet, which is a very small piece of paper that will have important information for the test on it, and can easily be

---

[29] Some blame the play for bad student discipline in Egypt, since it was very popular among teens, and every student tries to imitate its actors.

hidden on the student, so that they may use it in secret during the exam. A private teacher, most often, will go to the house of the student to tutor and some charge such a high fee, that students will sometimes split the costs by sharing a single tutor. In this cartoon the fee is raised for the approach of the exam, usually students don't start taking private lessons in regular years, until after the second half of the year, while in exam years (grades six, nine and twelve), they usually start sooner, some even before the start of the year. Waiting longer can cost the students more money as teachers raise their fee as the exam date approaches, and there may be no room for new students.

Translation

Title: Tests

On right: "Private Teacher

Crying boy on left: "Student"

[N.B. *In this cartoon it appears that the tutor is spitefully taking advantage of his student and milking his student of money.*]

Culture

Arab kids are overloaded with big subjects and heavy books. The textbooks used in Arab schools come from the government. They are badly written and must be deciphered either by private teachers or with the help of outside books that explain the government curriculum in a clear and concise way. Relying solely on government books in studying a subject is almost impossible. Some critics of these textbooks ask why the government spends a fortune on incomprehensible textbooks that no one uses rather than on the authors of the easy-to-understand books.

Translation

Woman: I'm optimistic, Father of Ishmael. The government will ban two-trailer trucks to reduce road accidents. This means that the government is about to ban Ministry textbooks to reduce mental retardation!

Language

"Ministry textbooks" refers to government-issued textbooks from the Ministry of Education, which are notoriously poorly written.

Culture

This cartoon refers to the ban in Egypt of trucks with two trailers being drawn by a cab, with the second trailer attached to the first. The second trailer can swing dangerously, posing a significant danger to others. After public outcry following many accidents, the government decided to ban them.

This law is just one of a series of laws designed to make the perilous roads safer. A number of dangerous vehicles, such as the once common tick-took—a rickety form of three-wheeled taxi—now operate under restricted hours and only on certain streets in many Arab countries.

☪ Rather than use his actual name, the wife in the cartoon calls her husband "Father of Ishmael." This is a common practice in the Arab world, as husbands and wives will call each other by the names of their sons or daughters. People will often address their neighbors and close acquaintances in this way as well. To an extent, the practice derives from the fact that it is considered impolite to call out to a woman by name. Public rules of etiquette, then, are often seen to extend into the personal Arab home. Likewise, the family in the cartoon is dressed conservatively, and illustrates how many Arab people even dress modestly in the privacy of their own homes.

☪ In Arab countries, it is perfectly normal and acceptable for a man to appear in public in his pajamas. For trips to the corner store or for socializing with the neighbors, it is entirely common for a man to wear his pajamas. If he must venture farther, of course, he is expected to don proper clothing. However, in most Arab countries, women do not go out in public unless they are fully and appropriately attired.

There are two types of pajamas in the Arab world: one for summer, which is made of lighter materials; and one for winter, which is made of heavier, warmer materials. Many are patterned like the pajamas in the cartoon. While women do not possess pajamas per se, they do own long, comfortable gowns like the one shown above—the difference, of course, being that they cannot wear this gown out into public.

☪ The use of a low dining table as a desk is not uncommon among poorer Arab students.

On books: Curriculum

[This cartoon contrasts the physical burden borne by the typical Arab and Japanese students. The Arab child lugs an overloaded backpack brimming with books, pencils and other supplies, while his Japanese counterpart briskly walks with everything he needs on a laptop and CD.]

Culture

The Arab youth featured in the left hand panel illustrates the typical Gulf student's attire, which consists of a common Gulf Arab gown and sandals that bear one strap for the foot and a separate, smaller strap for the big toe. Notice, however, that the student is not wearing a guthra: thought to look foolish upon the very young, children do not begin wearing the *guthra* until they have reached adolescene.

Special school uniforms are the reserve of the more prestigious institutions: foreign language schools, military schools and privitate institutions. As to student attire outside of the Gulf, it largely depends upon where the student lives, as well as the economic and social status of his family. For example, the very impoverished often lack even backpacks, and commonly tote their books to school in emptied rice sacks that have been set aside for this express purpose. The wealthy, meanwhile, often possess Western name brand bags from the likes of Prada and Gucci.

In the Arab world, students are saddle with an abundance (or, some argue, an overabundance) of coursework between 1st and 6th; to this, many governments are now considering the addition of foreign language instruction to public school syllabi. However, this campaign has encountered problems due to the lack of qualified foreign language teachers.

In many Arab countries—in particular, those that border Israel, or the Doul Al-moujaha ("facing states"), and that would thus be hit first in the case of an Israeli offensive—have incorporated military training in their middle school and high school curricula. Dressed in modified military uniforms, students are instructed by drill segreants in the firing and maintanence of weaponry, self defense, and tactical theory.

Translation

Book: Curriculum
Left: Teacher
Right: Student

Culture

The curriculum followed in the Arab world is traditional in most of the wrong ways. The approach to the Arabic language is based on texts that are over a thousand years old, and good grades depend upon following these models slavishly. The Qur'an is inseparable from the language, the epitome of eloquence and grammatical perfection, so that all examples and models are based on Qur'anic verses and the even older *Mu'allaqat* (discussed later in this section). Foreign languages are taught through books and focus mainly on grammar and exercises, while science is based on learning facts and is seldom practical or involves laboratory work. On top of this the textbooks are very unappealing, written in stiff language, with old-fashioned illustration, and printed on poor-quality paper. None of this makes learning a stimulating experience and the majority of the material just has to be memorized—and here the teacher is forcing the curriculum into the pupil's head with a plunger.

Translation

Title: Studying and rote-learning.
Written on shirt: Student.

Culture

As mentioned above, the only way for most students to pass exams, which are vital to success, is by memorizing the material parrot-fashion and not to dream of a more interesting approach or wait for a more skillful teacher to come along.

Translation

Right to left: before the exam, duing the exam, after the exam.

Culture

Arab students and even their teachers have the attitude that what they need to do is just learn in order to pass the exam. The approach is to regurgitate what has been learned, and that is that. Many educators believe that education should not be like that and that students should learn what will stay with them and benefit them in the future.

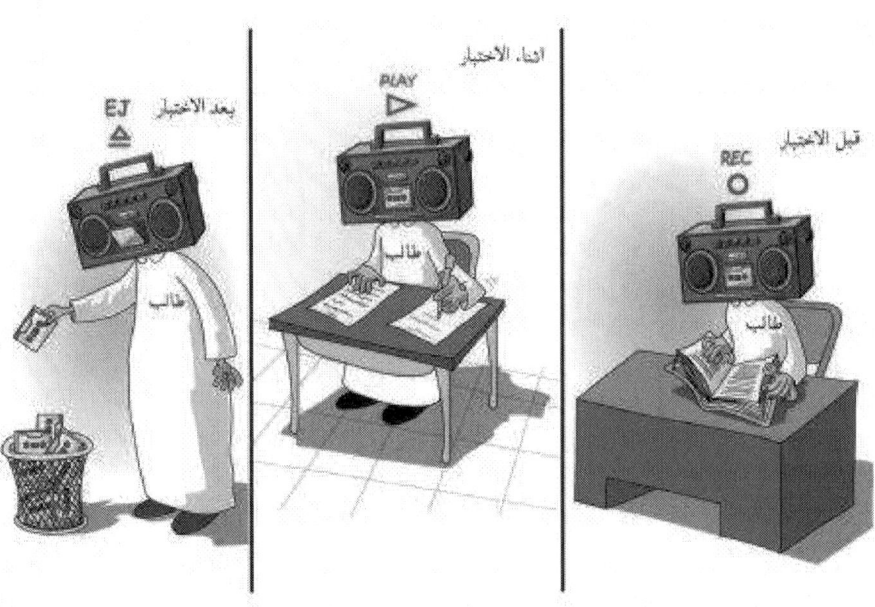

This is a page from an Arabic textbook teaching the English language.

Arab students cover much the same material as their American counterparts—math, chemistry, biology, etc. However, in Arab education systems, there exist additional fields of study not present in American schools. As you read through the following list of such courses, keep in mind that these are proper courses of studies, taught from textbooks and evaluated by the traditional means—tests, quizzes, papers and the like. Too, not all of the classes are present in all of the Arab countries, and some Arab countries will combine two of the classes below into one general course. Finally, with the exception of Saudi Arabia, 10% of the typical Arab student body is Christian; thus, when the time arises for the Islam-oriented topics that follow, the Christian students will usually be gathered together to study topics pertaining to their own faith.

2. Write about Jehan's weekend.

Thursday morning — read

Thursday afternoon — write

Thursday evening — visit

Friday morning — wake up

Friday afternoon — read

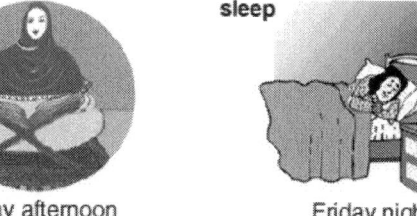
Friday night — sleep

a. Jihan reads a book on Thursday morning.
b. _____ c. _____
d. _____ e. _____
f. _____

Unless otherwise indicated, the courses below are taught between the 7th and 12th grades.

Monotheism

"Monotheism" explores the spectrum of religious practices and orientations that monotheistic worship prohibits and opposes. These include: the varieties of polytheism (the polytheism of fear, wherein a person fears some entity other than God; the polytheism of love, wherein the person loves some entity other than God; and the polytheism of reliance, wherein a person relies upon some entity other than God); idolatry; folk pagan artifacts such as fortune telling and the wearing of talismans; the glorifying of commemorative statues and memorials; the Arab "state of ignorance" prior to the revelation of the Qur'an; and the introduction of novel heretical doctrines to the pure, original faith.

Islamic Jurisprudence

"Islamic Jurisprudence" teaches the structure of the legal system, which is partitioned into five principle categories: religion, human life, progeny, private property and intellect. Islam teaches that these five categories constitute the cardinal virtues of man's worldly existence. Accordingly, the three most heinous crimes are thought to be polytheism, premeditated murder and adultery. "Islamic Jurisprudence" is not confined solely to elaborating the law, but rather examines the complexities of the law's application, including methods of crime prevention and the selection of adequate, commensurate punishments.

The Prophetic Era

Courses in "The Prophetic Era" examine: the socio-political milieu of pre-Islamic Arabia; the life of the Prophet Muhammad prior to his divine calling; the subsequent stages of his life, and the successive stages of his jihad; the four rightly guided caliphates; the numerous military expeditions which the four caliphates oversaw, including the reasons for their occurrence, and also their campaigns' aims and ultimate results; and the state system during the caliphate era, as well as the period's political, economic, cultural and scientific activity.

Traditional Methods and Techniques of Qur'anic Recitation

Studies in this field address the unique phonetics of the Qur'anic language, which can diverge radically from those present in regular speech.

Sayings of Prophet Muhammad

Courses in this area study the numerous issues attendant to the prophet's sayings, including: the methods whereby the hadith were preserved and transmitted; the guidelines by which one can discriminate true and false hadith; the link between the hadith and the Qur'an; and the importance of non-contradiction between hadith and the Qur'an.

Qur'anic Sciences

The "Qur'anic Sciences" encompass a wealth of topics culled from centuries of Qur'anic study. These include: the distinction between the *Qur'an* proper and the "Divine Sayings of God," supposed records of God's direct communiqués to prophets throughout the ages; the Qur'an's four names ("The Qur'an," "The Book," "The Revelation," "The Proof/Evidence") and three descriptions ("The Blessed," "The Manifested," "The Glorious,"), as well as proofs and explications of these various designations; why the Qur'an was revealed incrementally, over a period of twenty years; the manner in which the Qur'an was compiled; the Qur'an's division into thirty parts; the different calligraphies of the Qur'an; and the various stories contained within the text.

Additionally, the field covers a range of Qur'anic trivia, including: the number of *ayahs* (or verses) within the book (scholars have proposed 6,217, 6,220, 6,226 and 6,336, among other counts, the variations stemming from how one chooses to count *ayahs*—for example, if a line with a single word should be considered its own *ayah*, or belonging to the *ayah* that immediately precedes or succeeds it), the longest ayah ("Al Deen" from "The Cow") and the shortest ayah ("Yaseen," which also constitutes a full surah). (For the curious: the distinction between the Qur'an and the Sayings is that the latter were historically prone to redaction and alteration, while the former was not. Too, the Qur'an was revealed incrementally so as to allow time for memorization; at the time, literacy was rare—Muhammad himself was illiterate—and the primary mode of textual transmission was oral.)

Science of Inheritance

Examinations of Islam's labyrinthine, ornate inheritance system, such courses are typically reserved for juniors and seniors in high school. In opposition to the Western inheritance laws—which permit the indulgence of all varieties of whim, favoritism and fancy, no matter how frivolous (e.g. the bequeathing of a prodigious fortune to one's cherished poodle, to the exclusion of one's children and dependents)—

Islamic societies strictly delimit what one can and cannot do with one's wealth and possessions after one's death.

In pre-Islamic Arabia, conflicts over inheritance were badly contentious, and often became violent—in fact, numerous families suffered a bloody collapse through just these sorts of disputes. Islam sought to curtail this violence—and the social degradation it engendered—through the implementation of a vast, minutely elaborated system of inheritance, which strove to account for all possible situations. A given situation could be fairly simple or lavishly complex, and depended on a wealth of variables such as the number of relatives involved, their respective genders, their religious affiliations and their social statuses (imagine, for example, the intricacy involved adjudicating between, say, a Christian slave-wife and a Muslim niece, the deceased's sole living relatives). For every such situation, inheritance law tries not only to rule justly, but to do so in exact percentages. In a way, the system was intended not only as a means of lessening violence, but also as a corrective to the inequalities endemic in the old way of doing things, wherein a woman, for example, was prohibited from inheriting anything from any deceased relative.

Patriotism Education

"Patriotism Education" is confined primarily to the 1st through 6th grades, and is in fact far less Orwellian than the title would lead one to believe. In essence, it teaches the child to be a productive, upright citizen of his society—emphasizing the importance of punctuality, charity work and etiquette—and inculcates a healthy admiration for his country's history and culture (e.g. for its primary cultural exports, its role on the international stage). Too, it introduces the student to his country's unique, domestically manufactured commodities and natural resources, and underscores the importance of purchasing domestic products over foreign-made goods.

Household Economics

To an extent, "Household Economics" is analogous to American public education's "Home Economics," as it teaches the pupil a surfeit of useful homemaking tips. However, "Household Economics" diverges from its American counterpart in that it is intended solely for female students, and thus supplements the familiar content with material that is part woman's survival guide, part standard finishing school fare. In Household Economics, a girl will be introduced to the substance of her adult life, including etiquette (e.g. the proper way in which to walk, speak, sit, stand, eat, drink, sneeze, yawn, express condolences and congratulations, excuse oneself, laugh, share jokes, set the table, parent children and treat one's husband), homemaking (e.g. how to prepare popular, centrally important dishes; how to identify ripe, tasty fruits and vegetables; how to assess the freshness of eggs; how to successfully host guests; how to iron clothes, and clean and treat certain fabrics), and biology (e.g. female reproductive physiology; the nature of the menstrual cycle; how to lessen menstrual pain; how to clean menstrual blood; nutritional advice; and how to avoid obesity). As a rule, their textbooks will be written exclusively by other women, and never men. "Household Economics" is often taught to girls during middle school; this is chiefly because many women in the Arab world end their formal education with the 9th grade, and get married directly out of school.

Classical Arabic Calligraphy

As its title indicates, "Arabic Calligraphy" teaches the various calligraphic forms apposite to Arabic.

Interpretation of the Qur'an

"Interpretation of the Qur'an" is perhaps, more accurately, the *explication* of the Qur'an, providing the student with glosses on supposedly "difficult" vocabulary words and ostensibly difficult-to-scrutinize, or plainly inscrutable, passages from the text.

The Rules and Modes of Recitation of the Seven Imams

This topic is not uniformly present throughout Arab school systems; in fact, the extent of its presence is often directly proportional to the religiosity of the society in question. Thus, the study of the modes of the Seven Imams is ubiquitous in highly devout countries like Saudi Arabia, but largely lacking from standardized education in countries like Lebanon, which is home to a not-inconsiderable Christian population.

The topic focuses upon the seven traditional, authoritative "readings" of the *Qur'an*. The existence of *seven* "authoritative" readings may strike the Westerner as peculiar. In fact, this multiplicity of valid interpretations arose from the unique manner in which the *Qur'an* was set to writing—namely, lacking all diacritical marks. Thus, while the Arabic text of the Qur'an is in all seven traditions the same, the prescribed *pronunciation* of the text is not. This malleability with regard to pronunciation, it is said, was meant to accommodate the various local dialects present in Arabia during the era of the Prophet. Accordingly, each valid tradition, or "mode," can cite a complete record of its transmission—and thus, its validation—from Muhammad to the present. Students of the field must study and memorize the various transmitters' biographies, which include: the date of the transmitter's birth; those from whom he received the tradition, or his sheikhs; those to whom he bequeathed the tradition, or his disciples; and the date and circumstances of his death.

The seven modes disagree on topics and areas that might, to the novice, seem esoteric or obscure. For example: in adding diacritical marks, some traditions have diphthongized what others think ought to be assimilated, and vice versa; too, some traditions hold that one must utter two invocations ("I seek refuge in Allah" and "In the name of Allah, the (most) Gracious, the (most) Merciful.") at the beginning of each Qur'anic recitation, while others hold that only one is sufficient, and still others believe no invocation to be necessary at all.

Today, only one "reading" of the Qur'an is actively in use. This is that of the *Quraysh*, who were the dominant tribe within Mecca upon the appearance of Islam.

Translation

Top of board: Expression

Below: Your thoughts orally about the end of the school year.

[*The student proceeds to express his thoughts in a funny and poetic way.*]

Language

In Arabic, when a teacher asks for "expression," he means to write one's thoughts about a subject down. While there is no direct equivalent in American culture, it is similar to a teacher asking students to write a journal entry on a certain topic.

In the cartoon, the student responds to the teacher's request for a simple oral report with an extemporaneous declaration in poetic verse. In the Arab world, the ability to spontaneously compose and improvise verse is a highly coveted linguistic skill, a sure sign of intelligence and erudition. In part, then, the cartoon derives its humor from juxtaposing the teacher's simplistic assignment with the student's highbrow reply. However, humor also arises from the juxtaposition of the highbrow *form* of the student's speech (i.e. impromptu versifying) with the crude and colloquial *content* of what he is saying: should the teacher provide him with the answers to the upcoming final exam, he explains, he will be sure to pay the teacher well—and give him a free VHS, too, for good measure.

Culture

In addition to the final exam answers, the student also requests a good mark on his *"a'amal alsana"* which transliterates as "year work" and, though it lacks a direct correlate in English, generally signifies all academic work that does not fall under the midterm or final exams—for example, classroom participation, homework, and performance on pop quizzes.

The students and teacher in the cartoon are from Qatar, which one gleans from the specific nature of the *guthra* that each student wears.

The pride that some Arab youths take in their ability to extemporaneously compose verse is very similar to the pride that some American youths take in their ability to free-style rap.

Translation

"Mother, this is the modern way of studying; I'm studying with my colleagues for tomorrow's test by pal talk and chatting."

Culture

Around the world, mothers are not known for being particularly tech savvy, and Arab mothers are no exception.

Translation

"Mother! Don't get any closer, there's a virus!"

Translation

Title: (The right kind of desk for the right kind of student.)

(Starting at bottom and going backwards)

Left side: Sitting place of teacher[30]

The first desk: For those who are excellent students or have some type of complex. Each one of them is a brainbox. The teacher loves them because they erase the blackboard and will write for him [e.g. go up to the blackboard]. They are role models for the class.

The second desk: Type of students who deserve pity or are slow. Average in their studies, very polite, they try to prove their cleverness to the teacher.

The penultimate desk: They are average in mischief and troublemaking, and they are punchbags for the back row, weak in their studies, funny and cheats.

Final desk: They are always making trouble and know the topics well already, as they are repeating the grade. They don't have anything to do with studying and the teacher is scared of them.

[N.B. The brackets of the title indicate emphasis in Arabic.]

---

[30] Teachers sometimes sit not at their own desks but closer to the students to engage more fully, and also to make their presence felt more.

Language

The title is a play on a political slogan, launched in the early Sixties, "The right man for the right place," to combat corruption and nepotism and promising jobs based on qualifications and ability.

Translation

Thinker on right (title): Education Abroad

Thinker on left (title): Education at Home

The book he holds reads: The Ministry Book

Thinker on left: Horse, night, and desert know me (repeated three times)

Attacker and retreater, comer and dodger (repeated four times)

Rodin's statue "The Thinker," an emblem of deep and serious thought, is transformed into a dejected and depressed student, parroting archaic poetry from an Arab education ministry's text books.

Language

The first poetry verse that the bored Thinker repeats in the "Education at Home" section of the cartoon is the work of Imru'-al-Qays, (c. 500 CE — c. 550 CE). He was born in Nagid, Saudi Arabia and is regarded as the greatest poet of pre-Islamic times and one of the founders of Arabic poetry. He is the author of one of the seven *Mu'allaqat* collections of odes. The second verse that the bored thinker recites is the work of another great Arabic poet, Abu Tayeb al-Mutanabbi (915 CE-966 CE), who was born in Kufa, Iraq.

The *Mua'llaqat* odes are the seven greatest odes in Arabic tradition. The term *Mua'llaqat* literally means "Suspended ones," referring to their placement in pre-Islamic times hanging from the Kaabah, where the poets of the day displayed their works. This period is known as al-*Jahiliyya*, or "The Time of Ignorance," a term that is obviously understood to refer only to spiritual ignorance, given that this period saw the composition of such poetical masterpieces. The Arabian Peninsula was a patchwork of small tribal lands and kingdoms, each of which had a poet, or *Sha'ir*, whose task it was not only to glorify his tribe in verse but also to record its history and genealogy. This position carried enormous prestige, second only to the tribe's principal sheikh himself. These works are a fundamental part of Arab education, drilled into students as a means of perfecting their linguistic skills and lauded as foundational examples of fine composition, much as Shakespeare is in English-speaking countries.

Culture

The cartoon compares and contrasts education in the rest of the world and Arab countries.

Many rich Arabs will send their children abroad for their education, especially for their university studies though some travel for high school as well. Some governments will pay all the education expenses associated with sending students abroad in order for the best and the brightest to have better learning opportunities. Though the past few decades have altered this, at one time families in many countries were forced to send their children abroad for higher education for the simple reason that their home countries had no universities at all. It is generally held that Arab school and universities are slow to adopt innovative teaching styles and fall behind in teaching the methods of analytical thought that are needed to win the best jobs and compete internationally. Also, Arabs recognize that an education in a prestigious international school will give their children the opportunity to network with those who will likely go on to international prominence and influence.

☪ Understanding the Arabs of today requires an understanding of al-*Jahiliyyah*, since many characteristics of contemporary culture, both the good and the bad, have their roots in the period. Here is a brief review of this important era of Arab history.

☪ Many Arab government see sending their citizens abroad for their education as a way to combat Islamic fundementalism.

Jahiliyyah

Al Jahiliyyah refers to the era that preceded the rise of Islam, lasting for about a century and a half. This era was called *Jahilyyah*, meaning ignorance. The connotation of the word, however, is not of lacking knowledge, but is the opposite of mild-mannered, a sort of moral ignorance. The word derives from *jahela*, meaning *he did not know* or *he lost his temper*. This was one of the traits of Arab culture at the time, when war could be sparked by trivial actions and go on for years

1. Geography and Climate

The Arabian Peninsula is primarily a desert. There is widespread drought, but when it does experience rain the land becomes rather lush. The harsh environment made inhabitants subject to the whims of nature. Their manners and customs were defined by the environment in which they lived. During the period, they were famous for kindness, bravery and courage, loyalty, love of freedom, hatred of base morality, and they were the good Samaritans of the time. These traits still exist in today's culture, but their root was in the difficult climate of *al-Jahiliyyah*. The effect of it can also be seen on the content of literature of the time.

2. Social and Moral Life

The Arabs of *al-Jahiliyyah* were of two types, the town-dwellers, who represented the minority, and the nomads, who comprised the majority of the population. The urban people lived in houses and had a relatively steady life. They worked in cottage industries, agriculture, and trade and were represented mostly in the cities of Al-Hijaz and Yemen. The Quraysh tribe dominated Mecca, where, along with their allies, they represented most of the city's population. The nomadic people were also known as 'hair people' (*Ahl al-wahber*), which refers to the camel hair that they used to build their tents. Their life consisted of traveling and searching for pasture, as their livelihood depended on what their animals produced.

The Arabs of *al-Jahiliyyah* had a mixture of both high moral standards and poor character. The good morals were represented by respect of neighbors, kindness, bravery, honesty, loyalty, and protection of their fellow tribesmen. This respect for neighbor, however, was limited to one's own tribe, as the period was dominated by extreme tribalism, resulting in raiding, stealing, looting, female infanticide, excessive drinking and gambling.

Poetry of the time documented every aspect of Arabs' lives. It was the ancient record, chronicling war and peace, including travel and romance, with elements that might nowadays be in the press or on-line.

3. Political Life

The politically active Arabs of *al-Jahiliyyah* tended to live in cities, such as Mecca, and Emirates, such as the Emirate of Monzara and the Emirate of Ghsasent in the north of the peninsula, the Emirate of Kenda in the middle of the peninsula, and the Emirate of Saba and Houmir in the south. These states competed to attract the best poets and orators who were the public relations firms of the time, talking up their clients' achievements and good deeds to bolster their good reputations. This could lead to increased trade and business with other tribes. For this reason, Emirates would pay handsomely for the best poets to immortalize their achievements.

The other type of Arab had no interest in politics. These were tribes of nomads, each governed by a sheikh. He was usually a part of the cavalry and represented the best traits of the tribe, such as generosity, courage, eagerness to help, and, most importantly, eloquence. Every tribe had fighters, poets, and orators that satisfied the needs of the tribe and helped during peace and war, and it was the man who excelled in all these that would become the sheikh

4. Religious life

Most Arabs of *al-Jahiliyyah* were pagans who worshiped idols. The most significant were Allat, Houbel, El Ouza, and Manat, in addition to special idols that were kept in one's house. Some were fashioned out of pressed dates, or Ajwa, which were then eaten. Other Arabs worshiped the sun, moon, stars, while some worshiped fire. Small minorities were Christians or Jews, but most were not fully aware of religion. Some Arabs were repelled by what worshiping idols entailed, so they worshiped God in the Abrahamic tradition outside Judaism or Christianity, and they were called *hunafaa*.

5. Intellectual Life

The Arabs in the era of *al-Jahiliyya* had limited cultural and scientific knowledge, but it was suitable and sufficient for the desert environment. Illiteracy was common, but the period did not demand that level of knowledge.

6. Trade and Business of the *al-Jahiliyya* Arabs

Al Jahiliyya Arabs had many markets, known as souqs, in Naged, Al-Hijaz, Yemen, and Hadhramout. The three most famous were Oukaz, Medina, and Zi Almajaz. Usually the markets would fill up in the month leading up to al-Hijj and at the completion of business they would empty, attendees heading out on al-Hijj (a pilgrimage to Mecca, where the Kaabah was a shrine of idols). The market, however, was not restricted to business and trade. It functioned as a place to resolve conflict, exchange prisoners, and for diplomacy between tribes to occur. It also acted as a venue for poets, hired to glorify the accomplishments of tribes. It was a place to go for advice. If Dr. Phil or Jim Kramer had been alive it is in the market that they would have set up shop. During this month, a judge of poetry and oratory would set up in a red leather tent in each market, delivering advice or praise for poems delivered to him.

The market had a strong and profound effect on both Arabic language and culture. Most importantly, it homogenized tribal dialects, as the language of Quraysh, the largest tribe on the peninsula, became the tongue of business. The Quraysh dialect gained such prominence that it almost became the lingua franca of the region. When the Qur'an was revealed it was in this dialect that it was written.

Translation

Their way of talking to school children:

Obama: If you leave school, you will not fail, but the whole country will fail. The future of America depends on you and we are in need of each one of you to develop your abilities.

Our way of talking to school children:

Bureaucrat: Beware of the swine flu ... Take precautions against spreading the virus and don't sneeze in the face of the person next to you. And everybody carry soap with you!

Culture

This cartoon contrasts the attitude towards children of the American and Arab governments. The Arab official speaks to the school children in a belittling tone, as if they were simple-minded, while President Obama speaks to the school children of America in a way that recognizes that they are becoming adults. The cartoon urges Arab educators to be less patronizing and accept the individual worth of the students, thereby engaging Arab youth with their schooling and eventually benefitting the entire country.

Some westerners may be surprised to find that an Arab audience would be as familiar with the speeches of the American president as this cartoon implies. As it happens, the Arab world pays a great deal of attention to the speeches of American presidents, and furthermore, this goes beyond a people's natural interest in the thoughts of a major world leader. It is a long-standing practice amongst many Arab politicians to have the speeches of American presidents translated into Arabic and then to pinch the best lines for their own speeches, with appropriate adjustments. For example, the famous line about not asking what your country can do for you from Kennedy's Inaugural was eagerly taken up by Nasser, replacing "your country" with "Egypt;" so popular was Nasser's clever line that the government even turned it into a song. Unfortunately for the politicians, the translations are frequently hastily and shoddily done, and Arab politicians can find themselves led into gaffes in their eagerness to deliver a snappy line.

Translation

7 o'clock in the morning.
Right Sign: "To Riyadh (capital of Saudi Arabia)"
Left Sign: "To dormitory at al-Daria"
Under the bus: "No comment"

The humor of this cartoon is that all university students are going to Riyadh—where they will have fun in the city—instead of attending lectures and studying on their campus.

Note that the running student holds the end of his gown in his mouth. This echoes the Arabic maxim, "he took his tail in his teeth", which is used to refer to the act of running: in order to run successfully, one must lift the tail of his gown so that it doesn't interfere with his legs. In particular, the phrase refers to the act of running away, suddenly or hectically.

Culture

Playing Hooky

Arab students are expert at avoiding their schoolwork and take pride in the skill with which they sneak and play hooky. The diversions and attractions are endless, but going to the movies is a particularly popular pastime for truant students, so much so that police and truancy officers often patrol the ticket lines during morning screenings. The pleasures of a day of freedom do not come without risk, however. Students are allowed a maximum of thirty days' of unexplained absence, and if they exceed this limit they are expelled and are not permitted to enroll in another government school. Students in such cases must either seek a place in a private school or take up home-schooling. This policy can be manipulated by unscrupulous students in the final, twelfth grade. A student who is expelled from government school is still expected to pass his final exam, but rather than having his answers evaluated in comparison to his peers, the expelled student will submit his test with other home-schoolers. As most of these students will not score as well as most students from the formal education system, the student who only late in his career joined home school will look better in comparison and win higher scores in discretionary categories.

Co-ed Education in Saudi Arabia

Higher education in Saudi Arabia had always been separated by gender, but August 2009 saw the opening of Saudi Arabia's first fully integrated university. The multi-billion dollar King Abdullah Science and Technology Univeristy has state-of-the-art labs, the world's fourteenth fastest super computer, and one of the biggest endowments worldwide. The university boasts 817 students from 61 different countries, with 15% of the student population being Saudis. Many American universities, research institutes and companies—Babson College, Woods Hole Oceanographic Institute, Stanford University, Boeing and Dow Chemical, to name a few, are partnering with KAU.S.T. The step for women's education was vehemently opposed by conservative religious figures who considered it to be irretrievably openning the door to sin. In retaliation for such public criticism, King Abdullah dismissed one of his most prominent opponents Saad ben-Naser al-Shatrey, a member of the Council of Scientists, from his government posts. The spat intensified to the point that hackers hijacked the website of one of Saudi Arabia's leading newspapers, using the dismissal of al-Shatrey as evidence for the supposed spirit of irreligiousity seeping into Saudi life.

By building this university, Saudi Arabia has followed Dubai's example and has pursued the process of diversification of its economy. Dubai has been very successful in being recognized as more than just an oil producing country, and prior to its difficulties in late 2009, it had become a hub of financial and investment opportunities as well as a popular tourist destination. Dubai has succeeded in convincing the deans of of some of America's most prestigious universites, such as Harvard, Cornell and New York University, to open branches in the city.

☪ In Saudi Arabia, the staunch co-educational policies extend even to the textbooks. Even in the same subject, female students use different textbooks than do male students. There are a variety of reasons for this separation, from the content and images to the suitability and relevance of the topic itself.

Dormitories

At many major, urban Arab universities, there is a sharp divide between those students who live in dormitories, and those who continue to live at home. By and large, a dormitory residence is viewed as a mark of indigence, the refuge of those whose families lack the financial resources for city life. Most Arab dorms provide filthy, squalid living arrangements, and thus do much to foster this impression. They are eminently unaccommodating. A typical bed is a miniscule 5 ½ feet in length, and can bear only 130 lbs. without structural damage. And even if someone could use it for sleep, he would be doubtless awoken by the steady, unceasing stream of mosquitoes. One's belongings, meanwhile, are in constant jeopardy: the closets come with broken locks and busted door-knobs, and hall-monitors can, at any moment, for any reason, forcibly confiscate or search through one's possessions (for example, games such as chess, dominoes and playing cards are regularly seized for being "satanic" in nature.) The sole large gas-tank in the room rarely functions, but students are prohibited from using any electronic equipment in their rooms—including heaters. Life outside the bedroom is no better: the food is famously terrible, and residents are kept to a strict curfew: should one fail to return in time, he will be locked out of the dormitory, forced to wait until morning to reenter.

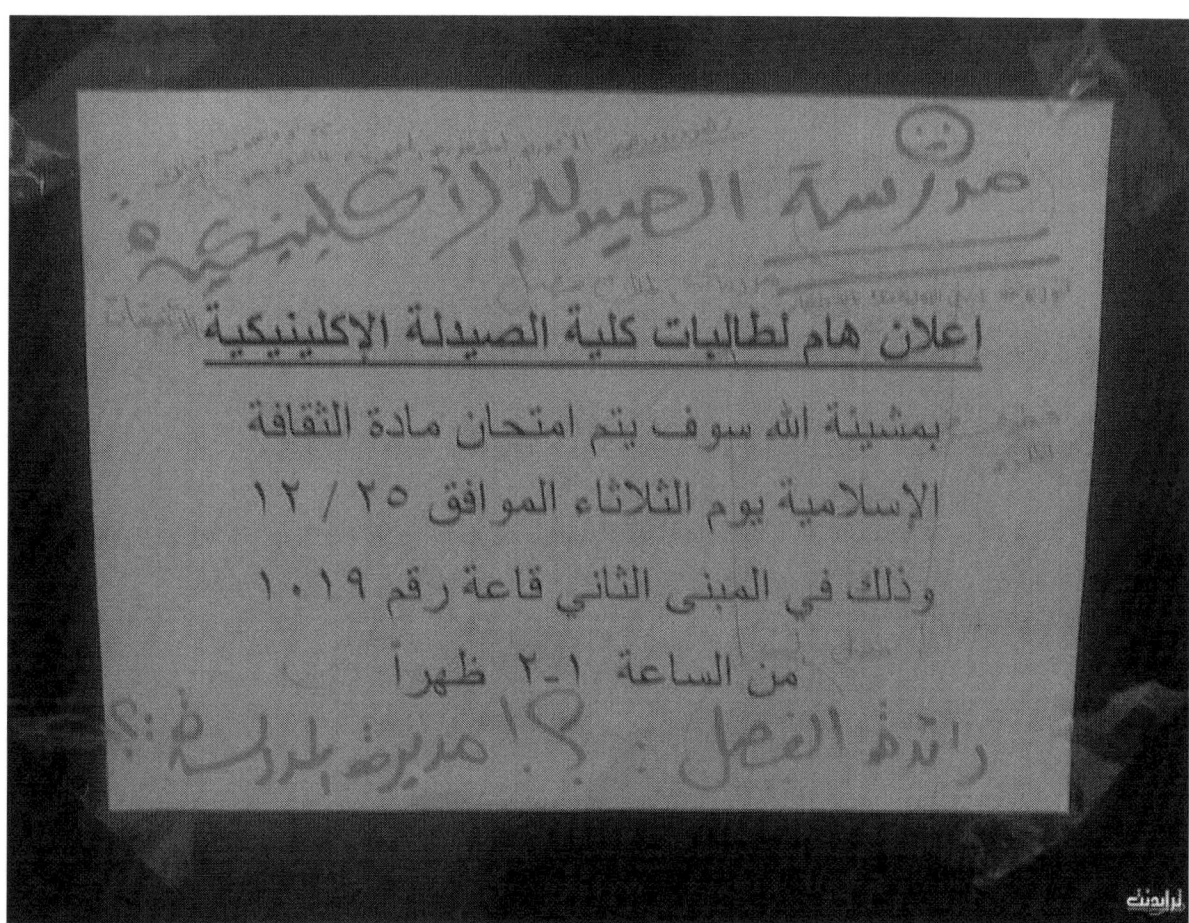

Translation

Printed text: An important announcement for the [female] students of the clinical pharmaceutical college: God willing, the Islamic culture exam will take place on Tuesday, 12/25 at the second building, Hall number 1019 from 1-2pm.

Handwritten Text:

Top: Clinical Pharmaceutical School

Bottom: Class [Female] Leader: School [Female] Principal

Culture

This is an announcement for the female students of a clinical pharmaceutical college regarding the upcoming Islamic Culture exam.

As here in America, wily students scribble funny notes on school posters. In this particular announcement, one student has changed the word *college* to *school*, thus debasing the institution. On the bottom, she is asking where are the names of the people who made the announcement and the name of the headmaster or the principal of the school that should approve it.

In the Arab education system, all-female schools will also have all female faculty and staff members; everyone from the custodians to the principals will be female.

☪On a number of occasions, newspapers reported that male paramedics were denied access to a female student in the throes of medical emergency; more than once, the student died. In most instances, the school administration barred paramedics because the girls within were improperly covered; too, they did not want a male paramedic to treat a female patient. This has happened in both schools and universities.

Religion is taught as a mandatory subject in all levels of the Arab education system until college and in some conservative Arab countries will continue to be mandatory throughout college. There are separate classes taught for Muslims and Christians; when it is time for religion class, the Muslim students will remain in the classroom, while the Christian students will go to another room to be taught.

In Arabic language, when writing dates the day will come before the month, so December 25th would be written as 25/12. *Zohr,* the Arabic word for the time at the middle of the day, carries a range of nuances. Whereas the English "noon" has become disconnected from the high point of the sun's progress and is now regulated by the clock, the sun's peak still determines the *zohr*, which is the time for the second of the daily prayers. Furthermore, *zohr* encompasses the entire mid-day period to around 3 p.m., during which that prayer can be performed.

Translation

Title: *During summer vacation*
On the signs, the students spell out the word "boredom."

Culture

In the Arab world, a student's options during his summer vacation are substantially limited. First, there is no concept of a "summer job" or a "part-time job," and what most Westerners would consider part-time employment—say, at

the register in McDonald's—is occupied year-round with full-time, very qualified workers. Secondly, there exist severe travel restrictions in most Arab countries, which were established in the wake of the

September 11th attacks. As most governments won't grant a full seven-year passport until a citizen has completed his military duties—or, in the case of women and male only-children, their civil service obligation—students are left to scramble for temporary "student passports," which expire after six months. They must also apply for a visa, a process which entails an extensive background check that can take longer than the summer vacation itself. On the off-chance that one does secure a visa in a timely fashion, travel costs often prove exorbitant and prohibitive. A few lucky students travel abroad to Europe, and find work there. Others travel domestically, visiting vibrant coastal towns—but the cost of such outings is likewise prohibitive. Accordingly, most students pass their vacations at home—sleeping through the day, spending all night with friends. For entertainment during these long, hot, interminable days of summer, there are a number of open-air movie theaters, wherein a student can wile away the hours. However, the social clubs—which offer athletics, leisure and socializing, and are similar to American country clubs—are the reserve of the very wealthy. Of course, these activities apply to those fortunate enough to have passed their final exams. Those who did not must spend the summer studying for re-instatement exams, which are held a few weeks before school starts.

☪ Drifting (*tufheet* in Arabic) is a sport of making dangerous, acrobatic moves with a car while moving at high speeds, twisting and swerving a car on the streets,

This perilous pastime is very popular among rich and bored young men, who have the financial means to buy the most powerful and expensive cars in the world and who consider drifting a worthwhile test of a driver's skill. They engage in drifting both in drag racing and also on the Arab highways, and making it a major cause of accidents, especially in Saudi Arabia. One specific type of car trick is aptly called "the death movement" and involves speeding to around 115mph and then suddenly maneuvering it onto its side two wheels, finally skidding to a stop. Also popular amongst these devil-may-care motorists are rounds of "chicken," or speeding two cares directly towards one another with the first to pull away declared the loser for his failure of nerve.

☪ The Gulf area has an extraordinarily high percentage of car ownership; more than 100,000 new cars are sold every year in Saudi Arabia alone, and one in two Kuwaitis own a car. There are around 3 million cars in Saudi Arabia for its population of 21 million, a high number next to comparable countries, especially considering that half the population is not allowed to drive.

17 — High School Exam

Translation

Title: How to Pass the High School Exam

Man with the coat: Professor Albert Einstein

Man with the wig: Sir Isaac Newton

Man by door: "Would you like more coffee, Mr. Isaac?"

Culture

Passing the High School Exam is not enough, students have to excel in it in order to be able to go to a good university. The competition is fierce and private tutoring from a good teacher is an important factor in attaining success. The cartoon suggests that private tutoring from the most brilliant minds is required for success in the exam

☪ It is customary for the parents of students to be extremely hospitable to tutors by plying them with food and drinks and always checking to see if they need anything. This is done to ensure that the tutor does a good job. This custom extends to all paid workers in the home (e.g. plumbers and carpenters) who are also offered cigarettes in addition to drinks. Meals are always offered if a mealtime coincides with the time spent working in the home.

☪ The High School exam is the Freddy Kruger of the Arab world, putting fear in the eyes of students. It is not unusual in the month of June to find headlines mentioning the death of students, who have killed themselves after performing poorly in the exam. In a country such as Egypt, the exam can be taken by as many as a million youngsters, and students and families commit themselves fully to doing well on these tests, as entrance to the top colleges (such as those for medicine, pharmaceuticals, economics, engineering, and political science) depend on the outcome. Most students prepare themselves very well for the exam, but limit their studies to the curriculum and go to take it fully confident they will perform well, since they have spent the past few months preparing, testing, and retesting themselves on the material in the curriculum. When they finally enter the exam hall, and find a question that is "outside of the curriculum" panic sets in that can freeze their thinking. They can see their parents' hopes and dreams evaporating before their eyes. This feeling is not limited to individual students, but starts from a single student's expression of shock and panic, and spreads throughout the hall and through the building. The building will fill with shocked and screaming students, and this is when tragedies occur, when a distraught student can try to kill himself or herself by jumping out of a window. The panic can also spread to the street, since concerned parents will come along to provide emotional support and wait outside for their children to finish the exam. Upon hearing the screams from the building, panic hits them as well.

This panic manifests itself in screaming, anger, hysterical crying, leaping from windows, or cutting oneself with broken glass from windows. The families outside sometimes break into the secured building, attempting to figure out what is happening to their screaming children. There can even be demonstrations in front of the Education Ministry, against the Minister and his staff for creating such challenging tests. When the Egyptian Minister of Education said he would personally visit any student who scored ninety percent or more on the exam, many parents considered this boast of the exam's difficulty to be a belligerent challenge. Some went to police stations in order to file a report against the Minister and his administrators. Many people begged the president to interfere on their behalf, so as to save them from the horror of the High School exam. Added to this is the strange situation by which the top marks may well be in excess of 100% as the exams can include optional questions for candidates who wish to show their ability.

Other parents threaten to not allow their children to take the test until something is done about its difficulty. Some legislators have even called for an inquiry into the inclusion of questions that were outside the scope of the curriculum. The trouble with an exam that adheres strictly to material covered in the classroom is that the level of preparation by students is such that many would receive perfect scores, and the truly gifted would be no different from the relatively studious. This line of argument is not accepted by those who want to see the students who have learned the given material succeed no matter what. In this picture a father, who has been waiting with other parents for his daughter, reacts angrily to her news that the exam included material outside of curriculum, as she sobs uncontrollably.

To resolve the issue of widespread anger and complaints, two to three days after the exam is taken, Ministry of Education officials sample a number of the exam scripts and will always announce good scores, thus assuaging any residual anger. However, the results that appear two months later will bear very little relationship to these samples, and may well be significantly lower. Over the years, those following the exam have seen no relation between the perceived difficulty of the exam and quality of student scores. Some years students and parents may complain a lot, but scores are high, while a year where there is little frustration may see a fall in scores. The Ministry may also decide to weight marking so that questions that were answered poorly will be allocated fewer marks.

Translation

Title: High school exams

Child: Father, the private tutor has arrived.

Language

In Arabic, when a person is likened to a saw, he is said to be "going up eating and going down eating." This refers to the motion of a saw, which cuts through any material no matter what direction it moves in. The saying is used to describe a person who makes money no matter what he is doing. The term "saw," however, carries bad connotations, comparable to the American slang term "hustler," but may also have connotations of jealousy on the part of the person using it.

Translation

Education minister: "Education is in good shape, people. The leak has happened because there's something wrong with the plumbing. Of course, our teachers made a leak proof exam."

The cartoon plays upon two meanings of the word "leak": the leak of a faucet, and the "leak" of information—in this case, exam materials.

Culture

High School Exam Leaks

The High School Exam is the the most important exam in the Arab world, as it is the exam that determines if a student has successfully completed his schooling. The results of this exam will have a profound effect on an Arab student's life much like the way an accumulated grade point average will affect a student's future plans. In the Arab world, it is not necessarily a college or university that holds prestige but rather the track that

does. Medical or engineering studies are regarded with the utmost esteem. If a student receives a high score on High School Exam, he will be encouraged to begin on the path to attaining the prestigious title of doctor or engineer, which will earn him the highest respects of society. If a student receives a low score, his future will likely not be as promising.

Arab families will spare no expense, ensuring that their children receive the highest scores on these exams by any means necessary. An Arab household with a student scheduled to take the High School Exam at the end of the academic year can be compared to a military training camp. The child himself is sequestered, and the rest of the family will change its lifestyle drastically to accommodate the child's preparation. They will stop receiving guests, taking vacations, avoid the room in which he's studying and even the rooms adjacent, keep the house quiet and will not participate in fun activities, so as to avoid tempting the student to join in. Generally speaking, the child will receive whatever he or she needs to pass the high school exam. The students themselves are under immense pressure because of this exam. Some may suffer nervous breakdowns or even commit suicide.

The exam results may reflect the disparities between classes, as the more money a family has, the better off their child will be. Wealthy families can hire expensive, experienced private tutors to help prepare their child. Poorer families will do their best to help their child, but they simply do not have the resources to hire the best tutors.

Sometimes the exams are leaked prior to the exam date. Copies of the exam can be obtained by the highest bidder, if he knows where to look. Israeli intelligence, Mossad, became aware of the importance of this exam to the Arabs and so, from 1967 to 1973, Mossad obtained the exam questions and broadcast them on the radio for the Arab students to hear. High School Exam leaks still occur in Arab countries. The actual exam paper arrives in sealed envelopes at school district offices twenty-four hours prior to the exam, after which the paper will be distributed to the individual schools and kept under the guardianship of a district manager. An unscrupulous district manager may be very tempted to leak the exam for the right amount of money.

Since the exam is sealed in an envelope, a manager who wants to leak the exam will take the envelope and use a small, sharp razor to make a tiny incision in the top corner of the envelope. The manager will then take a thin pencil and cover it with glue. Carefully, he will slide the pencil into the envelope and spin the pencil. This will cause the exam paper to wrap around the pencil, and if wrapped tight enough, the pencil and the exam paper will be small enough to pull through the hole in the envelope.

Translation

Title: Who stole the High School Exam?

Culture

Securing the High School Exam

The High School Exam is a countrywide test, and since a student's entire future may ride on the outcome, security procedures must be employed equal to those used for printing and storing bank notes or

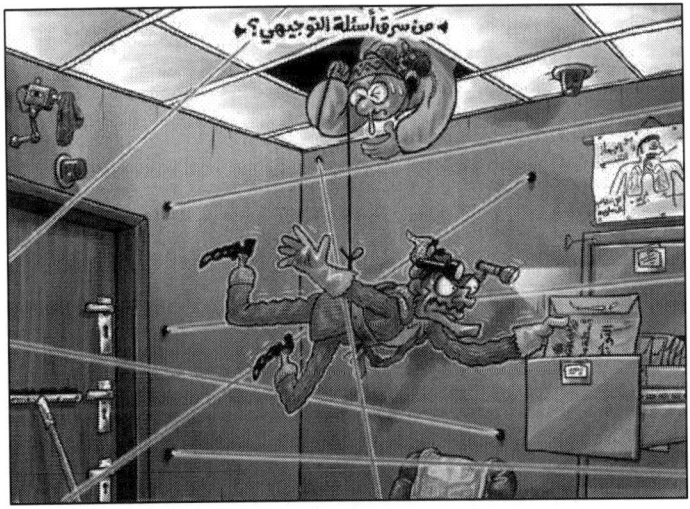

passports to prevent any leaking of questions. The entire process is overseen by the Minister of Education. Each subject section of the exam is written by a committee that is chosen from the best teachers in the country, as well as other experts on the subject who work for the Ministry of Education. The committee is under strict oversight for security, and the integrity and honesty of the members is made sure of.

Upon completion of creating the exam (which merits national news coverage), the final draft is transported to the "Secret Printer," of which there is only one, and the papers remain there unprinted until right before the exam, when hundreds of thousands of copies are published and distributed. The initial draft is under extensive security and is held at the printer's for safe keeping. This period of limbo, when the exam is written but unpublished, is generally about two weeks. All steps in the process from delivery of the draft onward are tightly scheduled.

While printing, all workers at the "Secret Printer" are prohibited from bringing cell phones, CDs, cameras, or anything that could transfer data outside the walls of the press. There is someone to log all activities of those working, and IT and maintenance personnel inside the facility must gain security clearance. The writers of the exam are allowed, at certain times, to enter the printer's and review the first printed version. They are assigned to a room, far from the publishing site and storage facility. No subject committee is given the same room or review time. After review, each room is swept to make sure no scrap paper has been left behind.

Once each subject is printed, all incorrectly printed copies are separated, along with draft papers, and stored in a secure location, inside the security perimeter of the building, until they can be destroyed.

The questions are then split and put in sealed envelopes for the locations where the tests will be taken. Boxed up, the name of the subject, name and location of exam site and dates of exams are stamped on the outside. The seal of the printer is finally pressed on each box. This process is overseen by a distribution committee. Each province has exam centers, separate from the test-taking sites, where the exams are stored upon delivery to the province, later to be distributed.

As in the U.S., schools are separated by grades, generally into three age-bands (primary, middle and high), with a building for each. By the time the exam is given, school is out so there is plenty of vacant space available for test takers, not only at high schools, and they are purposely assigned to schools that are not their own, so that they do not know any of the staff or faculty.

The president and committee members of the exam locations pick up the exams from their province's main distribution centers after providing verification of their identity and presenting a letter from the Ministry declaring their status as a committee member. Before leaving, they double-check that the proper number of exams were given.

Transportation of the Exam

The exam is moved by national police, who devise a plan for securing the boxes during the distribution to the different provinces. All working at the exam locations, both committee members and proctors or invigilators, are assigned to provinces that are not their home province. This is a point of contention for many teachers, assigned to locations very far from where they live. Some simply do not show up, but they are severely punished.

Distribution is overseen by various security departments, as the tests cross many borders, so each level of travel has different oversight. In one province it may have the local police, then after crossing the border it will receive new oversight from the new province's police. The exam arrives only thirty minutes prior to the scheduled start time. The distribution center for each district must be in the center to minimize travel time, and the caravan in which it travels has direct protection. The center also must be above ground level and it must have barred windows. Transportation of the exam occurs with buses used specifically for this purpose, accompanied by police. No private cars are allowed to move exams—though the press will publish "gotcha" photographs of officials breaking this stipulation.

Everything is carefully documented, and many entities are notified when distribution begins, including police and fire departments, so they can coordinate their efforts. All locks during this process must be new, and then destroyed after the exam is given. The exam is usually given two subjects per day, covering several weeks, and this process is repeated every day that the exam is given.

Translation

Title: The cancelling of the Tests.

Son: "Help me, father, they've canceled the High School Exam. What shall I do? Give me advice. Guide me."

Father: "I'll dedicate a song to you: 'We wrote what we wrote and alas, we lost what we wrote.'"

On the blackboard is a mixture of serious and funny writing. The serious writing refers to the subject the people are studying. The funny writing is a verse from a famous song by Umm Kalthoum under the square root (which is drawn right to left in Arabic), saying "you are unfair and criminal"—which could refer to the education officials who have canceled the exam. Under the blackboard there is a comment in the form of a question on the exam leak: "If five exams are leaked to three private schools, calculate the percentage of the leak."

The son has the crib written on his arm.

Written at the top of the blackboard, as is the norm, and never erased: "In The Name of Allah, the most compasionate, the most merciful."

Culture

When a major exam, such as the High School Exam, is leaked it will be canceled and students have to wait for the process of writing and printing the exam again before they can take it. The discovery of a leak generally occurs either during the final days of the exam, or after taking it. This is of course problematic for those who did not cheat and discover they must repeat the entire process a month later.

Radio programs will interview people on the street and at the end of the interview they will be invited to dedicate a song that is linked to their interview, so the father offers to dedicate a song that is appropriate to his son's situation.

In classrooms, unsupervised students will often write silly comments on the classroom blackboard at the end of the day or in a break, as if to cancel or contradict its usual contents.

Translation

On right: "Brother, what is the secret behind female students always beating us in high school? Most of the A-list is them."

On left: "There is no secret or watermelon. Honestly, girls focus on their study and we focus on girls."

Language

The Arabic phrase "no secret or watermelon (*batteeikh*)" means that there is no secret or anything else about the thing in question. The word "secret" can be replaced by any other word to deny the existence or the condition of the word in question. For example, "no love or watermelon" means that there is no love or anything else.

Culture

As here in America, girls in the Arab world are usually more serious than boys about studying. Often, they receive higher grades on a national level. The reason for this is the same as in America: girls are able to focus more than boys. Because girls in many Arab countries do not have as much freedom as boys (to go out to malls, have a boyfriend, etc.), they have a lot of time on their hands that they use for their studies.

☪ This is the picture of the top six scorers on the 2010 High School Exam in Egypt. As you can see, four of them are women. It is also notable that all of them come from small cities in more rural parts of Egypt, where life is slower with fewer opportunities for entertainment and distractions. Notice all of the girls are wearing Islamic attire. In Arab countries, they also give rankings of those with special needs, those in jail, and the blind. In these rankings, too, women dominate, with a woman topping the blind group as well.

Like these students, many of the most important and influential figures in the Arab world, from politicians to actors, writers and scientists, come from rural towns and villages.

Translation

Title: Home High School Diploma.
Man: "I don't think I'm going to get a good grade because I'm applying from home …Just a bedroom and a living room."

There are two methods of obtaining a high school diploma in some Arab countries: either one goes to school to study and receives a standard high school diploma as a result, or else one applies to sit the exam from outside the school system and obtains a diploma, similar to the GED in the United States. *Homes* is the name given to the second of these methods of entering the exam.

The cartoon plays upon this educational usage of the term "home," using the notion of a small or diminutive house—"just a bedroom and a living room"—as a metaphor for a lack of studying and preparation—and, consequently, a low grade.

Language

The terms "homes" or "from home" could also be used to refer to incompetent person professionally, like referring to a self-study doctor for example.

Culture

Those who apply to sit the exam from outside the school system, as *Homes*, are usually those who cannot attend school in the normal manner, including prisoners, the sick, those who have been expelled, foreigners and a variety of other minor categories. What distinguishes them all is that they will generally score poorly compared with regular students, since they have not had the specialized preparation and their life-circumstances probably also militate against effective study. These exams are usually marked separately from the rest, so that the graders are not too severe in their grading, as they might be if they came upon a script among a pile of those from well-prepared school students. This separate marking has been exploited by wily tacticians who will put themselves into this category in order to shine—which they do by getting themselves expelled, either through excessive absence, or through by breaking the rules in a sufficiently heinous fashion. They have to be confident that they will not need to re-enter the school system for a retake, so it can be something of a calculated gamble.

Translation

Title: A warning to our dear high school seniors whose failure is expected this year.

Right panel:

Boy smashing cell phone: God damn Rome! I failed!

Middle panel:

No, no, it's impossible! Boo hoo hoo.

Left panel:

Boy eating newspaper.

Text underneath: Learning you've failed your exams via phone or Internet can result in harm and financial loss you'd be better without.

[Final panel:] Choose the safest and cheapest method, and learn it from the newspapers.

Language

The boy smashing his cell phone damns "Rome" in his frustration because saying, vaguely, "God damn!" is impossible in Arabic. In outbursts like this, Arabic speakers direct their curses at some neutral focus — no one near him is likely to be offended that he has damned the far-off, Italian city.

Culture

It is impossible to overstress the importance of the High School Exam to students, since it will determine what paths are open to them for their future. Reactions are therefore extreme, even if it is only because their grades are a little lower than expected.

The easiest method of finding out the exam results is to go to the school, and the school, anticipating emotional reactions, usually hangs the results on the school gates or a fence. The school also announces the results through a loud-speaker, and they are effectively anonymized as each candidate has a distinctive "seating number." Those who go to the school gates in person are usually those who are fairly confident, and many people will send a family member to find out. The results will also be published in a national newspaper, while the national radio station will also broadcast the whole roster of results, province by province. Nowadays the results can be picked up via the Internet or mobile telephone. The cartoon here warns about learning one's results via a breakable device, and the consequent physical or financial pain.

As for the lucky few who attain top grades at a national level (like the six students in the photograph above) they will usually receive a personal call from the Minister of Education, and will be showered with gifts from government ministries, newspapers, and the establishment, and will become celebrities for a while. Most importantly, the doors of any university and any faculty will be open to them. In most cases, however, their level of excellence is not matched in their university careers, so that they seldom achieve the best degrees. Part of the reason for this is that the methods that served well in school may no longer work for university, but another part is the jealousy of university professors who like to cut these high-achievers down to size.

18 — Work Place and Bureaucracy

Translation

Title: The Employee's Breakfast.

On the floor: "Document [Requires processing by an employee]."

Nameplate on desk: "Division Manager."

People squeezed behind the door: Citizens

White container on top of file cabinet: "Salt."

Culture

Arab employees usually have breakfast at work after the start of the business day. People usually get to work between 7 and 8 a.m. and the clock here indicates that it is already 9—which explains the throng of people outside, waiting impatiently to conduct their business. Usually, co-workers and supervisors gather to eat together at the desk of one of the employees. It is considered very rude to interrupt a person's meal, especially if this person has the authority to delay your business. In this type of situation, a smart citizen would wish the civil servants a healthy appetite and wait somewhere out of sight until they have finished eating. The same goes for other personal activities, such as praying, that an employee may engage in. Some of the cartoons that follow offer nuggets of advice about how to expedite dealings with officialdom.

☪ As this picture and the following one show, the Arab breakfast is a heavy meal that can sustain people through the day, since the concept of the lunch break has not yet caught on, and the average worker will not eat before the end of the workday, usually around 3 p.m., and many will wait until they return home to have it. Breakfast is therefore the meal that they are most likely to eat outside of the home. Food items could include fava beans, felafel, eggs, feta cheese (most likely), hot peppers, tomato, cucumber, salad, tahini, vegetable pickles and split bea soup (depending on the season). Bread is staple and the average person will eat at least two rounds of bread similar in style to pita, but twice the size. Arabs most like to drink tea, according to the method called *talqima*, where the leaves are put in cold water and brought to the boil making a strong, dark tea, as can be seen here brewing on an electric stove while the breakfast is eaten. The breakfast is meant to give energy and warmth since they usually don't eat a heavy dinner and their morning commute could be taxing. For those who don't have the opportunity to eat with their fellow workers at their desks, will usually have to make do with a quick stop at a street vendor or restaurant. Arabs usually wash their mouth with soap and water after eating.

Prayer Time in Work Places

Many restaurants, coffee shops, supermarkets, malls, businesses, and government offices will stop work during prayer time. Usually it takes between fifteen minutes and a half hour to perform prayers and resume operation. These breaks usually occur during *zuhr* (noon) and *asr* (afternoon) prayers, because these occur during working hours. In malls, restaurants, supermarkets, and shops they will announce that the store will be closed for the duration of prayer time. The store keepers usually close the store while the shoppers are inside, which annoys many because they can't leave and women, especially, do not like finding themselves alone with foreigners or non-Muslims. Women may also feel threatened due to the fear that a fire or other emergency will occur during prayer time, and they will be unable to leave the store and find safety.

Usually the clients in a government office will stay and wait until the employees have finished their prayers and supplications. The employees pray beside their desks if there is no other place available, but many businesses and large establishments set a place aside for their employees and customers to pray during the day. Places of prayer outside of mosques are plentiful in the Arab world, in government offices, airports, and large malls, and these areas are like mini-mosques. These will not have an official imam, but anyone who memorizes Qur'anic verses can act as imam, or leader of the prayer, and will be helped by the others present if his memory falters.

If you are a Muslim client at a government office and prayer time comes, it is not courteous to pray in the same office space with employee who is praying, so he will forego his prayers and wait, or leave for prayers. Usually when someone who has been at prayer returns to his work or desk, the client who has been waiting will greet him with "*Haramun*," which means "sanctuary," and refers to the holy site of the Kaabah in Mecca or the burial-place of the Prophet in Medina. The sanctuary in Kaabah is a place of immunity and safety, as no harm may come to anything inside it. *Haramun* means that the speaker and the person will pray together in Mecca or Medina. The appropriate answer to this is "*jamaan*," "together."

Prayer is not protected as such, so the same strictures do not apply areas where it is not practical to take a break, such as banks and financial businesses, in general in the private sector, or where the manager is unsympathetic—a Christian or non-religious boss is under no obligation to allow employees to be absent from their posts at prayer-time.

Translation

Title: The Return of the Female Teachers. The sign above the doorway reads "Girl's School.

Culture

Government employee breakfasts pale in comparison to those organized by women teachers. As seen in this and the previous cartoon, it is not unusual for Arab teachers and workers, especialy those who work for the government and cannot be fired easily, to enjoy a large meal at their desks prior to beginning work. Both men and women bring food to share with their co-workers. As is common, these teachers wake early in the morning to cook food that has been specified in a schedule that tells each person what dish she is bringing on any given day. If a person fails to bring the food that was assigned to her, the other teachers will be very angry and make it clear that she has let them down. The children will likely eat sandwiches that their mothers have packed for them. Even though pita is by far the most common bread in Arab countries, it doesn't hold up well when packed in advance, so schoolchildren's sandwiches are usually made with thick Italian bread.

☪ Note the woman carrying a container of food on top of her head. For walking longer distances, Arab women will often carry objects in this way to leave their hands free. Many times they will wind a scarf around their heads to aid with balancing round objects, such as baskets. This technique also provides a cushion for their heads. This practice is well pronounced in the countryside where female farmers must travel between their fields and homes and allows them to carry larger amounts of goods in a single trip. The skill of headbalancing is a point of great pride for many Arab women and has been celebrated as an artform, readily seen in the Shamadan dance. This performance involves elements of belly dancing, while the performer carries a large burning candellabra atop her head.

☪ The Saudi teachers have been driven to school with their giant trays of food by chauffeurs. Like all females, small girls must be entirely coverd, but their faces and hair can be showing. Their cars will most likely be large American models, especially the luxury SUVs, such as the Suburban and Escalade, since they prefer cars that can accommodate a large family and plenty of belongings.

Translation

Title: Business Hours During Ramadan

Boss: "Excellent, excellent, today there are five fasting and two non-fasting. Everyone can leave early except Abu Mahjoub and Abu Muhammad, may God bless you. Dismissed."

The employees are sticking their tongues out to prove that they are keeping their Ramadan fast (a fasting person will have a dry tongue). Though effective, such a test is usually reserved for children). One of those two who has been ordered to stay has tongue that is not dry and the other's is black, indicating he ate something.

Culture

There are fringe benefits that go along with fasting, such as a shorter workday, so some people may say they are fasting when they aren't.

As the cartoon shows, Ramadan fasts have a great effect on work schedules. Business hours change during Ramadan to accommodate the different sleeping-waking pattern brought on by fasting. Usually, the work day will end around 3 p.m. to give people time to go home and prepare food. The work day will also start later because people must wake up and have a meal at least an hour before sunrise. Shops stay open later at night to accommodate patrons who prefer shopping after breaking their fast and watching TV or listening to the radio.

In private-sector companies in which the management has leeway about how long to stay open and how long to require the staff to work, non-Muslim workers can often continue their usual schedule, which is why, in the cartoon, some workers are dismissed and others—those who are not fasting—carry on with their work day.

Translation

"Hypocritical employee keeps warming up (his tongue) before going in."
On door: "Manager"

Culture

In Islam, hypocrisy (in Arabic, *nifāk*) is mentioned several times in the Qur'an as one of the worst sins, and hypocrites are promised the worst of punishments by God. Islamic extremists equate hypocrisy in times of war with spying and punish hypocrites by execution.

Hypocrisy is not regarded in the same light in Arab countries and America. In addition to the normal definition of this word, in Islam, an additional meaning defines hypocrites as those people who pretend to be friends or allies of Muslims, while, in actuality, they are willing to do anything possible to harm Muslims. It is for this reason that God promises to mete out the severest punishments to hypocrites.

Translation

"Believe me my dear manager, the fondness I have for you in my heart is as much as the hair on my head."

Culture

As anywhere, employees will sweet-talk their manager the best they can. In countries where men wear a headdress, they can take it off while at their office (just in case you thought they wore it all the time). They do wear it in the street however.

18 — Work Place and Bureaucracy

Translation

Title: Government Internet

Official: Here is the signature. Get lost, we have work to do. Close the door behind you.

Citizen: Indeed, brother. Since you've gotten the Internet, everything has become faster.

Sign on wall reads: Bright Anger

Language

"Bright Anger" is a verse from the patriotic song *Zahrat al-Madaen* ("The Rose of All Cities") by the Lebanese singer Fayrouz, who is the second most famous Arab singer after Umm Kalthoum. The song describes the anger of Arabs toward the occupation of Jerusalem.

In Arabic when something is compared to a rose, such as "The rose of all cities" or "The rose of youth," it means that it is the best of all.

The cartoon juxtaposes the anger that Arabs feel towards the occupation of Palestine with the anger that government employees feel towards citizens interrupting their daily routine. From the looks on the employees' faces, we can imagine what they are looking at, and why they would rather get through their official work quickly.

Culture

Like many official entities, Arab governments have begun using online services to ease citizen interaction. Their bureaucracies are convoluted, so that finding what is needed and where and who can help can be a very involved process. The hope is that the Internet will make the government more efficient, as well as reducing opportunities for bribery and corruption. They also hope to cut down the amount of traffic on the streets, but since most Arabs do not have computers at home, and therefore rely on Internet cafés, this entails going somewhere other than home—so adding to traffic. The country that has had the greatest success in implementing digital government has been Tunisia.

☪ The man on the far right with the cup of tea on a tray is the "Office Boy," a grown man who cleans the office, makes tea for the employees and their guests, he sells tax stamps, and if there is bribery going on in the office he can work as a go between for the government employees and the citizens.

Translation

Gentleman on right: "I can't stamp the document. You have to get it signed first."
Gentleman on the left: "I can't sign the document. You have to get it stamped first."

Culture

Arab citizens deal with bureaucracy every day and this daily frustration is part of the problem, as it schools people to be uncooperative and unhelpful themselves. They experience what Joseph Heller called "Catch 22." For an outsider, this looks like a sadistic way of treating citizens. Those in authority take pleasure in seeing people bewildered by regulations, but they do not generally intend torture: their aim is to secure a bribe, after which they will give the petitioner what he or she came for. If everything worked smoothly and people could complete their business without bureaucracy, there would be no need to pay bribes. As you can see from the citizen's face here, it is the ordinary people who need to interact with government and need the assistance of these officials. If you are rich you don't have to deal with these rules, but if you are poor they are frustrating beyond Western belief, so that people whose lives are already hard feel powerless to change their fates. Authority is ruthless, as a long history of dictatorship has reinforced, so people are taught to go with the flow and not resist, to learn the resignation and patience which Islam also enjoins. So people are patient and hope for eventual change.

☪ The shabby appearance of the citizen looking for his paper-work to be done is emblematic of the condition of the average person, *mowaten mutHoun*, "crushed citizen," who is suffering on every front: prices are high, health care is not adequately available, public transport is humiliating and borders on daily torture, and when he comes into contact with the vast bureaucracy of the government a new door of suffering and frustration opens up. As the following cartoon shows, "common sense" doesn't exist in the government dictionary.

Translation

On the paper: Application for apartment

Official: "Your application has been denied, respected one. What proof do you have for me that you are one of the victims of Al Doweiqa?"

Language

Arabic has a wide variety of terms of address, each with shades and subtlties that must be observed to avoid giving offense. "Respected one" serves, superficially, to mark respect and a degree of deference, yet it also implies a warning: there is an implicit reminder that he who is so addressed should control himself and not react in a rash manner that might be shameful and lose him respect. The bureaucrat in the cartoon uses it to ensure that the bandaged man does not become belligerent when his application is turned down.

Culture

In the fall of 2008, a large boulder from the Mokattam Mountain in Cairo came loose and fell down on Al Doweiqa, a shanty town below it, killing scores of people and injuring many more. The Egyptian government was very slow to respond and, as indicated in this cartoon, denied benefits to those who obviously needed them.

Translation

Title: Signing of an Official Document.

Right panel, above door: "Government Administration." Paper in hand, "Official document."

Left panel, on clothes: Various signatures with the title of the signee underneath.

Culture

Bueracracy in Arab countries is ridiculously complicated. When you look at any official document at its final stage, it will look like this cacophany of signatures and stamps.

Translation

Title: The Skills to Get Your Business Done

[*Clockwise from top right*]

[*In the text bubble pointing to the flies swarming around the man*]: Don't shower for a month. Eat onions and garlic. Don't clip your nails. This will make them get rid of you quickly and move your papers along fast.

[*In the bubble pointing to the man's full hand*]: Be ready for auxiliary services: a pen, Packet Fine, lighter, Marlboro airport, aspirin, and a new ring tone.

Nameplate: Wael Travolta

[*In the bubble pointing to the nameplate*]: Try to find out the last name of the person who handles your papers and take it from there: "How are you doing my uncle? How are you?" [After all,] We're not in Switzerland.

[*In the bubble pointing to the man's gently wagging, pointing finger*]: Try discreetly to attract his attention to your paperwork.

[*Pointing to the water bottle*]: Don't risk asking him for a pen or glass of water or looking at your watch; this could delay your papers considerably.

[*Pointing to the man's mouth*]: Say a lot of "baize wiping," such as the following: may God give you good health, may God give you strength and bon appetite.

[*And pointing to the man's mournful mien*]: Have a look of sadness and misery on your face so that he will feel sorry for you.

[*N.B. In Arab countries, influential people traditionally had desks covered in green baize cloth. This is the origin of the expression, "wiping the baize," literally meaning wiping a desk clean, but figuratively signifying a toadying effort to cajole one's way into a powerful man's approval.*]

The bureaucrat's name is an incongruous contradiction: the given name, "Wael," is an old, traditional Arab name, and his surname, "Travolta," is . . . not. To most Arabs, John Travolta is still Tony Manero, the preternaturally stylish and urban dancing phenomenon from *Saturday Night Fever*. This is probably not what the bureaucrat is like.

Culture

This cartoon pokes fun at the unbearable bureaucracy in Arab countries and the special skills required to get your paper work processed. The advice given to the man to speed up his paper work mentions the following:

Pen: Those who deal with Arab bureaucrats take every opportunity to expedite matters. To this end, a savvy suppliant will have a pen at the ready and immediately offer it for the bureaucrat's use in order to save time waiting for him to shuffle about his desk, looking for his own. As the pen thus offered is not returned, it also functions as a small bribe, and, therefore, high-quality pens are often more effective.

Packet Fine: "Packet Fine" is to the Arab world what Kleenex is to the Western, i.e. a brand name that has entered the language as a generic term for soft, disposable, facial tissue. Arabs often use such products to mop sweat as they soldier through the region's hot climate.

Lighter: Smoking is generally permitted in Arab offices. It is difficult, however, efficiently to carry out desk work while enjoying a cigarette, so bureaucrats' cigarettes are often lit and relegated, smoldering, to an ashtray. Their cigarettes are typically produced by Arab companies and are low-quality, so they quickly fizzle out when not being actively smoked. Therefore, someone hoping to deal with an Arab bureaucrat should have a lighter handy in order to assist with a re-light.

Marlboro airport: The citizen in the cartoon is also advised to bring with him a packet of Marlboro "airport" cigarettes as an additional offering. "Airport" signifies that they were bought in a duty-free shop in the airport and are high-quality, foreign-made Marlboros. Multinational companies like Marlboro often produce a different style of goods for Arab markets, and though these are generally favored over the products of local Arab companies, connoisseurs prefer the standard, Western-style product available only in duty-free shops.

Aspirin: A low-level bureaucrat's environment is loud, stressful, and busy, so many citizens may find their paperwork delayed by workers' headaches. Along with the other items mentioned in the cartoon, it is wise, therefore, to come with aspirin at the ready as an offering and palliative.

A new ringtone: As in the West and, indeed, all over the world, cell phones are ubiquitous in the Arab world. A new and interesting ringtone, therefore, can pique interest and begin a personal conversation, helping to forge a deeper rapport between the man behind and the man in front of the desk.

☪ The reference to Switzerland indicates how that country is considered as a pinnacle of impersonal, efficient Western business. Unlike dealings with Swiss disinterested efficiency, a warm greeting and a pleasant disposition can have a great effect on one's progress through Arab red tape.

☪ Family names are an important source of information about new acquaintances in Arab countries. Traditionally, people have been less prone to move from ancestral homelands, keeping families together through the generations. Therefore, upon meeting someone for the first time, one is often able to tell something of his background and status purely from his family name.

☪ In most Arab countries, it is the custom to eat, shake hands, wave a greeting with the right hand while the left hand reserved for certain "hygienic functions" or blowing the nose. It is impolite to offer the left hand for a handshake or to wave a greeting. Also according to the Qur'an, those who receive the book of their deeds on judgment day in the left hand will end up in hell. A Muslim will say in his prayer "O God, do not give me my book in my left hand, nor behind my back."

Greetings

Greetings are very important and you can't just walk by someone silently the way we do in America. So ingrained is the importance of a greeting to mark an entry or crossing of a threshold that Arabs traditionally will greet themselves when alone, speaking the customary formulae as though being greeted by God. The standard verbal Islamic greeting, often accompanied by a handshake, is, "*As salaamu alaikum wa rahmatullahi wa barakatuhu*," meaning, "Peace be upon you and His mercy and His blessing," or just the first half. It is said like "Hello" upon encountering someone. To respond or reply, one simply reverses it to, "*Alaikum salaamu*." Saying this greeting will dissolve hostility towards you. If you watch the news, you always see American soldiers in Afghanistan and Iraq saying this greeting to local people. Some people also use this greeting in answering telephone calls. A Muslim, however, when he receives this salutation from a person of another religion, sometimes replies, "And on you" (*Wa-'aleykum*).

Handshakes, though regarded as important, are not usually as firm as those of Europeans or Americans. Most Arabs shake hands every time they meet and every time they leave. This applies whether meeting on the street, in an office, at a conference, in a restaurant, or at home. If sitting down, it is proper to rise when shaking hands as well as when an esteemed person enters the room. If the handshake you receive when leaving somebody is longer than the one you received when first meeting, it indicates that you've made a good impression.

The general formal address for a man is *sayyed* ("sir"), which is easy to remember because both start with "S." The formal address for a woman is *sayeeda* ("ma'am") or *sayedity* ("my lady"), or Arab women can be addressed using the French word, *madame*. These formal addresses are followed by the person's name. Senior members of the society are called *sheikh* followed by the person's name. *Sheikh* (referring to a man) or *sheikhah* (referring to a woman) in modern Arabic usually refers to a person deeply versed in religion and Sharia law, one who recites the Qur'an professionally, or one who teaches others to do so.

When greeted, it is highly improper for an Arab man to remain seated, and he must stand up to return it. Greetings usually are returned either by repeating the same words or adding something to them. Within Arab culture, people are encouraged to start the greeting quickly and it is said that the better of the two is the first to greet. The etiquette regarding greetings is simple:

- Young people are encouraged to initiate the greeting when encountering older people.
- The person entering a location is supposed to start the greeting.
- It is very rude not to return a greeting at all. The culture dictates that if you were greeted you should then return the greeting with a better one. Even if you don't like the person who greeted you or whom you are supposed to greet, you are still required to say a greeting.
- Arab people tend to stress the replies with reference to being grateful to Allah. That is why many replies to greetings or to common expressions give thanks or show gratitude to Allah, as can be seen in other cartoons.

Arab punctiliousness about greetings extends as far as making it a point of courtesy to mark the change of a person's state with stock phrases of felicitation. Cleansing, purging, or purifying actions such as bathing, using the toilet, cutting hair, or wearing new clothes all come with associated phrases of well-wishing which can either be uttered upon first encounter after the change has taken place or in anticipation of the change if one will not be present afterwards. For example, if Muhammad leaves Ali to dress in a new suit and, while Muhammad is changing, Ali intends to leave, Ali will first tell Muhammad, "May you wear your new outfit in health"; but if Ali is planning to stay till Muhammad reappears, Ali will probably wait. These ritualized expressions of goodwill operate much as Americans saying "bless you" to someone who has sneezed.

Translation

Title: Solitaire!

On door: "Computer department"

Down on the door: "Raid."

Employee: "Hello sir, you've come at the right time. I'm working on a graph that represents the increase of productivity in the current month."

Language

Arabic graphs, like its writing, read from right to left. Therefore, if the manager believes the employee's excues, he not only thinks that his employee is innocent, but also that his company's overall productivity is improving.

The Arabic word for "raid," borrowed from police vocabulary, is comically over-blown for the situation depicted in the cartoon. In addition, it would not be uncommon for a company manager to be computer-illiterate, so the employee may, improbably, get away with his ruse.

Culture

As in America, employees in the Arab world have the same habits of playing computer games during work hours. Knocking on doors is courtesy not practiced in the work place since they considered a public area.

As you see from the cartoon, smoking is permitted in the work place in some Arab countries. Governments believe that it may not be a good idea to enforce the smoking bans everywhere, since smoking is a form of outlet for anger and is so entrenched in that culture that if people stopped smoking their frustration would be directed toward the establishment instead.

Translation

Sign above door: Business hours

Culture

This cartoon illustrates that some workers hate their jobs so much that they have to be dragged to work. It is easy to tell that many Arab employees hate their jobs and the monotony that come with it, pay is mediocre, offices are grim, weather is hot, most have jobs that are not related to what they studied at colleges and many people bring their home life into work place, this is slowly changing because of the unemployment affect and those who could land a job should strive to keep it.

Translation

Title: Summer Schedule...

Sign: Please do not disturb.

Desk: Government department.

Culture

During the summer months, the heat in Arab countries reaches oppressive temperatures. These extreme temperatures cause many people to feel lethargic, like the man in the above cartoon. By twelve or one o'clock in the afternoon, the heat will be at its highest temperature and because most offices do not have air conditioning, most workers will only want to sleep. Usually businesses will begin at seven in the morning and end at two in the afternoon, but during the summer months, it is not uncommon for businesses to begin at five in the morning and end at noon, so that they will be done before the temperatures get too high. These practices include government offices.

☪ Overall, Arab government employees are surprisingly underproductive: for example, the typical employee of the Egyptian government is estimated to work, on average, only 85 days each year.

☪ It is possible to distinguish an Arab person's origin by the color of his headdress. A checkered red-and-white headdress; called in Arabic *kufiya,* indicates a person from Saudi Arabia. Under this, an Arab man wears a small, close-fitting cap, slightly larger than a yarmulke. In the cartoon above, the slumbering employee is wearing this cap, while his *kufiya* is draped upon the nearby coat hanger.

☪ *Kufiyas* can be worn in a variety of ways, but many prefer to wear them on top of the head as a shield from the sun's strong rays. The derivation of the word "kufiya" is disputed, but the favored possibilities are the Iraqi city of Kufa—which was the traditional source of particularly fine *kufiyas* – or the word *"takou'uf,"* which means "roundness" and signifies the shape of the cloth on top of the head. Traditionally, *kufiyas* can be made of a variety of materials, including wool, flax, camel hair, cotton, and silk: cotton mixed with silk are favored for their breathability and lightness.

One wears one's *kufiya* with a long edge just over one's forehead so that the cloth drapes low over the back and sides of one's head. In addition to protecting one from the elements, this has the added advantage of providing an easy disguise, as either of the sides can be drawn up and over the lower portion of one's face.

Two variants on the *kufiya* that are commonly worn in the Gulf are the *ghutra* and the *sham'agh*. *Ghutra*s are extremely soft and made of nylon, silk, or wool. Unlike most *kufiyas*, they are a plain white or off-white, and with use, they take on the color of the dust of the desert, developing into the color from which the garment derives its name: *tagh'tear*. *Sham'agh*s, in contrast, have a regular checker-board pattern, with red, green, blue, or black squares set off against a white field. Saudi Arabia is particularly noted for the popularity of red *sham'aghs*, as you will have noticed in cartoons throughout this book.

When worn on the head, *kufiyas* are held in place with a thickly wrapped double band known as an *iqal*. These come in three varieties: *najdi*, *moukassab*, *esuid*. *Najdi* are brown *iqal* with decorative elements sewn in around the band, and *moukassab* have stiff, straight sides joined by tightly wound knobs of fabric, so that they form a regular polygon on one's head rather than a circular band. Both of these varieties have fallen into disuse, and the *esuid* dominates. It is a simple, black band made from the hair of a nanny goat. Though in modern times the *iqal* is primarily used to hold *kufiyas* in place, originally they also served to tie the forelegs of a camel to prevent its wandering off.

As the garment has become separated from its practical use, it has grown in symbolic value and now is taken to represent the wearer's honor, pride, and dignity. As such, it still serves a number of very important social functions in traditional, rural areas. Men in dire distress, for example, can plead for assistance by draping their *iqal* around the neck of a powerful personage from whom they require aid: this symbolically places the suppliant in the other's power. Such an abject request is usually granted, and only then do the involved parties discuss the particulars of the situation and possible resolutions. As a public badge of honor, it is expected that men who are considered to be disgraced will not wear it, at least until their dignity has been restored. Where honor killing is practiced, for example, a cuckolded man will forego their *iqal* until he has killed his offending wife.

Both the *kufiya* and the *iqal* are considered strictly masculine garments. The so-called sister of the *iqal* is the *osaba*, a length of cloth that women wrap around the top of their heads to keep their hair in place. The practice of wearing *osabas* is much like Western women's wearing of kerchiefs when engaged in strenuous labor, and they appear much the same. It is important to note that *osabas* are not considered to be part of the garb of devout Muslims, and they are not sufficient to fulfill the requirement that a woman keep her hair covered.

Translation

On chair: "Ministry of Social affairs"

Floor: "Applications for social help"

[*N.B. The newspaper is turned to the entertainment section.*]

Culture

In the Arab world, government is usually large and bureaucratic, and often times very inefficient. Many government employees engage in non work related activity during work hours—activities ranging from reading newspapers to leaving work to pray to even some women bringing vegetables to the office to clean to begin meal preparations—at the expense

of providing necessary services to citizen in need of them. The phrase "Come back tomorrow" is often heard in these government offices. In the cartoon, an employee at the Ministry of Social Affairs is doing a crossword puzzle, and neglects the many requests for help that are strewn about the floor of his office.

☪ Arab bureaucracy can be divided into tiers, and its ministries are not on equal footing with each other. The most bureaucratic ministries, which have the least qualified staff, deal with the lower segments of society. One such example would be the Ministry of Social Affairs. Other ministries—more efficient, with Western work ethic, and furnished with more impressive buildings—serve foreigners, diplomats, and the more privileged members of society. Examples of these ministries include the Ministry of the Exterior and the Ministry of Tourism. Manifestly, the motivation of the employees and the quality of the workplace improves along a continuum as the ministries are more removed from dealing with the society's needy citizens.

Translation

Electronic government:
Come back tomorrow
Agree, don't agree, cancel order

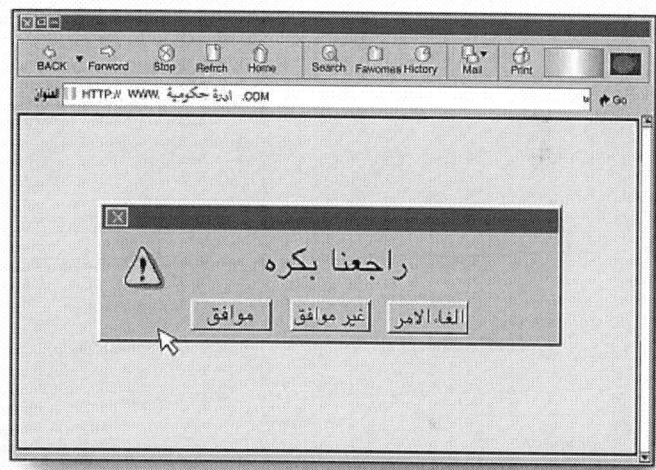

Even with the introduction of electronic government, in cyberspace one may still be instructed to "Come back tomorrow."

Culture

Arab governments implemented new technological interfaces to both expedite the bureaucratic process and minimize bribing.

Translation

Title: Strike of the Microbus Drivers and Train Conductors (In Arabic, train conductors are called train drivers.)

Pilot: "Ladies and gentlemen, please get off; I too am going on strike."

Culture

Since the recent introduction of democratic measures to some countries of the Arab world, such as Egypt, there has been a dramatic rise in the number of strikes, which had been practically unknown since the end of the Second World War. Strikes had been illegal in many Arab countries, with their organizers running the risk of the death penalty if they interrupted critical parts of the national economy. More recently there have been strikes to demand salary raises and improved working conditions, and in most cases the government has met these demands, which has encouraged others to strike, because they feel that this is the only way for their voices to be heard.

The execution of Mustafa Khamis and Muhammad al-Baqari

On August 12, 1952, the management of a factory in Kafr El-Dawwar, a major industrial city and municipality on the Nile Delta, transferred workers to the city of Koum Hamada in an unjustified disciplinary action. This, coupled with deterioration in pay and housing, and overall hopeless conditions, forced the workers into action. They were in the shadow of a new era and they believed action was justified in the wake of the recent revolution: the success of the July Officers (led by the future president of Egypt, Gamel Abdul Nasser) was fresh in their memories and revolutionary hopes were still being pushed by the propagandists, who declared support for farmers, workers, and promised the eradication of corruption and spread of justice.

When the workers thought that the situation and atmosphere were conducive to achieving their demands, a general strike was declared. All factory machinery was stopped, and crowds chanted, "Long live the national leader! Long live the Army Movement!" They were referring to Muhammad Naguib, the leader before he was ousted by his colleague, Nasser. To their surprise, the demonstrators found the police of the former regime surrounding them and firing, killing one. The demonstrating workers heard that the national leader was to pass by their factories, so they went out, calling on him to intervene. Upon arriving there, they found heavily armored police forces waiting for them. A bloody encounter ensued between the unarmed protesters and police. Tens were killed and hundreds arrested.

Gamal Abdul Nasser was the Minister of the Interior at the time, in charge of state police. A military tribunal was formed to put more than sixty protesters on trial, some of whom were in their early teens. Two of those arrested were Mustafa Khamis (a laborer) and Muhammad al-Baqari (a watchman), accused of inciting the demonstration. The resultant trial was little more than a show-trial, with these two main culprits yelling for lawyers throughout, claiming they were revolutionaries, calling for the national leader, and strong supporters of the spiritual movement. The judge asked the assembled crowd if there were any lawyers among them. Mousa Sabry, a journalist, was at the trial and held a license to practice law. He offered to defend the two, but his defense implicated them more than helped them, and he later became very famous and an intimate of both Presidents Nasser and Sadat.

The trial went on for four days with little evidence and no real defense, ending with the handing out of the death penalty to Mustafa Khamis, 18 years old, and Muhammad al-Baqari, who supported five children and whose mother was penniless and forced to sell radishes in the street to help support Muhammad's family. Ten life sentences with hard labor as well as several equally harsh, but shorter sentences were also handed down for other protesters. At the city's sports club, the workers were forced to sit in a large circle under the watch of heavily armed soldiers while listening in shock to the horrifying sentences from loudspeakers.

A congress of the revolution's leaders agreed on the sentences, and Naguib approved them, despite his belief that they were innocent, after Abdul Nasser convinced him of the need to deter such mutinies so no one would dare to repeat them. On September 7 both men were executed, with the media widely covering the event. Since then, no one dared to strike for a very long time until recent times.

Translation

"The manager is traveling. Everybody's traveling. Who am I? I am the secretary."

For Arabs, this is a funny cartoon because the man claiming to be a secretary is a foreign-looking janitor. Typically, Southeast-Asian immigrants occupy positions low on the socioeconomic totem pole, so for a janitor to feign possessing a more exalted post is a humorous absurdity.

Culture

Positions that are usually occupied by women in America, such as secretarial positions, are instead generally occupied by men. Usually when people clean in Arab countries, they do so without shoes, particularly during mopping which follows sweeping. Mopping is an important part of the cleaning process in the Arab world, because of significant amounts of dust and sand that stick to and dirty surfaces everywhere.

Translation

Office boy + guy with middle school education + man with university degree & 20 years' experience = the same salary

Culture

Incomes do not correlate with experience and education. The deeply flawed educational system produces a large surplus of workers with degrees and ambitions, yet there are relatively few people who are willing to work in menial jobs. Arab culture is strongly prejudiced against blue-collar trades; the very word for such jobs (*mihnh*) is etymologically descended from a word meaning "disgraceful" and "shameful." Thus, perversely, supply and demand work to keep their incomes roughly the same, especially when countless additional sums are added to the official salaries of menial positions. For instance, office boys demand fees for their errands and refreshment deliveries, and also frequently function as conduits for passing bribes to higher-ranking officials—bribes off of which they naturally skim.

19 – Immigrants

Translation

"No to naturalization!"

Culture

The "naturalizing" of foreigners is a supremely unpopular throughout most of the Arab world. For example, a person might be born in a country and still be denied citizenship there because his parents are immigrants. The hostility toward naturalization

springs from a variety of sources. The typical Arab society is a closed society with a conservative, devoutly religious populace; while most tolerate foreigners as tourists, there is a widely held belief that foreign residents serve as a font of social degradation, introducing uncouth and iniquitous practices into the community. Also, there exist very real economic concerns: many Arab countries suffer from a state-wide dearth of funding for essential services, as well as severe unemployment, and local populations fear that foreigners will snatch-up both jobs and resources that are too scarce to begin with. (Here, the American reader should note the similarity to conservatism's anti-immigration discourse, which traces a noticeably similar line of argumentation.) The cartoon above originates in Bahrain, which today faces a unique naturalization crisis. Although predominantly Shiaa, Bahrain is ruled by Sunni powers. Intending to displace the Shiaa as the national majority, the Bahraini leader is now attempting to naturalize some 260,000 foreigners. As expected, opposition to the plan is both widespread and vociferous.

Translation

The arrival of a new batch…

[N.B. *The masks indicate that the men are thieves.*]

Culture

The influx of immigrants to oil-rich countries in the Gulf has been met with contempt by the Arab people. The Gulf countries are not known for their political correctness. In this cartoon, the arrival of new Bangladeshi laborers and workers is portrayed as the arrival of a new band of thieves. The passion with which Bangladeshis are hated by many Gulf Arabs is appalling: they are far and away the most reviled immigrant group, and their criminality is assumed.

Almost all Arabs in the Gulf countries dislike immigrants, both Arabs and non-Arabs. These countries have enacted laws that allow immigrants to be treated as virtual slaves. Mistreatment ranges from withholding their passports to prevent easy exit from the country without the consent of their employer/sponsor to denying them acceptable standards of housing, even if this was included in the original employment contract. As shown in the cartoon above, these immigrants are the first suspects in any crime or accident that occurs.

Citizens of the Gulf countries feel that they are losing their culture and language to immigrants, because in some of the countries, natives only constitute 20 percent of the population and are thus forced to speak English in order to accomplish anything. This situation can be dangerous, when immigrants assume a position such as a doctor, and must exchange vital information with a patient. Because of these circumstances and the rising rate of unemployment, some governments have begun to require the private sector to hire or maintain a certain number of native employees in order to obtain permission to hire foreigners. Arab families are allowed to bring in five individuals as domestics; however, families sometimes object to the idea of their children being raised by people from outside their culture. Some families sell these visas for money.

Bounties on Illegal Aliens

In the Arabian Gulf, antipathy toward illegal immigrants has reached a fever pitch. In order to assuage public outcry, some governments have enacted legislation offering financial incentives to all those who report illegal immigrants to the authorities. Not surprisingly, the new policy has attracted the attention of those looking to make a quick buck, and statistics show that six out of ten folks reported as "illegal" are, in fact, legal residents of the country in question.

In the Gulf, support for the legislation derives from a startling discovery: each year, illegal immigrants (who are typically employed in menial or domestic labor) send abroad a total of $60 billion — or 10% of the country's annual oil revenue—to their families back home. In other words, 10% of the annual oil revenue is not being injected into the domestic economy.

However, the Arabian Gulf finds itself in a tough position. Foreigners perform a veritable surfeit of duties deemed insufficiently dignified for the regular Arab citizen; more importantly, such foreigners fill a number of necessary functions that the Arab population is too small to execute on its own adequately. In fact, the organization of contemporary Gulf society presupposes the presence of a foreign-born working class—without which, for one, the typical Gulf family estate could not operate (e.g. no gardeners, no chauffeurs, no housekeepers) and, for another, women—heretofore prohibited from driving—could not attend work or go about their various daily chores (i.e. no chauffeurs or cab drivers). To that end, the maintenance of a foreign chauffer/cabbie population is considered both eminently pragmatic and plainly necessary: without it, women would need to be allowed to drive—and the sudden, exponential increase in cars on the road (for wives, second wives, daughters, maids etc.) would lead to unmanageable traffic problems.

Why Immigrants in Arab countries Resort to Crime

Despite the cartoon's implications, Bangladeshis are not, in fact, the Gulf's most criminally active immigrant group. According to security statistics from the region, that dubious honorific belongs to the Yeminis, followed, in order, by Pakistanis, Indians, Bangladeshis, Egyptians, the Sudanese and Indonesians. Conversely, the immigrant group with the lowest crime rate is the Tunisians. The most commonly committed crimes amongst Gulf immigrant groups are, in order: the manufacture and distribution of drugs; theft; illegal residence within the country; the forging of official documents; prostitution, sorcery and augury; and *uquq'*, or disobeying one's parents (a criminal offense within the Gulf).

The disproportionately high crime rate among immigrant groups within the Arabian Gulf has both a socio-historical cause and an economic cause. As to the former, the relationship between immigrants and natives is today characterized by a destructive, deeply entrenched mutual enmity. Immigrants view natives as bigoted, decadent, exclusionary and hateful, while natives consider immigrants to be lazy, unscrupulous, filthy and ungodly. To a degree, the immigrants are correct in their assessment: natives will treat them with scorn and derision, vocal in their eagerness to see mass-scale deportation. Natives will make no qualms about this portrayal: natives *do* distrust them, *do* mistreat them and *would* like to see hordes of immigrants sent packing. However, natives will argue that theirs is a measured and necessary reaction, commensurate with the destructive potential (and, often, actuality) posed by the immigrant presence to Gulf society. Their narrative goes thus: originally, upon the first waves of immigration, Gulf Arabs greeted the newcomers with open arms and open hearts. These were strangers in strange lands, and the natives wearied themselves in accommodating them. "Sure, the mechanic may have flubbed the tune-up job—but he's alone in a foreign country, and no doubt did his best; I'll give his full salary (he is, after all, trying to found a life for himself), and merely take my car elsewhere for the tune-up it needs." This spirit of generosity, they say, was based on the premise that it is incumbent upon the very fortunate to care for those less fortunate than they. God had blessed the people of Gulf with uncountable riches in oil wealth—so who were they to be withholding? Who were they to refrain from sharing what was, in the first place, merely a gift from above?

But these immigrants, as it turned out, had not boot-strapped the many miles from their far off homes (areas of vast, calamitous indigence) only to gently cobble together a fit, proper and upright life. Rather: they were brazen wastrels, tucked beneath the masks of kindly fools, leeching the good natives of all they were worth. Slipping into the country in the dark of night to make a quick buck and spend it on something fast and lewd. They have since been uncovered as scoundrels; they must be forced to leave.

At least, that's how the popular, native narrative goes. Not only did the immigrant population manipulate and dupe the native class (fixing higher prices, doing lazy, shoddy jobs etc.), but it bore along with a whole carnival of uncouth, theretofore unheard practices—practices that threatened the very fabric of society. All in all, according to the natives, they feared and reviled immigrants for the following ten reasons: one, immigrants would introduce a variety of foreign, distinctly un-Islamic lifestyles into the country; two, the immigrant class, comprised of a preponderance of single men, would invariably increase the number of "moral" or "sexual crimes" within the country; three, the widespread availability of cheap immigrant labor would drive down wages; four, the presence of non-native Arabic speakers would necessarily dilute the purity of the language—especially the domestic servants, who have the potential to corrupt the language of the master's children; six, due to their low wages and immodest habits, the immigrants would be chronically unclean, and even introduce new diseases into the country; seven, the resultant population growth would stress public service systems such as policing and medical care, to the extent that service workers, so preoccupied with immigrant needs, would be unable to provide urgent care to natives; eight, immigrants would overstay their visas; nine, immigrants would introduce into the society a host of foreign crimes, such as money-motivated murder; and, finally, immigrants would disenfranchise the native working class.

Yes, the native working class. Due to the regional impact of the global financial crisis at the close of the aughts, Gulf Arab countries launched campaigns to dispel cultural taboos on blue collar labor—after all, many more natives now required the even meager wages that such jobs afforded. Immigrants, however, drove down the market, and already occupied the variety of these positions. This, then, is the "economic reason" alluded to earlier in the discussion: in order to clear menial jobs for native citizens, many Gulf Arabs have begun to vociferously lobby for large scale disenfranchisement and deportation campaigns. In some Gulf countries, the majority of immigrants now live in caves, as public opinion is so aggressively against them that no one will rent them a room. Crime, then, is becoming one of their sole means of livelihood.

Of course, crime is a far less trying recourse when one despises one's victims. Even the earliest immigrants considered the younger generation of Gulf Arabs—who had not endured the pre-oil hardships—to be lazy, spoiled and idiotic. And, indeed, there was a fair degree of duping, manipulation and price-gauging at play. Nonetheless, the population of non-native Gulf residents—who, instead of "immigrants," are still commonly, and unironically, referred to as *imāla* ("the labor force")—are finding opportunity harder and harder to come by in their adoptive countries. Meanwhile, this turn toward crime—in some cases, violent crime—is just further exacerbating the already-hateful relationship between immigrants and natives. Recent headlines include: "Egyptian painter blackmails female Saudi doctor over affair with her sister"; "Arrested: 11-member Yemeni gang, committed to stealing Saudi oil;" "Bangladeshi gang kidnapping foreigners in Riyadh;" "Housekeeper's cleaver ends life of elderly female citizen;" "Bengali kills female citizen."

☪ Kuwait recently held public celebrations to mark the deportation of their last illegal, Bangladeshi immigrant.

Translation

Title: Saudization

Saudization refers to the national policy in Saudi Arabia to encourage employment of Saudi nationals in the public private sector, which, as of 2006, has been largely dominated by expatriate workers from both South and Southeast Asia. As of 2006, the program had been met with little success.

The Saudi government has enacted policies to promote Saudization, including warnings that "companies which fail to comply with Saudization regulations will not be awarded government contracts."

The headdress covering all the different nationalities is a foreign and funny concept for an Arab, since the idea of this form of inclusiveness is strange and ridiculous. While in America ads and messages readily depict a mixture of different races and backgrounds working together to achieve their goals and move forward, to the Arab this is an unusual concept since such efforts should be limited to *true* citizens of the country.

Culture

Saudization has so far failed to stem the influx of foreign workers into the country. This cartoon depicts the Saudi *guthra* (which is the Saudi head cover) covering everyone living in Saudi Arabia. When it comes to foreigners in these oil-rich Arab countries, political correctness is nonexistent; the native citizens hate the foreigners and have no qualms voicing their disdain for them. Despite the fact that these foreigners carry the economy forward, citizens consider foreigners to be the source of everything that ails their society. This cartoon does not depict a favorable attitude towards foreigners and makes fun of the failure of the policies. Unlike America, which favors inclusiveness, Saudi Arabia generally does not welcome foreigners and rarely awards them citizenship.

In order to satisfy their Saudization quotas, some unscrupulous companies deliberately neglect to report to the Social Security Department Saudi employees who resign or get fired. In fact, such companies find it more profitable to continue to pay taxes upon the departed employees than to actually operate within the Saudization requirements. This practice has significant, detrimental ramifications for the departed employee (who, of course, is ignorant to the whole scheme): if his new company learns, from the social security database, that the employee is "still active" at his old job, they will surely fire him. This is due to the fact that concurrent employment within a single field is often perceived as a conflict of interest.

Translation

On the right: "They demand the Saudization of the private sector while our government departmnets have a lot of foreigners: engineers, designers, even data-entry operators and typists."

On left: "Son of lawful. All of these foreigners work for the government and when their projects are finished, they are moved onto the next project. These people are auxiliary employees."

Language

Son of lawful means a good man. *Halal*, which means *lawful* in Arabic, can be used to describe anything that is permitted or allowed in Islam whether it is food, an act or anything. When you describe a person as the Son of lawful, it implies that the person is a legitimate son or daughter as opposed to son or daughter of *Haram*, which means unlawful in Islam. You can call facetiously someone the son of unlawful to describe someone who does not act in the most traditional way.

Culture

Two Saudi citizens discuss Saudization, the process by which Saudi people are given preference over foreigners for jobs. The cartoon represents the bewilderment of many Saudis as to the extent of Saudization's success and how it is not applied evenly.

☪ Even when companies comply with the law of hiring certain numbers of natives, the Saudi employees can find that they are not really welcome, whether it is for lack of skills or because foreign workers are reluctant to show them how the job is done for fear of doing themselves out of a job in the future (which is the aim of these laws). Many end up like this man,

sitting at a desk (the nameplate reads: *Saudization*) and spending the day doing nothing. Natives are not very eager to learn and not motivated to acquire the knowledge or skills needed to do their job.

☪ Kuwait has a similar law called *takwiit*, Law 1104 of 2008, known as the 10% law, that applies to non-governmental bodies, meaning that for a private company at least 10% of the workforce should be native. In any dealings with the government, the certificate that a company is complying with the law is vital — and otherwise the company faces a fine each time it fails to produce it.

Translation

Title: Saudization progress.

Native: Natives will be lost among them.

Sign: Vegetable Circle

Language

In Arabic, a "vegetable market" is sometimes called a "vegetable circle," named for the large crowd of people that circle around.

In this cartoon, the word used for "native" is, "the son of the homeland." In Arabic, this word has many different meanings: it could mean "native" (as it does above), or it could metaphorically stand for an "old-fashioned, all-around good guy."

Culture

The percentage of immigrants in some Arab countries is remarkably large, and many native citizens feel that they are gradually becoming the minority. Meanwhile, high levels of unemployment amongst the natives greatly heighten their resentment against the immigrants, as they feel unfairly cornered out of the jobs they need to provide for their families. Governments, too, are eager to develop a class of qualified natives to fill essential positions running the country, since immigrants are more likely to leave when the economy slows and the revenue from oil decreases.

☪ The term "Asian" in the Arab world generally refers to people from the Pakistan and Bangladesh, similar to its usage in Britain, though Indians are usually referred to separately; it does not apply to people from Far Eastern countries as it does in the United States. Most grocers from India, and most vegetable sellers are Asian, from Pakistan or Bangladesh, as are most tailors, restaurateurs, juice-bar owners, gas-station owners, and small construction company owners.

As for illegal workers they are referred to as "loose labor" or "strays," since they have no sponsor, and many will work in car washes.

☪ In many wealthy Arab countries, the majority of street vendors are foreigners, much to the chagrin of the natives, as demonstrated in the cartoon above. The cartoon to the right, entitled "50,000 Foreign Workers Enter the Saudi Labor Market Monthly," shows a man identified as "unemployed" wiping his eyes with a tissue from a box of tissues bearing the labels, "Tissues," "Good for all uses," and "Keep your house clean.". The used tissues scattered about him are labeled "Diploma" and "Bachelor Degree."

Language

The placing of the Arabic word for monthly within quotation marks is the equivalent of underlining it for emphasis.

Translation

Writing on boat's sails:
"Illegal immigration"
Caption next to man with lifesaver:
"Indeed, he who 'leaves his home…'"

Language

The famous Arabic proverb, "He who leaves his home loses his place in life" reflects the pervasive notion in Arab culture that for each person there is a

designated area in which he commands total respect, but that he risks losing that respect the farther away from it he travels. The saying is often applied to situations in which a traveler in a foreign land experiences xenophobia and is humiliated, but could just as easily be used to describe a scenario in which a man is somehow disrespected when he is out and about in his hometown, and just a short walk away from his own house.

Historically, Arabs have dreaded "ghurba," defined as "absence from one's homeland." As recently as several decades ago it was common for Arabs who had traveled only several dozen miles from their home to swear "on my ghurba" instead of, say, "by God." Unlike Westerners, Arabs will swear by something unpleasant, such as a disease or a length of time spent in hospital—anything that constitutes suffering. So the fact that an Arab would swear by his ghurba illustrates the gravity attached to the state of being away from one's home. The concept of ghurba has undergone dramatic changes in recent years as younger generations of Arabs conclude that the benefits of moving to a foreign land outweigh the negative feelings associated with leaving one's home. Though younger Arabs today may be more willing to emigrate from their home countries than their parents or grandparents were, they still feel the need to ease their ghurba by living in enclaves populated by their countrymen, rather than fully assimilating into the culture of their adopted countries.

The significance of attachment to homeland in Arab culture seems to play a major role in the Palestinian-Israeli conflict. Many Palestinians believe that one of the conditions of any peace treaty should be a guarantee that Palestinians who have lost their homes during the conflict be able to reclaim possession of the property they lost. Many Palestinians—even if they live abroad—keep the keys to the homes their families lost decades ago. A visitor to one of the many Palestinian-owned shops in Brooklyn's Bay Ridge neighborhood, home to a significant Arab-American population, will likely notice an old-fashioned key hanging from a wooden plaque cut in the shape of Old Palestine.

Young and unemployed Arabs from Egypt, Morocco, Tunisia, Algeria and other not so rich Arab countries, often try to smuggle themselves into Europe by the way of the Mediterranean Sea and often fail.

20 – Religion

Translation

Title: Case of Suspicion

[Notice the long beards and short moustaches on the two men on the right.]

Culture

The couple here are returning from a shopping trip under the harsh scrutiny of two men. Their long beards and very short moustaches identify them as religious fundamentalists, possibly even members of the Religious Police. Though the Religious Police (officially, "The Commission for the Promotion of Virtue and Prevention of Vice") are a Saudi group appointed to protect public morals, many unofficial fundamentalists think it their religious duty to ensure that religious laws are followed. Here, they are exasperated by many features of the couple: the affectionate closeness with which they walk, the woman's tightly fitting abbaya, her apparent use of eye make-up, and for that matter the chic shopping bags which suggest a western—or at least luxurious and western-style—store. All of these would be anathema to the fundamentalists, and with that jumping-point, their heads may well swirl with suspicions and doubts about the propriety of their relationship.

Faced with such "provocation," a censorious fundamentalist in the Arab world would take it upon himself to approach the offending couple, verify their relationship, and point out their failings. Usually, those stopped in this way often act politely and listen to the lecture, recognizing that the his critic at least believes that he is acting in their best interest. A polite receiver of this kind of a correction typically offers thanks for the concern, clarifies the questionable situation or admits a mistake, and promises to be more circumspect in future. The range of behaviors that will produce such an situation range from country to country and community to community, but wearing shorts, having a Western look, being a clean-shaven man, wearing headphones, whistling, and singing are all common ways to earn a dirty look or a censorious speech.

Many in the Arabic media are criticizing the strictness of religious men and imams in the Arab world. They call for such people to change the way they talk to those whom they think are misbehaving or acting immorally. Such strict and rude talk, the media believes, will scare people away from the religion rather than make them love it. Their loud denunciations of too-liberal men and too-immodest girls can be rude and unjustified, argue there critics. Many of these people have no religious authority, but they take it upon themselves to fix the society and bring it onto what they see as the right path.

Religious figures in the West tend to be overweight; recently, several studies have attributed this mostly to the high levels of stress and depression that accompany the religious profession. Muslim clerics and imams, as well as sheiks, tend to be rotund too, but for a different reason. As in most parts of the world, food in Arab countries signifies hospitality. As highly respected men, religious figures and sheikhs are frequently given great quantities of delicious food. As part of family celebrations, people often send plates of food to the mosque; they consider it charity and, if the imam or sheikh doesn't want it, he can give it to beggars who always congregate around the mosque's entrance . Over time, the meals create their trademark round bellies.

Translation

Man with stick: This is a heresy; you leave the sunnah of the *miswak* and take up this as a lord instead of Allah!

Man on the left: Woe unto you, this is a temptation.

Language

Miswak is a tooth-cleaning twig

made from the arak tree. Scientific studies have found it to be remarkably effective, but its importance to the cartoon is that Muhammad enthusiastically recommended it for dental hygiene.

When fundamentalists harangue people in this way, they generally drop their everyday dialect and adopt a formal classical Arabic such as one would use for a sermon. This is meant to add to their authority.

When the man in the center warns that toothbrush use "is a temptation," he means a temptation to those around the person using the toothbrush. He fears this one example of modern, irreligious dental hygiene will spread virally as more and more are seduced with toothbrushes.

In this cartoon, the fundamentalist speaks as if the toothbrush were being used as an idol, threatening to replace worship of God: the toothbrush as the Golden Calf.

Culture

Islamic fundamentalists have been known to abstain from using modern technology and comforts, feeling that they should imitate how early Muslims lived, in the days before modern inventions. Many use things like radio or television only for religious purposes—to listen to a broadcasted sermon, for example. The most extreme fundamentalists eschew everything from cars, to electricity, to paper money.

The Soviet Union's long war in Afghanistan was a great catalyst for the spread of religious fundamentalism, and this is reflected in the fundamentalists' clothing. Long beards and short dresses were originally the mode amongst conservative Afghanis, but when foreign Muslims, prompted by their governments' and American urging, swept in to repel the Soviets, many Muslims were inspired to turn more fundamentalist and to adopt the Afghan manner of dress.

Some beauty and hygiene products have been found to contain alcohol or pork by-products, so that they have been subject to condemnation by religious leaders. Many manufacturers have found that it is greatly to their advantage to advertise that their products are halal, with sales rising after Arab consumers have been reassured.

Translation

"Isn't she ashamed that she's not wearing hijab? Such ill-manners. "

[N.B. This is Cairo University in the background where Obama delivered his June 2009 speech. The two women on the right are wearing the hijab (hair coverings), and despite their provocative clothing, they think that the other woman is dressed inappropriately because her hair is not covered.]

Culture

There are two types of women who wear

hijab: the one who wears it the right way and with the right purpose in mind-to cover her body shape and follow the religious guidelines-and the one who wears it tightly and considers it a fashionable thing to do.

Islam does not forbid women to attend public prayers in a mosque, but The Prophet pronounced it better for them to pray in private. When they do enter the mosque, women are permitted to place themselves apart from and behind the men.

Translation

Man: You're confusing us: you're not wearing a *hijab* so that we might respect you, but neither are you one of *those* with whom we can flirt.

Culture

Generally speaking, Arab men like to flirt. They will not flirt with women wearing full Islamic attire, though, and opt to flirt with women who seem open to male attention because of their Western, more revealing style of dress. There are some women who combine the headdress, or "hijab," with more revealing clothing. This cartoon depicts a man who is confused by this. He sees a woman whose clothing represents an amalgamation of the two types of women with whom he is used to interacting, and he is frustrated because he is unsure of whether or not he ought to respect or flirt with her.

Translation

On top right: Wily Devil

On top of Alarm: "God is most great. God is the most great."

Devil: "Why the rush? You know there are 20 minutes left before the dawn prayer. Go ahead and sleep for 15 minutes and I'll wake you up."

On bottom: "I don't think it's going to happen."

Language

In the Islamic faith, "Allah is the most great," *Allahu Akbar*, is called *tekbeer*, the declaration of God's greatness, and is used on specific occasions, especially at the beginning of the *azan*, or the call to

prayer. It is also the first phrase said by a Muslim immediately before he engages in prayer. An act done on the behalf of God should always be put ahead of something unrelated to God, and this phrase literally states that the act to follow it is more important that the act being done previously. People at war or those about to do something challenging or life-threatening will say this phrase to mean that God, and his power, will be greater than the enemy or task. Some Muslims will use alarms that instead of ringing will repeat this phrase, as the alarms will often be set to go off at the time for prayer. Advancements in technology have made Muslim life easier. In addition to alarm clocks that remind a person when to pray, there are also prayer rugs that have a built in compass which points in the direction of Kaabah.

The first *azan* of the day also includes the exhortation that "Prayer is better than sleep," in recognition of the fact that it is not easy to get up for early prayers.

Culture

Muslims are required to pray five times a day. The dawn prayer is the hardest to perform because this is the time when you are in the deepest sleep of the night. In this cartoon, the wily devil tells the man to go back to sleep and that he'll wake him up in 15 minutes for the dawn prayer. This however, is unlikely to happen. Many visitors to the Middle East find that the sound of Azan at this time of the day is the most disturbing memory because of its early timing.

☪ Prayer is one of the five pillars of Islam. Each daily prayer has a window of time in which one is allowed to perform it: for example, the evening prayer may be performed any time from its onset until the dawn of the next day. The dawn prayer, however, has the shortest time period—no more than an hour—and is the most difficult to keep. It occurs in the middle of most peoples' "deep sleep" phase of slumber; too, given the lack of on-demand hot water in most Arab countries, the prerequisite ablutions often require that the practitioner endure bitter cold water

Al-Islam: The world's fastest-growing religion.

Muslims generally call the religion that Muhammad taught "Al-Islam. "Al-Eeman" and "Al-Deen" are the particular terms applied, respectively, to faith and to practical religion. The grand principles of the faith are expressed in two articles, the first of which is this "There is no deity but God." In various places throughout the Qur'an God is described as He, "Who created all things in heaven and in earth," "Who preserveth all things," and Who "decreeth all things;" "Who is without beginning, and without end." He is omnipotent, omniscient, and omni-present; He is one. His unity is declared in a short chapter of the Qur'an:

Say, He is God; one [God]. God is the Eternal. He begetteth not, nor is He begotten; and there is none equal unto Him. (112) *Al-Ikhlas-*(Sincerity)

The name for this singular deity is Allah. This refers to the name of God Himself, and not, as is often thought, to the idea of a god in general, which is *ilāh*. Thus, one may say that different religions have worshiped various *ilāh*s, such as the Norse Thor, the Greek Zeus, and the Islamic Allah. It is commonly supposed in the West that the Islamic *ilāh*, Allah, has 99 names, but this is an obscure and non-Qur'anic doctrine. The Qur'an itself gives a number of epithets and titles that might be used in addressing Him—such as "The Compassionate" and "The Merciful,"—but these are lesser than the specific name "Allah," and the notion of 99 names is nowhere in the Qur'an. Tradition adds one further name, too: the Secret

/the Great Name. This name is unknown to mankind, but if it were discovered and used in supplication, one would be sure of having one's wishes fulfilled.

In the Islamic faith, Jesus Christ (whose name should not be mentioned without adding, "On whom be peace") is believed to have been born miraculously of a chaste virgin without any natural father, to have been the Messiah, and to have been "the Word of God which He transmitted unto Mary, and a Spirit [proceeding] from Him." Nevertheless, Jesus is not called the Son of God, and no higher titles are given to him than those of a Prophet. The Gospel that Jesus preached was, over time, corrupted and has been superseded by the Qur'an, delivered by Muhammad.

Muslims believe that after *Seyyidna 'Eesa* ("our Lord Jesus") had fulfilled His mission, God took his body and his soul unto Himself to save him from the horrible fate that was planned for him on the cross and that another person, on whom God had stamped the likeness of Christ, was crucified in His stead. Though the Qur'an does not say as much, there is also a widespread belief amongst Muslims that Christ is to come again upon the Earth to affirm the Muslim religion, bring perfect peace and security after having killed Antichrist, and to be a sign of the approach of the last day.

The other grand article of the faith, which cannot be believed without the former, is this: "Muhammad is God's Messenger."

Muslims believe that Muhammad was the last and greatest of Prophets. Six of these—namely Adam, Noah, Abraham, Moses, Jesus, and Muhammad—are believed each to have received a revealed law, or system of religion and morality. That which was revealed to Adam, though, was abrogated by that of Noah; and each succeeding law, or code of laws, abrogated the preceding, though all are believed to have been the same in every essential point. Therefore, those who professed the Jewish religion from the time of Moses to that of Jesus were true believers, and those who professed the Christian religion (uncorrupted, as the Muslims say, by the tenet that Christ was the son of God) until the time of Muhammad are held, in like manner, to have been true believers. In all these cases save the last, though, time introduced corruption into these texts, so that the copies of the Pentateuch, the Psalms of David (which the Muslims also hold to be of divine origin), and the Gospels now existing are believed to have been so much altered as to contain very little of the true Word of God. The Qur'an alone is believed to have suffered no alteration whatsoever. "Surely, We have revealed the Reminder and We will assuredly be its guardian (against all corruption)." (Al-Hijr 15:9)

There are a number of other tenants in which it is incumbent on Muslims to believe. They should believe in the existence of angels and of good and evil *jinn*; the evil *jinn* being devils, whose chief is Iblees. Furthermore, they must have faith in the immortality of the soul, the general resurrection and judgment, in future rewards and punishments in Paradise and Hell, in the balance in which good and evil works shall be weighed, and in the bridge *Es-Sirat* (which extends over the midst of Hell, finer than a hair, and sharper than the edge of a sword), over which all must pass, and from which the wicked shall fall into Hell.

Translation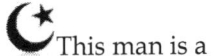

"Video clips are forbidden (haram) while people are fasting at Ramadan, especially Christina Aguilera's new song."

[N.B. Sheikhs often sit like this at mosques to give sermons or answer questions. "Haram" means prohibited, and "halal" means acceptable. Music videos are referred to as "video clips."]

☪ This man is a Qur'an-reciter, who will put his hands on his face like this, every time he recites from the Qur'an. He will usually be seated on a chair like the one in the above cartoon. While reciting the Qur'an from memory, he will rock gently from right to left. This rocking helps him keep the rhythm of the recitation. The hands on his face date back to the time before there were microphones and acted as a way to improve his delivery.

Culture

As in America, some religious figures in Arab countries do not practice what they preach. In this cartoon, the Sheikh asks his congregation not to watch something that he seems to watch.

Muslims can listen to religious sermons before the Friday prayer when attendance and prayer in a mosque is mandatory. The sermon on Friday occurs before Friday prayer and lasts about half an hour. The Imam goes up into the pulpit and delivers his sermon. Muslims can also listen to sermons on other days, but only at large mosques that have many people praying. The Imam sits on a large chair, as depicted in this cartoon, to deliver his sermon. This large chair is used by the person who presents the sermon or the person who recites the Qur'an. Worshipers sit shoeless on a carpet, which is generally green, in front of him and listen.

Friday, the Muslim Sabbath

Muslims celebrate the Sabbath on Friday. The tradition is held to date back to Adam himself, who is believed to have been created on Friday. Adam's death, as well, came on a Friday. That the Sabbath continues to be a crucial day is demonstrated by the prophecy that the general resurrection at the end of the world will occur on a Friday; this prophecy gives Friday its name *El-Gum'ah* (The Assembly). Muslims are not forbidden worldly business on the Sabbath except during the time of prayer.

Reading Chair

Designated Qur'an Reciters have the responsibility for the public recitation of the Qur'an. In modern times, most Arab countries have television and radio channels devoted to such recitation, and many Muslims make listening to it a part morning routine and they will also spend a few minutes listening in order to inaugurate a long journey. In mosques, the Reciter begins their work around half-an-hour before the next set of daily prayers. Listeners, ideally, attend in respectful silence as he reads out chosen passages, though more demonstrative listeners sometimes loudly express their rapture between verses, as though the Qur'an were a favorite song. In large, prestigious mosques, these recitations can be heard between all the prayers, but in humbler, less-busy institutions, the Reciter will only perform his duty before Friday prayers. In order that the Reciter may have a prominence that accords with his special and sacred function, he sits elevated in a special Reading Chair above the other worshipers on the floor. The Reading Chair is a wide and imposing piece of furniture, sturdily built and able to accommodate the Reciter as he sits cross-legged. A skilled Reciter can attain a high degree of celebrity and the most renowned command large fees for their services.

Recitation of the Qur'an

All Muslims who are reciting the Qur'an should make an effort to render the language as skillfully and beautifully as they are able. Not only are they expected to observe the poetic metre and finely worked construction of the text, but tradition has generated standard melodic chants that serve to regulate and embellish each Muslim's reading of the holy book.

A Description of Muslim Prayer

Muslims pray five times a day: at dawn, at noon, in the afternoon, at sunset, and in the evening. The prayer must face the Kaabah —a building— in Mecca in Saudi Arabia. If the person who is praying does not know where the Kaabah is, he can face anywhere he likes, but if he knows the direction of Mecca, it is mandatory for him to orient himself that way. Before a Muslim prays, he must clean himself ritually with water (ablutions) by washing his hands three times, gargling three times, sniffing water three times, washing his face three times, running his fingers through his hair three times, cleaning the ears with damp fingers three times, washing the neck three times, and washing his feet up to the heels three times. After this ritual, he may pray. He can make this process invalid if he passes gas, touches a woman, or has bad thoughts after completing the ritual. If any of these occur during the ritual, he must begin again. These ablutions allow the prayer both to pray and to read the Qur'an.

There are several types of prayers. The mandatory prayer that occurs five times a day is called the *fard*; this must be performed by every Muslim. Usually, Muslims know the time of these prayers by the *Azan*, or the call to prayer, a chant that any visitor to the Middle East and Arab countries will surely hear and remember. To perform these prayers, the person prays with his feet evenly spaced; he raises his hands and touches his forehead with his fingertips. When the arms are lowered, the hands must be clasped over the stomach, with the right hand on top of the left hand. (When the Pope recently visited a mosque and prayed the Muslim prayer, observers noticed that he placed his left hand over his right, which some consider insulting.) The person praying reads the opening of the Qur'an and a short surah in an audible voice. He places his hands on his knees, bends, and says a phrase glorifying God three times; he then straightens and repeats the praise. This process is then repeated with the person kneeling, and subsequently with the person prostrated on the ground.

This process is called *rek'ah*, and it can be repeated as many times as required.

During prayer time, you will occasionally see people in streets covered with rugs or newspapers, especially on Fridays, engaged in praying.

When Muslims assemble to perform prayer in a mosque, they arrange themselves in rows towards the Kiblah (that is, towards Mecca).

It is considered extremely sinful to interrupt a man engaged in his prayers.

The typical prayer time lasts about ten to fifteen minutes if performed in a mosque behind an imam in group prayer, and about five minutes if performed privately at home.

Each period of prayer ends when the next commences, excepting that of daybreak, which ends at sunrise. The prayers should be done as close as possible at the commencement of the periods above mentioned.

Visitors to the Muslim world are struck by the central role of prayers in daily life. In some countries such as Saudi Arabia, live commercials stop for praying. Even jewelry stores leave their display cases open and go to pray knowing that nobody will think about stealing (the punishment is cutting off a hand, which is performed in public).

Group Prayers

Muslims may pray individually or in groups. Friday noon prayers consist of two *rek'ahs* performed in a group, while groups prayers on other days and times are of the same number of *rek'ahs* as they would be if performed individually. Group prayers are similar to the ordinary prayers, the difference being that the people perform their postures in silence while they keep time with the Imam.

Other Prayers

Beyond the standard, required, five daily prayers, Muslims traditionally mark many occasions with prayer. Some specific occasions with associated prayers include: the two great festivals marking the end of Ramadan and the end of the pilgrimage, each of the nights of Ramadan, both solar and lunar eclipses, calls for rain, the beginnings of battle, setting out on pilgrimages and funerals.

Mosques in the Arab world

In the Arab world, there are literally thousands of mosques in every country, and all of them are within walking distance of each other. They range from sizes that can accommodate thousands of worshipers to smaller ones that can accommodate fewer than ten people. The word mosque, *masjid*, does not refer to the building, like a church, but rather to a place where prayer takes place. This means that a *masjid* is not confined to a building with four walls and can be anywhere that people engage in prayer. The word *masjid* refers to the place of prostration. During the time of the Prophet Muhammad, a *masjid* was literally four walls made of the leaves of a palm tree.

During the 1970s and 1980s the Arab world experienced an Islamic revival that resulted in a boom of building mosques. It had long been the government's duty to construct and maintain mosques, but in order to accommodate the surge of worshipers during the revival, the governments gave tax breaks to any landlords who included mosques in their buildings. The size of a mosque's congregation is largely dependent upon the fame of people buried in that mosque, often corresponding to their piety. The mosques that contain the remains of family members or close companions of the Prophet Muhammad (also known as the Four Rightly Guided Caliphs) have the most fame, after which come mosques of lesser renown. Accordingly, the mosques with the remains of extraordinarily pious people, *walee*, have the next biggest-sized congregations. Muslims often visit these mosques to be blessed by the person who is buried there. Superstition plays a role in these visits, for if a visitor has traveled from another city to a city where a pious person is buried and does not visit, it is believed that evil will befall him. These pious people are buried below a fenced-off monument in a rich metal: silver, brass polished like gold, or in the grandest cases, gold itself. Women and men both have access to the tombs; it is the only place in the mosque where genders can mix. When people visit these monuments, people may kiss the threshold, the windows, and the doors, and then they circle these monuments from left to right, reciting short surahs from the Qur'an and praying for whatever they want. The holiness of the site improves the chances of their prayers' being answered. People promise a *nadr*, vowing to sacrifice or give charity if their prayers are answered. Many of these *walee* and pious people have followers who celebrate their birthdays on a very large scale. The American ambassadors in the Arab world are known to go to these celebrations as a way of bonding with the population of the host country. These celebrations last for days—overnight people perform *zekr*, the chanting of religious songs and praising God repeatedly. These followers emulate the pious ones, most especially in their style of worship, following *tariqah*, which is repeating exactly the pious one's recorded style of worship.

Egypt possesses roughly 104,000 mosques, more than any other Arab country, and Egyptians are among the most pious people in the Arab world. The Saudis, though they are guardians of the Holy Site, are far less religious.

Supplicating God's help in a decision

Some Arab Muslims usually turn to the Qur'an for an answer when they are faced with a situation that requires a difficult decision. *Istikharah* is asking God to make plain what the right decision would be in order to please him. For example, if a woman has several suitors and a preference for one, she would ask God to give her a sign showing which one of those suitors is the one to choose, even though she may already have a preference. This is to ensure that her choice is pleasing to God first and foremost, instead of just pleasing to her. There are many ways of performing *istikharah*. One method is to hold any two points of the rosary beads, *sebhah*, after reciting the opening surah of the Qur'an three times, moving your finger down the rosary from right to left, say a prayer on each bead. For example, holding the first bead a person will say "I extol the perfection of Allah," while on the second bead, "praise be to Allah" and on the third bead, "there is no other god but Allah" and repeat this pattern of three prayers until reaching the last bead. If on the last bead, the person repeats the prayer he said on the first bead, then the decision will be favorable. So if there are three suitors, Muhammad, Ahmad and Mustafa and a woman prefers Muhammad, then she will perform this method of *istikharah*. If by the last bead she finds herself saying the prayer she made on the first bead, her decision to marry Muhammad is a favorable. This method can be applied to any decision that requires a difficult choice to make.

The second method is to read the *fat'Hah*, or opening chapter of the Qur'an, three times and then read surah number 112, and close the book. Then, opening it to a random page, the 7th line of the right hand page gives the answer. If the line says something positive the decision is favorable. If the line's meaning indicates something negative, then the decision being made is not favorable in the eyes of God.

A third method follows the same method as the second, only instead of reading the 7th line on the right hand page, the person counts the number of times the letters *kha* and *sheen* appear on the page. The letter *kha* represents the word *khair*, which means goodness, and the letter *sheen* represents the *shar*, which means evil. If the letter *kha* appears more times than the letter *sheen* then the decision is favorable. If the opposite is the case, then the decision is not favorable in the eyes of God.

A fourth method of performing *istikharah* is interpreting dreams in order to make the decision pleasing to God. Upon lying down, right before sleep, a person will ask God to reveal to them a sign while they dream. This sign should be either something white, something green or water in order for the decision to be favorable. Supplicants should recite the *fat'Hah* 10 times, and then say "O God, favor our Lord (the title of *Seyyidna*, our Lord, is given by Muslims to prophets and other venerated persons) Muhammad" and repeat that prayer until they fall asleep.

The final method is to have an *istikharah* prayer, with two extra *rek'ahs* and indicate, in the ritual declaration of intention that precedes the normal prayer that these two *rek'ahs* are for the purposes of guiding the worshiper to make the right decision. The worshiper will then attempt to follow through on the choice he or she has made, but if obstacles present themselves, it is understood to be a sign that the intention to carry out the decision is unfavorable. So, in the case of the woman who wants to choose Muhammad, if she intends to meet Muhammad for lunch, if the weather is poor, or there are troubles with transportation that prevent her from reaching her destination, then it is to be understood that the decision to marry Muhammad is unfavorable in the eyes of God.

Al- Fat'Hah

al-Fat'Hah is the name given to the first surah of the Qur'an and derives from the verb *fataha*, which means "to open." al-Fat'Hah is recited for many reasons including: at the beginning of every *rek'ah*; in dedication to a deceased person, whether in simple remembrance or as part of a visit to his or her grave; to seal a pact or contract, such as one that forms a partnership, reconciles an old feud or conflict, or that agrees upon an engagement; or to solemnize the expression of a wish or hope. Reciting al-fat'Hah grants a person *hasana* and, if one dedicates it to another's soul, that *hasana* is granted not only to the reciter but also to the person for whom it was recited.

Hasana and Saiyeh'eh

Hasana is the Arabic name for the merits awarded to good deed. Islamic belief holds that all of one's deeds are noted by recording angels. At Judgment Day, one's virtuous actions—*hasana*—will be scored against one's sins—*saiyeh'eh*—, and the fate of one's soul will be determined accordingly. Meritorious actions, however, are held to have ten times the potency of misdeeds in this final reckoning.

Translation

Man holding gigantic money bag: "Zakat? I don't have any money to spare!"

Gentleman with Glasses:

The Department of *Zakat* [and Income Tax] (DZIT)

Language

In the Arabic language, alms for the poor are known as *zakat*. Giving *zakat* is mandatory, and Arab people have the option of letting the Department of *Zakat* [and Income Tax] (DZIT) collect it along with their taxes, through charities, or by personally giving it to the poor. The households without the time or resources to calculate how much of their income should be given as *zakat* can rely on the DZIT or banks to determine how much should be given. These governmental entities will then find needy families to give the *zakat* to.

Culture

Zakat evaders, like tax evaders in the U.S., are companies or organizations that try to pay as little zakat as possible by cooking their books. Some companies will declare that their income is much smaller than it is in reality, or that they are using some real estate that they are not, as zakat is not paid on used property. Usually this process of cooking the books occurs at the end of the fiscal year, which generally coincides with the end of the calendar year. Most businesses willingly pay their zakat, but they make it so they have to pay as little as possible. Some do not pay them at all, thinking that the *sadaqah* (charity) given during the year is the same as zakat. Some actually pay more than they should, which, in Islam, is not viewed as better than paying the minimal amount. There are business owners who will consider what they give to their relatives, brothers and sister, of donations and gifts as part of the zakat, since he convinces himself they are poor. Others give their zakat to their employees as bonuses, but he doesn't call it zakat in order not to embarrass them. On the other hand, he is not fair to them in regards to overtime and other fringe benefits. There are others that do not pay zakat, believing that their state taxes pay for the zakat.

Translation

Title: The fatwah of breast-feeding adults.
Man: "I'm just here to breastfeed, not for anything, God forbid, I brought some cookies and I just need some breast milk for breakfast."

Culture

Fatwah means an Islamic legal or advisory opinion. The practice of issuing fatwahs has reached ridiculous heights. This cartoon criticizes a fatwah that was widely covered in the media because of its absurdity. The fatwah addressed the issue of mixing the genders in the workplace, because some Islamic scholars contended that Islam prohibits a man and a woman from being alone together in a room in a work-related capacity. The scholar who issued the fatwah said that in order for a man and a woman to be together in a room by themselves in the workplace legally, the woman would have to breastfeed her

colleague, which would create a familial bond between them. Needless to say, this fatwah was widely considered to be ridiculous, and the scholar had to retract his statement by saying that this situation occurred once, under very particular circumstances. Even this explanation was criticized. This cartoon is an example of the ridicule that greeted this incident.

Translation

Cow to man: "Don't be scared you idiot. I am your wife, I only look like this because I breastfed so many of my colleagues at work today."

Arabs usually look with amusement at those wearing pajamas or jalabaya with a matching night cap because that is the same uniform worn by patients in mental hospitals, by Jewish people in concentration camps, and by the Arab working class.

Translation

Top left corner: "Wily Devil"
Devil: "Hey sister, why are you so prudish? In the meantime this *skinny* girl Susie keeps picking up hot guys around her and you know you're better than her. But what can I say, you don't think right. She knows how to market herself and you are silly; you don't give the young guys any chance to see any part of you."

Culture

Arabs often publish cartoons showing the devil trying to tempt people to disobey their religious obligations, such as dressing in revealing clothes, staying longer in bed so that prayers are missed, and so forth.

Translation

Title: Alexandria Incidents
Snake spells out the phrase "religious strife."
Officer: "It's very clear that it came from abroad."

Culture

In October 2005, Muslims in the ancient Egyptian Mediterranean port city of Alexandria marched on St. George's Church to protest distribution of a DVD of a play performed by Copts two years ago. The play, "I Was Blind, But Now I Can See," depicted a Christian convert to Islam who is threatened with death by Muslim militants. The demonstration against this DVD caused clashes between Muslims and Christians, resulting in deaths and the destruction of property.

Sectarian violence between Christians and Muslims occurs all over the Arab world, but it is more pronounced in poor countries such as Egypt. Conflicts tend to be more deadly in the southern areas of the country than in the north. Most of this violence begins as conflicts between individuals and for reasons unrelated to religion. Disputes may be rooted in financial issues such as disputes over property, land use, or store ownership. Sometimes, conflict is sparked by a very trivial amount of money. Other reasons behind the violence are interfaith love relationships. Most of these simple disputes end violently, with hundreds of people on both sides fighting to the death. Many of these cases are resolved only when security forces intervene and arrest the perpetrators. Afterwards, the forces carry out an arbitration process between families that involves concessions on both sides in return for the release of those who were arrested. Some observers believe that sectarian violence throughout Arab countries is a part of a larger phenomenon of increasing violence in the Arab street, which can be seen on a daily basis on the pages of Arabic newspapers (these newspapers include separate pages called "Accident/Incident pages"). The deterioration of economic conditions has also contributed to the rise in sectarian violence, along with a culture of carrying guns. Even children know how to use machine guns. Additionally, when disputes arise and one party happens to be Christian and the other Muslim, the media fuels the fire by automatically characterizing the conflict as sectarian violence.

The first incident of sectarian violence in recent history occurred in 1972 in Egypt when the newly appointed pope of the Coptic faith challenged the late president Anwar al-Sadat over the authority to issue permits to build more churches that would accommodate the growing Christian population. (In most Arab countries, the construction of churches or other houses of worship other than mosques is restricted by law and tradition; these restrictions range from outright prohibitions in Saudi Arabia to the requirement of presidential consent for construction in Egypt.)

When Amr Ibn El-Aas conquered Egypt in 642 CE, the inhabitants of the country were almost exclusively Copts. Some historians believe that the ease of Amr's conquest was due to the help of Egyptian Christians. Amr treated Christians with absolute tolerance and issued a decree guaranteeing the safety of their churches and freedom of worship. Unfortunately, subsequent caliphs did not follow in Amr's footsteps. Merely seventy years after the conquest of Egypt, the sufferings of the Christians began when all of the privileges granted to this group were revoked. As a result, many Egyptian Christians revolted to defend their rights, but were defeated and slaughtered mercilessly. In 722 CE, for the first time, monks were required to pay protection money to the government, worth a dinar. In return, the collectors branded the hand of those monks that paid with an iron stamp. If a monk's hands lacked these marks, his hands would be cut off. Other Christians were required to pay ten dinars, and anybody who did not pay and provide proof of payment was beheaded or beaten to death. A subsequent caliph, Yazid Ibn Abdel-Malik, ordered that the hand of every Copt be branded with the image of a lion and greatly increased their suffering. Again, the Copts revolted, and again, they were defeated and slaughtered. All the Coptic churches were seized and their priests and bishops exiled. Another caliph, Al-Motawakil, in 849 CE, ordered Copts to wear restrictive dress, which was very humiliating to their pride and societal status. After this caliph, in 996 CE, Al-Hakim ("the wise one") ordered all Christians to wear a five-pound wooden cross around their neck and garments that were entirely black. This may be the origin of the black clothing and cross necklace that many Christian priests wear today. The reason that Al-Hakim chose this color for Christians is because black is the most hated color in Muslim society. All the churches were confiscated, destroyed, and replaced by mosques. During this time, an extra tax was also imposed on all Christians living in a Muslim country. Because non-Muslims were not allowed to join the army, this extra tax was intended to pay for their own protection. The rationale behind not allowing non-Muslims to join the army was to prevent them from killing other Muslims in the case of a war with another Muslim country. Many Christians during this period converted to Islam.

In the United States, the relationship between Arab Christians and Arab Muslims is still uneasy. Recently, a Christian family was murdered in New Jersey and fingers were immediately pointed at Muslims, who were later exonerated, but only after leaving indelible marks on them. After 9/11, Arab Christians joined the War on Terror, publicly lambasted Muslims and their treatment of minorities, and organized demonstrations whenever the leader of a country that had a history of mistreating Christians visited Washington.

Arab Christians living in America are an important force in shaping U.S. Middle Eastern policy. They have pressured Congress to enact laws that condemn religious intolerance and reduce trade ties and financial aid to any country that encroaches on its citizens' freedom of worship. Modern Christians' grievances against Arab countries are numerous and include restrictions on the construction of the churches, frequent attacks on Christian properties and houses of worship, the required statement of religion on identification cards, and restrictions on career advancement within the government. Additionally, some Muslims kidnap Christian girls and force them to marry Muslim men. Governments regularly attempt to assuage Christian fears, but the Arab population has begun to perceive the Christian population as aligned with the U.S. government, which is regarded as engaged in war with Islam, despite repeated assertions by George W. Bush and Obama that this is not the case.

In order to calm the fears of Christians, governments will occasionally publish pictures depicting a Christian priest and a Muslim sheikh embracing each other. Many people laugh at these photos, knowing that such deep-rooted problems cannot be solved by a single picture.

Translation

"What's the solution for cell phone ringtones in mosques?"

"The solution is cell phone companies shutting down the network during service."

Culture

In Arab countries, the nuisance of ringing cell phones is felt everywhere– even inside Mosques. Inside the mosque, Muslims are prohibited from talking in a voice more audible than a slight whisper, and so the sound of a cell phone ringing is quite disturbing to everyone. A person whose cellular phone rings and causes enough of a disturbance may be ejected from the mosque. Any activities beside praying or reading the Qur'an are prohibited. Some homeless people will sleep in the mosque, but right before prayer, someone will wake them by lightly tapping them with a tree branch or a thin stick. Panhandling is forbidden inside the mosque, and homeless people are directed outside the mosque where they can ask for money from people on their way out of the mosque.

Even if mosques are located in the busiest of neighborhoods, once prayer has begun, the neighborhood surrounding it becomes very quiet. Once the prayer has been completed, however, it is as though a switch was flipped. Once again, the hustle and bustle of the neighborhood can be heard. Merchants stand waiting outside the mosque waiting for the worshipers to leave in order to sell to them.

In the cartoon, the men share a physical closeness that is not very common elsewhere. In Arab countries, if a man is seen resting his head on another's thigh, for example, or if two men walk together hand in hand, there is no assumption made about the possibly inappropriate nature of their relationship.

☪ Arab Muslims are now using both Qur'anic verses and the Azan as ringtones, a practice which has inspired two opposing fatwahs. Those in support argue that the ringtones will help spread the Islamic faith, and keep the word of Allah fresh in the minds of the citizenry. Those who oppose the practice, meanwhile, argue that the typical person will answer the phone before the verse has been fully recited, thereby exhibiting disrespect and creating the potential for textual misinterpretations. Additionally, they fear that the recitation of the Azan might confuse the public, who are accustomed to hearing it only at specific hours of the day.

Translation

Title: Night of Decree
Man on prayer-rug: O Lord, enable me to get married before I die, O Lord!

Language

When a Muslim prays to God, he invokes Him both at the beginning and the end of the prayer. The verb "to know" in Arabic can also mean "to enable."

🧔 Saying that you want to accomplish something before you die can be both a humorous and serious wish. Usually this kind of wish is reserved for serious hopes when the end of life is approaching, as in an older man wishing to perform Hijj before he dies. When it is said by a younger man for something that can be accomplished but is difficult in his situation, humor is invoked. This man is poor, evidenced by the patches on his clothes, so the prospect of getting married (which involves financial security, an apartment, and so forth) can appear to him a farfetched dream.

Culture

Laylat al-Qadr, called the Night of Power, the Night of Decree, or the Night of Measures, is the holiest night in Islam, called by the Qur'an "better than one thousand months." It is believed that the archangel Gabriel—called in Islam The Spirit—descends to Earth accompanied by a host of angels. Also, *Laylat al-Qadr* is the night on which the first word—"Read!"—of the Qur'an was revealed to Muhammad. However, no human knows exactly on what night it falls, only that it is one of the last ten days of Ramadan.

☪ In prayer, cleanliness is required not only of the worshiper, but also of the surface upon which he prays, be it the ground, mat, rug, robe, or whatever else it may be. If one is unable to find or afford anything more formal, the bare ground is considered sufficiently clean, if dry. In such a case, the dust which adheres to the nose and forehead in prostration is regarded as a devout ornament to the believer's face and, therefore, not wiped off immediately. Some kind of covering for the ground, however, is preferable. This may be as simple as a cloak or any other garment that one can decently remove to spread on the ground. Ideally, though, one uses a prayer-rug (called *sejadeh*), a four to five foot-long rug used exclusively for devotional purposes. It is decorated with a directional pattern, often a woven minaret, the point of which is turned towards Mecca. One is always positioned at the base of this design, thereby ensuring that one's feet never rest where one touches one's head. The design never incorporates any verses from the Qur'an, as it would be disrespectful to put God's word on the ground. To preserve the sanctity of his *sejadeh*, a Muslim must roll it up upon completing his prayers; according to tradition, the Devil sneaks in and prays on any *sejadeh* left unrolled.

Each of the five daily prayers, described previously, is described as having a certain number of *rek'ahs*, or inclinations of the head. Furthermore, each of these five prayers can include two varieties of prayer, the obligatory, or *fard*, and the optional, or *sunnah*. At all times, the number of *rek'ahs* permitted is prescribed for both *fard* and *sunnah*. Morning prayers have two *sunnah* and two *fard*. At noon and afternoon prayers, there are four *sunnah* and four *fard*. In the evening, there are two *sunnah* and three *fard*. Then, the night-prayers (or *'eshë*) have four *sunnah* and four *fard*, and two *sunnah* again. Finally, one may also perform three *rek'ah* single or separate prayers, called *witr*. These may be performed at any time in the night, including immediately after the *'eshë* prayers, but they are more meritorious if done late in the night.

It is reckoned sinful to pass immediately before a person engaged in prayer. Worshipers typically place their shoes at the front end of the space on which they pray, be it the ground or *sejadeh*, to mark the space over which people should not cross.

As demonstrated by his patched-up robes, the man praying in the cartoon is poorly off, which is why he needs divine help in order to marry. Marriage is very expensive for an Arab man; not only must he be able to support his wife in a suitable home, but he also must bear the expense of providing a dowry. Though as an Arab, he is likely stuck without a turn in his luck, were he living in some non-Arab Muslim countries such as Pakistan and India, he might have better chances: some of these non-Arab Muslim women are able to offer their groom a dowry instead of vice-versa, a custom which helps otherwise undesirable women find a match.

Translation

1. They distract the youth of the nation with the World Cup (Mondial)!
2. And broadcast shots of naked female fans!
3. And they extort the poor by monopolizing and revoking free broadcasting.
4. Glorify teams and flags of occupying and appropriating nations!

All of this doesn't justify the jamming of Al-Jazeera Sport Channel Plus, and we demand the government to open an investigation into this sinister and shameful crime!

The paper in his hand contains a statement of protest against whoever jammed the Al-Jazeera sports broadcasts.

Language

In panel number four, the imam is referring to the countries that are presently occupying Muslim nations, such as the United States (in Iraq and Afghanistan) and other members of NATO.

Culture

This "firebrand imam" criticizes the conduct of his country's government in his sermon. Usually such imams galvanize their listeners by addressing immoral and irreligious conduct by society and the government, but are not inciting violence; these sermons will typically fall on a receptive ear, because the audience tends to be socially or economically vulnerable to extremist influences (not unlike the members of fundamentalist churches in the United States). The discontent of their audiences can be particularly agitated by the perception that God is punishing the people for the follies of the society. The Prophet Muhammad said in the Hadith that "whenever a Muslim witnesses anything morally abominable, they are to change it by 'hand' or by 'tongue', or by 'heart', and this is the weakest of faith." It is thus incumbent on a Muslim who sees an ailment of his society to ameliorate it, first "by hand." This means to physically get engaged, though not necessarily by force. A Muslim listener to one of these firebrand imams may already be self-selected as inclined to interpret "by hand" to mean violent intercession, and so when an affront against his religious or moral sense is brought to his attention, he is as a good Muslim to act, first and foremost, for its rectification. This, when coupled with a subject psychologically inclined to interpret "by hand" violently, can then result in what are designated to be "terroristic" actions by the West, similar to those who bomb abortion clinics when influenced by Christian demagoguery. Malcolm X's famous maxim of "by any means necessary" conveys a similar philosophy: a Muslim is permitted whatever means are available to accomplish crucial goals. Most Arab governments prohibit such sermons from taking place. This cartoon is funny because in panels one through four, the imam is making typical critiques of the corruption and decadence of the youth, but ends by objecting to the restrictions placed on an Al-Jazeera channel, which itself broadcasts the World Cup.

One may ascertain the difference between a regular imam and a firebrand imam by their clothes, as well as their degree of anger (most of the time, the beard of a firebrand imam would also be grown longer). In the above cartoon, the imam is quite angrily animated. Most of these imams usually began in small mosques in impoverished areas of town, where the audience was poor and disenfranchised. These audiences are by nature illiterate and unworldy, and hence take the imam's words unskeptically and at face value. After the imam gains notoriety, people travel considerably longer distances to see and hear him, and he would eventually travel to larger cities for bigger audiences. At this point, he would appear on the government's radar and be ordered to tone down his rhetoric; if their order is not complied with, he could face trumped up charges and be jailed. After his release, he would then proceed to do most of his work underground, disseminating cassettes with his sermons on them. Ironically, post 9/11, Arab governments cracked down on these imams and their audiences, yet before 9/11 these same people were offered political asylum and support by the United States on the grounds of free speech.

Many governments no longer permits extemporaneous sermons. They are to be written beforehand and approved so as to be better controlled. Firebrand imams generally perform their largely improvised sermons for about an hour.

21 – Begging

Translation

On man: "Demolished income employee"

Language

The words *maHdoud*, "demolished," and *mahdoud*, "limited" have only one letter different, and descibing someone as having a demolished income humorously indicates that it is even less than limited.

Culture

It is a well-known fact that in Arab countries the panhandler "owns half of the country" (Arabic proverb), as Arabs are so generous that the man who has no qualms about begging will end up with more money than the givers. Unlike their Western counterparts, Arab beggars expect a certain level of charity and will reproach someone who gives too little, even giving it back to say that it seems the giver's need is greater, but when the beggar is given enough, he will pay for the giver until he is no longer in sight. Many stories are published in the newspapers about beggars who are discovered to have large amounts of money stashed in their houses when they die. In this cartoon the panhandler offers money to the employee who certainly makes less money than him.

The equivalent of "Can you spare any change?" "Have you got a dime?" would be, in Arabic:

لله يا محسنيين حسنه قليله تمنع بلاوي كثيره

which means: "For Allah's sake, charitable one, a small act of kindness (*hasana*) can prevent a lot of misfortune." The reason for this is the belief that an act of kindness, a good turn or deed, can avert calamity, in a Muslim kind of "instant karma."

Translation

"Such a silly panhandler. He's saying, 'May God not lay your body in any land.' Why? Does he want me to die drowning in a ferry accident?"

The panhandler's prayer can be taken in two ways: it could mean "May God never make you seriously sick, so that you take to your bed," while it could also mean "May God not let you be buried in a place far from your land." The man takes the second meaning, rather than the more common first meaning, which is a prayer of thanks from a grateful inferior.

Language

"May God not…" implies that if the beggar isn't given charity then the fate that he is praying to avert may happen—a kind of subtle pressure or threat. So the man is saying that the beggar is praying for him to die by drowning if he does not give him the charity.

Culture

In 2006, a ferry crossing the Red Sea from Egypt to Saudi Arabia sank in a terrible accident, killing more than a thousand people. For a long time, no one was held accountable for this catastrophe and the incident became an infamous demonstration of the callous self-regard of the upper classes of Egyptian society—not least the owners of the ferry and the Egyptian government—who failed to uphold safety standards, to respond promptly and rescue the victims, or finally to prosecute those responsible. Incidents Such as this one and the one in the cartoon below, which deals with a railway disaster, are depressingly common in Arab countries. The entrenched inequality of the economies, the public's lack of political engagement, and the boldness with which corruption and crime are flaunted and rewarded by the power structure have alienated many Arabs from their own governments, leaving them feeling disenfranchised and apathetic. Disengaged from their own lives and communities, it is all-too-easy for a person to fall into the stupid lapses of judgment or derelictions of duty that lead to these devastating accidents.

An example is shown in following cartoon, which refers to a railroad accident a few years after the ferry disaster. Rather than run over a valuable cow, which could ruin a family or upset a whole village, a train-driver stopped his train. An express was coming up behind and ran into the back of the stationary train, causing many casualties and deaths.

Translation

Title: This edition's quiz

Subtitle (between bars): What mistakes exist in this picture? If you know the right answer, send it to The Ministry of Transit and Transportation.

Voice from inside the farthest train car: Move your bag, I want to sleep.

Two men sitting on top of the farthest train car: I have a ticket, but it is cleaner up here.

Guy with mustache: They wanted me to buy the train, but who in their right mind would buy it?

Man smiling and gesturing: And this is the area where the train rolled over twice.

Man bending the track tracks: Do you know how much a kilo of iron goes for?

Train conductor (from inside first car): Do you know what this thing is for?

People talking inside the second car back:

The people on the right side of the car:

"I'm getting off at the end of the line."
"You mean judgment day?"

The people on the left side of the car:

"Do you see this historical achievement? The faucet is new!"
"Allah is greater."

Man asleep on the middle train car: ZZZZZ

Translation

Title: Old-time caricature

Panhandler: "Please give me *Hasana, Baih*. May God give the United Nations a long life, for your sake."

Language

This cartoon makes fun of the obese wife by likening her to the United Nations.[31] Although making fun of obese people is considered to be in poor taste in the United States, Arab culture has no qualms about this type of humor

Baih, Basha, Afinedim, Hanim, and *Efendee* are titles from the Turkish era that Egyptians still use today in addressing others with respect. The revolution of 1952 abolished these titles, on the grounds they referred to a bygone era and discriminated between people. Nowadays their use is more widespread than before, especially to address high-ranking police officers and again the elite. Other Arabs mock the Egyptian use of these titles;[32] so it is used as shorthand to label an Egyptian in cartoons.

Hasana means charity or a good deed in Arabic.

Culture

Panhandling is a widespread phenomenon in Arab countries. Panhandlers concentrate on areas around mosques, especially those that are large and located in mid-town areas, due to the high concentration of religious visitors who will willingly donate to help the destitute. Panhandling in Arab countries is similar to organized crime where the head of the gang recruits, conditions, and assigns would-be beggars to specific areas of the city. It is a very lucrative operation, and usually the head of the gang receives a larger cut of the earnings in exchange for providing shelter, food, and protection to his employees. Some of them are so ruthless that they will permanently injure some of their employees to insure cooperation and future income. Usually these bosses recruit young runaways and single women because they are seen as the most lucrative. Some of these gangs are so organized that their operations extend across borders. The gang boss can afford to buy airfare and documentation to allow his employees passage from one country to another (ex. Saudi Arabia and Libya). The arrests of these gangs are usually big news in the Arabic media since many people, despite their charitable nature, complain about them and their appearance in tourist areas, as illustrated by the next cartoon.

Panhandling and begging becomes more widespread during Ramadan, as people feel more charitable and the gates of Heaven are open for people to repent.

---

[31] See "4 — Dating and Getting Married," p.62.
[32] See "Arab Leaders," p.227.- *Title*: The Catalogue of Royal Disguises

Translation

Title: The round-up of a gang teaching panhandling.

Blackboard: "Panhandling Science."

"Satisfying the customer."

Instructor: "You say to the customer, "May God grants you success, and may you become the most corrupt person in the world. And may He watch over you until you arrive in London rich and safe. He is all able and kind."

Culture

London is the gateway city of choice for crooked Arab businesspeople, who upon hearing that they are about to be indicted for a crime, use their connections to escape to London.

The instructor is teaching his student beggars how to give the best prayer to their charitable donors. In Arab culture, the beggars begin praying when they see a potential donor. The amount of the donation is based on the quality of the prayer, and so a very good prayer is valuable. With this blessing, the instructor prays that God will help make the donor very rich by leading them down a path familiar to many Arabs. In recent years, many unscrupulous business people have made huge fortunes illegally, defaulted on loans, or engaged in substandard construction and then fled to London thereby escaping prosecution.

☪Panhandlers don't always wear shabby clothes and a look of indignation. In some countries they dress very nicely and find that this not only brings them more money than their poor looking counterparts, but also affords them some measure of protection from the police. In some areas, the issue has become so serious that police departments have created specialized anti-panhandling units to control the situation.

Translation

Gentleman on right: "Panhandler"
Gentleman on left: "Panhandler Vice Squad"

Culture

To improve the quality of life, some Arab countries ineffectively try to crack down on panhandlers. The way Arabs look at panhandlers is differently than Americans. Arabs will gladly help them; being charitable to panhandlers is a religious duty. This makes panhandling worthwhile to continue, thus making panhandling difficult to eliminate.

Translation

Sign on car: Dear panhandlers: Don't come any closer—this car is not paid off yet, the house is rented, and the prices are on fire!

Culture

Panhandling is an art in Arab countries, and panhandlers target each person walking by. For example, if a panhandler sees a young woman coming, he would say, "O daughter, give me charity for God's sake, so God may help you find the right husband." Or if he

sees an old man, he might say, "O father, give me something so God may guarantee you health," or, "May you recover from illness." When he sees a student with books under his arm, he would say "may you pass your exam;" if he sees a husband and wife, "O mister, give me charity for God's sake so God may protect the lady for you;" and so on from case to case. Panhandlers will assess his mark's situation and spontaneously improvise a prayer for his or her circumstances. Eventually, those with some resources will travel to more prosperous areas to beg, going to evermore bustling cities or even emigrating to wealthy countries.

Rather than roaming the streets, panhandlers mostly stay stationary on the sidewalks. People of means avoid mass transit and so anyone on a bus or subway is unlikely to be able to give much, and at any rate, the vehicles are so crowded as to make begging impracticable. As beggars sit on the sidewalk, they attempt to make themselves look as pathetic as possible to inspire compassion in merciful passers-by. Some are driven to mutilate themselves, disfiguring their bodies or amputating limbs in order to look more pitiable. Female panhandlers will beg with their babies and children to demonstrate their need. Despite these appeals to human sympathy in practice, the ideal conceptualization of charity, to the Arab mindset, is to give not out of compassion but rather out of obligation to God. There are two types of charity giving for Islamic religion. The first is *zakat*, alms-giving, which is mandatory and calculated as a percentage of your savings. The second is *sadaqah*, charity, which is not mandatory. It is mentioned many times in the Qur'an, and is considered as important as praying. One of the goals of fasting in Ramadan is to feel the hunger that indigents feel.

☪People who are in extraordinary need and who are not beggars by profession can seek assistance in the mosque. Immediately after the end of the prayer and before people start to leave, they loudly describe their situation and their need. Usually, many of worshippers are eager to help these deserving cases.

Translation

Title: What the similarity

Culture

In the Arab world, traffic lights serve as small, vibrant centers of commerce and activity. In addition to the many ubiquitous panhandlers, there are people selling newspapers, chewing-gum, Kleenex, jasmine necklaces, and many other products as well. The newspaper salesmen are there largely in the morning, broadcasting the top headlines to the passing crowds; as the day moves on, they peter out, and other salesmen take their place. The typical sale is fast, frantic and somewhat dangerous. As the car slows, the vendor approaches the driver: in a matter of a few fast seconds, he must secure the sale, receive the payment, return the change, and get his tip. One will often see vendors running alongside a car as the customer, pressured by a busy intersection, picks up speed—trying to make sure the change is correct, or that his tip is sufficiently ample. Some vendors are actually pimps in disguise; if their customer is a foreigner, they will drop the ruse of chewing-gum sales and offer their real services.

The speed with which the street vendors, squeegee men and beggars appear at the traffic stop, do their business and then disappear is compared to the efficiency of a race crew at a Formula-One pit stop. Note that the handicapped squeegee man left his crutch at the roadside to get down on his knees and wipe the fender, and elicit more compassion and charity.

22 – The Internet

Translation

Title: Free Internet

Culture

Internet access is expensive but unreliable, often out for hours at a time, and taking months to get connected. Many people refuse to pay for what is a bad service, but still want the connection (almost universally in the form of DSL technology). Wireless access offers a form of solution, but there have been no places where it has been readily available (such as coffee shops or libraries), so it is not uncommon to see people roaming the streets with laptops looking for an unsecured signal.

Until recently most people with wireless did not use password protection. This was largely deliberate, since allowing access to others was a form of generosity and a good deed that would be rewarded by God. The Prophet instructed his followers to be open-handed to their neighbors and someone who found that his neighbor had installed wireless but put a password on it would regard this as the sign of a bad person. There is also a Hadith where the Prophet says that when a Muslim leaves his horse or camel, he should "tether it and trust [God]" – this leads to an attitude that if something is not "tethered" or secured it is free to be used by others, so using another person's Internet signal is not stealing. This has changed, however, with awareness that an unprotected signal leaves the owner's Internet habits and computer accessible to others, including the authorities, so that concern over privacy is winning out over generosity.

The mess in the apartment identifies the men as probably unemployed, while readers would immediately take the posture of the man on the left as indicating hemorrhoids or piles – and automatically funny.

Savvy companies that play to an international audience on the internet alter their content to fit different national audiences. This screenshot from the Egypt' Google commemorates the 100th birthday of the Nobel-laureate Naguib Mahfouz.

Translation

Title: Internet Addiction

(Right to left)

Panel Two: "Volume: Mute"

Panel Three: (*Arrow points to*) "Delete."

Panel Four: "Confirm Delete. Do you want to delete all items in trash bin? Yes. No. Cancel command." (*Arrow points to "Yes."*)

Culture

Although the Internet is seen as a source of temptation and corrupting influences, Arabs are enthralled by what it brings to their lives. While Arab culture used to restrict the movement of information, Arabs have now been exposed to everything; all taboos are out in the open. Conservative elements no doubt dislike this wide dissemination of information, but this has been a life-changing technology for the average person. Now, when given the opportunity to use the Internet, they become lost in it for hours. The emergence of it in the region was not gradual, so while the West's introduction was rather slow, moving from text based to multi-media over a decade, the transformation in the Arab region was extremely fast, shifting from nothing to our contemporary version almost instantly. Everything has been profoundly affected by this evolution: social, political, and religious spheres of life all have been reshaped.

Translation

"Marriage by way of Internet"

Culture

A large part of society is closed, and the sexes do not have much opportunity to freely meet one another. In countries such as Lebanon and Iraq, this situation is coupled with the security concerns about going out and curfews. As a result, both men and women have turned to the Internet to find a potential spouse. This method of meeting has its drawbacks, though. Arabs who advertise their desire for marriage on the Internet may embellish their profiles to appear more desirable. This is much the same as in America, where people may edit their pictures or misrepresent themselves in their profiles. In Arab countries, the projection of wealth is often a source of problems with Internet dating — a woman may wear a lot of jewelry in their pictures, intentionally overstating her family's wealth. There is often the presumption that simply because someone has an Internet profile his or her family is well off, because of the high costs of computers and Internet access in the Arab world — but this is often erroneous.

Marriage by proxy

In the event that an Arab man is interested in a woman whom he has met over the Internet and who lives in another country, he can marry her with the help of an intermediary, who serves as an agent. After they are legally married, she is able to travel to live with him in his country. These marriages often end, however, upon discovery of embellishments to the truth.

☪ The role of the Internet and the way that it now pervades everyday life can be seen in the many cartoons in other sections of this book where it is an important feature.

23 – Heat

Culture

The Arab world is famous for its intense heat. In 2010, two Arab cities were recorded to be the 2nd and 3rd hottest cities in the world, with the Saudi city of Jeddah reaching the temperature of 52.3°C and DoHa in Qatar reached 50.4°C. Summer temperatures can reach above 50°C, over 120°F, and the average is between 37 and 48°C, 100 and 120°F, and dust is abundant. Due to the desert climate, the heat is always dry and thus a bit more tolerable—a small stroke of good fortune for inhabitants.

☾✶ Despite the weather, Arabs still maintain their traditional dress outside the home. In the gulf countries, for example, men wear a pair of long underwear, pants, an undershirt, and a *jilbab*. On their heads, they wear a small round cap, a *shemagh* over the cap, fastened in place with an *iqal*. Luckily, these clothes are made in lighter fabrics and colors in the summer. In the comfort of their own homes though, men often strip down to their underwear, to the dismay of their wives!

Translation

Title: Atwa Reached His Boiling Point

Atwa to the sun: Hey, what do you think about coming inside?

Because of unfavorable conditions on the street (noise, dust, garbage, etc.), if you meet someone near your house and start to have a conversation, once the chat has gone on for a length of time or conditions make it uncomfortable, it's proper to invite the other person into your home to continue. As is often the case an invitation should usually be refused, so it can effectively mean the opposite of what it says—inviting someone in means that you want to say goodbye. The man is impatient with the sun, which has been blazing for so long, and he invites it into his home, actually meaning that it should go away.³³

☪ The hose hanging out the window is common in Arab bathrooms, which normally have two: a long one for cleaning the floors and a shorter one used in lieu of toilet paper to clean oneself when one uses a traditional toilet, which is a porcelain bowl with footholds that one squats over to use.

Culture

A sincere invitation is indicated by the host's insistence—the person's tone of voice and body language.

☪ When coming to another person's house, whether for a visit or any other reason, visitors should always declare their presence, and this is stipulated by the Qur'an³⁴. Since traditionally most doors are usually left open and there is often no bell to ring, coming to an Arab house may not be like visiting a Western house, and visitors will clap or call out to signal their presence, though not the person's name. It is particularly important for men to make their presence known, so that they do not take any women of the house unawares, since they will usually be uncovered within their own home. If a man has been left alone by his host and hears a sound of anyone else approaching, he should cough loudly or clap, to show that he is there. If people are seated when a guest enters, they will rise, although it is a politeness to indicate that they need not get up, with downward pressure in the handshake or a hand upon the host's shoulder.

Young people do not usually want to take the trouble of complicated etiquettes and may whistle to each other from out in the street, often quite far away, to let their friends know that they are coming.

Translation

Title: People in the heat

The box says: Air conditioner

Barber: What's the story? This is the fourth time you've come to cut your hair today.

Customer: What can I do? This last hair really bothers me. Cut it, but slowly.

Culture

Suffering through the worst of summer heat, Arabs go to great lengths to find patches of coolness. Centuries of tradition have led to home designs that maximize the potential for breezes and cool surfaces; many Arabs flee their beds in the hottest nights and sleep on the cool tiles of their floors.

---

³³ See further consideration of invitations in "2 — Social Life", p40.
³⁴ "O ye who believe! enter not houses other than your own, until ye have asked permission and saluted those in them: that is best for you, in order that ye may heed (what is seemly)." Al-Qur'an, 024.027 (*An-Noor* [The Light]).

Electric fans have been widely embraced, but air conditioners are beyond most people's means. Simply because they cannot afford to have them in the house does not mean, however, that Arabs do not relish the relief of an active A/C. Many Arabs try to plan their days to include stops in air-conditioned stores, fancy restaraunts, hotel lobbies, or airline offices. The man in this cartoon is being very particular about his hair cut to lengthen the time that he can take advantage of the cool air in his barber's.

Translation

Title: Dear citizen, If there is a blackout at the height of noon [middle of the day], please follow the following instructions

1. Gather all members of your family and calm them down.

2. Choose one of them to be the savior. The man thinks, "*akara bakra.*"

3. Punch the chosen one on the nose.

4. This will lead to his being hospitalized and the hospital has extra generators. All of you will enjoy air conditioning, free lunch and TV.

Language

"*Akara bakra*" is the Arabic equivalent of the English rhyme, "Eenie meenie miny mo." Every Arab country has it is own version of this rhyme.
Tagh is the sound attributed to a gun shot in Arabic, and the sound in frame 3 above the child, *Trrragh*, is an extended version, as the child is hit.

Culture

Air conditioning has become an almost essential part of daily life in the Arab world, especially the Gulf countries, which fortunately are the ones best able to afford it. This cartoon and the one that follows deal with the problems caused by the unreliability of the electricity supply.

Translation

Title: How long will these blackouts last?

Air conditioning unit: "I'm so sorry. I don't want to stop working but the electrical current has been cut from outside."

Culture

Blackouts are so frequent in some Arab countries that it is essential for Arab houses to have candles and kerosene lamps in the event of electricity loss. Traditional Arab architecture uses the circulation of air within the building to keep some coolness, so there are no exterior windows and the rooms face onto an internal courtyard, where there is a fountain and greenery. Modern architecture with more limits on space cannot use these techniques, but there are other methods of mitigating the heat without using air conditioning. People will plant trees in front of their houses and are very protective of them; they also spray their outside walls with water to use the effect of evaporation; houses usually have balconies; floors are tiled with terracotta which is cool to the touch, rather than wood, and mopping the floor is another way of cooling the house; the windows have shutters that can be pulled to during the height of the day; men usually wear only underwear inside the house. In the street most Arabs use umbrellas as protection against the sun, and would be amazed to know that they can also be used for the rain. All stores without exception have awnings that can be extended as the sun moves higher into the sky, and every storeowner will plant two trees by the entrance in front of the shop to provide shade, where they will sit while waiting for customers. They are also expected to spray the sidewalk and road in front of their shop, to keep the dust down and to help cool the air.

None of this necessarily helps when people are trying to get to sleep, and by evening time the house will be warmer than the outside, so if the heat is really too oppressive people will move to the balconies to sleep or the roof if it is available, or may even go to a nearby park, until the cooler night air takes over and they are able to move back inside.

☪ The fire hydrant, the unofficial source of cooling in poorer American neighborhoods, is not available in most countries. Fire trucks are usually equipped with water tanks and building materials have traditionally not been flammable (most use brick and tile), so an average person could go years without seeing either a fire or fire truck. Nowadays there are more fires: flammable materials used in small industry are often treated carelessly in hot conditions and confined spaces; flammable waste can be left baking in the sun; in homes, electric circuits are overloaded, poorly maintained, and left unattended — a prime culprit is air conditioning left on all day.

☪ Heat can also cause tires to explode, leading to accidents. Because of the heat, work outdoors normally stops between noon and 3 p.m., leaving many towns and cities practically deserted during the middle of the day.

24 – Reminiscing

Translation

Right: "Old-time marriage"

Left: "And now…"

[N.B. In times of yore, before the discovery of oil, Arabs were very poor and could do without a lot of things that they now depend on.]

 Notice that it is the man is not the happy one.

Culture

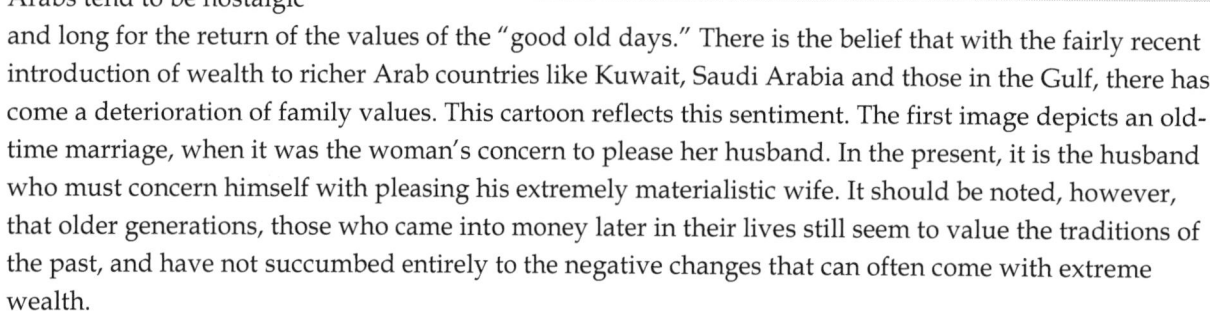

Arabs tend to be nostalgic and long for the return of the values of the "good old days." There is the belief that with the fairly recent introduction of wealth to richer Arab countries like Kuwait, Saudi Arabia and those in the Gulf, there has come a deterioration of family values. This cartoon reflects this sentiment. The first image depicts an old-time marriage, when it was the woman's concern to please her husband. In the present, it is the husband who must concern himself with pleasing his extremely materialistic wife. It should be noted, however, that older generations, those who came into money later in their lives still seem to value the traditions of the past, and have not succumbed entirely to the negative changes that can often come with extreme wealth.

Translation

Title: The Prices

On Calendar: Year 2040

"The whole world is blessed less… where are the days when everything was cheap? One egg was five pounds and a pair of pigeons was 140 pounds."

Language

In Arabic, the term "blessed" is synonymous with "abundance." For instance, when a person's money is "blessed" that person enjoys an abundance of wealth.

Conversely, if a person is "blessed less," then that money will be spent within a short amount of time.

In Arabic "the whole world" is *donya*, which also means "everything," "everybody" or an impersonal "it," so the man's comment could be "Everything is less blessed" or "Things are less blessed."

In some Arabic dialects, the word *goes*, not only means "pair," but also "walnuts," or "husband."

Culture

Nowadays the price of food is unusually high in some Arab countries and is steadily increasing. This cartoon depicts two elderly gentlemen in the year 2040, at a time when the prices have increased so much, that people will reminisce about food prices in 2010.

☪ Eggs can be sold individually, usually at an egg-store that only sells them, and have stands displaying eggs arranged on beds of straw, like a hen's nest, according to size and quality. As for "a pair of pigeons," a pair or brace is the normal way to buy pigeons, which are considered a delicacy, especially boiled and served with *mulukhiya* or stuffed and roasted. Squabs are also very popular.

Translation

"Yes kids. It is something edible and red with some fat in it. Sometimes they make it into a hamburger (*kufta*)."

Culture

In some countries in the Arab world, meat is very expensive and thus unavailable to those without much money. This cartoon depicts a poor elderly man telling his grandchildren about meat. The children listen to their grandfather enthralled, as though he is telling tales from a time long ago, for they have never been able to have meat and are very intrigued by his description of it. The most expensive meat in the Arab world is turkey.

Finding meat surprisingly cheap, Arab immigrants to America eat an unusually high quantity of beef. As a consequence, they often develop gout, the "Disease of Kings" as it is known in the Arab world.

Translation

Disguised as squiggles in a plummetting chart (reading from right to left, naturally), this cartoon charts the

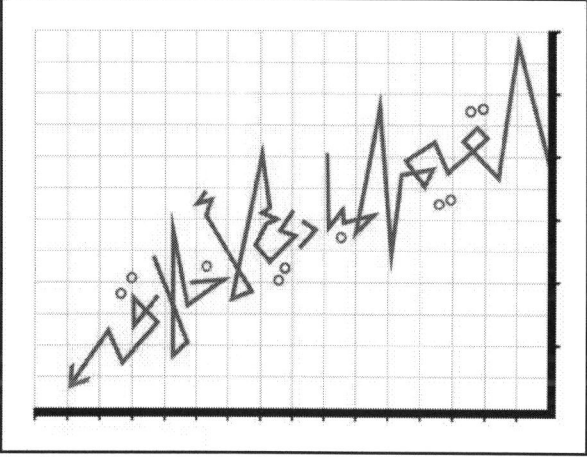

plummetting condition of: the values, the principles, the morals

Culture

Arabs generally take a very dim view of the moral state of their society, and surveys of civilization are characterized by extravagant self-reproach. The tendency is to focus on the misfortunes of the Arab world, which leads to the conviction that God must be meting punishment for shortcomings, which strengthens the focus on calamities, and so on.

Translation

Title: Allah, have mercy on your grandfather.

Frame 1: He can't survive without sending messages every day: "*Bring the donkey with you.*"

Frame 2: The receiver dish is the most important thing in his life.

Frame 3: And his donkey was wireless, walking behind him without a rope: "*Praise be to Allah in any way.*"

Language

"Allah has mercy on [name]" is slightly more flexible in Arabic than in English. If the name of God, Allah, comes first it indicates that the person is dead, whereas the verb comes first when the phrase is used after someone has sneezed—"Bless you." It can also be used to refer to earlier times, usually to upbraid someone who has changed and become arrogant, either because of money or good fortune, following the form, "Allah have mercy on the days when…" or "Allah have mercy on your father who…" or, as here, "Allah have mercy on your grandfather."

 The donkey blinkers have the symbol used for "Wi fi."

Culture

The grandfather doesn't have much but he is going home happy. The cartoon doesn't emphasize what the man lacked, but rather suggests that he had the same things in a different but simpler way.

Translation

Right: "Was long ago"
Left: "But now"

☪ Arab men always reminisce about the days when they were in charge, and you will find many cartoons that make fun of the emasculated men. Many factors have contibuted to this lost dominance: Arabs blame foreign influences from TV and the Internet, the economy, education, and that at home the father no longer has the authority he used to.

Translation

Title: (Top panel) Singing a long time ago. (Bottom panel) Singing now.

Culture

This cartoon is criticizing the vocal quality of contemporary Arab singers. As in Western culture, professional singers in previous years were talented and possessed very striking voices that were the focal point of the music. This is no longer the situation, as Western influence has diminished the vocalist's importance in popular music. Due to technological advances, these younger singers are able to perform even when they do not possess a voice which is traditionally considered "good."

Back in the old days, eloquent lyrics combined with a good voice were the norm in the Arab music scene. But now, even if you have a good voice, it is hard to find good lyrics. Many Arabs are saddened because they remember the "Golden Age" of singing. Arabs also use nicknames for their singers that are related to their voices: for example, Abdel Halim Hafez was called "Al-Aandalib Al- Asmar," the "The Tan/Brown Nightingale," and Sabah is known as "The Blackbird."

Translation

Upper Title: Titles long ago

Frame 1: Umm Kalthoum, "The Lady"

Frame 2: Fairuz, "The Queen"

Frame 3: Sabah, "The Blackbird"

Lower Title: Titles now

Frame 1: Not Yet, "The Mother of Bedsheets!"

Frame 2: Silicone More Criminal, "The Mother of Ah…Ah…Ah!"

Frame 3: Trivial, "The Mother of Oh…Oh…Oh!"

Language

The real names of the singers in the lower row of panels have been adapted to turn them into ordinary words in Arabic, satirizing them and as a sign of disrespect.

Culture

The three singers in top row are icons who stand out in Arab culture and they are generally appreciated both for their talent and for their contribution the Arab world. The dignity of their public and private behavior, their love for their country, shown partly through patriotic songs and charity work, inspired a true passion in their audiences that goes beyond simply liking their music. Umm Kalthoum was a classical Arab singer of unparalleled talent from Egypt, and it was said that two things united Arabs, their language and Umm Kalthoum. After the defeat of Egypt in the 1967 war with Israel, many people said that the defeat was the result of an obsession with soccer and Umm Kalthoum, and she herself seems to have felt a sense of guilt and dedicated hugely successful world tours to raising money for the war effort. Fairuz, a Lebanese singer, is also famous for her moving patriotic songs, as well as the more standard romantic fare. As for Sabah, her music was somewhat lighter, but her place within Arab culture was such that, when she fell upon hard times in later years, the Syrian president offered to support her. The three singers in the lower row—Alicia, Nancy Agram, Haifa—achieved a high level of popularity in the early 2000s, but were little more than Arab versions of international pop-music.

Translation

Upper (Ramadan then)

Man on far right: "Do you watch Nelly's riddles or Sherihan's?"

Other man: "Uncle Fouad.'

From the mosque: "Allah is the most great."

Stall sign: A kilo costs five pounds.

Side: Ramadan is blessed.

Manhole cover: Cairo province.

Lower (Ramadan now)

Man on far right: "Do you watch *A Man and Six Women*, *Son of Arandaley*, or *Tamir and Shauqiya*. Or *The Egyptians* or *Al Adham* or *Happiness Merchant*, or *War of the Spies* or *Nights* or *Nightmares* or *Abouda is a trade mark* or…"

Man with a reefer: I watch *You Tube*.

Mosque turned into Ramadan tent: "Allah on loving you!"

Sign on tent: We have *shisha* with *kunafa* (type of pastry).

Stall sign: One piece costs five pounds

Side: Ramadan is still blessed.

Manhole cover: Minstry of Agriculture.

Language

The phrase "Allah on [something]" means "How wonderful [something] is!" and the name of Allah on its own can be used to express admiration and sense of wonder, whether the context is explicitly religious or not.

Mixing up religion with debauchery

Religious ejaculations often interrupt conversation upon trivial and even licentious subjects in Arab society, and sometimes in such a manner that a person not well acquainted with the culture might imagine that they intended to make a jest of religion. The name of Allah is frequently introduced in songs about women and romance, as here in the song that accompanies the belly-dancer. This is certainly not done with any blasphemous motive, but from the habit of often mentioning the name of the Deity in vain, and of praising Him on every trifling occasion of surprise, or in testimony of admiration of anything uncommon. Thus, the first sight of a charming girl may provoke the exclamation, "Extolled be He who formed thee, O full moon!" and this and many similar expressions are common in songs and odes.

Culture

Ramadan celebration then and now

The transformation of how Ramadan is celebrated nowadays is constantly criticized in the media for the lack of spirituality and excessive secular activity that even in a regular month would be frowned upon. There is something of the same in complaints in Europe and America about how commercialized Christmas has become.

The gap between the two scenes shown here is probably some forty years—2010 and circa 1970.

The Two Men

In both cartoons the two men on the right are discussing the entertainment available during Ramadan. In the past people were content with what was on offer, though it was more limited. The entertainment would start shortly after the *iftar*, when people would be at home and relaxing after eating, which ensured a captive audience. The shows centered on *fawazeer*, riddles, where a popular actor or actress performed a sketch or a song as a clue each night, and listeners or viewers had to figure out the answer. At the end of the month they would send in their response and have a chance of winning a prize. These shows were on both television and radio, and the first man is asking about riddle shows on television on the two channels available, while the second says he has been listening to a riddle show on the radio.

There have always also been soap operas, *musalsalat*, that are just for Ramadan and last the thirty days of the month, but these are not mentioned in the first scene. In the second, however, the man mentions a whole list of them, most available via satellite, but his companion has not been watching television since he prefers YouTube on the Internet.

The men's clothes have become more Western with ripped jeans and are generally more casual in style, while one of them is smoking what appears to be a large joint of marijuana.

The Mosque and Ramadan Tent

In the mosque during Ramadan, Muslims may spend the night performing prayers called *tarawiyaH*, which means that they bring calm and happiness. These prayers, an addition to normal practice, come after the last mandatory prayer of the day, and are special to Ramadan. People go to the mosque more frequently during Ramadan than the rest of the year, and here the cartoon shows the call to prayer, *Allahu akbar*, a form that is only used for the mandatory prayers, and the optional *tarawiyaH* will continue after this final prayer. During the rest of the year the mosque will close its doors after the last prayer has been performed, whereas during Ramadan the doors will stay open all night, and the *tarawiyaH* can last throughout the night.

This contrasts with the scene below, which shows that the frequent visits are now to a Ramadan tent; inside the tent people are sitting and watching a belly-dancer, rather than standing and kneeling for prayer. The man approaching the tent is laughing, in contrast with more sober gait of the man going to the mosque, while the sign on the tent advertises hookah/*shisha*, satirically flavored with a Ramadan dessert—it is as if it were donut-flavored tobacco. The mosque's call has been replaced by a cheap romantic song, with Allah's name used in a colloquial expression rather than in prayer. In place of the crescent-topped dome, there is a satellite dish.

The lantern outside the mosque evokes the innocent entertainment, because they are carried by children who twirl them while singing Ramadan songs. This is replaced by the hookah pipe outside the tent, while the lanterns on sale are no longer traditional but in the form of novelty items.

☪The Ramadan tent is a new feature, only two or three decades old. Originally put up as annexes to large mosques to accommodate the extra worshipers during Ramadan, other groups and bodies started to erect them for their own members in order to create a space for religious purposes, and later some elements of entertainment were added. Over time, therefore, they have developed from religious spaces to mixed religious and entertainment to, now, completely secular places for entertainment during Ramadan.

The Sewer

The manhole cover in the first picture is stamped with "Cairo Province," which is standard, while the second one is labeled "Ministry of Agriculture" and "Ministry of Irrigation," in reference to using sewage water to irrigate crops—hence the plant shoot that is coming out of the drains rather than the cockroach, which is now on the stall selling food.

The Stall

The stall is selling some form of fruit or vegetables, and back in earlier times the food was cheap enough that it sold at 5 pounds a kilo, whereas now 5 pounds will only buy a single piece. The two women who are standing by the stall have been transformed in the period between the two pictures—in each case modern counterpart is dressed in a more extreme fashion. In the earlier scene, one woman wears a *hijab* while the other has her hair uncovered but is otherwise dressed conservatively; in the modern scene, one woman is in full niqab, with only her eyes showing, while the other is dressed in tight jeans and t-shirt, with a tattoo on her arm. The lanterns, already mentioned, would have been produced locally in the old days and are probably now imported from China.

The last ten days of Ramadan

The moon—only shown in the lower cartoon—is waning, which indicates that it is almost the end of the month. The "Night of Power," the night of the revelation of the Qur'an, is commemorated during the last ten days of Ramadan, although it is uncertain exactly which day it falls upon, so that the whole period is observed as one of especial holiness. This night of late Ramadan should be when religious observance is reaching a peak, but has instead become a time when people's minds are focused on soap-opera plotlines and exotic flavors of *shishah*.

Translation

Upper row title: Masters of progress and enlightenment at the start of the last century.

Lower row title: Masters of degradation and trivialization at the beginning of this century.

Culture

This cartoon also compares two sets of people past and present. The comparison is hardly fair since it juxtaposes intellectual heavyweights with figures from pop culture. However, the cartoon draws attention to the people who are in the public eye and are looked upon as role models. The lower row shows a range of contemporary television personalities, representing a general trend and the faces could easily be other people, but the figures in the top row are important individuals, who shaped the Arab world and are worth commenting on briefly.

Rifaa al-Tahtawi (1801–1873) was an Egyptian, who is famous as an intellectual, writer, teacher, translator, and Egyptologist. Tahtawi wrote about Western cultures and sought to find some form of reconciliation and understanding between the civilizations of Islam and the West. Sent to France by Muhammad Ali, the Turkish ruler of Egypt, to study science, he learnt French and translated some of the best of political and historical works, including a biography of Peter the Great and Montesquieu's *Considerations on the Causes of the Grandeur and Decadence of the Romans*. He was the founder of the School of Translation in 1835, al-Alsoun, one of the most prestigious schools of language, which still exists. He was involved with fostering the study of science, law, literature and Egyptology. His work influenced many later scholars, including Muhammad Abduh.

Jamal-al-din al-Afghani (1838–1897), Egyptian, was a political activist and Islamic ideologist in the Muslim world of the second half of the nineteenth century, who traveled extensively in the Islamic world and whose influence was felt in the Middle East, South Asia and Europe. He was one of the founders of Islamic Modernism, advocating pan-Islamic unity as a response to Western presence in Muslim world.

Muhammad Abduh (1849–1905) was an Egyptian jurist, religious scholar and liberal reformer. He is often regarded as the main founder of Islamic Modernism. He went to Paris in 1880 and partnered Jamal-al-din al-Afghani in publishing a newspaper named *al-'Orwa al-Wothqa*, "The Strong Handle."[35] He returned to Egypt in 1889 and became a member of the Assembly of Legislative Counseling, until his death in 1905. He was engaged in Islamic reform and issued hundreds of fatwahs on economic and political affairs, the position of women and the relationship of science and religion.

Qasim Amin (1863–1908) was also an Egyptian jurist and one of the founders of the Egyptian national movement and Cairo University. He is called "the Liberator of Women" for advocating the granting of equal rights to women, including voting and education.

These men have always been held up as examples to young children, with their names used for schools and their lives included as part of the school curriculum in the Arab world.

---

[35] Al-Qur'an, 031.022 (*Luqman* [Luqman]) and 002.256 (*Al-Baqara* [The Cow]); it means that Muslims should hold on as much as they can to Islam, the strong handle.

In the second volume

The themes examined here are extended and supplemented in the companion volume, where there is a greater focus on the problems facing the modern Arab world. These range from the age-old practices of *wasta* (string-pulling and nepotism) and *rushwa* (bribery), to problems over water and power supplies, to protest boycotts. The second volume also takes a long hard look at the thorn in the side (or "dagger in the heart") of the Arab world, Israel, showing the variety and evolution of attitudes to it. On a lighter note, there are examinations of celebrations and entertainment, while the importance of religion is represented by looks at Ramadan and the Hijj.

Topics in Volume Two

- Children
- Flirting
- Dowry
- *Wasta* (string-pulling)
- Celebrations
- Ramadan
- Hijj
- Growth
- Oil
- Boycotts
- Democracy
- Arab Flags
- Israel and Other Foreign Policy Issues
- Housing
- Bread-lines and Shortages
- Water and Electricity
- Prices
- Consumer Protection
- Unemployment
- Violence in Schools
- Drugs and Smoking
- Peculiarly Arab Crimes
- Terrorists in Drag
- *Rushwa* (bribery)
- Hospitals
- Maids and Chauffeurs
- Traffic
- Street Food Vendors
- Entertainment
- Travel
- Rich Arabs
- Us and Them

Index

9

9/11 · 4, 42, 124, 271, 273, 287, 297, 298, 309, 314, 437, 442

A

Abbaya · 63, 140, 190, 191, 208, 224, 225, 423
Abdel Halim Hafez · 461
Abu · 124
Abu Ghraib · 9, 293, 297
Academia · 3
Afghanistan · 238, 260, 261, 263, 274, 275, 285, 319, 406, 425, 441
Ajem · 8
al Mounasa'ha—the Saudi Counseling Program · 266
al-Aandalib al- Asmar · 461
Alexandria · 50, 436
Algeria · 2, 102, 115, 188, 221, 270, 342, 422
Alias · 123
Alms · 101, 239, 434, 449
al-Qaeda · 260
American-Style · 63, 64, 234, 263, 284, 312, 355
Arab Dream · 4
Arab Leaders' Way of Dressing · 223
Arab Names · 100, 102, 121, 123, 125
Arab Sense of Humor · 50
Arab Summits · 225, 230
Arab Wedding Night · 85
Arabiya · 296
Arabs' Respect for Their Names · 125
Arafat · 225
Astaghfir Allah · 56
Astrology · 132
Attar · 143

B

Baghdad · 137, 305, 306
Bait al-Ansar · 260
Balfour Declaration · 300, 301
Bangladeshis · 8, 415, 416
Barber · 42, 455
Bars · 29
Beehives · 356
Bilal · 7
Bishara al-Khoury · 56
Black Market for Dollars · 326
Blackouts · 457
Blair · 279, 303, 304
Body Language · 14, 455
Bounties on Illegal Aliens · 415
Brag · 74, 118
Bright Anger · 401
Bukhari · 70
Burqu' · 97
Bush · 9, 123, 224, 238, 240, 272, 273, 279, 290, 291, 294, 295, 297, 308, 309, 310, 311, 312, 313, 314, 315, 317, 319, 321, 438

C

Cairo · 9, 10, 19, 50, 205, 220, 230, 237, 294, 307, 403, 425, 463, 465, 467
Calligraphy · 371
Camel'S Hump · 208
Camels' Continuing Role in Arab Countries · 334
Carriage of Food · 70
Charms · 134
Conspiracy Thinking · 104, 298, 299, 301
Constructive Chaos and the New Middle East · 290
Corruption · 2, 104, 125, 221, 236, 240, 315, 376, 401, 412, 428, 442, 444
Cramming in the Mosque · 353
Cultural Centers · 2
Cultural Change · 187
Curricula · 3, 367
Curriculum · 8, 360, 365, 367, 386, 387, 467
Cursing · 18, 47, 125

D

Dayan · 50
Death Row · 343
Demanding Satisfaction · 129
Department of Education · 353, 354, 360
Disgracing the Family · 17
Dormitories · 382
Dove of Peace · 320
Drifting · 385
DSL · 451

E

Eddeh · 150, 151, 157
Education in Prison · 42
Eid · 118, 119, 135, 141, 159, 248
Empty Quarter · 24
Envy · 133
Es-Sirat · 428
Executioner · 41, 251, 252, 253, 343

F

Fallujah · 306, 307
Fard · 430, 440
Fat'Hah · 433
FataH · 220, 225, 261, 291
Father Allows Me · 16
Fatwah · 72, 73, 86, 114, 168, 175, 189, 234, 250, 282, 435
Fawazeer · 464
Female Hairdressers · 43
Female Infanticide · 183
Fitna, Temptation · 281
Flipping the Bird · 32
Flogging · 12

Form Number 6 · 220
Franco · 339
Friday, the Muslim Sabbath · 430
Funeral · 95, 223, 303

G

Gas Cylinder · 33
Gaza · 54, 55, 232, 279, 287, 295
Girl is Reserved · 82
God Willing · 39, 120, 315, 316, 383
Gout · 459
Goza · 343
Greetings · 406
Groom Mix · 71
Groom's Breakfast · 70, 71
Ground Zero · 289, 290
Group Prayers · 431
Guardian · 79, 86, 95, 98, 105, 106, 114, 214, 215, 255, 428
Gulf Dress · 226
Guthra · 11, 34, 88, 367, 373, 418

H

Habiby · 26
Hadith · 32, 250, 288, 441, 451
Haggling · 144
Hairstyle · 15, 357
Hajj · 64, 220, 237
Hajjah · 64
Halal · 23, 69, 77, 126, 269, 425, 429
Hamas · 54, 55, 220, 225, 261, 291, 295
Hanafi · 69, 84, 151
Hanbali · 69
Hand Gestures in Disputes · 170
Haram · 23, 126, 213, 429
Hasana and Saiyeh'eh · 434
Hasheesh · 29, 30
Herbal Medicine · 143
Heresy · 12, 255, 282, 424
Hide-and-Seek · 48
Hijab · 28, 49, 67, 130, 134, 206, 209, 252, 296, 425, 426, 465
Hijj · 43, 68, 225, 379, 439, 468
Hijjra · 110
Hookah · 39, 48, 465

Hooky · 381
Hormones · 40
Hourglass · 328
House of Obedience · 115, 145
House of Occasions · 95
Household Economics · 371
Household Help · 68
Humor · 28, 30, 32, 36, 37, 50, 63, 70, 98, 131, 132, 137, 152, 163, 181, 310, 311, 314, 345, 350, 351, 373, 381, 439, 446
Hurra · 295, 296
Hygiene · 155

I

I Don't Change Brands · 31, 32
Ibl · 329
Iblees · 428
Iftar · 464
Ignore Me Pants · 12
Imam · 97, 234, 289, 310, 429, 431
Impotence · 114, 136, 137, 138
In Praise of Older Women · 76
In Sha' Allah · 39, 120, 316
Indians · 8, 416, 421
Infidel · 12, 269, 282, 355
Infiltrator · 6
Inflated Hijab · 209
Inflation · 164, 258
Inheritance · 79, 83, 106, 174, 186, 237, 238, 257, 370, 371
Intentions · 92
Intercession in Islam · 277
Interpretation of The Qur'an · 372
Iqal · 34, 226, 410, 454
Iraq · 7, 12, 115, 137, 221, 222, 225, 228, 230, 231, 232, 250, 251, 263, 273, 285, 293, 297, 299, 304, 306, 311, 313, 317, 319, 322, 377, 406, 441, 453
Islam · 427
Islamic Jurisprudence · 369
Israel · 10, 24, 54, 55, 222, 229, 230, 231, 234, 261, 285, 290, 294, 295, 296, 298, 302, 309, 316, 320, 321, 328, 342, 349, 367, 462, 468
Istikharah · 432

J

Jahiliyyah · 377
Jalabaya · 435
Jews · 8, 12, 301, 308, 378
Jihad · 255, 260, 268, 370
Jilbab · 226, 454
Jinn · 66, 135, 428
Jordan · 4, 53, 89, 105, 115, 169, 184, 221, 222, 223, 226, 228, 230, 245, 247, 249, 263, 270, 304

K

Kaabah · 86, 135, 234, 251, 252, 279, 325, 377, 379, 397, 427, 430
Kafalah · 37
Katb al-Kitab · 98
Kinship · 57, 91
Kufiya · 225, 409, 410
Kufta · 459
Kuwait · 34, 102, 115, 209, 219, 221, 222, 226, 232, 298, 304, 308, 417, 420, 458

L

Laylat al-Qadr · 439
Lebanon · 2, 4, 7, 22, 53, 105, 110, 115, 188, 206, 221, 231, 270, 285, 290, 292, 296, 322, 327, 372, 453
Lingerie · 206
Logos · 3, 46
London · 447
Love and Hate for the Sake of Allah · 355
Luqman · 87, 467

M

Ma Sha' Allah · 120
Maasil · 39
Mahfouz · 125, 137, 329, 451
Maliki · 69, 151
Mansaf · 38, 249
Marriage By Proxy · 453
Marriage of First Cousins · 77

Martyr · 94, 245, 248, 283
Masturbation andSexual Purity · 86
Mazoon · 68, 69, 95, 96, 97, 106, 107, 185
Mecca · 110, 135, 296, 300, 372, 378, 379, 397, 430, 431, 440
Mehbash · 247
Men Seeking Women · 49
Men Snatcher · 180
Milka · 97, 98, 99
Misyar · 126
Mo'zen · 7
Monotheism · 369
Moon,Arab And, · 110
Morocco · 2, 4, 22, 102, 188, 221, 224, 316, 422
Mosques in the Arab World · 432
Mother of Ah…Ah…Ah · 462
Mother of All Battles · 64
Mother of Bedsheets · 462
Mother of Disgust · 64
Mother of Misery · 64
Mother of Oh…Oh…Oh · 462
Mother of Problems · 64
Mother-in-Law · 23, 85, 140, 141, 197
Motorcycle · 316
Mua'llaqat · 377
Mubarak · 9, 83, 124, 138, 220, 224, 232, 237, 238, 239, 240, 241, 243, 273, 304
Mujahedeen · 260, 275, 307
Mukhallafat En-Nebee · 307
Muslim Prayer · 430

N

Nafaqa · 126
Naksa · 342
Name is Two Muhammads · 100
Naming System · 100
Naseeb · 111
Nashiz · 151
Native-Foreigner Marriages · 103
Neutral Names · 125
Night of Entrance · 85
Nile · 67, 412
Nobel · 8, 125, 325, 451
Noses' Love · 59
Nubia · 7

O

O Bride · 96
O Daughter · 448
O Father · 448
O Full Moon · 464
O God · 119, 242, 346, 406, 433
O Lord · 324, 439
O Mister · 448
O My Servants · 56
O My Uncle · 81, 99
O Peace · 193, 235, 284, 289
O Saddam · 246
O Son of Those Who · 1
O Soul of Your Mother · 52
Obama · 5, 6, 8, 9, 10, 237, 238, 240, 255, 270, 283, 292, 294, 297, 312, 315, 321, 324, 325, 380, 425, 438
Oil · 1, 24, 35, 54, 70, 102, 109, 110, 115, 123, 147, 149, 221, 232, 237, 268, 284, 287, 299, 302, 308, 328, 334, 354, 382, 415, 416, 417, 418, 420, 458
Oman · 103, 221
Origin of Conspiracy Thinking · 299

P

Pajamas · 13, 45, 366, 435
Palestinians · 54, 222, 230, 232, 285, 295, 297, 308, 422
Patriotism Education · 371
Pedophelia · 183
Perfume · 43, 71, 189, 191
Pluralist · 117
Police · 12, 166, 275, 423
Polygamy is the Solution · 118
Power Marriage · 83
Prayer · 7, 23, 28, 29, 53, 81, 134, 156, 199, 212, 234, 242, 243, 259, 280, 307, 325, 350, 353, 384, 397, 398, 406, 426, 427, 429, 430, 431, 432, 433, 438, 439, 440, 444, 447, 448, 449, 465
Prayer Bump · 260
Prayer Time in Work Places · 397
Praying for Leaders · 242

Premeditated Murder in Islamic Law · 256
Prophetic Era · 370
Public Baths · 19
Publications About Sex in the Arab World · 137

Q

Qawama · 76
Qazafi · 9, 100, 219, 220, 221, 223, 225, 234, 243, 312
Qisas, Diya and Afw · 256
Qismah · 111
Qur'an · 254
Qur'anic Recitation · 370
Qur'anic Sciences · 370

R

Racism · 6, 271, 283
Ramadan · 43, 81, 99, 101, 118, 119, 122, 158, 224, 399, 429, 431, 439, 446, 449, 463, 464, 465, 468
Rap · 373
Reading Chair · 430
Rebus · 44, 46
Recitation of the Qur'an · 430
Rek'ah · 431, 433, 440
Religious Police · 12, 191
Requirements for Marriage · 86
Restraining Order · 66
Revealing Clothing · 12
Rising Number of Unmarried Women · 91
Rosary · 92, 97, 244, 432
Rubaiyat · 123

S

Sadat · 7, 83, 207, 224, 226, 233, 234, 235, 240, 319, 412, 437
Saddam · 64, 100, 137, 225, 228, 231, 245, 246, 247, 248, 299, 304, 313, 314
Sand Clock · 328

Saudi Arabia · 7, 8, 24, 34, 35, 42, 63, 68, 78, 87, 98, 99, 100, 103, 104, 105, 106, 107, 115, 130, 164, 177, 180, 183, 188, 190, 191, 192, 195, 204, 206, 213, 221, 224, 226, 228, 231, 234, 251, 253, 258, 262, 267, 268, 269, 270, 304, 313, 319, 369, 372, 376, 381, 382, 385, 409, 410, 418, 430, 431, 437, 444, 446, 458
Saudization · 418, 419, 420
Sawa · 295
Sayings of Prophet Muhammad · 370
School of the Trouble Makers · 364
Science of Inheritance · 370
Sejadeh · 440
September 11th · 268, 271, 287, 385
Seventy-Two Virgins · 245
Sexual Relationships in the Arab World · 137
Shadow of a Man · 89, 90
Shafi · 69, 84, 151
Shahada · 252
Shaheed · 94
Sharia Law · 255
Sharon · 318
Shemagh · 226, 454
Shiaa · 126, 291, 322, 414
Shisha · 463, 465
Siesta · 127
Sin · 23
Six Days' War · 246
Slaves · 6, 7, 84, 101, 257, 325, 415
Sleeping Sponsor · 37
Somalia · 7, 221, 275, 277, 285
Son of Lawful · 11, 419
Spice-Dealer · 143
Spinster · 90, 91, 180
Sponsor · 36, 37, 415, 421
Staring · 190
Stigma · 29, 48, 74, 90, 91, 118, 124, 128, 253, 318, 320
Sudan · 4, 7, 42, 70, 115, 221, 222, 273, 285, 314, 338
Summit Clubs · 344
Sunnah · 68, 83, 96, 146, 156, 238, 250, 281, 282, 355, 424, 440
Supplicating God's Help in a Decision · 432

Swearing · 18

T

Tar · 46, 90
Tarawiyah · 464
Tashmees · 262
Textbooks · 3, 113, 218, 355, 360, 363, 364, 365, 367, 369, 371, 382
Tobacco · 39, 465
Tone of Voice · 87, 235, 455
Tunisia · 2, 22, 108, 115, 188, 221, 401, 422
Tutor · 363, 364, 365, 386, 388
TV · 4, 14, 57, 73, 143, 146, 162, 172, 212, 246, 249, 278, 295, 296, 336, 340, 344, 346, 400, 456, 461
Tying the Knot · 108

U

U.S. · 24, 63, 132, 226, 231, 263, 269, 274, 282, 284, 285, 288, 295, 301, 302, 304, 306, 309, 316, 317, 326, 329, 353, 361, 390, 434, 438
Ululation · 71, 95
Umm Kalthoum · 391, 401, 462
Umra · 68, 237
United Arab Emirates · 34, 53, 107, 115, 138, 209, 221, 226
Unsuitability · 104
USAID · 10

V

Valentine's Day · 64
Viagra · 137, 138, 187
Vocal Pitch · 86

W

War Camels · 334
War on Terror · 270, 273, 437
Wealthiest Arabs · 35

Weapons of Mass Destruction · 231, 304
Wedding · 44, 69, 70, 71, 76, 85, 89, 94, 95, 96, 97, 98, 99, 100, 115, 137, 143, 166, 179, 212, 214, 223
Western Names · 124, 125, 207
When Arabs Don't Kiss · 58
White House · 318
Who will Eat the Last Piece · 31
Who will Go First · 31
Who will Hang Up First · 31
Who will Pay · 31, 258
Witr · 440
Women Prevented from Marrying · 79
World Trade Center · 262, 271, 272, 287, 289

Y

Ya · 1, 3, 81, 235
Ya Salaam · 235
Yemen · 29, 42, 115, 221, 222, 225, 275, 325, 378, 379
Your Name is Your Enemy · 102

Z

Zagroutas · 87
Zakat · 434
Zamalek · 343
Zawahiri · 259, 265
Zemzem · 135

Printed in Poland
by Amazon Fulfillment
Poland Sp. z o.o., Wrocław